OM5030

Corporate Social Responsibility and Managerial Ethics

material excerpted from

MANAGING BUSINESS ETHICS

Linda K. Trevino
Kate A. Nelson

Copyright © 2005 by John Wiley & Sons, Inc.

All rights reserved.

No part of this publication may be reproduced, stored in a retrieval system or transmitted in any form or by any means, electronic, mechanical, photocopying, recording, scanning or otherwise, except as permitted under Sections 107 or 108 of the 1976 United States Copyright Act, without either the prior written permission of the Publisher, or authorization through payment of the appropriate per-copy fee to the Copyright Clearance Center, 222 Rosewood Drive, Danvers, MA 01923, (978) 750-8400, fax (978) 646-8600. Requests to the Publisher for permission should be addressed to the Permissions Department, John Wiley & Sons, Inc., 111 River Street, Hoboken, NJ 07030, (201) 748-6011, fax (201) 748-6008.

To order books or for customer service, please call 1(800)-CALL-WILEY (225-5945).

Printed in the United States of America.

ISBN 978-0-471-72754-5

10 9 8 7 6 5

BRIEF CONTENTS

ETHICS WITHIN THE BUSINESS CULTURE

CHAPTER 1 INTRODUCING STRAIGHT TALK ABOUT MANAGING BUSINESS ETHICS: WHERE WE'RE GOING AND WHY 2

CHAPTER 2 WHY BE ETHICAL? (WHY BOTHER? WHO CARES?) 22

COMMON ETHICAL DILEMMAS

CHAPTER 3 COMMON ETHICAL PROBLEMS 60

APPROACHES TO ETHICAL DECISION MAKING

CHAPTER 4 DECIDING WHAT'S RIGHT: A PRESCRIPTIVE APPROACH 88

CHAPTER 5 DECIDING WHAT'S RIGHT: A PSYCHOLOGICAL APPROACH 110

ETHICAL RESPONSIBILITIES OF MANAGERS I

CHAPTER 6 ETHICAL PROBLEMS OF MANAGERS 138

ETHICAL RESPONSIBILITIES OF MANAGERS II

CHAPTER 7 MANAGING FOR ETHICAL CONDUCT 161

ETHICAL PROBLEMS FACING ORGANIZATIONS

CHAPTER 8 ETHICAL PROBLEMS OF ORGANIZATIONS 194

CHAPTER 9 ETHICS AS ORGANIZATIONAL CULTURE 225

MANAGING ETHICAL PROGRAMS AT THE ORGANIZATIONAL LEVEL

CHAPTER 10 MANAGING ETHICS AND LEGAL COMPLIANCE 275

INDEX 316

CONTENTS

ETHICS WITHIN THE BUSINESS CULTURE

CHAPTER 1   INTRODUCING STRAIGHT TALK ABOUT MANAGING BUSINESS ETHICS: WHERE WE'RE GOING AND WHY   2

Introduction   **2**
Taking Away the Mystery   **3**
Moving beyond Cynicism   **3**
   Tools to Manage Unethical Behavior   **6**
   Focus on the Positive, the Ethical, and the Socially Responsible   **6**
Is Business Ethics Just a Fad?   **7**
Can Business Ethics Be Taught?   **8**
   Aren't Bad Apples the Cause of Ethical Problems in Organizations?   **8**
   Shouldn't Employees Already Know the Difference between Right and Wrong?   **10**
   Aren't Adults' Ethics Fully Formed and Unchangeable?   **11**
This Book Is about Managing Ethics   **14**
Bringing Ethics Down to Size   **16**
Ethics and the Law   **16**
How the Book Is Structured   **17**
Conclusion   **18**
Discussion Questions   **18**
Exercise: Your Cynicism Quotient   **19**
Notes   **19**

CHAPTER 2   WHY BE ETHICAL? (WHY BOTHER? WHO CARES?)   22

Introduction   **22**
Why Be Ethical? Why Bother? Who Cares?   **23**
The Motivation to Be Ethical   **23**
The Media Focus on Ethics and Corporate Reputation   **24**
Industries Care about Ethics   **26**
Executive Leaders Care about Ethics   **27**
Managers Care about Ethics   **28**

Employees Care about Ethics: Employee Attraction and Commitment **29**
Individuals Care about Ethics: Reputation Counts **30**
Does Society Care? Business and Social Responsibility **30**
  Economic Responsibilities **32**
  Legal Responsibilities **32**
  Ethical Responsibilities **32**
  Philanthropic Responsibilities **33**
Government Regulation of Business **34**
Is Socially Responsible Business Good Business? **36**
  Socially Responsible Investors **40**
  Avoiding the Costs of Criminal Liability **40**
  The Importance of Trust **43**
The Best and the Worst in Us **45**
Reflections **45**
Conclusion **50**
Discussion Questions **50**
Case: Merck and River Blindness **51**
Short Case **52**
Notes **53**
Appendix: How Fines Are Determined under the U.S. Sentencing Guidelines **56**

COMMON ETHICAL DILEMMAS

CHAPTER 3 *COMMON ETHICAL PROBLEMS* **60**

Introduction **60**
Human Resources Issues **61**
  Discrimination **62**
  Harassment, Sexual and Otherwise **64**
Conflicts of Interest **67**
  What Is It? **67**
  Why Is It an Ethical Problem? **69**
  Costs **70**
Customer Confidence Issues **70**
  What Is It? **70**
  Why Is It an Ethical Problem? **74**
  Costs **74**
Use of Corporate Resources **74**
  What Is It? **75**
  Why Is It an Ethical Problem? **78**
  Costs **78**

When All Else Fails: Blowing the Whistle   **78**
    When Do You Blow the Whistle?   **79**
    How to Blow the Whistle   **80**
Conclusion   **84**
Discussion Questions   **84**
Short Cases   **85**
    Human Resources Issue   **85**
    Conflict of Interest Issue   **85**
    Customer Confidence Issue   **85**
    Use of Corporate Resources Issue   **86**
Notes   **86**

APPROACHES TO ETHICAL DECISION MAKING

CHAPTER 4 *DECIDING WHAT'S RIGHT: A PRESCRIPTIVE APPROACH*   **88**

Introduction   **88**
    The Layoff   **88**
Prescriptive Approaches to Ethical Decision Making in Business   **89**
    Focus on Consequences (Consequentialist Theories)   **89**
    Focus on Duties, Obligations, and Principles (Deontological Theories)   **91**
    Focus on Integrity (Virtue Ethics)   **93**
Eight Steps to Sound Ethical Decision Making in Business   **94**
    Step One: Gather the Facts   **94**
    Step Two: Define the Ethical Issues   **95**
    Step Three: Identify the Affected Parties (the Stakeholders)   **96**
    Step Four: Identify the Consequences   **97**
    Step Five: Identify the Obligations   **98**
    Step Six: Consider Your Character and Integrity   **99**
    Step Seven: Think Creatively about Potential Actions   **99**
    Step Eight: Check Your Gut   **100**
Practical Preventive Medicine   **100**
    Doing Your Homework   **100**
    When You're Asked to Make a Snap Decision   **101**
Conclusion   **103**
Discussion Questions   **103**
Case: Pinto Fires   **105**
Short Case   **109**
Notes   **109**

CHAPTER 5 *DECIDING WHAT'S RIGHT:*
A PSYCHOLOGICAL APPROACH **110**

Introduction **110**
Moral Awareness and Moral Judgment **110**
Individual Differences, Moral Judgment, and Ethical Behavior **113**
   Cognitive Moral Development **113**
   Locus of Control **119**
Cognitive Barriers to Good Ethical Judgment **120**
   Script Processing: The Pinto Fires Case **120**
   Cost/Benefit Analysis **122**
   Thinking about Fact Gathering **123**
   Thinking about Consequences **124**
   Thinking about Integrity **126**
   Thinking about Your Gut **127**
Emotions in Ethical Decision Making **128**
Reflections on the Pinto Fires Case **129**
Conclusion **132**
Discussion Questions **133**
Short Case **134**
Notes **134**

ETHICAL RESPONSIBILITIES OF MANAGERS I

CHAPTER 6 *ETHICAL PROBLEMS OF MANAGERS* **138**

Introduction **138**
Managing the "Basics" **138**
   Hiring and Work Assignments **138**
   Performance Evaluation **140**
   Discipline **142**
   Terminations **144**
Managing a Diverse Workforce **146**
   Diversity **147**
   Harassment **148**
   Family and Personal Issues **149**
The Manager as a Lens **152**
   The Buck Stops with Managers **152**
   Managers Are Role Models **155**
Managing Up and Across **155**

Honesty Is Rule One **156**
Standards Go Both Ways **157**
Conclusion **158**
Discussion Questions **158**
Short Cases **159**
Employment Basics **159**
Managing a Diverse Workforce **159**
Managing Up and Across **159**
Notes **160**

ETHICAL RESPONSIBILITIES OF MANAGERS II

CHAPTER 7 MANAGING FOR ETHICAL CONDUCT **161**

Introduction **161**
In Business, Ethics Is about Behavior **161**
Practical Advice for Managers about Ethical Behavior **162**
Our Multiple Ethical Selves **162**
The Kenneth Lay Example **163**
The Dennis Levine Example **164**
Practical Advice for Managers about Multiple Ethical Selves **165**
Reward Systems **165**
People Do What's Rewarded and Avoid Doing What's Punished **165**
How Reward Systems Can Encourage Unethical Behavior **166**
Practical Advice for Managers about Reward Systems **167**
Recognize the Power of Indirect Rewards and Punishments **168**
Can You Really Reward Ethical Behavior? **170**
What About Punishment? **170**
Practical Advice for Managers about Punishment **172**
"Everyone's Doing It" **173**
People Follow Group Norms **173**
Rationalizing Unethical Behavior **173**
Pressure to Go Along **174**
Practical Advice for Managers about Group Norms **174**
People Fulfill Assigned Roles **175**
The Zimbardo Prison Experiment **176**
Roles at Work **177**
Conflicting Roles Can Lead to Unethical Behavior **177**
Roles Can Support Ethical Behavior **178**
Practical Advice for Managers about Roles **178**
People Do What They're Told **179**

The Milgram Experiments **179**
　　Obedience to Authority at Work **180**
　　Practical Advice for Managers about Obedience to Authority **180**
Responsibility Is Diffused in Organizations **181**
　　"Don't Worry—We're Taking Care of Everything" **181**
　　Diffusing Responsibility in Groups **182**
　　Diffusing Responsibility by Dividing Responsibility **182**
　　Diffusing Responsibility by Creating Psychological Distance **184**
　　Practical Advice for Managers about Personal Responsibility **184**
Conclusion **185**
Discussion Questions **185**
Case: Sears, Roebuck, and Co.: The Auto Center Scandal **186**
Short Case **189**
Notes **190**

ETHICAL PROBLEMS FACING ORGANIZATIONS

CHAPTER 8　*ETHICAL PROBLEMS OF ORGANIZATIONS* **194**

Introduction **194**
Managing Stakeholders **195**
Ethics and Consumers **197**
　　Conflicts of Interest **198**
　　Product Safety **201**
　　Advertising **205**
Ethics and Employees **207**
　　Employee Safety **208**
　　Employee Downsizings **210**
Ethics and Shareholders **213**
Ethics and the Community **215**
Why Are These Ethical Issues? **218**
Costs **218**
Conclusion **219**
Discussion Questions **219**
Short Cases **220**
　Conflict of Interest **220**
　Product Safety **220**
　Advertising **221**
　Shareholders **221**
　Community **222**
Notes **223**

CHAPTER 9 *ETHICS AS ORGANIZATIONAL CULTURE* **225**

Introduction **225**
A "Cookie Cutter" Approach Won't Work **225**
    Organizations Don't Have Cookie-Cutter Ethical Problems **225**
    Cookie-Cutter Programs Are Superficial **226**
    "Ethics for a Day" Breeds Cynicism **226**
    Proactively Develop an Ethical Organizational Culture **226**
Organizational Ethics as a Cultural Phenomenon **228**
    What Is Culture? **228**
    Strong versus Weak Cultures **228**
    How Culture Influences Behavior: Socialization and Internalization **229**
Formal Cultural Systems **230**
    Executive Leadership **230**
    Selection Systems **237**
    Organizational Structure **238**
    Values and Mission Statements, Policies and Codes **240**
    Reward Systems **243**
    Orientation and Training Programs **247**
    Decision-Making Processes **247**
Informal Cultural Systems **249**
    Norms: "The Way We Do Things Around Here" **249**
    Heroes and Role Models **250**
    Rituals **251**
    Myths and Stories **251**
    Language **253**
Developing and Changing the Ethical Culture **255**
A Cultural Approach to Changing Organizational Ethics **257**
    A Cultural Systems View **257**
    A Long-Term View **257**
    Assumptions about People **258**
    Diagnosis: The Ethical Culture Audit **258**
    Ethical Culture Change Intervention **260**
The Ethics of Managing Organizational Ethics **262**
Conclusion **262**
Discussion Questions **262**
Case: VideoTek Corporation **263**
Case: Culture Change at Texaco **267**
Case: An Unethical Culture in Need of Change: TAP Pharmaceuticals **270**
Notes **271**

MANAGING ETHICAL PROGRAMS AT THE ORGANIZATIONAL LEVEL

CHAPTER 10 *MANAGING ETHICS AND LEGAL COMPLIANCE* 275

Introduction **275**
Structuring Ethics Management **276**
   Managing Ethics: The Corporate Ethics Office **276**
   Ethics Officers **277**
   The Ethics Infrastructure **278**
   The Corporate Ethics Committee **279**
Communicating Ethics **280**
   Basic Communications Principles **280**
   Evaluating the Current State of Ethics Communications **283**
   Multiple Communications Channels for Formal Ethics Communication **284**
   A Novel Approach to Ethics Communication at USAA **286**
   Mission or Values Statements **290**
   Policy Manuals **291**
   Codes of Conduct **292**
   Communicating Senior Management Commitment to Ethics **294**
   Formal and Informal Systems to Resolve Questions and Report Ethical Concerns **302**
Using the Reward System to Reinforce the Ethics Message **304**
Evaluating the Ethics Program **306**
   Surveys **307**
Values or Compliance Approaches **308**
Globalizing an Ethics Program **310**
Conclusion **312**
Discussion Questions **312**
Case: What's Wrong with This Picture **313**
Notes **314**

INDEX **316**

ETHICS WITHIN THE BUSINESS CULTURE

CHAPTER 1

INTRODUCING STRAIGHT TALK ABOUT MANAGING BUSINESS ETHICS: WHERE WE'RE GOING AND WHY

INTRODUCTION

This book began with a fortuitous phone call back in 1987 that resulted in a friendship. Linda Treviño, professor of organizational behavior at Penn State University, noticed a small article on the front page of *The Wall Street Journal*. The piece described a game to teach business ethics that had been developed at Citicorp, the nation's largest commercial bank at the time. As someone who teaches ethics to business students, and who cares deeply about preparing students to think about ethics and manage their conduct in corporations, she decided to find out more about Citicorp's game. She called the game's developer, Kate Nelson, who was then a vice president and head of human resources communications at Citicorp. The rest, as they say, is history.

We began a dialogue and, over time, discovered that we had a lot in common. We had both learned that many students—whether on a campus or in a corporation—felt intimidated by the subject of ethics. We had both listened to their frustrations: "Why does this have to be so mysterious? This is hopeless; there's nothing we can do about the behavior of people who report to us. Give us some guidance. Tell us what we should be doing. Don't frame business ethics in terms of Aristotle. Tell us what will be expected of us at General Electric, Ford, and Bank of America. Advise us on what to do when something goes wrong, and how to prevent that from happening." In many ways, this book is a response to those concerns.

Before writing the book, however, we had to make several decisions. First, would such a big undertaking be a worthwhile effort? Could we take the mystery out of business ethics? Could we address the cynicism that we had both encountered? Did we have something unique to say? Would it make any difference? We became convinced that we could write a book that would teach something unique, and that we could do it in a fun and practical way.

TAKING AWAY THE MYSTERY

We want to take the mystery out of business ethics. In other situations (romance, for example?) mystery may stimulate interest. But mystery only serves to make ethics inaccessible to most students and managers. For most people, the word "ethics" means something esoteric and far removed from reality. But organizational ethics isn't mysterious. It's about *us*—people making decisions in organizations every day. All of us belong to organizations. We're members of schools, fraternities, sororities, clubs, sports teams, religious organizations, and work organizations. As members of these organizations, we frequently find ourselves facing ethical dilemmas—*situations concerning right and wrong where values are in conflict.*

As a student, you may have observed a friend cheating and wondered what to do. Which is the more important value—sticking by a friend, or complying with the honor code that requires you to turn in a cheater? In a work setting, perhaps you've been tempted to do something you believe is wrong (for example, lie to a customer about a delivery date) because your boss encourages you to focus on short-term financial results. Which is more important—honesty to the customer or adherence to your supervisor's expectations? Loyalty is an important value for most of us. But, what happens when one of your employees (a good friend) hasn't been meeting agreed-on performance expectations for some time? Which is more important—loyalty to the organization or loyalty to your friend? All of these examples represent values in conflict. All are ethical dilemmas.

Until about fifteen years ago, so little was known about the topic of organizational ethics that a book like this probably couldn't have been written. With rare exceptions, knowledge was limited to a few surveys saying that, yes, ethics is a problem in organizations. But in recent years, researchers have begun to rigorously study organizational ethics as social science. Although there is much left to learn, we're beginning to understand the factors that influence ethical conduct in organizations, and what works and what doesn't in ethics management. That's the kind of information we'll share with you so that you'll understand yourself and others better, and you'll be a better manager who will understand how to influence others' behavior in an ethical direction.

MOVING BEYOND CYNICISM

Cynicism has become an epidemic throughout society and is manifested in a "contemptuous mistrust" of business leaders.[1] Irving Kristol, writer, educator, and editor, said, "One of the reasons the large corporations find it so difficult to persuade the public of anything is that the public always suspects them of engaging in clever public relations instead of simply telling the truth."[2] Such cynical attitudes toward business have been exacerbated by repeated organizational restructurings, accompanied by high executive compensation and layoffs.[3] Many believe that executives are not being held accountable for bad management decisions and the pain they inflict on employees as a result. Recent business scandals and the accompanying questions about the accuracy of financial statements and the trustworthiness of investment analysts have contributed to widespread cynicism about business ethics.

In 2000, the Ethics Resource Center, a nonprofit educational organization, conducted its National Business Ethics Survey, a nationally representative survey of 1,500 U.S. employees. The researchers found that more than one of every eight employees reports feeling pressure to compromise ethical standards. And most of the employees who feel such pressure say that the pressure comes from supervisors and top management.[4]

Since the classic studies of business ethics conducted in the 1960s and 1970s,[5] managers have repeatedly reported their own cynicism—the pressure they feel to compromise their personal ethical standards on the job—and they're even more cynical about their peers' ethics than their own.[6] They blame business's preoccupation with gain, the lack of reinforcement of ethical behavior, competition, the existence of generally accepted unethical practices in certain industries, a sense that only results are important to superiors, and the ineffective enforcement of ethics codes. Among all managers, those at lower levels have reported feeling the most pressure to compromise their ethics.[7]

Many of our readers are business school students, the future managers of business enterprises. Surveys suggest that many business students believe that they'll be expected to check their ethics at the corporate door or that they will be pressured to compromise their own ethical standards in order to succeed.[8] The entertainment industry may be partially responsible for students' cynical view of American business. Think about the depiction of business and its leaders in movies and on television. The Media Research Center conducted a survey of 863 network TV sitcoms, dramas, and movies from 1995 to early 1997. Nearly 30 percent of the criminal characters in these programs were business owners or corporate executives. Entrepreneurs were represented as drug dealers (*Beverly Hills, 90210*), kidnappers (*Nash Bridges*) or sellers of defective gear to the military.[9] *Fortune* magazine called this "the rise of corporate villainy in prime time."[10] More recent movies with a negative message about corporate America include *Civil Action, The Insider,* and *Erin Brockovich.* Academic research on the representation of business in movies suggests that cynicism toward American business increased after study participants viewed the film *Roger & Me,* which depicted ruthless plant closings and layoffs at General Motors.[11] Imagine the cumulative effect of viewing countless movies and television programs that portray business as corrupt and business leaders as ruthless and unethical.

Surely, the factor that has contributed the most to student cynicism in recent years is the highly visible behavior of some of the nation's leading corporations and executives whose activities have garnered so much space in the business press and on the evening news. How do you watch hour after hour of congressional hearings into the activities—clearly unethical and likely illegal—of Enron and not walk away a bit jaded? How can you not be cynical when you read about the finance professionals at Merrill Lynch who laughed it up over the stocks they were trashing to one another on e-mail as they were touting them to clients? How can you help but wonder about the ethics of business when you read about pharmaceutical companies bribing doctors to prescribe their products with all-expense paid trips to exotic locations? In 2001 and 2002, all you had to do was read the newspaper to feel cynical, and business school students are no exception.

An Aspen Institute study of over 2,000 MBA students who graduated in 2001 from 13 leading international business schools provides insight into MBA students' attitudes. The three-wave survey followed the students from entry into their graduate programs through graduation. It found that MBA students anticipate facing difficult values conflicts in their jobs, suggesting cynicism about ethics in the workplace. Most said that they would leave a company whose values were inconsistent with their own rather than speak up or try to promote change from within. Although about two-thirds of the students said that operating according to a strong ethical code was the mark of a well-run company, surprisingly only about ten percent of students said that a company's ethical standards would be an important factor when considering job offers. Students overwhelmingly named challenging and diverse job responsibilities as the most important factor in job selection.[12]

For our cynical readers, we want to help by doing two things: (1) empowering managers with the tools they need to address ethical problems and manage for ethical behavior and (2) providing positive examples of people and organizations who are "doing things right." We agree with Coach Joe Paterno, Penn State's legendary football coach whose program is known for integrity. He said this in response to our questions about cynicism: "I don't care what cynical people say. I don't really pay attention. These are small people who ... don't have the confidence or courage to do it the right way. And when they see someone doing it the right way, deep down they feel guilty. They'd rather say that it can't be done ... that everybody cheats. I hear that all the time. 'Fine,' I say. 'You think what you want.' I know what I do. People around me know. You've got to just run your organization. You can't worry about what these cynical people say."

Finally, we can't leave a discussion of cynicism without talking about the events of September 11, 2001, and their potential effect on attitudes toward American business. While the business scandals of 2001–2002 left many cynical, the events of September 11, 2001, also brought out the best in many individuals and businesses. All of us have read about the care, compassion, and assistance given by countless American firms to those who were harmed by the terrorist attacks. Few firms were hit as hard as Sandler O'Neill & Partners, a small but very profitable Wall Street investment bank that lost 66 of its 171 employees on September 11, including two of the firm's leading partners. The firm's offices had been on the 104th floor of the World Trade Center. Despite its dire financial straits, the firm sent every deceased employee's family a check in the amount of the employee's salary through the end of the year and extended health-care benefits for five years. Bank of America quickly donated office space for the firm to use. Competitors sent commissions their way and freely gave the company essential information that was lost with the traders who had died. Bigger Wall Street firms took it upon themselves to include Sandler in their deals. The goal was simply to get Sandler some money and back on its feet.[13] This is only one of the many stories that point to the good that exists in the heart of American business. In this book, we will offer some of these positive stories to counterbalance the mostly negative stories portrayed in the media.

Tools to Manage Unethical Behavior

With so much focus on negative events, people can become cynical because they feel helpless to influence these events. They feel overwhelmed by the pressures they perceive to be pushing them and others inexorably toward self-interested behavior at the expense of their higher aspirations. The "mystery" of organizational ethics contributes to this feeling of helplessness. How can people do anything about something they don't understand? We hope to dispel this feeling of helplessness, and simultaneously reduce the cynicism by offering conceptual and practical tools for managing ethics.

Focus on the Positive, the Ethical, and the Socially Responsible

We would also like to focus on the positive and the ethical in people and in organizations. We're not Pollyannas, but we see plenty of positive evidence and real-world examples that inspire us to keep ourselves and our organizations moving in a positive and ethical direction.

Ethical conduct is alive and well at work. In an *Industry Week* survey, three out of four respondents claimed that their company's code of ethics, or ethics in general, actually means something to them in their day-to-day work.[14] Similarly, the Ethics Resource Center's 2000 survey of business ethics found that about seventy percent of respondents from for-profit organizations have *never* observed conduct that either violated the law or the organization's own ethics standards. Only six percent of employees said that they had observed such misconduct often, and only about five percent said that they frequently experience pressure to compromise their company's ethical standards in order to achieve business objectives. More than seventy percent of employees said that the values of honesty, respect, and trust are applied frequently in their workplace. Finally, about eighty-five percent of employees said that supervisors and executives in their organization model ethical business behavior. Clearly, most employees are having a positive ethical experience at work. You might want to conduct your own survey among the people you know. Ask them these questions and see what they say. If your findings are similar to those reported above, perhaps you will begin to question the widespread cynicism conveyed by the media and pay more attention to the many examples of positive and ethical business behavior.[15]

From a social responsibility perspective, many organizations are acknowledging that they're not islands, isolated from the larger communities that surround them. In fact, they know that they function best within healthy communities. The leaders of these organizations have been referred to as "enlightened capitalists."[16] They reject the notion that business's sole responsibility is to maximize profits. Although they're true believers in the free market system, these "enlightened capitalists" acknowledge that the free market system can also produce negative side effects such as pollution and "poverty-amid-plenty."[17] They believe that it's better for business to voluntarily help solve these problems than to be forced to do so by the government. One corporate lawyer estimated that one new law results in 200 to 300 pages of regulations, all of which have to be followed by the corporations affected by the law. Furthermore, enlightened business leaders argue that business has a responsibility to address certain social problems because of its unique abilities, and because a healthy social environment is a prerequisite for a healthy business environment. Therefore, they maintain that when a business serves its multiple stakeholders best (i.e., customers, employees, the community—essentially, any party who has a stake in what the organization does and how it performs), it also serves its shareholders best in the long run.[18]

IS BUSINESS ETHICS JUST A FAD?

Management researchers began to study business ethics during the 1960s by conducting surveys of managers' attitudes toward business ethics.[19] Some thought that business ethics was just a fad then (related to media attention to the burgeoning consumer rights movement, for example) and that interest in the topic would quickly fade. But research has found that management fads generally last only about 10 years,[20] and interest in business ethics has climbed for more than 40 years. This interest is fueled in part by regular media coverage of ethical lapses in the business community. Examples include the federal savings and loan disaster, Wall Street insider trading scandals, Archer Daniels Midland's price fixing, Denny's and Texaco's racial discrimination, Mitsubishi's sexual harassment, the tobacco industry's nicotine-spiking of cigarettes, the Ford/Firestone tire and automobile safety controversy, the Enron/Arthur Andersen debacle, WorldCom, Adelphia (unfortunately, the list is long).

But ethical lapses aren't limited to business; such problems affect every institution of our society. For example, in the 1970s the Watergate scandal focused attention on ethical problems in government. This focus continued with questions about the faulty decision making that led to the Challenger disaster, check-writing scandals in Congress, Irangate, Whitewater, sexual harassment in the military, questionable election fund-raising tactics, and the sex scandals in the Clinton White House.

Religious, educational, philanthropic, and sports organizations haven't been immune. Catholic priests (and other religious leaders) have sexually abused children, students have cheated on exams and plagiarized papers, philanthropic organizations have spent contributors' funds irresponsibly, student athletes have run afoul of National Collegiate Athletic Association (NCAA) rules, and Olympic judges have been accused of fixing scores. Although we don't want to leave it to the media to define ethical business practice, the media's continuing interest in ethical issues suggests that ethics isn't just a fad.

Articles and books have proliferated in the academic and professional press, suggesting that these communities are becoming increasingly interested in ethics as well. And organizations of every kind are addressing the "ethics problem" in a number of ways. Many of them are establishing high-level ethics committees, drafting codes of ethical conduct, and conducting ethics training programs. Such ethics initiatives have increased quite steadily since the 1970s.[21] The Ethics Resource Center 2000 survey found that 79 percent of respondents reported that their companies have a written set of ethical standards (compared with 60 percent in 1994).[22]

The wider American community also seems very interested in ethics and values these days. An ethicist writes a column for the Sunday *New York Times* and appears regularly on National Public Radio. Character education has also been growing in the public schools with multiple public and private initiatives. So, while there is certainly a focus on the negative—the ethical lapses—there also seems to be a need in our society to focus on the positive. We want to celebrate ethical "heroes" in private and public life and we are anxious to discuss and teach our children positive ethical values.

As we've seen, interest in ethics reflects the reality of life in all sectors of our society, and it has continued to grow over the past 40 years. Of course, ethical lapses are a part of human behavior that's here to stay. That's one reason why we wrote this book. If the ethics "problem" isn't just a fad, then managers have an ongoing concern that they must anticipate, understand, and manage. We also believe that the interest in ethics as a positive force hasn't been adequately tapped in the business world. Although they do not get as much media attention, there are many positive examples of business people doing good and doing well. We want to share those too.

CAN BUSINESS ETHICS BE TAUGHT?

Before launching a book-writing effort, we also needed to be convinced that we could actually teach our readers something. Despite growing interest in ethics and ethics training, dissenters from both the business and academic communities have raised questions about whether ethics can or should be taught. Felix Rohatyn, a noted New York investment banker, said that ethics can't be taught past the age of 10. Lester Thurow, former dean of the Massachusetts Institute of Technology's Sloan School of Management, echoed this view when he stated that business schools can do little if students haven't already learned ethics from their families, clergy, previous schools, or employers.[23]

In the wake of the insider trading scandals of the 1980s, Thurow and a chief operating officer of a large Wall Street investment firm claimed on a television news program that educational institutions or business organizations could have done little about the unethical individuals who participated in insider trading. These people just hadn't been raised with the proper values.

If they're correct, ethics education is a waste of time and money. "Bad apples" are just tainted people who can't be trained or rehabilitated. Therefore, resources should be devoted to identifying and discarding bad apples, not educating them. We disagree, and the evidence is on our side.

Aren't Bad Apples the Cause of Ethical Problems in Organizations?

In part, the belief that ethics can't be taught is driven by the assumption that ethical problems are caused by such "bad apples" and that unethical behavior in organizations can be traced to a few bad apples that spoil it for the rest of us. According to this belief, people are good or bad when they join organizations. The organizations are powerless to change these folks, so they should focus on hiring good people and weeding out the bad ones who somehow slip through the selection process.

This bad apple idea[24] is appealing in part because unethical behavior can then be blamed on a few bad individuals. Although it's unpleasant to fire people, it's relatively easier to search for and discard a few bad apples than to search for some organizational problem that caused the apple to rot.

Garry Trudeau's (1987) Doonesbury cartoon treatment of Dennis Levine, who was convicted of insider trading in the 1980s, reflected this bad apple view. In the cartoon, Levine is totally unresponsive to an ethics counselor's attempts to appeal to his sense of morality.

> Scot, Ethics Counselor: "... and since everyone else was doing it, you figured using insider information was okay?"
>
> Levine: "Yeah, like the golden rule says."
>
> Scot: "Uh, the golden rule? Which golden rule is that?"
>
> Levine: "Do unto others before they do it unto you first."
>
> Scot: "Okay, ethically, you seem to be a little rusty ... Why don't we review a few basic moral questions, okay? What's the opposite of wrong?"
>
> Levine: "Poor."

Trudeau portrays Levine as a bad apple who is totally unresponsive to the counselor's attempt to appeal to some basic understanding of right and wrong. Trudeau's Levine just doesn't "get it." Later, however, in an article he wrote for *Fortune* magazine,[25] the former Wall Street trader acknowledged that he knew he was doing something very wrong and deserved the punishment he received. You'll read more about Dennis Levine in Chapter 7.

Despite the appeal of the bad apple idea, "character" is a poorly defined concept, and when people talk about it, they rarely define what they mean. They're probably referring to a complex combination of traits that are thought to guide individual behavior in ethical dilemma situations. If character guides ethical conduct, training shouldn't make much difference because character is thought to be relatively stable, meaning that it's difficult to change, persists over time, and guides behavior across different contexts. Character develops slowly as a result of upbringing and the accumulation of values that are transmitted by schools, families, friends, and religious organizations. Therefore, the idea is that people come to educational institutions or work organizations with an already defined good or poor character. Good apples will be good and bad apples will be bad.

In fact, people do have predispositions to behave ethically or unethically (we'll talk about these in Chapter 5). And sociopaths can certainly slip into organizations with the sole intent of helping themselves to the organization's resources, cheating customers, and feathering their own nests at the expense of others. They have little interest in "doing the right thing." When this type of individual shows up in your organization, the best thing to do is to discard the bad apple and make an example of the incident to those who remain.

But discarding bad apples generally won't solve an organization's problem with unethical behavior. The organization must scrutinize itself to determine if there's something rotten inside the organization that's spoiling the apples. Although all the facts are not yet in, information to date suggests that both Enron and Arthur Andersen had cultures that encouraged unethical behavior. Enron allowed (and perhaps encouraged) unethical behavior throughout the organization, and Arthur Andersen's actions with a series of clients is still under scrutiny from law enforcement and regulatory agencies. You'll learn in this book that most people are not guided by a strict internal moral compass. Rather, they look outside themselves—to their environment—for cues about how to think and behave. This is particularly true when circumstances are ambiguous or unclear as they are in many ethical dilemma situations. At work, the organizational culture transmits many cues about how one should think and act. Executive leadership, norms, role models, reward systems, and many other components of the management context (Chapter 7) and organizational culture (Chapter 9) combine to let people know what's expected. Although much more subtle, this is as much an educational process as explicit ethics training.

So, our view is that apples often turn bad because they're spoiled by "bad barrels"—that something in the organization not only condones, but may even expect, unethical behavior. These are not bad folks to begin with. But their behavior can easily turn bad if they believe that their boss or their organization expects them to behave unethically. In this view, an organization that's serious about supporting ethical behavior and preventing misconduct must delve deeply into its own management systems and cultural norms and practices to search for systemic causes of unethical behavior. Management must take responsibility for the messages it sends or fails to send about what's expected. If ethics problems are rooted in the organization's culture, discarding a few bad apples without changing that culture isn't going to solve the problem. An effective and lasting solution will rely on management's systematic attention to all aspects of the organization's culture and what it is explicitly or implicitly "teaching" organizational members.

This question about the source of ethical and unethical behavior reflects the broader "nature/nurture" debate in psychology. Are we more the result of our genes (nature) or our environments (nurture)? Most studies find that behavior results from both nature *and* nurture. So, when it comes to ethical/unethical behavior, the answer is not either/or, but *and*. Individuals do come to organizations with predispositions that influence their behavior, but the work environment can also have a large impact.

Shouldn't Employees Already Know the Difference between Right and Wrong?

A belief associated with the good/bad apple idea is that any individual of good character should already know right from wrong and should be able to be ethical without special training—that a lifetime of socialization from parents and religious institutions should prepare people to be ethical at work. You probably think of yourself as an individual of good character. So, think about the following real dilemma.

You're the VP of a medium-sized organization that uses chemicals in its production processes. In good faith, you've hired a highly competent scientist to ensure that your company complies with all environmental laws and safety regulations. This individual informs you that a chemical the company now uses in some quantity is not yet on the approved EPA list, although it's scheduled to be placed on the approved list in about three months because it's been found to be safe. You can't produce your product without this chemical, yet regulations say that you're not supposed to use the chemical until it's officially approved. Waiting for approval would require shutting down the plant for three months, putting hundreds of people out of work, and threatening the company's very survival. What should you do?

The solution isn't clear, and good character isn't enough to guide decision-making in this case. As with all ethical dilemmas, values are in conflict here—obeying the letter of the law versus keeping the plant open and saving jobs. The decision is complicated by the fact that the chemical has been found to be safe and is expected to be approved in a matter of months. As in many of today's business decisions, this complex issue requires the development of occupation-specific skills and abilities. For example, some knowledge in the area of chemistry, worker safety, and environmental laws and regulations would be essential. Basic good intentions and a good upbringing aren't enough.

James Rest, a scholar in the areas of professional ethics and ethics education, argues convincingly that "to assume that any 20-year-old of good general character can function ethically in professional situations is no more warranted than assuming that any logical 20-year-old can function as a lawyer without special education."[26] Good general character (whatever that means) doesn't prepare an individual to deal with the very special ethical problems that are likely to arise in one's career. Individuals must be trained to recognize and solve the unique ethical problems of their particular occupation. That's why many professional schools (business, law, medicine and others) have added ethics courses to their curricula and why most large business organizations now conduct ethics training for their employees.

So, although individual characteristics are a factor in determining ethical behavior, good character alone simply doesn't prepare people for the special ethical problems they're likely to face in their jobs or professions. Special training can prepare them to anticipate these problems, recognize ethical dilemmas when they see them, and provide them with frameworks for thinking about ethical issues in the context of their unique jobs and organizations.

Aren't Adults' Ethics Fully Formed and Unchangeable?

Another false assumption guiding the view that business ethics can't be taught is the belief that one's ethics are fully formed and unchangeable by the time one is old enough to enter college or a job. However, moral psychology research has found that this is definitely not the case. Children and young adults develop moral judgment through a complex process of social interaction with peers, parents, and other significant persons, and this development continues at least through young adulthood. In fact, young adults in their twenties and thirties in moral development educational programs have been found to advance in moral reasoning even more than younger individuals.[27] Given that most people enter professional education programs and corporations as young adults, the opportunity to influence their moral reasoning clearly exists.

Business school students may need ethics training more than most because research has shown they have ranked lower in moral reasoning than students in philosophy, political science, law, medicine, and dentistry.[28] Also, undergraduate business students and those aiming for a business career have been found to be more likely to engage in academic cheating (test cheating, plagiarism, etc.) than students in other majors or those headed toward other careers.[29] At a minimum, professional ethics education can direct attention to the ambiguities and ethical gray areas that are easily overlooked without it. Consider this comment from a 27-year-old Harvard student after a required nine-session module in decision making and ethical values at the beginning of the Harvard MBA program.

> Before, [when] I looked at a problem in the business world, I never consciously examined the ethical issues in play. It was always subconscious and I hope that I somewhat got it. But that [ethics] was never even a consideration. But now, when I look at a problem, I have to look at the impact. I'm going to put in this new ten-million-dollar project. What's going to be the impact on the people that live in the area and the environment.... It's opened my mind up on those things. It's also made me more aware of situations where I might be walking down the wrong path and getting in deeper and deeper, to where I can't pull back.[30]

It should be clear from the above arguments that ethics can indeed be taught. Ethical behavior relies on more than good character. Although good upbringing may provide a kind of moral compass that can help the individual determine the right direction and then follow through on a decision to do the right thing, it's certainly not the only factor determining ethical conduct. In today's highly complex organizations, individuals need additional guidance. They can be trained to recognize the ethical dilemmas that are likely to arise in their jobs; the rules, laws, and norms that apply in that context; reasoning strategies that can be used to arrive at the best ethical decision; and an understanding of the complexities of organizational life that can conflict with one's desire to do the right thing. For example, businesses that do defense-related work are expected to comply with a multitude of laws and regulations that go far beyond what the average person could be expected to know.

The question of whether ethics should be taught remains. Many still believe that ethics is a personal issue that should be left to individuals. They believe that attempts to teach ethics are inappropriate efforts to impose certain values and to control behavior, much like attempts to proselytize about religion. But we believe that employers have a real responsibility to teach employees what they need to know to recognize and deal with ethical issues they are likely to face at work. Failing to help employees recognize the risks in their jobs is like failing to teach a machinist how to operate a machine properly. Both situations can result in harm, and that's just poor management.

DEFINING ETHICS Some of the controversy about whether ethics can or should be taught may stem from disagreement about what we mean by ethics. Ethics can be defined as "a set of moral principles or values," a definition that portrays ethics as highly personal and relative. I have my moral principles, you have yours, and neither of us should try to impose our ethics on the other.

But our definition of ethics—the principles, norms, and standards of conduct governing an individual or group—focuses on conduct. We expect employers to establish guidelines for work-related conduct, including what time to arrive and leave the workplace, whether smoking is allowed on the premises, how customers are to be treated, and how quickly work should be done. Guidelines about ethical conduct aren't much different. Many employers spend a lot of time and money developing policies for a range of employee activities, from how to fill out expense reports to what kind of client gifts are acceptable, to what constitutes a conflict of interest or bribe. If we use this definition, ethics becomes an extension of good management. Leaders identify appropriate and inappropriate conduct, and they communicate their expectations to employees through ethics codes, training programs, and other communication channels.

In most cases, individual employees will agree with their company's expectations and policies. For example, who would disagree that it's wrong to steal company property, lie to customers, dump cancerous chemicals in the local stream, or comply with regulations on defense contracts? At times, however, an employee may find the organization's standards inconsistent with his or her own moral values or principles. For example, a highly religious employee of a health maintenance organization may object to offering abortion as an alternative when providing genetic counseling to pregnant women. Or a highly devoted environmentalist may believe that his or her organization should go beyond the minimum standards of environmental law when making decisions about how much to spend on new technology or on environmental cleanup efforts. These individuals may be able to influence their employers' policies. Otherwise, the person's only recourse may be to leave the organization for one that is a better values match.

GOOD CONTROL OR BAD CONTROL? Whether or not we prefer to admit it, our ethical conduct is influenced (and, to a large degree, controlled) by our environment. In work settings, leaders, managers, and the entire cultural context are an important source of this influence and guidance. If, as managers, we allow employees to drift along without our guidance, we're unintentionally allowing them to be "controlled" by others. If this happens, we're contributing to the creation of "loose cannons" who can put the entire organization at risk. Guidance regarding ethical conduct is an important aspect of controlling employee behavior. It can provide essential information about organizational rules and policies, and guidance about behavior that is considered to be appropriate or inappropriate in a variety of situations.

But should organizations be "controlling" their employees in this way? B.F. Skinner,[31] the renowned late psychologist, argued that it's all right, even preferable, to intentionally control behavior. He believed that all behavior is controlled, intentionally or unintentionally. Therefore, what was needed was more intentional control, not less. Similarly, ethical and unethical behavior in organizations is already being controlled explicitly or implicitly by the existing organizational culture (see Chapter 9). Therefore, organizations that neglect to teach their members "ethical" behavior may be tacitly encouraging "unethical behavior" through benign neglect. It's management's responsibility to provide explicit guidance through direct management and through the organization's formal and informal cultural systems. The supervisor who attempts to influence the ethical behavior of subordinates should be viewed not as a meddler but as a part of the natural management process.

To summarize, we believe that educational institutions and work organizations should teach people about ethics and guide them in an ethical direction. Adults are open to, and generally welcome, this type of guidance. Ethical problems are not caused entirely by bad apples. They're also the product of "bad barrels"—organizational systems that either encourage unethical behavior or merely allow it to occur. Making ethical decisions in today's complex organizations isn't easy. Good intentions and a good upbringing aren't enough. The special knowledge and skill required to make good ethical decisions in a particular job and organizational setting may be different from what's needed to resolve personal ethical dilemmas, and this knowledge and skill must be taught and cultivated.

THIS BOOK IS ABOUT MANAGING ETHICS

Now that we've (hopefully) convinced you that ethics is a worthwhile topic that can and should be taught, we need to discuss our somewhat unique approach to teaching business ethics. This book takes a managerial approach. Between us, we have many years of experience in management, in consulting, and in management teaching and research. Based on this experience, we begin with the assumption that business ethics is essentially about human behavior, and that if we understand human behavior in an organizational context, we can better understand and manage our own and others' ethical conduct. Kent Druyvesteyn was vice president for ethics at General Dynamics from 1985 to 1993 and one of the first "ethics officers" in an American company. He made a clear distinction between philosophy and management in his many talks with students and executives over the years. As he put it, "I am not a philosopher and I am not here to talk about philosophy. Ethics is about conduct."

We agree with Mr. Druyvesteyn. After years of study and experience, we're convinced that a management approach to organizational ethics is needed. As with any other management problem, managers need to understand why people behave the way they do so that they can influence this behavior. Most managers want the people with whom they work to be productive, to produce high quality products, to treat customers well, and to do all of this in a highly ethical manner. They also want and need help accomplishing these goals.

Therefore, we rely on a managerial approach to understanding business ethics. We introduce concepts that can be used to guide managers who want to understand their own ethical behavior and the behavior of others in the organization. And we provide practical guidance to those who wish to lead their department or organization in an ethical direction.

First, we're defining ethical behavior in business as behavior that is consistent with the principles, norms, and standards of business practice that have been agreed upon by society. Although some disagreement exists about what these principles, norms, and standards should be, we believe that there is more agreement than disagreement. Many of the standards have been codified into law. Others can be found in company and industry codes of conduct and international trade agreements.

The ethical decision-making process illustrated in Figure 1.1 involves three basic steps: moral awareness (recognizing the existence of an ethical dilemma), moral judgment (deciding what's right), and ethical behavior (taking action to do the right thing). We propose that all of these steps are influenced by two types of factors: characteristics of individuals and characteristics of organizations. Most ethics texts focus on individual decision making. They teach about philosophical theories that can help individuals analyze the ethics of a given situation to make good moral judgments (the middle stage in the process). The idea is that ethical behavior will improve if people acquire these conceptual tools that can help them make sound ethical decisions. Business people know that deciding what's right represents an essential part of organizational ethics, and we agree. Therefore, we introduce some of the most useful philosophical theories designed to guide moral judgment in Chapter 4. But we also believe that acquiring these decision-making tools provides only a small part of the knowledge needed to improve business ethics. Sometimes people aren't even aware that they are facing an ethical dilemma. That's why moral awareness is considered the first stage in the ethical decision-making process. Even if they are aware that they're facing an ethical dilemma, cognitive limitations and biases often limit their ability to make the best moral judgment (see Chapter 5). Furthermore, even when people know the right thing to do, they often find it difficult to do the right thing because of group or organizational pressures. Therefore, our approach focuses on individuals and organizations—on ways

FIGURE 1.1 The Ethical Decision Making Process

to manage your own conduct and the conduct of other people in the organization, especially those who report to you. (Chapter 7 covers group and organizational influences, and Chapter 9 emphasizes the role of organizational culture.)

As the figure shows, we believe that ethical behavior is affected by both the characteristics of individuals and the characteristics of organizations. But we emphasize organizational factors in this book because those are the factors managers can most influence.

BRINGING ETHICS DOWN TO SIZE

Most ethics texts focus almost exclusively on "big" dilemmas that reflect a corporate position: "Should the company market this product or do business in this particular country? Are executive compensation plans fair and equitable?" We include corporate-level examples, too, because they're important. But this book is also loaded with examples that reflect the ethical dilemmas facing individual employees and managers at all levels (see especially Chapters 3 and 6). "Should you blow the whistle on your employer? Should you accept a gift from a supplier? Should you hire your spouse's company to provide an important service to your firm?" These are the kinds of ethical dilemmas people face every day in work organizations and the kinds of problems that can short-circuit individual careers if they're mishandled.

ETHICS AND THE LAW

You'll find many references to the law in the pages that follow. By including these references, we certainly don't mean to imply that the only guiding principle for deciding what's right should be whatever is legal. Perhaps the easiest way to think about the relationship between business ethics and the law is in terms of a Venn diagram (see Figure 1.2). If we think of the law as reflecting society's minimum norms and standards of business conduct, we can see that there is a great deal of overlap between what's legal and what's ethical. Therefore, most people believe that law-abiding behavior is also ethical behavior. But there are many standards of conduct agreed upon by society that are not codified in law. For example, some conflicts of interest may be legal, but they are generally considered to be unethical in our society and are commonly prohibited in codes of ethics. So, the domain of ethics includes the law but extends beyond it to include the ethical standards and issues that the law does not address. Finally, there are times when you might encounter a law that you believe is unethical. For example, racial discrimination was legal in the United States for a long time. But racial discrimination was and is highly unethical. Similarly, many companies do business in developing countries with few, if any, laws regulating environmental pollution or labor conditions. These companies have to decide whether to adhere to ethical standards that are higher than the legal standards in those countries. Therefore, the legal and ethical domains certainly overlap to a large degree, but not completely. It is conceivable to think of something as being legal and unethical, or unethical but not covered by any law.

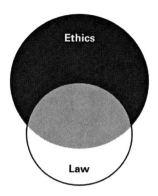

FIGURE 1.2   Relationship between Ethics and Law

HOW THE BOOK IS STRUCTURED

This chapter of the book introduces our approach. Chapter 2 begins with (and attempts to answer) the question many students ask: "Why Be Ethical? Why Bother, Who Cares?" We give concrete examples showing that people at all levels (from employees to managers to society) care about ethics, and that your success in business can depend on how well you can manage ethics.

The sections "Common Ethical Dilemmas" and "Approaches to Ethical Decision Making" focus on ethics from an individual perspective. Chapter 3 categorizes the common ethical problems individuals face at work. Chapter 4 presents the reader with an overview of some basic philosophical theories that have formed the underpinning for the traditional study of business ethics. It also suggests a list of practical decision-making steps individuals can follow to evaluate an ethical dilemma and decide on a course of action. Chapter 5 presents a more psychological approach to individual ethical decision making. It provides a kind of "reality check" for Chapter 4, suggesting that human cognitive biases can interfere with the ideal decision-making process (see Figure 1.1). Chapter 5 also suggests that people do have predispositions to behave in certain ways when faced with ethical dilemmas.

In the sections "Ethical Responsibilities of Managers I" and "Ethical Responsibilities of Managers II", we develop our management perspective on business ethics. Chapter 6 presents some common ethical problems managers face when dealing with their subordinates, their superiors, and their peers and provides advice on what factors to consider when you're confronted with one of them. Chapter 7, "Managing for Ethical Conduct," introduces management concepts that can help explain the group and organizational pressures that influence people to behave ethically or unethically. We also provide practical advice for managers about how to use these management concepts to encourage ethical conduct and discourage unethical conduct in their employees.

The next section entitled "Ethical Problems Facing Organizations." It begins with a chapter entitled "Ethical Problems of Organizations." Although some people question whether corporations are moral entities, there are clearly ethical issues that can be classified as organizational rather than managerial. This chapter classifies those, using a stakeholder perspective, and provides examples. Chapter 9 focuses on business ethics as a phenomenon of organizational culture. It provides a comprehensive overview of how an organization can build a culture that reflects a concern for ethics, and how it can change its culture to be more supportive of ethical conduct. This chapter also emphasizes the importance of executive ethical leadership for the creation of a strong ethical culture. The final section is entitled "Managing Ethical Programs at the Organizational Level." Its chapter is entitled "Managing Ethics and Legal Compliance" which follows with practical advice on how organizations can design an ethics infrastructure, and effective communications and training programs. It also includes examples of the programs various companies have implemented to encourage ethical conduct among their employees. Many of these examples resulted from interviews we conducted with top managers in these companies.

CONCLUSION

We hope that reading this book gives you a better understanding of how you can encourage ethical business behavior in yourself and others. It's critically important that we all understand ethics because good ethics represents the very essence of a civilized society. Ethics is the bedrock on which all of our relationships are built; it's about how we relate to our employers, our employees, our co-workers, our customers, our communities, our suppliers, and one another. Ethics is not about the connection we have to other beings—we are all connected—rather, it's about the quality of that connection. That's the real bottom line.

DISCUSSION QUESTIONS

1. Before reading this chapter, did you think of ethics as "just a fad"? Why or why not? What do you think now? Why?
2. Have you been cynical about business and its leaders? Why or why not? (See the following cynicism exercise.) How does cynicism affect you, as a business student or as a manager?
3. We defined ethical behavior as "behavior that is consistent with the principles, norms, and standards of business practice that have been agreed upon by society." What happens if society hasn't agreed (as when new technologies come on the scene or strong differences of opinion exist)? And what happens if you're doing business in a society different from your own? How would you define ethical behavior then?
4. Cite an example of unethical conduct you have observed in a work setting. Was it the fault of a "bad apple," was there something rotten in the organization that

6. Cite an example of a situation you're familiar with where the "right" answer just wasn't obvious. What would a decision maker need to know in order to arrive at an acceptable solution?
7. Are you convinced that business ethics can and should be taught? Why or why not?

EXERCISE

Your Cynicism Quotient

Answer the following questions as honestly as you can. Circle the number between 1 and 5 that best represents your own beliefs about business.

	Strongly Disagree				Strongly Agree
1. Financial gain is all that counts in business.	1	2	3	4	5
2. Ethical standards must be compromised in business practice.	1	2	3	4	5
3. The more financially successful the business person, the more unethical the behavior.	1	2	3	4	5
4. Moral values are irrelevant in business.	1	2	3	4	5
5. The business world has its own rules.	1	2	3	4	5
6. Business persons care only about making profit.	1	2	3	4	5
7. Business is like a game one plays to win.	1	2	3	4	5
8. In business, people will do anything to further their own interest.	1	2	3	4	5
9. Competition forces business managers to resort to shady practices.	1	2	3	4	5
10. The profit motive pressures managers to compromise their ethical concerns.	1	2	3	4	5
	Strongly Disagree				Strongly Agree

Add the total number of points. The maximum is 50 points. Total _____.

The higher your score, the more cynical you are about ethical business practice. Think about the reasons for your responses. Be prepared to discuss them in class.

NOTES

1. O'Toole, J. 1991. Do good, do well: The business enterprise trust awards. *California Management Review* (spring): 9–24.
2. Olasky, M. N. 1985, 1986. Ministers or panderers: Issues raised by the public relations society code of standards. *Journal of Mass Media Ethics* 1 (1).
3. Andersson, Lynne M. Employee cynicism: An examination using a contract violation framework. *Human Relations,* New York; Nov 1996; Vol. 49, Iss. 11; pg. 1395, 24 pgs.

4. Joseph, J. 2000. Ethics Resource Center's 2000 National Business Ethics Survey Volume: How Employees Perceive Ethics at Work. Washington, D.C.: Ethics Resource Center.
5. Baumhart, R. C. 1961. How ethical are businessmen? *Harvard Business Review* 39 (4): 6–8.; Brenner, S. N., and Molander, E. A. 1977. Is the ethics of business changing? *Harvard Business Review* 55: 57–71.
6. Carroll, B. 1975. Linking business ethics to behavior in organizations. *S. A. M. Advanced Management Journal* 43: 3, 4–11. Jones, T. M., and Gautschi, F. H. 1988. Will the ethics of business change? A survey of future executives. *Journal of Business Ethics* 7: 231–248. Lincoln, D. J., Pressley, M. M., and Little, T. 1982. Ethical beliefs and personal values of top level executives. *Journal of Business Research* 10: 475–487. Posner, B. Z., and Schmidt, W. H. 1987. Ethics in American companies; A managerial perspective. *Journal of Business Ethics* 6: 383–391. Posner, B. Z., and Schmidt, W. H. 1992. Values and the American manager. *California Management Review,* Spring: 80–94
7. Baumhart, R. C. 1961. How ethical are businessmen? *Harvard Business Review* 39 (4): 6–8; Baumhart, R. C. 1968. An honest profit: What businessmen say about ethics in business. New York: Holt, Rinehart and Winston. Brenner, S. N., and Molander, E. A. 1977. Is the ethics of business changing? *Harvard Business Review* 55: 57–71.
8. Wood, J. A., Longenecker, J. G., McKinney, J. A., and Moore, C. W. 1988. Ethical attitudes of students and business professionals: A study of moral reasoning. *Journal of Business Ethics* 7: 249–257. DeSalvia, D. N., and Gemmill, G. R. 1971. An exploratory study of the personal value systems of college students and managers. *Academy of Management Journal* 14: 227–238. Lane, M. S., Schaupp, D., and Parsons, B. 1988. Pygmalion effect. *Journal of Business Ethics* 7: 223–229. Fulmer, R. M. 1968. Business ethics: A view from the campus. *Personnel Administrator* 45 (2): 31–39. Jones, T. M., and Gautschi, F. H. 1988. Will the ethics of business change? A survey of future executives. *Journal of Business Ethics* 7, 231–248.
9. Elber, L. 1997. Bad guys wear business suits: Businessmen and women get a bad rap on television. *(State College, PA) Centre Daily Times,* June 27: 22C.
10. *Fortune.* 1997. Villains of prime time: Business is TVs newest bad guy. *Fortune,* July 7: 32.
11. Bateman, T. S., Sakano, T., and Fujita, M. 1992. Roger, me, and my attitude: Film propaganda and cynicism toward corporate leadership. *Journal of Applied Psychology* 77: 768–771.
12. The Aspen Institute. 2002. Where will they lead? MBA student attitudes about business and society.
13. Brooker, K. 2002. Starting over. *Fortune.* January 21: 50–68.
14. Benson, T. E. 1991. Industry ethics edge upward. *Industry Week,* September 16: 18, 20.
15. Joseph, J. 2000. Ethics Resource Center's 2000 National Business Ethics Survey Volume: How Employees Perceive Ethics at Work. Washington, D.C.: Ethics Resource Center.
16. O'Toole, J. 1991. Do good, do well: The business enterprise trust awards. *California Management Review,* Spring: 9–24.
17. Ibid.
18. Ibid.
19. Baumhart, R. C. 1961. How ethical are businessmen? *Harvard Business Review* 39 (4): 6–8.
20. Abrahamson, E. 1996. Management fashion. Academy of Management Review, 21: 254–285.
21. Weaver, G., Treviño, L.K., and Cochran, P. 1999. Corporate ethics practices in the mid-1990s: An empirical study of the Fortune 1000. *Journal of Business Ethics,* 18 (3), 283–294.
22. Joseph, J. 2000. Ethics Resource Center's 2000 National Business Ethics Survey Volume: How Employees Perceive Ethics at Work. Washington, D.C.: Ethics Resource Center.
23. Fineman, J. 1994. Virtuecrats. *Newsweek,* June 13: 31–36. Levin, M. 1990, Ethics courses: Useless. *New York Times,* November 25. Hanson, K. O. 1988. Why we teach ethics in business school. *Stanford Business School Magazine,* February: 14–16.
24. Treviño, L. K., and Youngblood, A. 1990. Bad apples in bad barrels: A causal analysis of ethical decision-making behavior. *Journal of Applied Psychology* 75 (4): 378–385.
25. Levine, D. B. 1990. The inside story of an inside trader. *Fortune,* May 21: 80–89.

26. Rest, J. R., and Thoma, S. J. 1986. Educational programs and interventions. In *Moral development: Advances in research and theory,* edited by J. Rest. New York: Praeger, 59–88.
27. Rest, J. R. 1987. Moral judgement: An interesting variable for higher education research. Paper for the Annual Convention for the Association for the Study of Higher Education, Baltimore, MD: November 21.
28. McCabe, D., and Treviño, L. K. 1993. Academic dishonesty: Honor codes and other situational influences. *Journal of Higher Education* 64: 522–538.
29. McCabe, D. & Trevino, L. K. 1995. Cheating among business students: A challenge for business leaders and educators. *Journal of Management Education,* 19 (2): 205–218.
30. Piper, T. R., Gentile, M.C., and Parks, S. D. 1993. Can ethics be taught? Boston: Harvard Business School.
31. Skinner, B. F. 1971. *Beyond freedom and dignity.* New York: Knopf.

CHAPTER 2

WHY BE ETHICAL? (WHY BOTHER? WHO CARES?)

INTRODUCTION

It's impossible to know what John might have accomplished if he had lived. Since he was a brilliant young tax lawyer, he might have helped you structure your finances or defended you in court. Since he came from a prominent, civic-minded family, he likely would have been a respected community leader. He surely would have been the friendly, decent kind of neighbor you leave your key with when you leave town. Unfortunately, we'll never know.

We haven't fabricated John's story to make a point. He was a son, a brother, a husband, and he became a father one month after he died at age 32 in December 1978. He died because some of the people who worked for a leading corporation never thought about how their product could affect him. If they did think about it, they didn't care enough to protect John and the thousands of other people who were injured or died as a result of being exposed to asbestos.

John's asbestos exposure occurred during a summer job he held between college and law school. He spent a few weeks that summer unloading sheets of asbestos at a hardware store in Utica, New York. While the dangers of asbestos exposure were largely unknown to the general public back in the late 1960s, the dangers were well known to the people who made it. The manufacturer knew before John was born that asbestos could cause fatal lung diseases and cancers in the workers who handled it. But for decades no one was warned. And John—who had been named a partner in a prestigious Park Avenue law firm just before he died—paid a terrible price, along with ship builders, brake repairers, and tens of thousands of others who worked with the deadly material. Many died young, and many died awful deaths. During the months that John valiantly struggled to live, his doctors couldn't understand how this handsome young attorney contracted a rare cancer that was almost unknown among white-collar workers. It wasn't until his autopsy revealed asbestos fibers in his lungs and intestinal tract that John's father remembered that seemingly harmless summer job so many years before. (John's story is told in *From This Day Forward*, by Nancy Rossi, his widow.)

WHY BE ETHICAL? WHY BOTHER? WHO CARES?

As workers, we should care about ethics because most of us prefer to work for ethical organizations. We want to feel good about ourselves and the work we do. As managers, we must be concerned about the ethics of the people who report to us. More than just our jobs depend on this concern—recent legislation has made managers liable for the criminal activities of their subordinates. Organizations must care about ethics because workers depend on them to help define the boundaries of acceptable and unacceptable behavior. Also, ethical lapses can cost an organization dearly in shattered customer confidence, increased government regulation, and huge fines.

But, most important, we as individuals must care about ethics. Regardless of what kind of jobs we hold, we are human beings first. We must care enough to protect people like John. We must care about the babies who sipped "apple" juice that contained no apples and the women who were maimed by birth control devices and the people who had their retirement savings wiped out by the greed of a few high-placed swindlers at Enron and other firms. These people are our parents, spouses, siblings, children, and friends. We live in a world community and we're all inextricably connected to each other and to the environment that surrounds us. Our future depends on our caring enough.

THE MOTIVATION TO BE ETHICAL

Classical economists assume that practically all human behavior, including altruism, is motivated solely by self-interest—that humans are purely rational economic actors who make choices solely on the basis of cold cost/benefit analyses. But there is much evidence to suggest that people also act for altruistic or moral purposes that seem to have little to do with cost/benefit analyses.[1] For example, people will mail back lost wallets to strangers, cash and all; help strangers in distress; and donate blood marrow for strangers or a kidney to a family member.

In his book *The Moral Dimension,* Etzioni[2] cited many more examples and research evidence to document his claim that human action has two distinct sources: the pursuit of self-interest, and moral commitments. Accordingly, most human decisions are based on ethical and emotional considerations as well as rational economic self-interest. People are motivated by both economic and moral concerns.

Therefore, we begin this chapter with an important assumption—that, as members of society, all of us have moral and ethical concerns as well as self-interested economic concerns. You will see in this chapter that people and organizations care about ethics for reasons that stem from both of these sources. For example, organizations may be interested in being ethical in order to avoid criminal liability or a bad reputation, or they may be interested in being ethical because they believe it's the right thing to do.

THE MEDIA FOCUS ON ETHICS AND CORPORATE REPUTATION

If you believe that the media focus attention on issues people care about, then lots of people must care about ethics. In recent years, the media spotlight has focused on serious ethical lapses in every type of organization—business, government, educational, religious, sports, and others. We've all heard about senior managers who line their pockets at employees' expense, auditors who overlook serious accounting problems, investment analysts who sell stocks they know to be in trouble, insider traders, businesses that overcharge the government, government employees who steal or misuse funds, academics who falsify their research results, students who cheat, ministers who steal from their congregations, priests who abuse children, athletes who take bribes or use performance-enhancing drugs, and companies that lie to their customers.

Hollywood, society's most powerful image-maker, has generally portrayed business people as sleazy, greedy, and heartless. Who can forget J.R. Ewing, who "slithered across the TV screen as the vile head of Ewing Oil" on the TV series *Dallas,* or Michael Douglas as Gordon Gecko, the unscrupulous corporate raider who corrupted a young stockbroker in the classic film *Wall Street*?[3] More recent Hollywood examples include harsh portrayals of business in *Boiler Room, Glengarry Glen Ross, The Insider,* and *Erin Brockovich.* Charles Brown, former chairman of AT&T, asked, "When was the last time you watched a TV sitcom in which a business person was the hero?"[4]

But can the media really influence an organization's image? The answer is yes. Since 1982, *Fortune* magazine has conducted an annual "most admired corporations" survey, based on ratings provided by senior executives, outside directors, and financial analysts. Using these survey results along with additional data, an academic study investigated the relationship between media coverage and change in corporate image or reputation.[5] Overall, more positive media coverage meant a more positive corporate reputation. And for companies that began with poor reputations, positive media exposure was associated with significant image improvements.

Does reputation really matter? According to *Business Week,* "business has a huge stake in the way the rest of society perceives its ethical standards." On the negative side, scandals give business "a black eye"[6] and cost money. For example, in response to media reports that raised questions about Dow Corning's breast implants, the stock of Corning, Inc., one of the two corporate parents, declined by about 15 percent, despite the fact that the implants represented only around 1 percent of Dow Corning's business, and insurance coverage seemed adequate to cover potential lawsuits.[7] Similarly, Exxon faced years of negative media scrutiny after the Exxon Valdez oil spill. And Monsanto was blindsided by protesters' hostile reaction to its genetically altered seeds. In response to protesters' demonstrations against genetically modified products at the "Battle in Seattle" (protests against the World Trade Organization meeting in Seattle in 2001), Monsanto and other biotechnology firms have been hard at work portraying themselves as helping farmers and consumers as well as shareholders.[8]

Business isn't the only kind of organization that can be negatively affected by media exposure and a bad reputation. Since the 1940s, the United Way has been the "blue chip of charities." In 1992, the United Way's reputation as a trusted community philanthropic organization was severely damaged when the extravagances of its leader were aired in the press. President William Aramony resigned amid charges of nepotism and misuse of agency funds to support his lavish lifestyle. For the United Way, reputation translates into dollars contributed to its funding coffers. After the scandal, the organization (both at national and community levels) struggled to regain its lost public trust. Reports suggested that the United Way network raised $66 million less in 1992 than it did in 1991. In attempts to regain the public trust, United Way appointed a new president, implemented new cost controls and accountability measures, and established an ethics program. For United Way, "doing business differently" came to be seen as a matter of the organization's survival.[9] The organization reeled from the scandal for years as donors gave less.[10]

Similarly, sexual abuse by Roman Catholic priests and the hierarchy's efforts to cover it up have had a devastating effect on the reputation of the Church. The scandals have profoundly damaged the trust of the faithful and the ability of the Church to act as a moral authority.

On a more positive note, a favorable corporate reputation "may enable firms to charge premium prices, attract better applicants, enhance their access to capital markets, and attract investors."[11] In its March 2, 1998 issue, *Fortune* reported that if an investor had bought $1,000 worth of stock in its top ten most admired companies and reinvested the dividends, that investment would have compounded into $146,419—three times more than a similar investment in the Standard & Poor's 500 would have produced over the same time period. But top financial performance alone does not get a company into the ranks of the "most admired." The most admired companies have great leaders and outstanding employee relations, and they have stayed out of legal and ethical trouble. In 2002, Southwest Airlines once again appeared on *Fortune*'s list of America's most admired companies. Herb Kelleher, the chairman of the board, said, "We pay just as good wages and benefits as other airlines, but our costs are lower because our productivity is higher, which is achieved through the dedicated energy of our people. It's sheer willpower—no mechanical tricks." In explaining how Southwest can empty and refill a plane in 20 minutes when it takes other airlines an hour, Kelleher said, "We've got exactly the same equipment. The difference is, when a plane pulls into a gate, our people run to meet it." The leaders of the most admired companies are in love with their businesses; Kelleher said, "I love it, I love it—I sure as heck do."[12] Kelleher uses the word "love" a lot and sees it as key to the successful corporate culture. As an example, post September 11, 2001, Southwest employees organized an effort to donate part of their pay to the company. The company didn't even have to ask. The airline's success has continued in the post-September 11 environment as it continues to fill planes and remain profitable in an industry that has reeled from the effects of the terrorist attacks.[13]

The media generally ignores the millions of routine but ethical transactions that must occur every day if society is to function effectively. However, the media spotlight does shine on those particularly positive or negative events that are considered to be newsworthy. Organizations that find themselves in this spotlight will find their reputations either enhanced or sullied.

INDUSTRIES CARE ABOUT ETHICS

In some industries, companies have joined together in voluntary efforts to promote ethical conduct among organizations in the industry. The most prominent among these efforts are the Defense Industry Initiative and Responsible Care, an initiative of the Chemical Manufacturers Association. A cynic might say that these initiatives are aimed solely at preventing more intrusive government regulation and that companies in these industries don't truly "care" about ethics. Certainly, these types of initiatives have generally begun in response to a scandal or crisis. But over the years, they tend to take on a life of their own. Members internalize beliefs about appropriate conduct, hire support staff, and develop structures for enforcement that become institutionalized among member organizations. Research evidence suggests that industry attention to social issues is an important influence on company behavior. When an industry pays attention to particular stakeholder concerns (for example, in industry publications), companies in that industry are much more likely to respond to those concerns.[14]

The Defense Industry Initiative on Business Conduct and Ethics (DII) is a major voluntary industry initiative. It is described on the organization's Web site (www.dii.org) as "a consortium of U.S. defense industry contractors which subscribes to a set of principles for achieving high standards of business ethics and conduct." It developed out of the President's Blue Ribbon Commission on Defense Management (the Packard Commission), which was convened after a number of defense-industry scandals in the early 1980s. In 1986, the commission concluded that the industry could be improved by focusing on corporate self-governance. A number of companies voluntarily joined together to "embrace and promote ethical business conduct," and their work together continues today. As of July 2001, 48 companies were signatories, and, as such, they have agreed to live according to the following obligations:

- Adopt a written code of conduct
- Conduct employees' orientation and training with respect to the code
- Provide employees a mechanism to express concerns about corporate compliance with procurement laws and regulations
- Adopt procedures for voluntary disclosure of violations of federal procurement laws
- Participate in Best Practices Forums
- Publish information that shows each Signatory's commitment to the above

The organization hosts a two-day Best Practices Forum each year, with participation from the industry's prime customer, the Department of Defense. It also hosts workshops on specific topics, including an annual one-day workshop to train ethics professionals, and publishes an annual report to the public and government summarizing DII activities.

Responsible Care, a voluntary initiative of the chemical industry, was launched in the U.S. in 1988, in response to major accidents such as the 1984 disaster at a Union Carbide plant in Bhopal, India. Its aim is to secure the public's trust in the chemical industry by demonstrating responsible corporate citizenship. Members subscribe to a voluntary code of conduct that is monitored and enforced by the Chemical Manufacturers Association. The codes cover the following areas: community awareness and emergency response, pollution prevention, safe distribution of chemicals in transit, employee health and safety, and safe handling of chemicals from manufacture through disposal. The codes and policies extend beyond legal compliance and focus on continuous improvement, communication with external stakeholders, and training of suppliers on the standards.[15]

EXECUTIVE LEADERS CARE ABOUT ETHICS

Some of us are understandably cynical about CEO ethics after the widely publicized scandals, huge compensation packages, and CEO "perp walks" of 2002. But many business executives do care about ethics in their own organizations and about business's image in society.

John Akers, former chairman of the board of IBM, wrote that "No society anywhere will compete very long or successfully with people stabbing each other in the back; with people trying to steal from each other; with everything requiring notarized confirmation because you can't trust the other fellow; with every little squabble ending in litigation; and with government writing reams of regulatory legislation, tying business hand and foot to keep it honest.... There is no escaping this fact; the greater the measure of mutual trust and confidence in the ethics of a society, the greater its economic strength."[16]

Robert D. Haas, chairman of the board of Levi Strauss & Co., discussed the importance of company values this way:

> Levi has always treated people fairly and cared about their welfare. The usual term is "paternalism." But it is more than paternalism, really—a genuine concern for people and a recognition that people make this business successful.
>
> In the past, however, that tradition was viewed as something separate from how we ran the business. We always talked about the "hard stuff" and the "soft stuff." The soft stuff was the company's commitment to our work force. And the hard stuff was what really mattered; getting pants out the door.
>
> What we've learned is that the soft stuff and the hard stuff are becoming increasingly intertwined. A company's values—what it stands for, what its people believe in—are crucial to its competitive success. Indeed, values drive the business.... Values are where the hard stuff and the soft stuff come together.[17]

Joe Paterno, Penn State University's legendary football coach, said the following in an interview about his program's reputation for integrity.

> It makes good sense to be ethical—to be honest. If there's a rule, I insist that we adhere to the rule. If my people say, "Hey the other guy is breaking the

rule," I say in the short run, it may hurt us, but in the long run we'll be way ahead of them. It may mean we have to work a little harder. Instead of calling on ten players to recruit five, we may have to call on fifteen or twenty.... It's certainly doable, because we're doing it. I don't care if it's in football or in business. You've got to have enough guts and enough confidence in your ability to do it right.... There's a difference between success and excellence in the sense that it's easy to make money. It's easy to win. You can manipulate, cut corners. But, I think you have to have a standard that you believe in and stay with it. We're in it for the long run. This isn't a get-rich-quick kind of operation. If we were in business, we wouldn't play games with the company to get the stock up in the next three years. We'd be in it for the long haul. And, we'd be a better company. Once you establish that, the stockholders or the fans love you.

We believe that, although intertwined with the "hard stuff," organizational ethics is a distinct managerial concern that must be addressed by management at all levels of the organization. Top management's role is particularly important. The leaders of America's business organizations don't "leap from bed in the morning in order to maximize the risk-adjusted present value of streams of future cash flows." Their role is "not simply financial and administrative, but social, political, and moral."[18] This book will provide insight into this moral leadership role and its importance in creating and maintaining the organization's ethical culture (see Chapter 9).

MANAGERS CARE ABOUT ETHICS

Managers care about ethics in part because they face the thorny problem of how to prevent and manage unethical behavior in their ranks. Ask any manager for examples and be prepared to spend the day. As just one example of self-interested unethical behavior, the U.S. Chamber of Commerce estimates that workplace theft costs U.S. businesses between $20 billion and $40 billion each year, and employees are thought to be responsible for much of it.[19] In addition to self-interested behavior, employees may engage in unethical behavior because they think (rightly or wrongly) that it's expected or that their behavior is justified because they've been treated unfairly. Or, they simply may not know that they are doing something that's considered to be unethical.[20]

Whatever its source, subordinates' unethical behavior is a management problem that won't go away. It may become even more of a challenge as restructuring reduces management layers, leaving fewer managers to supervise more workers. With more workers to supervise, the manager can't directly observe behavior. Restructuring also increases the number of part-time or contingency workers. These workers are likely to feel less loyalty to the organization and may be more prone to engage in unethical behaviors such as theft.

Furthermore, more workers may cross the ethical/unethical behavior line in response to fierce business competition and strict focus on the bottom line. Employees may believe that they can help the company succeed (at least in the short term) by fudging sales figures, abusing competitors, or shortchanging customers.

Those who are potential layoff candidates are also more likely to flirt with impropriety.[21] Many perceive the message to be "reaching objectives is what matters and how you get there isn't that important."[22] Therefore, today's managers may have to work even harder to communicate that ethical conduct is expected, even in the midst of aggressive competition.

Finally, many managers understand the positive long-term benefit a reputation for ethics can bring to business dealings. Carl Skooglund, former vice president and ethics director at Texas Instruments, had this to say:

> There are very positive, even competitive, reasons to be ethical. If you walk into a relationship and somebody says, "I know you, I know your track record, I can trust you," that's important. Two years ago, in a survey that we sent out to employees, I received an anonymous comment from somebody who said, "A reputation for ethics which is beyond reproach is a silent partner in all business negotiations." I agree and it works in all personal and business relationships. An unethical company is very difficult to do business with. You can't trust them. You're never sure if a commitment's a commitment. At TI, our customers have told us that they can be sure of one thing: Once TI commits, we're going to break our tail to make it happen. That's an easy company to do business with.

EMPLOYEES CARE ABOUT ETHICS: EMPLOYEE ATTRACTION AND COMMITMENT

Organizations are concerned about their ability to hire and retain the best workers. The evidence suggests that employees are more attracted to and more committed to ethical organizations. "People who know that they are working for something larger with a more noble purpose can be expected to be loyal and dependable, and, at a minimum, more inspired."[23]

Graduating students at more than one hundred colleges and universities now sign or recite the "Graduation Pledge," in which they promise to "take into account the social and environmental consequences of any job" they consider. They also pledge to "try to improve these aspects of any organizations" where they work. Elite universities such as Harvard and Cornell are participating. Prospective employers should be very interested in these graduates and their concerns that go beyond just making a living.[24]

Recent surveys confirm that it may be important to consider how potential and current employees are affected by an organization's ethics. In a survey conducted by *Working Woman* magazine, "a strong majority of those polled said that they would not work for a company with a history of environmental accidents, insider trading or worker accidents, or a law firm that defends known racketeers."[25] In another survey conducted by a national opinion research firm, ethical corporate behavior, honest company communications, and respectful treatment ranked among employees' five top-ranked goals, before good pay, which was eleventh on the list, and job security, which ranked fourteenth. Ethical corporate behavior was ranked so high because "workers translate the ethics of the company into how they're personally treated." People "want to be proud of where they work." They "don't want to work for bandits, and when companies get negative publicity for their activities, workers suffer."[26]

Academic studies have also found that workers are more attracted to socially responsible firms.[27] They are also more committed to organizations that have a "benevolent climate"—one that focuses on the welfare of employees and the community, while organizational commitment is lower in "egoistic" climates (based on self-interest and people being out for themselves). Employees are also more committed to organizations whose top managers represent high ethical standards and whose reward systems support ethical conduct and discipline unethical conduct.[28] Yet another survey found that managers who believed their senior management to be credible (i.e., honest and competent) reported positive attachments to their organization.[29]

INDIVIDUALS CARE ABOUT ETHICS: REPUTATION COUNTS

Employees are not just organizational drones. They are individual human beings who are concerned about their relationships and their personal reputations. In today's work environment, success depends on one's ability to work effectively with others. Trust greases the wheels of working relationships with peers across departments and on project teams. We disagree with the old adage that "nice guys (or gals) finish last." If it looks like bad guys (or gals) come out ahead, this is generally a short-run result. A reputation for being difficult to work with, dishonest, or mean often catches up with you as co-workers withhold important information and promotions go to others. Given the importance of relationships to effectiveness in business today, one's reputation for integrity is an essential ingredient for success and personal satisfaction.

In our interview with Carl Skooglund, he talked about a story he used to tell college recruits who visited Texas Instruments.

> I quote Helen Hayes... She made a statement that applies to anybody who is a parent, a teacher, a manager, a supervisor, a spouse, anybody who is in a position of trust. She said, "When they call you a star, you are obligated to conduct yourself above reproach. People give you their hearts and their trust, and you have no right to let them down." I tell the recruits, look, there are going to be decisions you have to make. There are going to be times when things will be given to you. There are going to be times when things will be taken away—perhaps even your job. But throughout your professional life, there is one thing that nobody can ever take away from you unless you make the decision to let them take it away from you, and that is your integrity.

DOES SOCIETY CARE? BUSINESS AND SOCIAL RESPONSIBILITY

Most of this book is about ethics inside organizations. But we also need to consider business's role in society and whether business has social as well as financial responsibilities. A rich literature on corporate social performance suggests reasons why corporations must be socially, as well as financially, responsible.[30] First, from an economic perspective, business must use its power responsibly or risk losing it. Businesses are responsible to multiple stakeholders. Recall that a stakeholder was defined in Chapter 1 as any party (e.g., customers, employees, suppliers, the government, stockholders, the community) who has a stake in what the organization does and how it performs.[31] These stakeholders often have the power to interfere with a firm's autonomy and economic freedom. For example, employees can strike, customers can boycott products, protesters can bring bad publicity, and the government can pass laws and regulate a firm's activities. In this economic perspective on social responsibility, corporations must be socially responsible in order to avoid economic harm and in order to maintain the legitimacy granted by society.[32]

A second duty-based perspective argues that businesses have an ethical responsibility to stakeholders that goes beyond avoiding economic harm. Responsible executives have a duty to care about justice and stakeholder rights because, as part of society, it is simply the right thing to do. This perspective supports corporate policies and practices that go beyond legal or regulatory requirements, such as the development of quality products that contribute to societal welfare, human resource practices that treat employees fairly, manufacturing processes that protect the environment, and contributions to help the firm's community. These policies and practices may "pay," especially in the long term. For example, the best employees may be attracted to firms that treat people well. But those who argue for the duty-based perspective would say that the positive duty exists whether or not an economic payoff results.[33]

Obviously, the biggest corporate social responsibility challenges come when ethical responsibility and economic responsibility conflict. For example, if the long-term economic interests of the firm require that employees be laid off, a duty-based perspective would require that the layoffs be carried out in a fair and just manner.

Corporate social responsibility (CSR) has been conceptualized as a pyramid constituting four kinds of responsibility that must be considered simultaneously: economic, legal, ethical, and philanthropic.[34] (See Figure 2.1.)

FIGURE 2.1 Corporate Social Responsibility Pyramid
Reprinted with permission from the Foundation for the School of Business at Indiana University, *Business Horizons*, July/August, 1991.

Economic Responsibilities

Economic responsibilities refer to business's primary function as a producer of goods and services that consumers need and want, while making an acceptable profit. This responsibility is considered to be primary, because without financial viability the other responsibilities become moot issues.

Economist Milton Friedman is the best-known proponent of the argument that management's sole responsibility is to maximize profits for shareholders. Yet even he states that management should "make as much money as possible while conforming to the basic rules of society, both those embodied in the law and those embodied in ethical custom."[35] Interestingly, this statement tacitly embraces two of the three additional components of the corporate social responsibility pyramid: legal responsibility and ethical responsibility.

Legal Responsibilities

In addition to its economic responsibilities, business is expected to carry out its work in accordance with the law and government regulations. The law guiding business practice can be viewed as a fundamental precept of the free enterprise system and as coexisting with economic responsibilities. As we said in Chapter 1, the law can also be viewed as representing society's minimum norms and standards of business conduct.

Ethical Responsibilities

Obviously, not every societal expectation has been codified into law. Therefore, ethical responsibilities encompass the more general responsibility to do what's right and avoid harm. There are many good examples of companies going beyond legal requirements to fulfill what they perceive to be ethical responsibilities. For example, Levi Strauss says on its Web site (www.levistrauss.com) that it was the "first multinational company to develop a comprehensive code of conduct" designed to ensure that the company's workers "anywhere in the world are safe, and treated with dignity and respect." Further, the company's commitment to diversity began in the 1940s, well before the Civil Rights Act of 1964.

In another example, Abbott Laboratories, a pharmaceutical firm, has gone beyond its legal responsibilities to provide its AIDS tests and protease inhibitor drugs at no profit in 35 African countries (www.abbott.com). In a speech to the 2002 Conference Board (a global membership organization that brings executives together and disseminates knowledge about management) meeting on ethics, Abbott chief executive officer Miles D. White talked about his recent visit to Africa and his concern that providing these drugs at cost was still too expensive for the AIDS victims who desperately need them to survive. He also discussed the challenge of balancing the demands of multiple stakeholders, from some stockholders who believe that "their" money should not be spent on such philanthropic endeavors to activist groups and other stockholders who believe that the company, because of its knowledge and wealth, has special obligations to help those in need.

Johns Manville, a manufacturer of specialty building products, now goes beyond its legal responsibilities with regard to product safety—perhaps not surprisingly, given its problematic history (more than 150,000 lawsuits alleging health problems from exposure to asbestos). In addition to complying with U.S. law by placing warning labels on all of its fiberglass products, the company also places warning labels on fiberglass products being shipped to Japan. Such warnings are not required by local law, and the company was even advised against it by the Japanese government because the warnings might result in cancer fears. Tom Stephens, former chairman, president, and chief executive officer, said, "But a human being in Japan is no different from a human being in the U.S. We told them we had a policy. We had to have a label." Although the company lost 40 percent of its sales to Japan in one year, it was later able to rebuild its Japanese business.[36] Thus, the ethical responsibility category frequently intersects with the legal category, pushing the expansion of legal responsibilities, and placing expectations on business persons to function at a level above the law.

It can be costly not to anticipate societal expectations about what's ethical. For example, on St. Patrick's Day 2000, The Home Depot found itself scurrying for cover. Activists from the Rainforest Action Network used the company's own public address system to embarrass the company, broadcasting storewide announcements in multiple stores like "On aisle seven you'll find mahogany ripped from the heart of the Amazon." Despite the profitability of selling mahogany furniture, the firm had to ask itself whether it was ethical to sell mahogany, a vital resource in rainforests.[37]

In 1993, when GM claimed that its sidesaddle fuel tank design (placed outside the truck frame in order to carry more fuel) met all federal regulations, a Georgia jury apparently wasn't convinced that the company had met its ethical obligation to avoid harm. In the case of a 17-year-old who was killed when his pickup truck's gas tank exploded, the jury found the company negligent and awarded the boy's parents over $100 million in punitive damages.

Philanthropic Responsibilities

Finally, philanthropic responsibilities engage the corporation's participation in activities that promote human welfare or goodwill. This generally includes donations of time and money, such as donations to the United Way or mentoring programs for disadvantaged youth. Because philanthropy is considered by many people to be a voluntary or discretionary aspect of corporate social responsibility, failure to be philanthropic is generally not considered to be unethical and some may question whether it is a "responsibility" at all. On the other hand, in American culture, those with wealth (including wealthy businesses) are expected to share their good fortune and are offered tax incentives for doing so. Andrew Carnegie, the nineteenth-century steel baron who gave millions to charity, said, "He who dies rich dies thus disgraced." He believed that the rich were morally obligated to give their riches to the community and they should do so during their lifetime.[38] In a 1990s version of the same belief, broadcasting tycoon Ted Turner pledged $1 billion to the United Nations in 1997 to help refugees, and he challenged other wealthy business people to follow his lead. An even more astounding figure is the $24 billion endowment created by Microsoft founder Bill Gates and his family. The Bill & Melinda Gates Foundation, run by Bill's father, William H. Gates Sr., has become the largest foundation in history and its main goal is to bridge the gap in human health that exists between the developed and developing world (see www.gatesfoundation.org). It took a while for Gates to join the ranks of philanthropists, but he eventually learned that in American society, those with the most resources are expected to help those who are less fortunate. He jumped on board and hasn't looked back. These modern-day philanthropists are ambitious, strategic, and global in their charitable giving. They are actively involved in tackling huge global ills such as cancer, the AIDS epidemic, and they demand accountability and results.[39] If one believes in philanthropic responsibility for corporations, obvious questions include what types of initiatives make most sense, how much to invest in them, how to monitor and evaluate them, and whether to pay for philanthropic initiatives through a firm's operating budget or a foundation. Unfortunately, little research exists to help us answer these questions.[40]

GOVERNMENT REGULATION OF BUSINESS

Government regulation is one way that society shows it cares about responsible conduct in business. Consider recent changes in health care in the United States. Market forces have helped to reduce inflation in health care costs as managed care companies compete for patients. But citizens have called upon state and federal government to intervene with regulations that limit the financial incentives these companies can give to doctors and that bar them from excluding people with preexisting medical conditions. In *Everything for Sale: The Virtues and Limits of Markets* (Knopf, 1997), author Robert Kuttner argues that regulation is necessary because, as a society, we have commitments to certain public purposes such as universal access to electricity (even in unprofitable rural areas) and health insurance (even for otherwise uninsurable cancer or AIDS patients). Furthermore, circumstances exist when consumers don't have choices, as when there is only one local cable-TV company or when economies of scale make competition inefficient. (For example, it wouldn't be efficient to string multiple power lines to every home.) Sometimes, in order to create competition, monopolies (such as the former AT&T) need to be restrained through regulation. Finally, government is responsible for preventing serious risks to our system (for example, by regulating the financial services and electricity industries) and for holding companies accountable for the "externalities" they create. *Externalities are costs to society, such as air and water pollution, that are produced by companies but that are not reflected in the company's cost structure.*[41] As consumers, we rely on our representatives in government to hold companies accountable for their actions. We want to be sure that our air, food, and water are safe, that airlines don't skimp on maintenance, security, or pilot training, and that physicians who work for managed care companies put patient care ahead of profits.

In the post Enron/Andersen/WorldCom/Tyco/Adelphia environment, business is bracing for a regulatory backlash that is supported by many in the public. In recent years, the push to deregulate business had been quite successful. But, interestingly, deregulated businesses (e.g., telecommunications, energy, banking) have been in the forefront of the scandals. Enron clearly took advantage of the lack of regulation of its energy trading business to influence government officials and play games with the numbers.[42] The management of Enron, and its auditors and lawyers, failed to play by the ethical rules guiding American business. Perhaps as a result of these monumental ethical failings, a *Business Week*/Harris poll conducted in January 2002 found that the percentage of people who said they had "hardly any" confidence in business executives nearly doubled from 13 percent in 1999 to 24 percent in 2002. Seventy-nine percent of these survey respondents believed that senior executives put their own interests ahead of those of employees and shareholders. In a February 2002 survey conducted by the Opinion Research Corporation, 43 percent of active, individual investors had less confidence in the stock market in the aftermath of Enron, and only 23 percent of U.S. investors believed strongly in the stock market's ability to reflect the fair value of stocks.[43]

It's no wonder then that the New York Stock Exchange led the pack calling for reform. Its new reforms, passed in August 2002, enforce corporate board and audit independence. Congress passed the Sarbanes-Oxley Act legislating corporate governance and accounting reform in July 2002. Among other things, the law sets up a new oversight board for the accounting industry, requires that companies change their auditors every five years, reduces the range of services auditors can offer, and bars senior executives from selling stock during certain time periods.[44] In addition, CEOs and CFOs of public companies are now required to certify the accuracy of their financial statements, which they did for the first time in August 2002. A false certification can get the executive a $5 million fine and up to 20 years in prison. Securities fraud is punishable with up to 25 years in jail, and shredding or destroying documents in federal investigations can get the perpetrator up to 20 years.[45] Large shareholders are also getting into the act. For example, the Vanguard Group, a large mutual fund company, sent a letter outlining its expectations to 450 companies whose shares it owns.[46] It isn't clear how much steam the move to increase regulation will maintain—memories can be short in Washington, D.C. But, it is clear that the regulatory movement has received a significant shot in the arm from these scandals and that the public wants more, not less, regulation.

Perhaps in an attempt to stave off regulation, in July 2002 the Pharmaceutical Research and Manufacturers of America (PhRMA) embraced new guidelines for how pharmaceutical sales representatives can market to physicians. For decades this has been fertile territory for conflicts of interest, and PhRMA's guidelines are the beginning of a cleanup. The new code specifically prohibits pharmaceutical sales reps from paying for a range of perks they have employed in the past to get access to physicians who make the decisions about which drugs to prescribe. The perks ranged from dinners to ski vacations, sporting events, cruises, and even paying for a physician to fill up his car at a service station—all in an attempt to get air time with the doctors. Although PhRMA has no enforcement provisions, many of the pharmaceutical companies are expected to take the new guidelines seriously. Executives from Merck, GlaxoSmithKlein, Wyeth Ayerst, and others have spoken publicly in support of the guidelines.[47] But the government was not content to leave the companies to regulate themselves on this issue. In September 2002, the Department of Health and Human Services issued similar guidelines prohibiting pharmaceutical companies from offering incentive payments of any other "tangible benefits" to reward the prescribing or purchasing of their drugs. Companies that flout the new standards can be investigated and prosecuted under federal fraud and kickback statutes.[48]

IS SOCIALLY RESPONSIBLE BUSINESS GOOD BUSINESS?

We don't have a perfect answer to this question. There's anecdotal evidence on both sides, and truly definitive research has not been done. We can probably all name individuals who have "gotten ahead" the unethical way. Despite our desire to believe otherwise, unethical managers can be successful and unethical organizations can be profitable, at least in the short term. On the other hand, one can also point to highly ethical organizations that have been extremely profitable. In an attempt to demonstrate a positive link between good ethics and firm financial performance, James Burke, former CEO of Johnson & Johnson, compiled a list of major companies with a reputation for ethics and social responsibility. The group, including such recognized names as Johnson & Johnson, Coca-Cola, Gerber, IBM, Deere, 3M, Xerox, J.C. Penney, and Pitney Bowes, grew at a rate of 11.3 percent annually from 1950 to 1990, while the growth rate for Dow Jones industrials as a whole was only 6.2 percent for the same period.[49]

Many business leaders argue that ethics pays in the long term. For example, Norman Augustine, retired chairman of Lockheed Martin, a large defense contractor, recounted a situation when the company's ethics were on the line. When competing on a government contract, the company received a brown paper bag containing their competitor's bid. They immediately turned it over to the U.S. government and told the competitor about it. The company lost the contract, employees lost jobs, and shareholders lost money—huge short-term losses. But Augustine is convinced that the loss was only short term. "We helped establish a reputation that, in the long run, will draw us business … it always pays off in the long term."

Over the last thirty years or so, 95 empirical studies have attempted to document the relationship between social responsibility and financial performance. These studies have shown both positive and negative relationships, although positive relationships predominate and there are few negative ones.[50] But, when positive correlations were found, it wasn't clear whether social responsibility led to increased financial performance or whether higher financial performance provided firms with more slack resources that they could then devote to social performance.

Recent research suggests that both may be true.[51] One study used an index of eight attributes of corporate social responsibility as rated by the firm Kinder, Lydenberg, Domini (KLD), an independent service that assesses corporate social performance of companies in the S&P 500, based on firms' responses to key stakeholder interests. Firms with strong financial performance were rated higher on corporate social performance, suggesting that companies that do well financially also allocate more resources to social concerns—they "do good by doing well." Those that are not in good financial health may not have the funds to engage in philanthropy or other discretionary social performance activities. The study also found that

financial performance depends on good social performance, sug
also "do well by doing good." The authors termed this the "good
ory," arguing that good social performance is related to other goo
tices. It is likely that these relationships are linked in what the
"virtuous circle" in which good corporate social performance feeds financial performance and good financial performance makes it possible to continue good corporate social performance. Clearly, being socially responsible doesn't harm the firm's bottom line as some economists have suggested in the past. In fact, the study's findings suggest that a firm's relationships with key stakeholders (e.g., employees, community, natural environment) are important to its financial performance.[52]

In a more recent study, researchers compared the 2001 "100 Best Corporate Citizens" (as measured by a synthesis of the KLD rankings) with *Business Week*'s financial rankings. Average financial performance of the 100 best corporate citizen firms was significantly better (more than ten percentage points higher) than the average financial performance of the rest of the S&P 500.[53] These firms also had higher rankings in *Fortune*'s 2001 reputation survey. Corporate citizenship was measured by rating companies' service to seven different stakeholder groups: stockholders, community, minorities and women, employees, environment, non–U.S. stakeholders, and customers.[54] Some studies have also focused on specific aspects of corporate social performance, such as family-friendly human resource policies. One recent study found that firms that made *Working Mother* magazine's list of "Most Family Friendly Companies" for the first time experienced significant, positive, abnormal stock market returns following the announcement that they were on the list.[55] Finally, researchers have found that a reputation for higher corporate social performance is associated with decreased firm financial risk.[56]

Research has also found that social irresponsibility and illegal corporate behavior are associated with substantial negative stock market returns. One study synthesized the results of 27 studies that covered over 2,000 incidents of socially irresponsible or illegal behavior. Across these studies, stock prices decreased significantly in response to socially irresponsible or illegal acts, thereby decreasing shareholder wealth.[57] These results suggest that there are definitely costs to being socially irresponsible.

The research we just reviewed supports the idea that social responsibility can be financially rewarding and risk reducing, and that irresponsibility can be costly. But social responsibility cannot compensate for a poor business strategy. Levi Strauss is a 150-year-old company that has long been known for social responsibility. But it recently experienced a slide in revenue that is just beginning to turn around. A new CEO, Phil Marineau, was hired from Pepsi North America and has initiated a turnaround strategy aimed at product innovation, the system of styles and sizes, as well as information technology initiatives to track sales. The best companies have both excellent business strategies as well as ethical and socially responsible business practices.

Finally, we would like to propose that business people may have another reason (besides financial performance) to believe in "good ethics" and social responsibility—because they're people first, who value their good reputations and the opinion of their friends, family, and community. They're guided by a moral compass that points them in an ethical direction, as well as a financial compass that points them ward consideration of the costs and benefits of a decision. As one businessperson put it, "I can only really speak for myself, and to me, my word is the most important thing in my life and my credibility as an individual is paramount. All the other success we have had is secondary."[58]

Ethicist Michael Josephson clearly separated good ethics from good business when he said:

> Goodness does not guarantee winning. And unless we can teach that to people, they are always going to look for the angle ... ethics [is a] separate, independent evaluation of conduct.... Ethics is like your skin—it goes with you everywhere. Ethics is a moral perspective that asks you to judge your conduct in terms of what's right and wrong, what's decent, what's good, what's honest, what's honorable. The reason to be ethical is simply that it's the right thing to do.[59]

You may have heard of Malden Mills, the Massachusetts manufacturer of Polarfleece and Polartec fabrics. On December 11, 1995, while the CEO was celebrating his seventieth birthday, the company experienced a catastrophic industrial fire that wiped out three of four factories in Lawrence, Massachusetts. The fourth building was saved due to the heroic efforts of twenty-seven union employees who fought the fire all night. No one was killed in the fire, thanks to the efforts of employees who checked attendance sheets, made a human chain, and dragged their fellow employees to safety. After the fire, CEO Aaron Feuerstein carried the welfare of his employees, customers, and the Lawrence community on his shoulders. "There is no way I would throw 3,000 workers into the street—no way I would take Lawrence, Massachusetts, and condemn them to economic oblivion."[60] He quickly announced that he would keep his 3,000 jobless employees on the payroll for a month, which he extended to two months, and then three months, while the factory was being rebuilt. Feuerstein paid out a total of more than $15 million in wages and benefits to jobless employees after the fire. Employees jumped to the challenge. Just a few weeks after the fire, productivity was higher than it had been before the fire because of employees' creativity and willingness to work "25 hours a day."[61] By summer, almost all of the employees had returned to work, and the 400 unemployed got extended health benefits, help finding work, and a promise of a job when the new plant opened. Feuerstein received accolades from the workforce and the media, and an invitation from President Bill Clinton to attend the State of the Union Address.

Many in the business community thought Feuerstein should have pocketed the insurance money and moved the company somewhere with lower labor costs, perhaps overseas. But *Fortune* magazine later praised Feuerstein as an astute businessman in his handling of the disaster. He treated his employees as an asset rather than an expense, cultivated their loyalty, and bet on the company's future. The decision to rebuild the factory was also a rational one because insurance covers the replacement cost of a factory only if it is rebuilt. If he hadn't replaced the factory, Feuerstein might have had to settle for the depreciated value of the burned building and its contents. And moving the factory overseas would have risked losing the quality advantage.

Finally, Feuerstein took advantage of a mountain of free media at[...] and *Parade* magazines, TV news magazines such as *Dateline*, a[...]

According to *Fortune*, "Any idiot with a strong enough stor[...] money, sometimes a lot of it, by slashing costs and milking custome[...], a company's reputation. But clearly that's not the way to make a lot of money for a long time. The way to do that is to create so much value that your customers wouldn't dream of looking for another supplier. Indeed, the idea is to build a value creation system of superior products, service, teamwork, productivity, and cooperation with the buyer."[63] This view jibes with Feuerstein's philosophy. In a 1997 talk to management professors at their annual Academy of Management meeting, Feuerstein said that his business objective is to win by creating a better-performing, higher-quality product that is different from what competitors are making. But to do that, you have to have the right people, trust, and understanding. You have to extend to your people the loyalty you want them to extend to you. Clearly, Feuerstein is an accomplished businessman. But he is also driven by deeply held moral beliefs. In that talk to business professors, he quoted the Bible (in Hebrew!) on the responsibility of a rich man not to praise himself for his riches, and to do kindness, justice, and charity in the community. Given his moral beliefs, he believed that he had no choice but to rebuild his factories.

In an unfortunate turn of events, Malden Mills was forced to file for bankruptcy under Chapter 11 when it ran short of cash in late 2001 due to the cost of rebuilding after the devastating fire. It remains to be seen whether the company will pull out of its current financial crisis. Feuerstein remains optimistic. Key customers have remained loyal (L.L. Bean, Patagonia, North Face, the U.S. Military), union employees have volunteered major concessions, and members of the general public (including local townspeople) have sent notes of encouragement and sometimes checks! *60 Minutes* aired a laudatory segment about Feuerstein and the company on March 24, 2002, and the company is working hard to develop new specialty products for growing markets including the American military. At press time, the company's Web site (www.polartec.com) was predicting a strong recovery. And, in response to support from consumers, the Web site offers them the opportunity to take the "Polartec Promise." It reads:

> I support companies who treat their employees with respect and dignity.
>
> I support companies who make world-class products in the USA.
>
> I support companies that demonstrate lasting commitment to their communities.
>
> I support companies that make products that are sensitive to our natural environment.
>
> I will show my support not only with words, but by purchasing at least one product manufactured out of genuine Polartec® performance fabrics in the coming weeks.

Feuerstein says that he didn't expect anything in return for his magnanimous behavior in 1995. He did it because it was right, not because there would be a payoff.[64] "There e times in business when you don't think of the financial consequences but of the human consequences."[65] So, to Feuerstein, the question "Is socially responsible business good business?" is tautological. Good business doesn't refer to just the financial bottom line. It refers to business that does well financially by producing products that meet customers' needs *and* by being responsible to employees and the community.

Socially Responsible Investors

Some shareholders care about both the financial and social bottom line of business. "Socially responsible" investors insist that their investments meet ethical as well as financial criteria. They "put their cash where their conscience is." Although the social criteria vary, many shun certain types of industries, such as nuclear energy, weapons, and tobacco, while they support companies that use energy wisely, protect the environment, and market safe products and services. They may also consider the firm's human resource practices such as female and minority advancement, day care, or profit-sharing. Books such as *The Better World Investment Guide*[66] provide ethical investors with specific company evaluations based on ethical criteria. A number of brokers, financial planners, and mutual funds are also now serving these investors' needs. A trade association, the Social Investment Forum (www.socialinvest.org), reported that socially responsible investing grew from $40 billion in 1984 to over $2 trillion in 2001. They list 230 mutual funds that use some sort of social screen, way up from the 168 funds identified in 1999, and in the down stock market, these funds have managed to keep investors better than other funds. Some of them have performed quite well. For example, the $443 million Calvert Social Investment Equity Fund, earned an average return of almost 7 percent a year over the past three years, compared with the Standard & Poor's 500 stock index average loss of over six percent a year.[67] What does this mean for business ethics? At least for this group of investors, shareholders' interests are no longer distinct from employee, customer, and community interests. They're all interconnected.[68] This concern for multiple stakeholders may be even more true in other countries than it is in the United States. In a recent Canadian survey, 74 percent of stockholders agreed that "Executives have a responsibility to take into account the impact their decisions have on employees, local communities, and the country as well as making profits."[69]

Avoiding the Costs of Criminal Liability

In addition to all of the other reasons for being ethical, the law presents a crystal clear cost-based reason.[70] Corporate criminal misconduct is costly. Firms' stock prices drop in the short term in response to announcements of allegations of corporate crime and in response to announced penalties.[71] Financial performance suffers significantly over the five years following a conviction.[72] Companies also often settle with prosecutors to avoid lengthy litigation. For example, in late 2002, the top ten U.S. brokerage firms (including Citigroup's Salomon Smith Barney unit, Goldman Sachs, and Credit Suisse First Boston) agreed to pay $1.44 billion in fines, completely separate their stock research from their investment banking operations, and pay for independent stock research. Merrill Lynch agreed to pay a $100 million fine earlier in 2002.

Until recently, criminal law focused on the individual defendant rather than the corporation, and fines on corporations were relatively modest. However, since the mid-1980s the trend has been toward increasing fines for both individuals and organizations convicted of felony crimes. Congress created the U.S. Sentencing Commission in 1984 in response to criticism of judicial discretion in sentencing and perceived disparities between sentences for "white-collar" and other types of crimes. In 1987, the Commission imposed federal sentencing guidelines for individual offenders. These guidelines limited judicial sentencing discretion and mandated some incarceration for virtually every felony offender.

In November 1991, the Commission issued new sentencing guidelines for organizations convicted of federal crimes. The organization can be convicted even if only one employee is caught breaking the law. The guidelines cover most federal crimes including fraud, antitrust, securities, tax, bribery, and money-laundering offenses, and they impose a schedule of mandatory fines. "Virtually without exception, the Guidelines require a convicted organization to make restitution and to pay a substantial fine (which is not tax deductible)."[73] The guidelines even include a provision calling for a "corporate death penalty." The provision was used by federal prosecutors in the case of American Precision Components Inc., a Farmingdale, New York, company that sold ordinary nuts and bolts to government contractors as highly tested space components.[74] The company agreed to divest all of its assets. Arthur Andersen, the former auditing firm that once "stood for integrity," put its stamp of approval on a long list of dirty books (e.g., Sunbeam, Waste Management, Enron, Global Crossing, Qwest, and WorldCom), and has now become the biggest case ever of corporate capital punishment.[75]

The sentencing guidelines use a "carrot and stick" approach to managing corporate crime. The carrot provides incentives to organizations to develop a strong internal control system to detect and manage illegal behavior. The stick provides for severe punishment for organizations that are convicted of crimes and were not proactively managing legal compliance within the organization. Fines and other sanctions vary widely depending on whether management reports itself and cooperates with investigative authorities and depending on whether the company has a program in place to prevent and detect illegal behavior. Therefore, the same crime can be subject to a wide range of penalties. The minimum fine under the guidelines is $250, and the maximum is $290 million or even more if the crime meets certain criteria. (For more specific information about how fines are determined, see Appendix: How Fines Are Determined under the U.S. Sentencing Guidelines at the end of this chapter.) The guidelines also provide that a defendant organization that doesn't have an effective legal compliance program should be put on corporate probation. Some of the recommended conditions of probation include requiring that the organization: publicize (at its own expense and as directed by the court) the fact of its conviction and the nature of the punishment; periodically report to the court regarding financial condition and operating results; submit to periodic, unannounced reviews of books and records, and interrogation of employees by court-appointed experts (paid by the organization); and inform the court of any material adverse change in business conditions or prospects.

According to the U.S. Sentencing Commission's reports (found at www.ussc.gov), more and more firms are being sentenced under the guidelines. Because the guidelines were not applied retroactively, they remained under the radar screen for a number of years. However, their impact has steadily increased and companies are paying attention. For example, in 1995, Con Edison was convicted of an environmental offense and was subject to probation that included onerous compliance requirements. In 1996, in what has come to be known as the Caremark decision, corporate boards of directors were put on notice to take the guidelines into account as part of their corporate governance responsibilities or face personal liability. In 1999, Hoffman-LaRoche was convicted of antitrust conspiracy charges and was fined $500 million, the largest criminal fine imposed in the United States, while Rhone Poulenc was granted amnesty because it reported the offense. In fiscal year 2000, 197 organizations were sentenced under the guidelines with fraud being the most frequent offense. And, in 2001, TAP Pharmaceuticals received the third largest fine ever imposed under the guidelines—$290 million.[76] (See Chapter 9 for more on the TAP Pharmaceuticals case.) A review of sentencing over the last ten years found that although the number of organizations sentenced remained stable, fine amounts increased substantially. For example, in 1990, the average fine was $167,214. In 2000, the average fine had risen to $3,225,462.[77]

Clearly, organizations have an incentive to develop effective legal compliance programs, and more and more organizations are doing so. In fact, the sentencing guidelines have influenced organizations to develop new job descriptions as well as new organizational programs and structures generally referred to as ethics and legal compliance programs. The Ethics Officer Association (www.eoa.org) was begun in 1992 with 12 members and now has nearly 800 members, suggesting that corporate America has embraced the approach promoted by the guidelines. Similarly, the Health Care Compliance Association has grown from two members in 1996 to over 2,000 today.[78] Although legal compliance programs in corporations vary somewhat depending upon the size and nature of the organization, the framework provided by the sentencing guidelines has steered their general development. The requirements include making legal compliance the responsibility of high-level officers, communicating rules through written materials and training, establishing monitoring and reporting systems, and disciplining offenders and those responsible for not detecting offenses (among other requirements). (See Table 2.1: Seven Requirements for Due Diligence and an Effective Compliance Program for the full list of requirements.) In addition, other government agencies are adopting similar "carrot and stick" approaches. For example, the EPA issued a policy in 2000 that provides similar incentives for firms to develop environmental compliance programs. And the U.S. Department of Health and Human Services has provided incentives for health care providers to develop legal compliance programs as well.[79]

It should be clear by now that the misconduct of a single employee can put an entire organization at risk and that the development of an effective compliance

FREE Business Checking •

America's Best Business Bank

98 Severna Ave

Julia

• Local Loans by Local People

Table 2.1 Seven Requirements for Due Diligence and an Effective Compliance Program

1. Establishing compliance standards reasonably capable of preventing criminal conduct
2. Assigning specific high-level individuals with responsibility to oversee those compliance standards
3. Exercising due care to ensure that discretionary authority is not delegated to individuals with a propensity to engage in illegality
4. Taking necessary steps to communicate compliance standards and procedures to all employees, with a special emphasis on training and the dissemination of manuals
5. Taking reasonable steps to achieve compliance with written standards through monitoring, auditing, and other systems designed to detect criminal conduct, including a reporting system free of retribution to employees who report criminal conduct
6. Consistently enforcing the organization's written standards through appropriate disciplinary mechanism, including, as appropriate, discipline of individuals responsible for failure to detect an offense
7. After an offense is detected, taking all reasonable steps to respond and to prevent future similar conduct

program can help an organization prevent trouble with the law. However, compliance programs are not equally effective, and the sentencing guidelines acknowledge that. Prosecutors have received guidance suggesting that they consider the effectiveness of an organization's compliance program—whether it is adequately designed, and whether it is working.[80] Employees can sometimes view compliance programs as symbols of management's mistrust or of management's attempt to cover itself at employees' expense. Employees are more likely to accept a compliance program and abide by it if it is seen as part of an organization's more positive focus on ethics and values.[81] We will talk more about specific organizations' ethics and compliance programs in Chapter 10.

The Importance of Trust

A more elusive benefit of ethics in organizations is trust. Although difficult to document, trust has both economic and moral value. Trust is essential in a service economy where all a firm has is its reputation for dependability and good service. Individuals and organizations build trust accounts that work something like a bank account.[82] You make deposits and build your trust reserve by being honest and by keeping commitments. You can draw on this account and even make mistakes as long as the reserve is maintained. Having a trust reserve allows the individual or organization the flexibility and freedom to act without scrutiny, saving a great deal of time and energy in all types of relationships. Imagine a marriage that is based on trust. The partners go about their daily business without feeling any need to check up on each other or to hire private detectives to confirm the other's whereabouts.[83] The same is true of trust-based business relationships where a handshake seals a deal, and a business partner's word is considered to be a contract. Corporations also build trust with their customers. Johnson & Johnson made a huge contribution to its trust account when it recalled all Tylenol from store shelves after the poisoning crisis in 1982 (a situation discussed in more detail in Chapter 8). Despite no recall requirement and huge recall costs, the company put its customers first. Trust may be even more important in efforts at global collaboration and alliances, and in cross-cultural management teams. Trust encourages open exchange of ideas and information, reduces the need for costly controls, allows for rapid adjustment to change, and is associated with willingness to work through cultural differences and difficulties.[84]

However, trust accounts are easily overdrawn. And when they are, all flexibility disappears. Every word and action is carefully checked and double checked for signs of dishonesty. In organizations, lawyers are hired, contracts are drawn up and signed, and CYA (cover your you-know-what) memos fly. Recent corporate ethics scandals have created a huge gap in the public's trust. In an essay for *Business Week,* titled "Can You Trust Anybody Anymore?," Bruce Nussbaum wrote:

> There are business scandals that are so vast and so penetrating that they profoundly shock our most deeply held beliefs about the honesty and integrity of our corporate culture. Enron Corp. is one of them. This financial disaster goes far beyond the failure of one big company. This is corruption on a massive scale. Tremendous harm has befallen innocent employees who have seen their retirement savings disappear as a few at the top cashed out. Terrible things have happened to the way business is conducted under the cloak of deregulation. Serious damage has been done to ethical codes of conduct held by once-trusted business professionals.... Investor confidence is critical to the success of our economic system ... People increasingly feel the game is rigged ... Who can come to the rescue? The reputations of many of the professionals who were counted on to safeguard the economic system lie in tatters ... What's to be done? ... The lesson from the Enron debacle should be to restore basic integrity to the bottom line, ethics to business professionals, and clout to overseers that even a deregulated economy need.[85]

The entire American business system relies upon the public's faith and trust. That trust has been shattered in a manner that could be extremely costly to society. The public considers the debacles at companies such as Enron, Arthur Andersen, Worldcom, Tyco, and Adelphia not as an anomaly, but as an example of the workings of a business culture that has lost its way. Unfortunately, all companies have been tainted by the scandals. Blue chip companies such as IBM and GE are now facing the close scrutiny and skepticism of shareholders as they are being asked to open their books and share much more information than has been recent practice.[86] Meeting profit projections or beating them by a penny is being viewed suspiciously as evidence of accounting chicanery rather than reliability.[87] Confidence and trust in the system must be restored, or access to capital (the engine of the entire system) could be cut off. The good news is that many corporations are responding. Boards of directors are replacing inside members with outsiders who are seen as more independent. Stock options are being expensed. CEO compensation packages that are seen as excessive are being cut. And executives are asking their people whether they are living by the "spirit of the law" as well as the letter of the law.[88]

THE BEST AND THE WORST IN US

The years 2001–2002 will be remembered as a time that brought out the best and the worst in us. First, from the terrorist acts of September 11, 2001, to the largest corporate scandals in history, we observed ourselves at our worst—people hurting other people without remorse. But, we also had an opportunity to see ourselves at our best. Read the accompanying "Reflections" piece by Renee Flemish, BS and MBA graduate of The Pennsylvania State University. Flemish held a variety of leadership roles in technology sales and marketing at AT&T and then led three Internet start-ups from ground floor to IPO or acquisition before 9-11. Flemish lived in New York and, after 9-11, she volunteered at The Salvation Army. Before long, her unique skills were recognized and she became executive director of the Salvation Army's World Trade Center Relief Program. In that role, she oversaw the coordination of the $80 million 9-11 program fund, led a team of ninety employees, and organized 2.5 million volunteer hours. She was also instrumental in establishing a new independent nonprofit consortium called the 9-11 United Services Group, designed to facilitate a coordinated approach among multiple relief agencies. In her role, Flemish saw how businesses responded to the tragedy and, at times, she saw people and businesses at their best. Flemish offers some thoughts about lessons we can all learn from this experience.

REFLECTIONS

By Renee Flemish

If the true test of character lies in our ability to gain strength from tragedy, then we passed the test.

An unprecedented humanitarian response followed the September 11th terrorist attacks. It was the single most catastrophic day in the history of any fire department in the nation as 343 firefighters gave their lives in the rescue attempts. In the days that followed, people lined up for blocks waiting to donate blood and thousands volunteered at Ground Zero to aid in the search, recovery, and cleanup efforts. Private contributions came in the form of goods and services, volunteerism, and cash. Trucks rolled in with pallets full of bottled water, flashlights, food, clothing, and toys. Space was donated for warehousing goods and fleets were donated for distribution of goods.

The city's airspace was restricted and F16 fighter jets blared overhead at Pier 94 where makeshift memorials covered the walls and death certificates were processed. Hundreds of people trained in crisis intervention and grief counseling came to work at Pier 94. Many of them never went home at night. Nothing in their medical, clinical, or theological training could have prepared them for this; still, they came to New York hoping to make a difference. People sought help without regard for our credentials. Early on, it became clear to all of us that what people mostly needed was someone who could listen and get things done.

In the year that followed, student organizations, church congregations and youth groups arrived from all fifty states to offer their support and feed the rescue workers on site. Citizens from the world over donated their time in New York City to try to comfort those who had lost loved ones and assist thousands more who lost their homes or jobs.

The people we saw were bond traders, electricians, investment bankers, and food service professionals. Some were near retirement and others were just getting started. They came from different neighborhoods and different countries, and they prayed in different languages and religions. As we listened to them, I realized that people are far more alike than they are different. They were men and women with families, friends, and dreams. After the terror attacks, they shared the same despair and are still picking up pieces of their lives more than a year after the devastating losses.

History could offer no appropriate paradigm to guide the emergency response to a disaster of such unprecedented scale. There were no existing systems to provide clear, reliable information to the thousands of traumatized victims, or to equip the nonprofit and governmental organizations working to manage the crisis at hand. Within a short time, it became resoundingly clear that more formalized coordination would be critical to ensure that those affected by the attacks on the World Trade Center received the help they needed—in both the short- and long-term—as quickly and effectively as possible. To foster this coordinated approach, we chartered the 9-11 United Services Group (USG), a not-for-profit consortium of thirteen human services organizations—including the American Red Cross in Greater New York, Safe Horizon, and The Salvation Army—working together on the front lines of the September 11th recovery effort.[1] This founding marked the first time New York City social service organizations joined forces to coordinate efforts on such a broad scale.

These coordinated efforts of the USG member agencies have resulted in approximately $750 million[2] being distributed or committed to approximately 70,000 individuals affected by the events of September 11th. The organizations continue to work one-on-one with more than 6,000 victims or family members to assist them in getting the help they need—including mental health services, employment assistance, health care services, and financial assistance. Since opening in September 2001, more than 150,000 calls have been received by the September 11th Support Hotline to pair individuals in need with one of over 160 case workers cross-trained in the full range of benefits and services available to individuals affected by the tragedy.

The Business Community's Role in Aiding the Recovery

The 9-11 USG charities faced the enormous challenge of creating a new infrastructure that would enable the efficient and compassionate distribution of September 11th assistance. As our nation's largest disaster response got underway, dedicated talent, functional expertise, and operational know-how emerged from the business, philanthropic, and government arenas. With nearly $1.4 billion in donated monies, the 9-11 USG became the focal point for service providers who wished to aid in the recovery effort. Rather than working as thirteen separate charities, the organizations combined their talents and bargaining strength to secure professional services from companies such as IBM, McKinsey, Merrill Lynch, Goldman Sachs, Morgan Stanley, and Skaaden Arps. Our professional-service needs included information technology, operations expertise, legal counsel, financial planning, Web site development, and language translation services, to name a few. The vast majority of these services were provided on a pro bono basis while others were deeply discounted or offered at cost.

Corporate partners came forward to aid the effort in a number of ways. Managerial talent was offered through senior executives who brought key contacts and longstanding business relationships that the charities were able to build on. For example, the chief executive of the

9–11 USG was also the vice chairman of Goldman Sachs. Along with private sector experience, these managers brought client and vendor relationships that were instrumental in advancing the recovery effort.

Bear Stearns donated an entire floor of their midtown offices to house the 9–11 Family Assistance Center. This inter-agency facility has served thousands of families with counseling, economic assistance and support group activities. Additionally, the investment banking division of Bear Sterns dedicated some of their brightest analysts to the 9–11 USG.

Wall Street was especially hard hit by the attacks with a number of firms directly and deeply affected with human and financial losses. The Financial Advisory Referral Program was formed with the participation of six such affected firms: American Express, JP Morgan Chase, Merrill Lynch, Morgan Stanley, Prudential Financial, and Salomon Smith Barney. These firms were selected on the basis of their size, investment expertise, and national presence. The program was designed to assist the families of victims in managing the money they may receive from the Federal Government's September 11th Victim Compensation Fund or other sources. For many families, managing large amounts of compensation money would be complex and risky, so financial education and advice are key to their making sound investment decisions. Participating advisors from each firm were experienced financial professionals who were selected by their institutions and who stepped forward to participate in the program. These advisors have been working one-on-one with families to tailor investment strategies and meet individualized needs ranging from estate planning to college savings. This program is a vital part of USG's mission to address the long-term needs of those affected by the attacks.

A shared goal of the USG and its corporate partners was to help clients navigate through myriad economic assistance and social service programs and tap into those that are most beneficial. In order for the thirteen charities to offer seamless service coordination, they had to be able to operate from a common technology platform. Technology partners provided reliable and widespread access to relevant programs and funds, helping to minimize red tape and facilitate service delivery. IBM was instrumental in helping to build an e-business environment that would speed service delivery while ensuring the highest security standards. Finally, operational needs such as payroll, email, staffing, and direct mail were also met through the contributions of corporate partners.

Motivating Factors: What's in It for Businesses?

Motivated by a sense of civic duty and humanitarian obligation to the community, corporate partners came voluntarily. Targeting the center of world commerce, the terrorists took aim at a lifestyle and philosophy defined by capitalism and free markets. A good deal of our national identity is invested in the spirit of corporate enterprise. Corporate contributors helped to reaffirm some of that spirit by lending talent and business expertise to the recovery effort.

"Anything you need" was the phrase we heard most often in the weeks following the attacks, as offers poured in from the private sector. Many offers came through corporations where volunteerism is fostered. Still others were spurred on by employees who approached senior management with a call to action. Self-driven and generous, the corporate contributors created goodwill with the community, customers, and employees.

As the charities worked to define business requirements, the open-ended offers began to take shape. The list of partners narrowed and service agreements were structured. Each of the partners took on specific deliverables that would ultimately define their role in aiding the recovery.

The charities and their business partners shared a unifying sense of urgency. Getting assistance to the people in need was the sole priority and motives were never questioned. Whatever the underlying motives, everyone was drawn together to a common purpose.

Nonetheless, observations in retrospect do suggest motivating factors that are not entirely selfless. Aiding the recovery provided firms with a number of opportunities. It was a chance to build new relationships while strengthening existing ones. In a soft market, client referrals and testimonials are vital to new business development. For some partners, media exposure was a serious draw as the charities routinely shared press conferences with Mayor Rudy Giuliani, and September 11th news filled the front page of *The New York Times*. Some businesses welcomed an occasion to test their professional expertise in uncharted territory. These contributors were motivated by the professional challenge and determined to go well beyond their conventional approaches. Understanding and addressing the business needs of the September 11th marketplace was a monumental task and extraordinary assignment. The partnerships also posed a rare opportunity for businesses to learn from leaders in the human services arena. The charities worked closely with the Federal Emergency Management Agency, the Office of Emergency Management, the New York City Mayor's Office and the New York State Attorney General. These linkages offered a unique learning opportunity for the businesses involved. In the most direct link to future business, corporate partners recognized that they were building a knowledge base that could be "productized" for future disaster relief opportunities. In the wake of another national crisis, future practitioners will rely on the lessons learned post September 11th. These corporate contributors are now better positioned in the disaster response arena and could respond more quickly in a future crisis.

In the days following the attacks, airwaves ran commercial free, and ad agencies were feeling the slowdown. In donating their services to build September 11th campaigns and Web sites, advertising firms were building their nonprofit portfolios while staving the inevitable layoffs. Business was particularly slow across the professional services sector. Budget cuts and the Arthur Andersen scandal left consulting firms in survival mode. Pressured to keep utilization rates up, consulting firms saw an opportunity to build a knowledge base by deploying a dedicated team to formulate and conduct a study of unmet needs.

Observations and Lessons Learned

Nonprofits traditionally have not been able to take full advantage of cutting-edge technology solutions. Unfortunately, clients are the ones to pay the price, as service delivery is hampered, new programs are slow to develop, and cross-charity collaboration is out of the question. The coordinated case management approach that served more than 70,000 affected individuals would not have been possible without the expertise of the technology partners, many of whom worked on a pro bono basis. As a result, donor monies were more directly available to clients, as the charities were able to build large-scale programs and the necessary infrastructure with minimal cash investments.

Firms with a cultural tradition of volunteerism and pro bono service were more apt to maintain the highest standards of client service. They consistently put their best talent forward and saw their commitments through to the finish. They did not discriminate between paying and pro bono or low margin clients. But a number of Web site designs and consulting projects fell short because the partners were unable to sustain the necessary investments or carry out their commitments. In the future, before stepping forward to provide assistance, corporations should carefully examine their motives and ability to deliver on their well-intended offers. For companies that do not have them, now is the time to establish policies on volunteerism and pro bono services. That way, if their services are needed in a future disaster (and hopefully they won't be), they'll be ready and able to deliver. In the meantime, managers and employees can reap the psychological and spiritual rewards derived from their organization's commitment to meeting their financial *and* their moral commitments.

What's So Different about Nonprofit Organizations?

In closing, it's interesting to reflect on some of the contrasts between corpo organizations. These differences, in my experience, are not subtle—they sh tem and the success measures and have a tangible effect on management sty

While we were working on the recovery programs, I thought it would be easy to ignore my emotions and focus instead on the business of running the operation. That is, after all, how we managed in the corporate world, and it had always worked for me. But September 11th was entirely different. Nothing was formulaic. Instinct and emotion permeated our thinking for we were in the business of healing and rebuilding. It was the most rigorous test of my leadership abilities and a culmination of all my prior experiences. Wherever possible, decisions were made without review boards and committees. There was no time for the planning sessions, iterative revisions, and approval cycles that generally go into a corporate budgeting decision or product marketing plan.

The nonprofit business model is fundamentally different from the for-profit model. Much as businesses rely on customers for revenue growth, nonprofits rely on donors to finance their charitable missions. Rather than profitability, a key performance metric for charities is the effective utilization of funds and keeping operating costs at a minimum. Nonprofits maintain a fiduciary responsibility to donors just as corporations do to their shareholders.

Corporate bottom lines are sometimes at odds with what's best for the customer, as organizational decisions are strongly guided by cost justification. Decisions can be shaped more by how Wall Street will interpret the news rather than by what's in the customer's best interest. In contrast, because the September 11th recovery programs were funded entirely through donations, we were accountable to the private citizens and organizations that made our efforts possible. Unhindered by concerns of what the analysts might make of our latest decision, our thinking and the services were entirely client-driven. With a deep sense of urgency and compassion, we focused on serving the critical needs of our clients and maximizing the utilization of donor contributions. The clients were the only reason we were in business and their well-being was the sole motivation for our programs.

Similarly, negotiations with other agencies were carried out in the spirit of doing what's best for the client. Parties left the negotiating table satisfied and accomplished in knowing that client needs were served to the very best of our combined abilities. As long as the resulting programs delivered the greatest possible service, there were no regrets over which agency took 51 percent and who got 49 percent.

Finally, in a welcome departure from the corporate world, I found that I could uphold the same principles at work as I did outside of work. Not only was it expected, but it was the self-guiding force that fueled the organization. Staying true to our core values gave us the energy, confidence and clarity that the recovery work demanded.

Notes: **1.** The founding USG member agencies are American Red Cross in Greater New York, Asian American Federation of New York, Black Agency Executives, Catholic Charities of the Archdiocese of New York, Catholic Charities of the Diocese of Brooklyn and Queens, Federation of Protestant Welfare Agencies, Hispanic Federation, Human Services Council, Mental Health Association of New York City, Safe Horizon, The Salvation Army, UJA-Federation of New York, and United Neighborhood Houses of New York. Independent agencies actively involved in USG Service Coordination include Asociacion Tepeyac, Brooklyn Bureau of Community Service, Center for Independence of the Disabled in New York, Children's Aid Society, Community Service Society, Legal Aid Society, and WTC Permanency Project. **2.** This number reflects the reported records of USG member organizations as of December 2002.

CONCLUSION

This chapter was designed to pique your interest in business ethics. Hopefully, we have convinced you that lots of people care about it, and that it's worth bothering about. We hope Renee Flemish's reflections inspire you to think about the role of business in society and not just during disasters. The remainder of the book aims to help you understand ethics from a managerial perspective, explaining how this aspect of the organizational world actually works and what you can do to manage it. It will also provide practical decision-making guidance for facing your own ethical decisions and for helping others do the same.

DISCUSSION QUESTIONS

1. Do you think business ethics/social responsibility is important? Why or why not?
2. Identify reasons why an organization would be interested in being ethical, and classify those reasons in terms of whether they represent moral motivation or economic motivation.
3. Choose a company and identify its key stakeholders.
4. Think about the four types of corporate social responsibility. Do you agree that they should be represented by a pyramid? Why or why not? What are the implications of stopping at a particular pyramid level? For example, would it be all right if a company took its sole responsibility to be financial responsibility to its shareholders? Financial responsibility and legal responsibility? Can you think of a better way to graphically represent a company's social responsibility?
5. Think about the television programs and films you've seen recently in which business was portrayed in some way. How were business and business people portrayed? Is there anything business could or should do to improve its media image? Some businesses try to stay out of the limelight. Why might that be? What do you think of that strategy?
6. Do you believe that employees are more attracted and committed to ethical organizations? Are you? Why or why not? Make a list of the companies you would prefer to work for and the reasons why. Are there also companies that you would refuse to work for? Why? Are there ethically "neutral" companies that don't belong on either list?
7. Do you think organizations should be concerned about the U.S. Sentencing Commission's sentencing guidelines? Should they be doing anything differently because of them?
8. Discuss the importance of trust in business. Can you cite examples? What happens when trust is lost?
9. What can we learn from the 9-11 tragedy about ourselves and about business?

CASE

MERCK AND RIVER BLINDNESS

Headquartered in New Jersey, Merck & Co. is one of the largest pharmaceutical companies in the world. In 1978, Merck was about to lose patent protection on its two best-selling prescription drugs. These medications had provided a significant part of Merck's $2 billion in annual sales. Because of imminent loss, Merck decided to pour millions into research to develop new medications. During just three years in the 1970s, the company invested over $1 billion in research and was rewarded with the discovery of four powerful medications. Profits, however, were never all that Merck cared about. In 1950, George W. Merck, then chairman of the company his father founded, said, "We try never to forget that medicine is for people. It is not for the profits. The profits follow, and if we have remembered that, they have never failed to appear. The better we have remembered that, the larger they have been." This philosophy was at the core of Merck & Co.'s value system.

River Blindness

The disease onchocerciasis, known as river blindness, is caused by parasitic worms that live in the small black flies that breed in and about fast-moving rivers in developing countries in the Middle East, Africa, and Latin America. When a person is bitten by a fly (and some people are bitten thousands of times a day), the larvae of the worm can enter the person's body. The worms can grow to almost two feet long and can cause grotesque growths on an infected person. The real trouble comes, however, when the worms begin to reproduce and release millions of microscopic baby worms into a person's system. The itching is so intense that some infected persons have committed suicide. As time passes, the larvae continue to cause severe problems, including blindness. In 1978, the World Health Organization estimated that more than 300,000 people were blind because of the disease, and another 18 million were infected. In 1978, the disease had no safe cure. There were two drugs that could kill the parasite, but both had serious, even fatal, side effects. The only measure being taken to combat river blindness was the spraying of infected rivers with insecticides in the hope of killing the flies. However, even this wasn't effective since the flies had built up immunity to the chemicals.

Merck's Ethical Quandary

Since it takes $200 million in research and 12 years to bring the average drug to market, the decision to pursue research is a complex one. Since resources are finite, dollars and time have to go to projects that hold the most promise, both in terms of making money so a company can continue to exist and in alleviating human suffering. This is an especially delicate issue when it comes to rare diseases, when a drug company's investment could probably never be recouped because the number of people who would buy the drug is so small. The problem with developing a drug to combat river blindness was the flip side of the "orphan" drug dilemma. There were certainly enough people suffering from the disease to justify the research, but since it was a disease afflicting people in some of the poorest parts of the word, those suffering from the disease could not pay for the medication.

In 1978, Merck was testing ivermectin, a drug for animals, to see if it could effectively kill parasites and worms. During this clinical testing, Merck discovered that the drug killed a parasite in horses that was very similar to the worm that caused river blindness in humans. This, therefore, was Merck's dilemma: Company scientists were encouraging the firm to invest in further research to determine if the drug could be adapted for safe use with humans, but Merck knew it would likely never be a profitable product.

Case Questions

1. Think about the definition of stakeholders from Chapter 1—any parties with a stake in the organization's actions or performance. Who are the stakeholders in this situation? How many can you list? On what basis would you rank them in importance?
2. What are the potential costs and benefits of such an investment?
3. If a safe and effective drug could be developed, the prospect of Merck's recouping its investment was almost zero. Could Merck justify such an investment to shareholders and the financial community? What criteria would be needed to help them make such a decision?
4. If Merck decided not to conduct further research, how would it justify such a decision to its scientists? How might the decision to develop the drug, or not to develop the drug, affect employee loyalty?
5. How would the media treat a decision to develop the drug? Not to develop the drug? How might either decision affect Merck's reputation?
6. Think about the decision in terms of the corporate social responsibility pyramid. Did Merck have an ethical obligation to proceed with development of the drug? Would it matter if the drug had only a small chance to cure river blindness? Does it depend upon how close the company was to achieving a cure, or how sure they were that they could achieve it? Or does this decision become a question of philanthropy?
7. How does Merck's value system fit into this decision?
8. If you were the senior executive of Merck, what would you do?

Source: Bollier, D. 1991. *Merck & Company.* Stanford, CA: The Business Enterprise Trust.

SHORT CASE

You have a long-standing consulting relationship with a large consumer products company. This company represents 50 percent of your consulting revenues and is clearly your most important client. The CEO has called to ask you to commit a significant amount of time over the next couple of months to assist with a large merger project. The company is merging with a large conglomerate whose primary business is the sale and distribution of tobacco products. The CEO is relying on you to assist in facilitating a smooth integration of the two companies. You promised yourself that, since your father died of lung cancer, you would never work for a tobacco company. Is there a way that you can accept the consulting assignment and still keep your promise to yourself? How will you handle this if you decide that you cannot work for the tobacco company?

NOTES

1. Etzioni, A. 1988. *The moral dimension: Toward a new economics.* New York: Free Press.
2. Ibid.
3. Grover, R. 1988. Bad guys wear pinstripes. *Business Week,* October 21: 61–63.
4. Quoted in Fusco, M.A.C. 1988. Ethics game plan: Taking the offensive. *Business Week* Careers, Spring/Summer: 51.
5. Wartick, S. L. 1992. The relationship between intense media exposure and change in corporate reputation. Spring: 33–49.
6. *Business Week.* 1988.Yes, business and ethics do go together. *Business Week,* February 15: 118.
7. Labich, K. 1992. The new crisis in business ethics. *Fortune,* April 20: 167–176.
8. Hess, C., and Hey, K. 2001. "Good" doesn't always mean "right." *Across the Board,* July/August.
9. Segal, T., and Del Valle, C. 1993. They didn't even give at the office. *Business Week,* January 25: 68–69.
10. Johnston, D.C. 1997. United Way, faced with fewer donors, is giving away less. *New York Times,* November 9: 1.
11. Fombrun, C., and Shanley, M. 1990. What's in a name? Reputation building and corporate strategy. *Academy of Management Journal,* 333: 233–256.
12. Stewart, Thomas A. 1998. America's most admired companies. *Fortune,* March 2: 71–82.
13. Colvin, G. 2001. What's love got to do with it? *Fortune,* November 12: 60.
14. Bergh, J. 2002. Do social movements matter to organizations? An institutional theory perspective on corporate responses to the contemporary environmental movement. Unpublished doctoral dissertation, The Pennsylvania State University.
15. Prakash, A. 2000. Responsible care: An assessment. *Business & Society* 39(2): 183–209.
16. Akers, J. F. 1989. Ethics and competitiveness: Putting first things first. *Sloan Management Review,* Winter: 69–71.
17. Howard, R. 1987. Values make the company: An interview with Robert Haas. In *@CT: Leaders on leadership,* edited by W. Bennis. Boston: Harvard Business School, 33–54.
18. Badaracco, J. L., Jr. 1992. Business ethics: Four spheres of executive responsibility. *California Management Review,* Spring: 64–79.
19. Zemke, R. 1986. Employee theft. How to cut your losses. *Training,* May: 74–78.
20. Collins, J. 1990. Why bad things happen to good companies and what can be done. *Business Horizons,* November–December: 18–22.
21. Hager, B. 1991. What's behind business' sudden fervor for ethics. *Business Week,* September 23: 65.
22. Labich, K. 1992. The new crisis in business ethics. *Fortune,* April 20: 167–176.
23. Channon, J. 1992. Creating esprit de corps. In *New traditions in business,* edited by J. Renesch. San Francisco: BerrettKoehler Publishers. 53–68.
24. *Business Week.* 2002. Get a job, save the planet. *Business Week,* May 6, p. 10.
25. Sandroff, R. 1990. How ethical is American business? *Working Woman,* September: 113–116.
26. Kleiman, C. 1989. Heading the list of worker wishes isn't more money! *The (Allentown, Penn.) Morning Call,* October 2: B10.
27. Greening, D.W., and Turban, D.B. 2000. Corporate social performance as a competitive advantage in attracting a quality workforce. *Business & Society* 39(3): 254–280.
28. Cullen, J. B., and Victor, B. 1993. The effects of ethical climates on organizational commitment: A multilevel analysis. Unpublished manuscript.

Turban, D. B., and Greening, D. W. 1997. Corporate social performance and organizational attractiveness to prospective employees. *Academy of Management Journal* 40: 658–672.

Treviño, L. K., Butterfield, K. D., and McCabe, D. 1998. The ethical context in organizations: Influences on employee attitudes and behaviors. *Business Ethics Quarterly.* 8 (3): 447–476.

29. Posner, B. Z., and Schmidt, W. H. 1992. Values and the American manager. *California Management Review,* Spring: 80–94.
30. Swanson, D. 1995. Addressing a theoretical problem by reorienting the corporate social performance model. *Academy of Management Review* 20: 43–64.
31. Freeman, E. 1984. *Strategic management: A stakeholder approach.* Boston: Pitman/Ballinger.
32. Davis, K. 1973. The case for and against business assumption of social responsibilities. *Academy of Management Journal* 16: 312–322.

    Wood, D. J. 1991. Corporate social performance revisited. *Academy of Management Review* 16: 691–718.
33. Swanson, 1995, op. cit.
34. Carroll, A. B. 1991. The pyramid of corporate social responsibility: Toward the moral management of organizational stakeholders. *Business Horizons* 34 (4): 39–48.
35. Friedman, M. 1970. The social responsibility of business is to increase its profits. *New York Times,* September 13: 122–126.
36. Hess, C., and Hey, K. 2001. "Good" doesn't always mean "right." *Across the Board,* July/August.
37. Singer, A. W. 1993. Can a company be too ethical? *Across the Board,* April: 17–22.
38. Byrne, J.A. 2002b. The new face of philanthropy. *Business Week,* December 2: 82–86.
39. Ibid.
40. Margolis, J.D., and Walsh, J.P. 2001b. Misery loves companies: Whither social initiatives by business? Unpublished working paper.
41. Kuttner, R. 1997. Everything for sale. *Fortune,* March 17: 92–94.
42. Nussbaum, B. 2002. Can you trust anybody anymore? *Business Week,* January 28: 31–32.
43. Towers Group, Inc. Press release, 5 March, 2002.
44. Murphy, C. 2002. D.C. gets it right. *Fortune,* Sept. 2: 38.
45. Fineman, H., and Isikoff, M. Laying down the law. *Newsweek,* August 5: 20–25.
46. Eichenwald, K. 2002. Even if heads roll, mistrust will live on. *New York Times* online, www.nytimes.com, October 6.
47. George, J. 2002. Big pharma kills doc giveaways. *Philadelphia Business Journal* 21 (19), June 28.
48. Pear, R. 2002. Drug industry is told to stop gifts to doctors. *New York Times* online, www.nytimes.com, October 1.
49. Labich, K. 1992. The new crisis in business ethics. *Fortune,* April 20: 167–176.
50. Aupperle, K. E. Carroll, A. B., and Hatfield, J. D. 1985. An empirical examination of the relationship between corporate social responsibility and profitability. *Academy of Management Journal* 28: 449–459.

    McGuire, J. B., Sundgren, A., and Scheeweis, T. 1988. Corporate social responsibility and firm financial performance. *Academy of Management Journal* 31: 854–872.

    Ullman, A. H. 1985. Data in search of a theory. a critical examination of the relationships among social performance, social disclosure, and economic performance of U.S. firms. *Academy of Management Review* 10: 3, 540–547.

    Margolis, J.D., and Walsh, J.P. 2001a. *People and profits? The search for a link between a company's social and financial performance.* Mahwah, NJ: Erlbaum.

    Margolis, J.D., and Walsh, J.P. 2001b. Misery loves companies: Whither social initiatives by business? Unpublished working paper.
51. Margolis, J.D., and Walsh, J.P. 2001a. *People and profits? The search for a link between a company's social and financial performance.* Mahwah, NJ: Erlbaum.

    Margolis, J.D., and Walsh, J.P. 2001b. Misery loves companies: Whither social initiatives by business? Unpublished working paper.
52. Waddock, S. A., and Graves, S. B. 1997. The corporate social performance-financial performance link. *Strategic Management Journal* 18: 303–319.

53. Verschoor, C., and Murphy, E. 2002. Best corporate citizens have better financial performance. *Strategic Finance* 83(7): 20.
54. Graves, S.J., Waddock, S. and Kelly, M. Getting there: The methodology behind the corporate citizenship rankings. *Business Ethics* 16 (2): 13.
55. Jones, R., and Murrell, A.J. 2001. Signaling positive corporate social performance: An event study of family friendly firms. *Business & Society* 40(1): 59–78.
56. Orlitzky, M., and Benjamin, J.D. 2001. Corporate social performance and firm risk: A meta-analytic review. *Business & Society* 40(4): 369–396.
57. Frooman, J. 1997. Socially irresponsible and illegal behavior and shareholder wealth. *Business & Society* 36 (3): 221–249.
58. Bhide, A., and Stevenson, H. H. 1990. Why be honest if honesty doesn't pay. *Harvard Business Review*, September–October: 121–129.
59. Josephson, Michael S. 1989. Ethics in a legalistic society. *Exchange,* Fall: 3–7.
60. Feuerestein, A.1997. Presentation at the Academy of Management annual meeting, Boston.
61. Ryan, M. 1996. They call their boss a hero. *Parade,* September 8: 4–5.
62. Teal, T. 1996. Not a fool, not a saint. *Fortune,* November 11: 201–204.
63. Ibid.
64. Seglin, J. 2002. The right thing: A boss saved them. Should they save him? *New York Times,* January 20.
65. Browning, L. 2001. Fire could not stop a mill, but debts may. *New York Times,* November 28: C1, C5.
66. Alperson, M., Marlin, A. T., Schorsch, J., and Will, R. 1991. *The better world investment guide.* New York: Prentice-Hall.
67. Scherreik, S. 2002. Following your conscience is just a few clicks away. *Business Week,* May 13: 116–118.
68. Melton, J. 1996. Responsible investing; $639 billion and counting. *Co-Op America Quarterly,* Spring: 13.
69. Verschoor, C., and Murphy, E. 2002. Best corporate citizens have better financial performance. *Strategic Finance* 83(7): 20.
70. Adapted from a speech given by attorney Steven Alan Reiss at the Conference Board meeting on business ethics, 1992.
71. Strachan, J. L., Smith, D. G., and Beedles, W. L. 1983. The price reaction to (alleged) corporate crime. *Financial Review* 18 (2): 121–132.
72. Baucus, M. S., and Baucus, D. 1997. Paying the piper: An empirical examination of longer-term financial consequences of illegal corporate behavior. *Academy of Management Journal* 40: 129–151.
73. Reiss, S. A. 1992. Speech given at the Conference Board meeting on business ethics, 1992.
74. *United States v. American Precision Components Inc.*, 93–450.
75. Byrne, J.A. 2002c. Fall from grace. *Business Week.* August 12: 50–56.
76. Kaplan, J.M. 2001. The sentencing guidelines: The first ten years. *Ethikos and Corporate Conduct Quarterly* 15(3): 1–4.
77. Murphy, D. 2002. The federal sentencing guidelines for organizations: A decade of promoting compliance and ethics. *Iowa Law Review* 87: 697–719.
78. Ibid.
79. Kaplan, J.M. 2001. The sentencing guidelines: The first ten years. *Ethikos and Corporate Conduct Quarterly* 15(3): 1–4.
80. Murphy, D. 2002. The federal sentencing guidelines for organizations: A decade of promoting compliance and ethics. *Iowa Law Review* 87: 697–719.
81. Treviño, L.K., Weaver, G.R., Gibson, D.G., and Toffler, B.L. Managing ethics and legal compliance: What works and what hurts. *California Management Review,* 41(2): 131–151.
82. Covey, S. R. 1989. *The 7 habits of highly effective people.* New York: Simon & Schuster.
83. Ibid.
84. Child, J. 2001. Trust—the fundamental bond in global collaboration. *Organizational Dynamics* 29(4): 274–288.

85. Nussbaum, B. 2002. Can you trust anybody anymore? *Business Week*, January 28: 31–32.
86. Byrne, J.A. 2002a. How to fix corporate governance. *Business Week*, May 6: 69–78.
87. Useem, J. 2002. In corporate America, it's cleanup time. *Fortune*, September 16: 62–72.
88. Ibid.

APPENDIX

How Fines Are Determined under the U.S. Sentencing Guidelines

Exact penalties are based on a base fine and the "culpability score" assigned by the court. The base fine is the greatest of the following: the pretax gain from the crime, the amount of intentional loss inflicted on the victim(s), and an amount based on the Sentencing Commission's ranking of the seriousness of the crime (ranging from $5,000 to $72.5 million). This amount is then multiplied by a number that depends on the culpability score. The culpability score ranges from 0 to 10, and the multipliers range from .05 to 4 (see Table 2.2: Method for Determining Minimum and Maximum Fines).

Every defendant starts at a culpability score of 5 and can move up or down depending on aggravating or mitigating factors (see Table 2.3: Factors That Can Increase or Decrease Culpability Scores for these factors). The presence of aggravating factors can cause the culpability score to increase. These aggravating factors include (1) organizational size, combined with the degree of participation, tolerance, or disregard for the criminal conduct by high-level personnel or substantial authority personnel in the firm, (2) prior history of similar criminal conduct, and (3) role in obstructing or impeding an investigation.

The presence of mitigating factors, however, can cause the culpability score to drop. In order to decrease the culpability score, the organization must have in place

Table 2.2 Method for Determining Minimum and Maximum Fines

Culpability Score	Minimum Multiplier	Maximum Multiplier
10 or more	2.00	4.00
9	1.80	3.60
8	1.60	3.20
7	1.40	2.80
6	1.20	2.40
5	1.00	2.00
4	0.80	1.60
3	0.60	1.20
2	0.40	0.80
1	0.20	0.40
0 or less	0.05	0.20

Table 2.3 Factors that Can Increase or Decrease Culpability Scores

Aggravating Factors: Result in an increase to the base level of 5
- The size of the organization coupled with the degree of participation, tolerance, or disregard for the criminal conduct by "high level personnel" or "substantial authority personnel." In a firm with greater than 5,000 employees, this factor can result in an increase of as much as 5 points.
- Prior history: Organizations that have been either civilly or criminally adjudicated to have committed similar conduct within the past five years can have up to 2 points added.
- Obstructing, impeding, (or attempting to obstruct or impede) during the investigation, prosecution, or something can result in 3 points added.

Mitigating Factors: Result in decreases from the base level of 5
- Having an effective program to prevent and detect violations of the law can result in a downward departure of 3 points.
- Self-reporting, cooperating, and accepting responsibility for the criminal conduct can result in a downward departure of 5 points.

an "effective program to prevent and detect violations of the law." If the court determines that the organization has such a program, 3 points can be removed from the base culpability score of 5. Besides having an effective compliance program in place, the culpability score can be substantially reduced if the organization reports the criminal conduct promptly after becoming aware of the offense and before government investigation. According to the guidelines, an organization that reports its own misconduct, cooperates with authorities, and accepts responsibility can have as many as 5 points subtracted from the base culpability level of 5.

The mitigating factors that reduce the culpability score have important implications for the way companies manage ethical conduct. For example, many believe that overseeing an "effective" program for preventing and detecting legal violations is a full-time job for at least one person. It would likely involve the development of a conduct code, training programs, scrutiny of reward systems, the development of communication systems, detection systems, and so on. Practical information about how organizations are actually implementing ethics programs will be discussed in more detail in Chapter 10.

COMMON ETHICAL DILEMMAS

CHAPTER 3

COMMON ETHICAL PROBLEMS

INTRODUCTION

The bad news about business ethics: Your career can be irrevocably damaged if you mishandle an ethical issue. But there's also good news: Many ethical issues in business are quite predictable. You can be fairly certain that during the course of your career, you'll run into myriad ethical problems such as a customer who asks for a special deal or terms, or questions about the appropriate use of corporate resources, or discrimination of one sort or another. Since many ethical issues are somewhat predictable, you have a better chance of dealing appropriately with ethical problems if you think about what's likely to happen before it occurs.

Before we get into a discussion of ethical issues, however, it's important to look at the relationship that exists between you and your employer. Although most people don't sign a contract on the day they join a company or organization, there is a contractual relationship of sorts between workers and employers. Both parties have expectations, and rights, and offer consideration to the other. Your employer pays you in salary and benefits to perform a job, and your organization expects you to behave in a certain way; you have a responsibility to be "part of the family" and exhibit loyalty and other corporate "virtues" and to refrain from other, less desirable behaviors. On the other hand, you expect not only a salary for the work you perform, but also a certain modicum of fairness. Most people expect employers to treat them decently and to provide an appropriate work environment. Whenever we discuss the employer/employee contract in this chapter, it's this complicated set of expectations that we're referring to.

So what are some typical ethical problems? We've compiled some of the more obvious dilemmas and have divided them into broad categories, including human resources issues, conflicts of interest, customer confidence issues, and the use of corporate resources. We will address a number of specific topics under each broad category. To make it easy to follow, each topic contains the following information:

- What is it? A definition of the issue.
- Why is it an ethical problem?
- Professional costs and possible penalties for ethical or legal transgressions.
- Special notes and some topics may include important information related to the topic.

HUMAN RESOURCES ISSUES

It's difficult to overstate how important it is for a company to effectively manage its people. Human resources—the employees who make up an organization—are any corporation's most important and expensive investment, and are the underpinning of an organization's success or failure. Barbara Toffler[1] found that 66 percent of the ethical issues encountered by the managers she interviewed involved managing human resources or internal organizational processes. In addition, the widest legal exposure for many companies may involve violations or perceived violations of the employer/employee contract.

In the United States, there's currently a shortage of workers to fill highly skilled jobs. McKinsey & Company describe this phenomenon as being a "War for Talent." In 1998, McKinsey conducted a yearlong study of 77 companies and 6,600 managers, who concluded that the most significant business challenge over the next 20 years will be recruiting, retaining, and inspiring talent. Specifically, companies are eager to find and keep highly skilled workers who can perform in a global economy, who are technologically savvy, and who can adapt quickly to change.[2] As a result, corporations are actively designing workplaces that attract, motivate, and retain qualified employees. Companies are eager to be "employers of choice." While the McKinsey study was conducted in boom times, the resulting bear market in 2001 and beyond made it even more imperative for companies to keep their most promising talent.

Probably the most effective way to retain qualified employees is to create a working environment where people feel appreciated. People who like to come to work may be significantly more productive than workers who feel their efforts are unappreciated, their management doesn't care about them, or their ideas don't count. Productivity, which is at the very heart of competitiveness, can exist only when employees are respected by management and when employees are encouraged to respect one another.

We use the term *human resources issues* to describe the problems that occur when people work together. They can include privacy, discrimination, sexual and other types of harassment, performance evaluation, hiring, firing, or simply "how people get along." (Performance evaluation including appraisals, discipline, hiring, firing, and layoffs will be discussed in Chapter 6.)

The word to remember when considering human resources issues is fairness, and most corporate policy is constructed to build fairness into the system. When we talk about fairness, we mean equity, reciprocity, and impartiality—the way most people think about what is "fair."[3] Something is said to be equitable when something is divided between two people according to the worth and gains of the two individuals: "If they received equal shares, did they work equally hard?" Most people think it's unfair when two people have performed the same duty but receive a different share of the reward. Another measure of fairness is reciprocity, or the fairness of exchanges: "You did this for me and I'll do that for you." Most people perceive it as being unfair if one person fails to hold up his or her part of a bargain. The third measure of fairness is impartiality: "Is the person who's going to listen to my story biased in some way, or has he or she prejudged the situation?" Most people think of fairness as being inconsistent with prejudice and bias.

Most protective legislation and corporate human resources policy try to incorporate those elements. The goal is to hire, treat, promote, appraise, and lay off or fire employees based solely on their qualifications and not on factors like sex, race, or age. The goal is to level the playing field and create a fair environment where performance is the only factor that counts (equity), where employer/employee expectations are understood and met (reciprocity), and where prejudice and bias are not factors (impartiality).

Discrimination

> You and Lisa met five years ago when you were hired into the management training program of a large utility. Although you're now in different parts of the organization, you have managed to stay close over the years. Lisa recently had a baby and plans to take advantage of the full six months of maternity leave the company offers. She told you that she's definitely coming back to work after her leave and that her department has promised to hold her job for her. Meanwhile, you've seen a posting for her job on the company's Web site. You run into one of Lisa's colleagues in the hall and ask about the posting. He says, "Oh yeah, they're going to fill that job. But don't tell Lisa. She's got five more months to be a happy mom. Besides, they'll find something for her to do if she decides to come back."

Since discrimination by race, religion, national origin, sex, and age is prohibited by federal law in the United States, many companies have defined policies prohibiting any kind of discrimination. Unfortunately, there can be quite a gulf between where corporate policy leaves off and reality begins. When people from various backgrounds get together to provide a service or manufacture a product, there surely will be people who have conscious or unconscious biases toward various groups, and others who are simply ignorant of the effect their behavior has on others.

WHAT IS IT? Discrimination occurs whenever something other than qualifications affects how an employee is treated. Unequal treatment, usually unfavorable, can take many forms. Older workers who suddenly find themselves reporting to younger ones can be resentful since they feel younger workers lack experience. Younger employees can be tempted to ignore advice from older workers, who they feel are "out of touch." The attitudes toward age will most likely become increasingly important over the next decade as the general population grows older.

Racial, ethnic, religious, or sexual stereotypes can creep into the behavior of even the most sophisticated individuals. The importance of being able to manage different types of people can't be overstated. In the United States, ethnic and racial minorities are growing faster than the population as a whole. By the year 2000, almost 85 percent of the new entrants into the workforce were expected to be women, minorities, or immigrants.[4]

In the case involving Lisa, the new mother, her maternity leave could result in discrimination. Although pregnant employees are protected by law (see "Why Is It an Ethical Problem?" which follows), in this case her time away from her job is clearly being viewed as a liability. Of course, employers have the right to replace workers who are on extended leaves because of illness, disability, or other reasons such as finishing an education. The problem in Lisa's case is that her department seems to be doing an end run around her by keeping her in the dark while her job is filled. If Lisa knew what the department's plans were, she might shorten her leave, or arrange a part-time working situation for a few months. But unless you, her colleague, tell her what you have found out, the job she left won't be the one she comes back to. It's simply not fair to keep Lisa in the dark.

Discrimination can be a subtle or not-so-subtle factor not only in working relationships, but also in hiring, promotions, and layoff decisions. People who don't fit a "corporate profile" may be passed over for advancement because they're female, or a member of a minority group, or too old, or for other reasons that may or may not be covered in protectionist legislation. Surely there are many barriers in the workplace, not just the glass ceiling that refers to barriers to female advancement. There probably are also barriers for people who are over 50 years old, or who have medical problems, or who are short, disabled, overweight, bearded, balding, or homosexual—any quality that varies from the "norm." And some employers create job requirements that could automatically eliminate certain employees, not because of their qualifications, but because of personal circumstances.

WHY IS IT AN ETHICAL PROBLEM? Discrimination is an ethical issue—beyond any legal protections—because it's at the core of fairness in the workplace. Fairness is a critical commodity because it's viewed in the United States as an "inalienable" right.[5] Our government has attempted to ensure fairness and justice; the word "trust" is on every piece of currency, and the Pledge of Allegiance declares "with liberty and justice for all." In addition, our entire legal system has justice and the protection of individual rights as its cornerstone. Consequently, people expect fairness from organizations in general, but specifically from their employers.

COSTS Victims of discrimination can file under Title VII of the Civil Rights Act of 1964 with the Equal Employment Opportunity Commission (EEOC), or bring suit under tort or contract law. This legislation specifically prohibits discrimination based on race, religion, sex, color, and national origin. Groups specifically protected by Title VII include women, African Americans, Hispanics, Native Americans, and Asian-Pacific Islanders. (Some states and local communities have added more protections—like sexual orientation and marital status—to that list.) The Pregnancy Discrimination Act of 1978 prohibits discrimination against pregnant women. The 1967 Age Discrimination in Employment Act extends protection to people 40 years of age and older. The 1973 Rehabilitation Act was the first federal legislation to protect disabled

Americans against discrimination by federal, state, local governments, agencies, and contractors. The Americans with Disabilities Act (ADA) of 1990 extended protection to the private sector by requiring all companies with more than 15 employees to make reasonable accommodations in order to employ workers with disabilities. Although the law doesn't list conditions or diseases that are protected—since people react differently to disease, some may be disabled and some may not be—some conditions are specifically included or excluded. HIV infection, for example, is considered a disability, and people who have it are protected by the ADA law.

Discrimination lawsuits can be costly for employers not simply in terms of legal fees and damages and media coverage. The morale of victims certainly suffers as they endure discrimination lawsuits, but the morale of other employees can also suffer. Imagine how the thousands of employees of Texaco must have felt when their company was under siege for a discrimination lawsuit. (You'll read more about this case in Chapter 6.) It's embarrassing for employees when the company they work for is publicly accused of wrongdoing.

If you're an individual accused of discriminating against another employee, the least you'll endure is an investigation. If you're found guilty, you'll probably be penalized or even fired. If you're found innocent, you or your accuser will most likely be counseled about your behavior and its effects, and one or both of you may be transferred to another area. If you manage someone who has been accused of discrimination, expect a lot of questions concerning why you were unaware of it or tolerated it. If you were aware of it and didn't do anything about it, be prepared for disciplinary action, particularly if a lawsuit results.

SPECIAL NOTE   The many programs that train employees to "value diversity" can seem to be at odds with the efforts to assimilate various groups and especially with the laws and policies that prohibit discrimination. Learning to appreciate differences flies in the face of what many of us are taught from the time we're children, that we should "fit in." Not only are many of us taught to downplay our own uniqueness in an effort to blend in, but also we're taught to ignore differences in other people. We usually are taught "not to notice" different colors, religions, accents, ways of dressing, and physical disabilities or abilities. Even sexual differences, which can be hard to ignore, have been played down in the not-too-distant past.

Valuing diversity means treating people equally while incorporating their diverse ideas. Discrimination means treating people unequally because they are, or appear to be, different. Valuing diversity is a positive action, while discrimination is a negative action. Valuing diversity tries to incorporate more fairness into the system, while discrimination incorporates unfairness into the system. The key to valuing diversity is understanding that different doesn't mean deficient and it doesn't mean less. Different means different.

Harassment, Sexual and Otherwise

The U.S. Senate confirmation hearings of Clarence Thomas's nomination to the Supreme Court in October 1991 (where the nominee was accused of sexual harassment by his former employee, Anita Hill) focused American business and workers on the issue of sexual harassment as perhaps nothing else has. One result of that incident was an increase in the number of corporations offering sexual harassment training to sensitize employees to the issue. The Equal Employment Opportunity Commission now requires all organizations with more than 15 employees to have a sexual harassment policy and to train employees in these issues. Another result was a growing apprehension on the part of employees, especially men, toward workers of the opposite sex. Sometimes the line between friendly and offensive is blurry.

> One of your co-workers is Joanne, a computer whiz with an offbeat style and a great sense of humor. Two of Joanne's favorite "targets" are you and Bill, another co-worker who tends to be quite standoffish in his business relationships. Joanne is the department clown and is forever goading you and Bill; you, because you're a great audience and clearly think she's hilarious; Bill, because she likes to try to get him to be more approachable. Joanne frequently alludes to sexual subjects and has called both you and Bill "little alley cats" and "studs." While Joanne's behavior doesn't offend you at all, you're surprised when Bill approaches you in the men's room and bitterly complains about Joanne's constant teasing.

WHAT IS IT? Sexual harassment is defined as unwelcome sexually oriented behavior that makes someone feel uncomfortable at work. It usually involves behavior by someone of higher status toward someone of lower status or power.

Federal law has defined two types of sexual harassment: *quid pro quo* and *hostile work environment*. Quid pro quo means that sexual favors are a requirement—or appear to be a requirement—for advancement in the workplace. Hostile work environment means that a worker has been made to feel uncomfortable because of unwelcome actions or comments relating to sexuality. This type of sexual harassment is especially murky because sexual harassment of this type is like beauty: It's in the eye of the beholder. What constitutes sexual harassment for one person may not for another. Putting your arm around a person's shoulder may feel like harassment to one individual, and someone else may be comfortable with such a gesture. This type of sexual harassment includes not only physical gestures but also remarks of a sexual nature—even compliments—and displays of sexually provocative material, like nude or revealing photographs displayed in an office.

In both types of sexual harassment, the decision about whether the behavior constitutes harassment is determined from the point of view of a "reasonable" person and the harasser's intentions aren't considered, which is why sexual harassment issues can be confusing. Since sexual harassment is determined by the reaction of the victim, you have to consider not what you mean by your comments or actions, but how they might be interpreted by the other person.

Most people will readily agree that kissing someone or patting someone on their rear end could be construed by some as being sexual harassment. But are you sexually harassing someone if you compliment her appearance, or touch his arm, or make jokes of a sexual nature? In Joanne's case, she hasn't done a very good job of considering exactly who her audience is and how each of her two co-workers might react to her jokes. While you might think it's funny to be called a little stud, Joanne probably should think more carefully about how someone like Bill might react to being called a name with sexual connotations. Is Joanne out of line? Is Bill overreacting? According to the law, it doesn't matter if you and Joanne think Bill is overreacting. The yardstick used to determine whether sexual harassment occurred will be how uncomfortable a reasonable person would be with Joanne's comments, and not what Joanne intended with her remarks. How Bill *felt* will be considered more than what Joanne *intended*.

WHY IS IT AN ETHICAL PROBLEM? Harassment (sexual or otherwise) is considered to be a form of discrimination and is therefore an ethical issue because it unfairly focuses job satisfaction, advancement, or retention on a factor other than the ability to do the job. Most instances of sexual harassment have nothing to do with romance and everything to do with power and fairness.

COSTS Victims of sexual harassment can file under Title VII of the Civil Rights Act of 1964 with the Equal Employment Opportunity Commission (EEOC), or bring suit under tort or contract law. An employer can be held liable for an employee's sexual harassment activities if the employer had knowledge of the conduct and did nothing to correct it. As a result, most companies take a sexual harassment charge very seriously.

Most companies will launch an immediate investigation if someone is accused of sexually harassing another employee. If this is a first-time event and the incident that prompted it is not determined to be lewd or assaultive—think of the scenario featuring Joanne that was discussed earlier—the employee may be warned, disciplined, or transferred to another area. (However, in some major companies a first-time offense is enough to get someone fired.) If the behavior is judged to be lewd or forceful, or if there's evidence that the employee has demonstrated a pattern of behavior, the employee will most likely be fired, and often very quickly. (One corporation was able to conduct an investigation, find evidence of a pattern, and terminate the harasser in less than 48 hours.) If the accused is found innocent, or if it's determined that a misunderstanding exists between the two parties, the accused and the accuser will probably be counseled by human resources professionals and, if necessary, one of them may be transferred to another area. The manager of a sexual harasser can expect a lot of questions. If the manager was aware of harassment and didn't do anything about it, he or she should be prepared for disciplinary action, particularly if a lawsuit results.

Nearly a third of the claims filed with the EEOC are sexual harassment claims. And sexual harassment lawsuits are very expensive for corporations. Awards to victims have been substantial, as is the toll such charges can take on co-worker's morale and on the ability to hire qualified candidates. For example, in June 1998, Mitsubishi Motor's North American division agreed to pay $34 million to settle its sexual harassment case. The settlement was based on charges brought by 350 female factory workers at an Illinois factory. The women alleged that co-workers and supervisors kissed and fondled them, called them "whores" and "bitches," posted sexual graffiti and pornography, demanded sex, and retaliated if they refused. They also complained that managers did nothing to stop the harassment. In addition to paying the fine,

Mitsubishi fired 20 workers and disciplined others, agreed to provide mandatory sexual harassment training, to revise its sexual harassment policy, and to investigate future sexual harassment allegations within three weeks of a complaint.

CONFLICTS OF INTEREST

People and corporations are naturally involved in a tangle of relationships—both personal and professional. Your personal reputation, and the reputation of your company, are inextricably tied to how well you handle relationships with other employees, customers, consultants, vendors, family, and friends. Your ability to act impartially, and look as if you are acting impartially, is key to your fulfilling your end of the employer/employee contract.

> Your daughter is applying to a prestigious university. Since admission to the school is difficult, your daughter has planned the process carefully. She has consistently achieved high marks, taken preparatory courses for entrance exams, and has participated in various extracurricular activities. When you tell one of your best customers about her activities, he offers to write her a letter of recommendation. He's an alumnus of the school and is one of its most active fundraisers. Although he's a customer, you also regularly play golf together, and your families have socialized together on occasion.

What Is It?

A conflict of interest occurs when your judgment or objectivity is compromised. The appearance of a conflict of interest—when a third party could think your judgment has been compromised—is generally considered to be just as damaging as an actual conflict.

The current poster child for conflicts of interest surely must be Enron. (The complete description of the Enron/Arthur Andersen debacle is in Chapter 8.) Now that we have gotten a glimpse of "life at Enron" before its undignified collapse in late 2001, we see conflicts of interest at every turn. CFO Andrew Fastow created financial partnerships to hide Enron debt and from which he allegedly collected $30 million in management fees.[6] Wendy Gramm (wife of former U.S. Senator from Texas, Phil Gramm), took her seat on Enron's board of directors just five weeks after resigning as head of the Commodities Futures Trading Commission, where she strong-armed her colleagues into approving a crucial regulatory exemption that benefited Enron.[7] President Jeffrey Skilling hired his girlfriend, later his wife, as corporate secretary of Enron for an annual salary of $600,000.[8]

These incidents and others have been trumpeted by the media, which has used the long series of conflicts as evidence of the Enron executives' culpability. It seems that the folks at Enron never considered how their activities would look plastered across the front pages of America's newspapers, or perhaps they were too arrogant to care. Most reasonable people believe that Enron's spider web of unsavory relationships certainly influenced decisions and judgments—the classic definition of a conflict.

In the case of a customer offering to do a favor for you—or your daughter or other member of your family—some of the questions you'll need to ask yourself include: Would your customer's offer influence your business relationship? Could someone think your business judgment had been compromised by accepting your customer's offer? Is your relationship more than just a business one, so that accepting an offer could be interpreted as a simple act of friendship?

Some corporations have a policy that permits the acceptance of favors from customers or vendors if there's also a "friendship" present; and friendship is usually defined by these companies as a long-standing relationship that's well known in the community. For example, in small towns where everyone knows everyone else, many customers will also be friends and it's unrealistic to expect anything else. Other organizations (including government agencies) would discourage accepting a favor like this one under any circumstances. Things to consider when making your decision in this case include: how long you've been friends with your customer, how well known the relationship is in your community, his knowledge of your daughter's qualifications, and whether your customer expects anything in return for his recommendation or if the letter is simply a gesture of friendship with no strings attached. How would his recommendation be perceived by others?

Almost every business situation can involve conflicts of interest. A conflict can occur when a vendor lavishly entertains you or when you entertain a customer—if the object is influence. Both situations could prompt an observer to think that a special deal or advantageous terms are part of the relationship. Conflicts of interest can occur when people who report to you observe that you have an especially close friendship with one of their co-workers. Conflicts can occur when you're asked to judge the creditworthiness of your neighbor or if you perform consulting work for your employer's competitor. They can involve accepting hand-tooled cowboy boots from an advertising agency, being sponsored for membership in an exclusive private club by a consulting company, or allowing a supplier to give you a discount on equipment for your home when you place an order for your office.

Common conflicts of interest include overt or covert bribes and the trading of influence or privileged information.

OVERT BRIBES OR KICKBACKS Anything that could be considered a bribe or kickback is a clear conflict of interest. It doesn't matter whether the bribe or kickback is in the form of money or something else of substantial value that is offered in exchange for access to specific products, services, or influence.

SUBTLE "BRIBES" These can be interpreted to include gifts and entertainment. Most corporate policy places a ceiling of $25 to $100 on the gifts employees can accept from, or give to, customers or vendors. Reciprocity is one yardstick used for determining whether entertainment is acceptable. If you can't reciprocate with the same kind of entertainment being offered to you, it's probably inappropriate to accept it. For example, if a supplier offers you tickets to the Super Bowl, or a weekend of golf, or dinner for four at a $200-per-person restaurant, its probably inappropriate for you to accept under any circumstances. The emphasis on reciprocity is to maintain a fair, even playing field for all suppliers, so that you (as a purchaser) will be unbiased when making a decision about a supplier. As mentioned earlier, both reciprocity and impartiality are elements of fairness.

Accepting discounts on personal items from a vendor will also be interpreted as a conflict. The formula to use when determining whether to accept a discount is simple: If it's a formal arrangement between your company and a supplier and it's offered to all employees, it's probably acceptable; if the discount is being extended only to *you*, it's not acceptable.

INFLUENCE Your relationship with someone by itself can constitute a conflict of interest. For example, if you're in charge of purchasing corporate advertising and your cousin or neighbor or college friend owns an advertising agency, it will be considered a conflict if you make the decision to hire that firm. That doesn't preclude the firm from bidding, but it does preclude you from making the decision. If a decision involves anyone with whom you have a personal relationship, you should ask someone else to make it. Another way to avoid the appearance of a conflict in a situation like this one, which is charged with issues of partiality, is to arrange for a "blind" competition, where the identity of various bidders is known only by someone not involved in the decision-making process. However, since any decision made by you in such a case will be suspect—even in blind evaluations—you should include other employees in the decision-making process.

PRIVILEGED INFORMATION As an employee, you're naturally privy to information that would be valuable to your employer's competitors. That's why its generally considered a conflict of interest if you hold a full-time job for ABC Insurance Company and decide to do some consulting work for XYZ Insurance Company. There are certainly exceptions to this rule of thumb: If you're a computer programmer at Green's Restaurant, it probably isn't a conflict to wait on tables at Red's Restaurant. Two factors could make such a situation acceptable: if the work you perform at your second job doesn't compromise the work you do at your first one, and if both employers are aware of your activities.

In addition, it can appear as if you're involved in a conflict if you and a close relative or friend work for competitors or if one of you works for an organization—such as a media company—that might have a particular interest in your company's activities. For example, if you work as an investment banker for Goldman Sachs and your sister holds the same position at Salomon Smith Barney, you both should alert your managers to the situation. These are potential problems that can be defused when your manager knows about the relationship. Full disclosure removes substantial risk.

Why Is It an Ethical Problem?

The basis of every personal and corporate relationship is trust, and it exists only when individuals and corporations feel that they're being treated fairly, openly, and on the same terms as everyone else. Conflicts of interest erode trust by making it look as if special favors will be extended for special friends and that attitude can enhance one relationship, but at the expense of all others.

Costs

Depending on the offense, myriad federal and state laws cover conflicts of interest. Certain professions, such as banking, accounting, law, religion, and medicine, have special obligations—often spelled out in professional codes of ethics—commonly referred to as "fiduciary" responsibilities. These professions are widely known as "trust" professions, meaning that these practitioners have been entrusted with sensitive, confidential information about their clients. Fiduciary responsibilities concern the obligations resulting from relationships that have their basis in faith, trust, and confidence.

If you're suspected of a conflict of interest, the least you can expect is an investigation by your company. If it determines that your behavior demonstrates a conflict or the appearance of a conflict, you may be warned, disciplined, or even fired depending on the nature of your behavior. If you've accepted a bribe or kickback, you could face termination and even arrest. Being involved in a conflict of interest means that your judgment has been compromised and it can severely damage your professional reputation.

CUSTOMER CONFIDENCE ISSUES

We've all heard the saying, "The customer is always right," and companies like L.L. Bean and Wal-Mart have benefited by weaving that slogan into the fabric of their corporate cultures. But excellent customer service is more than being able to return a defective refrigerator or having cheerful customer service representatives (although that helps). Excellent customer service also means providing a quality product or service at a fair price, honestly representing the product or service, and protecting the customer's privacy.

What Is It?

Customer confidence issues include a range of topics including confidentiality, product safety and effectiveness, truth in advertising, and special fiduciary responsibilities.

> You work for a consulting company in Atlanta. Your team has recently completed an analysis of Big Co., including sales projections for the next five years. You're working late one night when you receive a call from an executive vice president at Big Co. in Los Angeles, who asks you to immediately fax to her a summary of your team's report. When you locate the report, you discover that your team leader has stamped "For internal use only" on the report cover. Your team leader is on a hiking vacation and you know it would be impossible to locate him. Big Co. has a long-standing relationship with your company and has paid substantial fees for your company's services.

CONFIDENTIALITY Privacy is a basic customer right. Privacy and the obligation to keep customer information in confidence often go beyond protecting sales projections or financial information. It can also mean keeping in strict confidence information concerning acquisitions, mergers, relocations, layoffs, or an executive's health or marital problems. In some industries, confidentiality is so important an issue that companies prohibit their employees from publicly acknowledging a customer relationship. In the financial services industry, for example, it's common practice to refuse to divulge that XYZ Company is even a customer.

In the case involving Big Co., an executive is demanding access to a confidential report. First, are you absolutely certain that the caller is indeed a Big Co. executive? If you have verified her identity, do you know whether she has clearance from Big Co. to examine your team's report? If she does have clearance, is your team's report in a format that your company wants to share with Big Co., or does it need revision? Whenever you see "For internal use only," that's what it means, and it can be enormously risky to release the report to anyone—including the customer—without permission from someone within your company who has responsibility for that client. In a case like this one, you should track down someone who's in a position of authority in your company—your manager's manager perhaps—before you override the warning on the report and release any information.

On occasion, third parties may ask for customer information. For example, a reporter or a client may ask you about customer trends. It's never acceptable to discuss specific companies or individuals with a third party, or provide any information that might enable a third party to identify a specific customer. If you want to provide information, you can offer aggregate data from a number of companies, as long as the data provided doesn't allow any one customer to be identified.

> You're the head of marketing for a small pharmaceutical company that has just discovered a very promising drug for the treatment of Alzheimer's disease. You have spent months designing a marketing campaign that contains printed materials and medication sample kits for distribution to almost every family physician and gerontologist in the country. As the materials are being loaded into cartons for delivery to your company's representatives, your assistant tells you that she has noticed a typographical error in the literature that could mislead physicians and their patients. In the section that discusses side effects, diarrhea and gastrointestinal problems are listed as having a probability of 2 percent. It should have read 20 percent. This error appears on virtually every piece of the literature and kits, and ads containing the mistake are already on press in several consumer magazines.

PRODUCT SAFETY Another basic customer right is product safety, and there's probably no issue that will more seriously affect a corporate or an individual's reputation. When we think of product safety, we usually think of it as being an organizational issue. But many of the ethical disasters that have product safety as the core issue started out as small problems that mushroomed. Especially in service businesses, where the "products" are delivered by individuals to individuals, product safety is a critical issue. As a result, product safety is every employee's issue, as well as being an organizational issue. (We'll read more about this as an organizational problem in Chapter 8.)

In the case concerning the typographical error about a new drug's side effects, the head of marketing faces a nasty dilemma. If she reproduces all of the printed material, it surely will be at a very great cost to this small company, and it will result in a significant delay in getting the drug to physicians. However, since many elderly people are prone to gastrointestinal upsets and many can become very ill and even die as a result, this typo is a significant one and the material cannot go out as is. Certainly the ideal solution would be to redo all of the marketing materials. However, if time and financial considerations prohibit that, there are other solutions. One solution might be to quickly produce a "correction" to be inserted into every kit. Also, a letter could be distributed to every physician with an explanation of the correction, as well as a discussion of how important quality and full disclosure are to your company. This solution will still be costly, but not nearly as costly as doing nothing and letting the kits go out with an error. What do you suppose would be the cost of even one wrongful death lawsuit? How about a class action? How about the accompanying publicity?

In another case, a large financial firm was excoriated in 1994 when its brokers sold shares in questionable partnerships to individual investors, who later lost substantial sums on their investments in the partnerships. As a result, the firm not only suffered repeated lashings in the press, but it paid enormous fines as well, and its reputation has suffered greatly. In 2002, Merrill Lynch was fined $100 million after it was shown that some of its Internet analysts publicly urged investors to buy stocks that they were privately calling "pieces of junk," "dogs" and worse in e-mails to one another.[9] Although these may not be the kinds of situations we ordinarily think of when we consider product safety, people have suffered profound losses because a firm's salespeople overstated the soundness of a "product." In these cases the product was advice, and the public, the press, and the courts deemed once again that the "safety" of a product or service is an important consumer right.

TRUTH IN ADVERTISING There are many salespeople who simply exaggerate their product's (or service's) benefits to consumers. Do fast sports cars automatically turn every young man into a James Dean? Will investing in a certain bond ensure you a safe retirement? Hype is generally a part of most sales pitches, and most consumers expect a certain amount of hype. There are other cases, however, when fudging the truth about a product is more than just hype—it's unfair. (Like product safety, truth in advertising is an issue for both organizations and individuals.)

Imagine that your financial firm is offering a new issue—a corporate bond with an expected yield of 7 to 7.5 percent. In the past, offerings like this one have generally been good investments for clients, and you have sold the issue to dozens of large and small clients. You're leaving on a two-week vacation and only have a few hours left in the office, when your firm announces that the yield for the bond has been reduced; the high end will now be no more than 7 percent. The last day of the issue will be next week, while you're away on vacation. What should you do?

The fact is that your customers have been misled (albeit unintentionally) about the yield on that particular bond, and now you are under an obligation to tell the truth about the instrument before the issue closes. Why? Because another basic consumer right is to be told the truth about the products and services purchased. Failure to tell the truth about a product can be devastating for an organization, and it also can cause big problems for the company employees who are involved in perpetuating the false information.

SPECIAL FIDUCIARY RESPONSIBILITIES As discussed earlier in this chapter, certain professions, such as banking, accounting, law, religion, and medicine, have special obligations to customers, which are commonly referred to as fiduciary responsibilities. The law and the judicial system have recognized these special obligations, and they are spelled out in the codes of ethics for those professions. Fiduciary responsibilities hold these professionals to a high standard, and when they violate those responsibilities, the punishment is often harsh. For example, some of the employees of Arthur Andersen's Houston office failed Enron shareholders when they allowed the high-risk accounting practices used by Enron to continue. Although David Duncan, leader of the Andersen auditing team at Enron, warned the Enron board of directors in 1999 that the firm's accounting practices were "high risk," he apparently did not take the extra steps that would have been required to get the board to take action (in fact, the board did nothing in response to his warning.[10] For example, Duncan could have threatened to withdraw Andersen's services or to turn the company in. At the time, this would have looked risky because Enron might have simply fired the auditors and Andersen would have lost a huge client. But, in hindsight, exercising appropriate fiduciary responsibility could have saved two companies, thousands of jobs, and a huge amount of shareholder wealth. One of the early accountants of Arthur Andersen, Al Bows, who established the Arthur Andersen office in Atlanta in 1941, said that the founder of his old company, the original Arthur Andersen, would be "disgusted with what these guys did to his company." Bows went on to tell a story about a big juice company in Atlanta. He discovered that "the CEO was starting another juice company on the side to profit for himself. I told him he'd better cut it out or I'd turn him in. He stopped. But he was mad".[11] Of course, Bows is describing the fiduciary responsibilities of accountants—one of which is to ensure the financial integrity of publicly-traded companies. When Arthur Andersen employees breached their fiduciary responsibilities in 2001, they contributed to the collapse of a major company.

Here's another case:

> For 12 years, you've been the financial advisor for an elderly man in his late 70s who is an active investor of his own portfolio and for a trust that will benefit his two children. In the last few months, you've noticed a subtle, yet marked, change in his behavior. He has become increasingly forgetful, has become uncharacteristically argumentative, and seems to have difficulty understanding some very basic aspects of his transactions. He has asked you to invest a sizable portion of his portfolio and the trust in what you consider to be a very risky bond offering. You are frank about your misgivings. He blasts you and says that if you don't buy the bonds, he'll take his business elsewhere.

If you work for a large electronics chain, it's not your responsibility to assess the mental stability of a customer who's purchasing a new television. You're selling; he's buying. However, individuals in fiduciary professions have a responsibility to protect their customer's assets—and that entails "knowing" their customers; frequently, that can mean assessing behavior and saving customers from themselves. In this case, if a customer wants to make a risky investment against your advice, there's little you can do but wish him or her well. Who knows? You might be wrong, and the customer might make a fortune. However, if a financial professional sees clear signs of incompetence in a long-time customer who's suddenly interested in making a risky bet, he or she is under some obligation to seek help. The case involving the mental stability of a long-time customer is one of the most common dilemmas encountered by financial advisors. The advisor could try again to dissuade the client from making the investment, or involve the firm's senior management in negotiations with the client. The advisor could contact a member of the client's family—one of the children perhaps—and explain his or her reservations. The advisor could also possibly contact the client's lawyer or accountant, who also would be bound by confidentiality constraints because of the fiduciary nature of their professions. However, most financial executives will agree that something must be done to try to help this long-time customer.

Why Is It an Ethical Problem?

We use the term *customer confidence issues* as an umbrella to address the wide range of topics that can affect your relationship with your customer. These are ethical issues because they revolve around fairness, honesty, and respect for others and customer relationships can't survive without those basics of trust.

Costs

There are severe corporate and individual penalties regarding truth in advertising and product safety, and more may be on the way. In addition to fines and imprisonment, the publicity in cases where product safety is a factor is generally staggering, as is the public's reaction. Even if a company is exonerated in the long run, the publicity generated by these situations can be seriously damaging, and it can take years for a company to recover, especially if there's evidence of wrongdoing and consumers feel that the organization has violated a public trust. As in the case of Arthur Andersen, the public and regulatory reaction to a breach of fiduciary trust can be swift and fatal.

The fastest way to lose customers or clients is to violate their basic rights to honesty, a quality product or service, or confidentiality. And, obviously, losing customers will short-circuit any career. In addition, if you belong to a profession with special fiduciary responsibilities, violating customer trust or confidentiality can result in disciplinary action or censure.

USE OF CORPORATE RESOURCES

As discussed in the introduction, you and your employer have a special relationship, and each owes the other a modicum of loyalty based on that relationship. In addition, since you're a corporate representative, you're considered an "agent" of your company. This means that your actions can be considered as actions of the corporation. This section of the chapter presents the flip side of the above section on human resources issues—your employer's responsibilities to you are described in that section, and your responsibilities to your employer are described here.

What Is It?

The use of corporate resources involves your fulfilling your end of the employer/employee "contract." It means being truthful with your employer and management and being responsible in the use of corporate resources, including its finances and reputation.

> A young woman who works for you is moving with her husband to another city, where she'll be looking for a new job. She's an excellent worker and when she asks you for a reference, you're glad to do it for her. She specifically asks for a written recommendation on your corporate letterhead.

USE OF CORPORATE REPUTATION Whenever you identify yourself as an employee of your company, people can infer that you are speaking on behalf of it, which is why you have to be careful how you link yourself to your company. For example, if you use corporate letterhead to write a recommendation for someone or simply to complain to the telephone company, it can be construed as a "corporate" position. Consequently, corporate letterhead should be used only for corporate business. If, as in the case of the recommendation, you need to identify yourself as an employee, use your personal stationery and attach your business card. The objective is to differentiate between your personal opinions and any official stance of your organization.

Recommendations, in particular, present a challenge for employers and individuals. Many companies attempt to check with former employers when hiring someone. This can present a problem since most companies prohibit their personnel from officially supplying this type of information because of lawsuits that have resulted from employer-supplied recommendations. (Many employers will supply only the following information concerning former employees: name, date of employment, and job title. And most employers will require the former employee's written consent before they supply any salary information to a third party.)

Similarly, if you're asked to make a speech, write an article, serve on the board of a nonprofit organization, or participate in any activity that would identify you (and your personal opinions) with your company, be sure to get permission from your manager, the legal department, or human resources. You may unwittingly be supporting a position or organization with which your company may not wish to be associated. For example, while it might seem like a great idea for you to serve on the board of your local ASPCA, if you work for a pharmaceutical company that tests drugs on animals, you may be placing your employer in an embarrassing position. Of course, you can serve on the board as a private citizen, but not as an employee of XYZ Drug Company unless you've received corporate authorization.

> You're an employment counselor at a large outplacement firm. Your company is currently negotiating with Black Company to provide outplacement services to 500 employees who are about to lose their jobs as the result of a layoff. Your neighbor and good friend is a reporter for the local newspaper, who mentions to you over coffee one Saturday that she's writing a story about Black Company. According to her sources, 1,500 employees are about to lose their jobs. You know her numbers are incorrect. Should you tell her?

Dealing with the press—even when the reporter is a friend or relative—is a tricky business and shouldn't be attempted by a novice. In a case like the one above, where you may think your friendly reporter might have incorrect numbers, silence is truly the best policy. Her numbers may in fact be correct, and your numbers may represent only the employees who are eligible for outplacement services, not the total number who are losing their jobs.

Another issue that can be confusing to business people is what "off the record" means. For the most part, off the record means that a reporter won't quote you directly or attribute any remarks to you. You can't, however, tell a reporter that your remarks are off the record after the fact. The way to tell a reporter that remarks are off the record is to inform him or her before you offer your information. But the very best way to make sure something is off the record is to keep your mouth shut in the first place. Reporters with the best of intentions can very innocently get their sources into trouble by providing information that only the source would know, thereby identifying the source.

If you are contacted by the press, immediately alert your company's public relations department. Unless you're trained to answer press inquiries and receive authorization to do it, you should never comment to the press. It's easy to innocently supply confidential information or cast a negative light on your company when you're untrained to deal with probing or ambiguous questions posed by a skilled journalist.

> You've been working very long hours on a special project for the chairman of your company. Your company policy states that employees who work more than 12 hours in one day may be driven home by a company car at company expense. Policy also states that employees who work longer than two hours past the regular end of their day can have a meal delivered to the office at company expense. You and your colleagues who are also working on the project are arriving at the office at 8:00 A.M. and order dinner at 7:00 P.M.; then you enjoy dinner and conversation for an hour and are driven home by company cars. Is this OK?

CORPORATE FINANCIAL RESOURCES In a game entitled "Where Do You Draw the Line: An Ethics Game," produced by Simile II, players explore the differences between taking $10 worth of pencils from their company and distributing them to poor children, making $10 worth of personal long-distance calls at work, and taking $10 from their company's petty cash drawer. Is there a difference among these scenarios, or are they pretty much the same thing? Most people eventually conclude that all of them, regardless of the employee's intentions, involve stealing $10 worth of corporate resources. The bottom line is that corporate equipment and services should be used only for company business. Whether it involves making personal phone calls, padding expense reports, appropriating office supplies, sending personal mail through the company mail room, or using copy equipment to print a flyer for your scout troop, personal or inappropriate use of corporate resources is unethical and violates most corporate policy.

In a case like the one above where you and colleagues are working long hours to complete a special project for the company's chairman, you are following corporate policy to the letter, so your actions are probably acceptable to most organizations. However, if you and your co-workers are stretching out the last hour of dinner so that you can take a company car home, you're getting into ethical hot water. Are you also stretching out their work in order to have a free meal? If you would have no problem explaining your actions to the chairman, or if you wouldn't mind if he or she sat in on one of those dinner hours, then the meals and the cars are perfectly acceptable. The important thing is to treat your company's resources with as much care as you would your own.

> Your manager is being transferred to another division of the company in early January. He calls a meeting in early November and asks that every department head delay processing all invoices until after January 1. He wants to keep expenses low and revenues high so that his last quarter in your area shows maximum revenue.

PROVIDING HONEST INFORMATION Another key issue concerns truth. Although everyone will agree that telling the truth is important, someday you may have a manager who says something like, "These numbers look too negative—let's readjust them so it looks better to senior management." Many managers feel it necessary to put a positive spin on financials before submitting them up through the ranks. As a result, some companies have suffered serious financial penalties because their numbers have been positively spun on so many succeeding levels, they bear no resemblance to reality by the time they reach the top. "Fudging" numbers can have serious consequences since senior management may make crucial decisions based on flawed data. (Corporations are fined by regulators if inaccurate financial information is submitted to regulators or incorporated into formal financial statements.) If you're asked to skew any kind of corporate information, you may want to consult with someone outside of your chain of command such as the legal, human resources, or audit department.

In the case about a manager wishing to delay paying expenses until after he leaves the area, such creative bookkeeping not only harms the person who is taking his place in January, it also harms the suppliers who are relying on prompt payment of their invoices. It's grossly unfair to ask suppliers to wait almost 60 extra days before getting paid. One solution might be to approach the other department heads and gain their cooperation in refusing to follow your manager's request. Another course of action would be to relate the incident to the audit department, who would surely be interested in your manager's shenanigans.

Why Is It an Ethical Problem?

Your use of corporate resources is an ethical issue because it represents fulfilling your end of the employer/employee contract, and its roots are in fairness and honesty.

Costs

Obviously, if you've stolen corporate assets or filed an inflated expense report, you'll almost certainly be fired, and you may be arrested. If you have divulged confidential information to another corporation (as in supplying a recommendation for a former employee), your company may be placed at risk for a lawsuit.

If you fail to uphold your end of the employer/employee loyalty contract, your career at your company can be short-circuited. Most corporate cultures place tremendous importance on honesty, loyalty, and teamwork. Generally, successful corporations are communities, where a sense of family has been encouraged. Just as family members try to protect one another and keep family information private, the company community tries to encourage the same behavior. Individuals who violate the "family" trust by squandering resources, being dishonest, or misusing the "family" reputation, are frequently isolated or even banished.

WHEN ALL ELSE FAILS: BLOWING THE WHISTLE

A section on ethics and the individual wouldn't be complete without a discussion of what happens when you suspect wrongdoing within your organization. If your organization's activities are keeping you awake at night, you may have to report it—blow the whistle—and you need to proceed with great caution.

How *not* to blow the whistle might be best illustrated in a case that involves a high-level investment banker who discovered that some of his colleagues were engaged in unethical dealings with several customers. The investment banker brought the situation to the attention of his manager, who told him to forget it. Determined to raise the issue, the banker wrote an irate memo outlining the situation and naming names to his company's CEO. The banker copied the memo to several other top managers. Even though there were only three levels of management between the banker and the CEO, and even though the banker was right about his colleagues and they were eventually fired, the banker was also fired.

In another large, multinational company, a young trainee in an Asian country felt he was being treated unfairly by his local management. In a pique of anger, he wrote a long message outlining his grievances on his company's electronic mail system. Although he addressed his message to the company CEO, president, and head of human resources (all three senior managers were based in New York), he copied everyone else on the system—approximately 30,000 managers worldwide. The trainee was fired, not because of the message, but because of how he communicated it. The head of human resources commented, "He was being groomed for management, and we couldn't have someone with such poor judgment in that role. If he had complained only to senior management, he would have been heard, he would have been protected, and we would have corrected the situation. After copying the world with his complaint, we felt he was a loose cannon and we had no choice but to get him out."

Unless you want to be branded as someone with poor judgment, you have to be very careful about how you raise ethical concerns. Usually, the CEO is one of your last resorts, and he or she should be approached only after you've exhausted every other internal resource and are ready to go outside the company to resolve the issue. An exception to this would be in a company like PPG Industries, where the former CEO, Vince Sarni, asked and encouraged employees to contact him directly with issues. A hotline for that purpose sat on his desk, and he personally answered that phone. Warren Buffett, the CEO of Berkshire Hathaway, also used the "call me" approach when he served as a director of Salomon Brothers back in 1991. As the company became embroiled in a bid-rigging scandal (see Chapter 8 for the details), Buffett stepped in as interim CEO. He wrote a letter to Salomon Brothers managers that said, "Here's my home phone number in Omaha. If you see anything unethical, give me a call." Managers did call him and they were able to devise a plan to save Salomon Brothers from Andersen's fate.[12]

So how do you blow the whistle? First, let's talk about when.

> A long-time customer approaches you for financing for a new business venture. The customer offers as collateral a piece of property he has purchased in a rural location for the purpose of building a housing development. You send an appraiser to the property and he accidentally discovers that this property holds toxic waste. You're sure this customer is unaware of the waste; in fact, the waste is migrating and in a few years will invade the water table under a nearby farmer's fields. You explain the situation to your manager, who naturally instructs you to refuse to accept the property as collateral, but he also forbids you to mention the toxic waste to the customer. "Let them find out about it themselves," he says. Do you alert the customer to the toxic waste? Do you alert government regulators?

When Do You Blow the Whistle?

Let's assume first that your concern involves a serious issue. Reporting toxic materials, for example, is a serious issue, because of the potential for harm. A colleague padding an expense report a bit probably isn't as serious. Once you've informed your manager about a fudged expense report, your responsibility is probably fulfilled. However, one colleague fudging an expense report is a far cry from a group of employees systematically altering all of their expense reports with their manager's knowledge. If you suspect something of that magnitude, of course you should report it to someone outside of your chain of command such as your internal auditor.

Many might disagree with this approach, but few people in business have the time to be "on patrol." Once a manager is alerted, it's his or her responsibility to deal with issues like expense reports, except in extraordinary circumstances. This could be termed "picking your battles," and responding appropriately to your gut feelings. Chapter 4 will provide detailed decision-making tools that can help you decide what to do in a particular ethical dilemma. But, for now, let's consider a number of simple triggers that can help you to determine if an issue is serious.

Some of the triggers to help you determine if an issue is serious enough to be raised beyond your immediate manager include an issue that involves truth, employee or customer (or other stakeholder) rights, trust, harm, your personal reputation or the reputation of your organization, and whether the law is being broken or compromised. In the toxic dump case, for example, harm could certainly result, customer (and other stakeholder) rights are involved, your organization's reputation is at risk, a public trust may be violated, and law may very well be compromised or broken if you keep quiet about toxic wastes under a proposed housing development. A situation like that has all the earmarks of a serious ethical dilemma.

Suppose your manager asks you to supply inaccurate numbers in a financial report to another level of management. That situation involves not only a breach of truth, but also potential harm and could damage your reputation. It's a serious issue that you'll probably want to report.

How to Blow the Whistle

Let's assume that you're dealing with a serious issue, you've assembled the facts, they're accurate to the best of your knowledge, you've asked your peers or your manager for advice, and there's a law or company policy about to be violated or one of the other triggers discussed earlier indicates a serious problem. Now what?

1. APPROACH YOUR IMMEDIATE MANAGER FIRST. If your manager tells you to ignore a situation or belittles your concern, approach him or her again. The second time you approach your manager, you may want to write a memo and spell out your concerns in black and white so it's more difficult for your manager to ignore or dismiss them. Frequently, writing a memo will be enough to convince your manager that this is serious and you'll get a more favorable response. You should also do some soul searching to make sure your decision to pursue this issue is an objective one, and not based in any feeling of revenge you might have for your manager, coworkers, or company. Also, you should find out exactly how your company wants issues raised and if there is a special process for doing it. If there is, follow the process to the letter.[13]

2. DISCUSS THE ISSUE WITH YOUR FAMILY. Since any whistle-blowing activity can affect not only you, but also your family, it's imperative that they know what's going on. It's also the time to document your activities. Obtain copies of correspondence that relate to the issue and any memos you've written in an attempt to alert management. Keep a diary to track activities related to the issue and describe any conversations you've had concerning the issue.[14]

3. TAKE IT TO THE NEXT LEVEL. If you receive no satisfaction from your manager, it's time to go to the next level of management. The most diplomatic way of going around your manager is to say to your manager something like, "I feel so strongly about this that I'd like a meeting with you and your manager to discuss it." The positive aspect of asking your manager to go with you to the next level is that he or she won't feel betrayed and you'll appear to be a team player. The negative aspect is that your manager may forbid you to approach his or her manager. If that happens, or if you're still not satisfied after meeting with the next level of management, you'll need to consider going outside of your chain of command.

4. CONTACT YOUR COMPANY'S ETHICS OFFICER OR OMBUDSMAN. Find out if your state has any special legislation regarding whistle-blowing. Your state may have legislative protection for whistle-blowers, but it may require you to follow certain procedures in order for you to be protected.[15]

5. CONSIDER GOING OUTSIDE YOUR CHAIN OF COMMAND. If your company has no formal ethics department, think about other areas that would be receptive to your concerns. If your issue is human resources related—if it involves relationships or activities within your company like discrimination or sexual harassment—approach your human resources officer or department. If the issue is business related—if it involves external relationships such as those with customers, suppliers, regulators—you can still approach human resources, but a better choice would probably be the legal department or your company's internal auditors. Obviously, if the issue involves the law or an actual or potential legal issue, you should contact the legal department. And if the issue concerns a financial matter, it's probably better to approach your organization's auditors. Most auditors have a system of internal checks they can trigger that will confirm or refute your suspicions and even protect you. Also, some auditors in some industries have an underground network of sorts; there are relationships that exist among auditors from various organizations. They can investigate situations very quietly and keep the situation from blowing out of proportion if that's indicated and appropriate.

Since the role of human resources, legal, and audit departments is to protect the corporation, they should be receptive to any concerns that could put the company at risk. If, however, the activity you're concerned about has been approved or condoned by the highest levels of management, these internal departments may be inclined to go along with "business as usual." And since their role is to protect the company, you are likely to find that their first allegiance is to the company, and not to you.

It's usually safe to approach these departments, but it's not completely without risk. You can reduce the risk if you can persuade one or more of your colleagues to join you in the process. Having an ally can encourage lawyers and auditors to take you more seriously. It also may be wise to consult your personal lawyer at this point in the process. According to Hoffman and Moore, your attorney can "help you determine if the wrongdoing violates the law, aid you in documenting information about it, inform you of any laws you might be breaking in documenting it, assist you in deciding to whom to report it, make sure reports are filed on time, and help you protect yourself against retaliation."[16]

Once you've approached your management, the ethics office (if your company has one), and human resources, legal, or audit, you should have received some satisfaction. The vast majority of whistle-blowing cases are resolved at one of those levels. However, if you're still concerned, the risks to you personally escalate significantly from this point on. Your last resort within your company would be your organization's senior management, including the CEO, president, or board of directors. Obviously, you should contact whoever has a reputation for being most approachable. Understand that your immediate management will most likely be irate if you approach senior management. However, if you're right about your concerns, you may end up a big hero if the issue you're raising is a localized problem and senior management is unaware of what's going on.

Before contacting your senior management, be sure to have your facts straight and documented. (This is where a diary and copies of correspondence will be useful.) If you're wrong, few people are going to understand or forgive you. You may be harassed, reprimanded, penalized, or there may be some pretext found to fire you. However, there is evidence that you can contact the CEO and keep your job. For example, Sherron Watkins, vice president of corporate development at Enron, still had her job at Enron one year after CEO Ken Lay received her fearful letter about accounting irregularities and months after the executive team resigned. However, she wrote her letter to the CEO and not to the local newspapers.[17]

6. GO OUTSIDE OF THE COMPANY. If you've raised the concern all the way to the top of your company, still have a job, and are still unsatisfied, your only choice now is to go outside. If your company is part of a regulated industry, like defense contractors and commercial banks, you can contact the regulators who are charged with overseeing your industry. Or you can contact the press. However, if you've already contacted numerous individuals in your company about the issue, it won't take a genius to figure out who is talking outside of the company. Even if you contact the press or the regulators anonymously, your co-workers probably will know it's you.

Recent legislation has made it easier and more lucrative for employees to blow the whistle to regulators when companies are government contractors or when the federal government has somehow been defrauded. Under the False Claims Act, whistle-blowers who report corporate wrongdoing to prosecutors can be awarded 15 to 30 percent of whatever damages the federal government recovers, which are to be three times the damages the government has sustained. Since the government recovered $1.13 billion in the 1990s, this has become a powerful incentive for some employees to tell all to prosecutors.[18]

In 2002, Congress passed the Sarbanes-Oxley Act, which, among other things, provides whistle-blowers in publicly traded companies with revolutionary new protections if they "make a disclosure to a supervisor, law-enforcement agency, or congressional investigator that could have a 'material impact' on the value of a company's shares".[19] Under the law, board committees must set up procedures for hearing whistle-blower concerns; executives who retaliate can be held criminally liable and can go to prison for up to ten years; the Labor Department can force a company to rehire a whistle-blower who has been fired; and workers who have been fired can request a jury trial after six months. Corporate attorneys are now required to report misconduct to top management and to the board if executives don't respond. But, unlike the False Claims Act, the new law does not provide for financial incentives. And, employees at private companies are not protected.

For additional guidance about whistle-blowing, there are several Web sites that can answer myriad questions; just use the key word "whistleblower" on your Internet search engine.

7. LEAVE THE COMPANY. There are situations that might be so disturbing to you that you may have no alternative but to quit your job. The toxic dump situation described earlier might be one of those situations. Frankly, the stress involved in blowing the whistle is so intense that you might consider quitting your job after step 3 or 4.

Whistle-blowing is so stressful that in one study, one-third of the whistle-blowers surveyed would advise other people not to blow the whistle at all.[20] Senator Charles Grassey likened whistle-blowers to "a skunk at a picnic."[21] Many people, however, would find it extremely difficult, and perhaps impossible, to live with certain situations on their conscience. The knowledge of a toxic dump about to poison private wells would probably be almost impossible for most people to live with. When knowledge becomes unbearable, blowing the whistle and ultimately quitting your job may be the only solution.

Unfortunately, 2002 provided lots of opportunities for whistle-blowing. *Business Week* called 2002 the "Year of the Whistleblower," highlighting the role of Joe Speaker, a manager at Rite-Aid (and son of a former Pennsylvania Attorney General) who alerted the audit committee of the board to accounting chicanery at the firm. Martin Grass, the former CEO and chairman, and three lieutenants are scheduled to go on trial in 2003.[22] *Time* magazine named Cynthia Cooper, Coleen Rowley, and Sherron Watkins "persons of the year," for their "exceptional guts and sense." Watkins was the vice president at Enron who first brought improper accounting methods to the attention of chairman Kenneth Lay and later testified before Congress where, she says, she "broke out in a cold sweat." Coleen Rowley is the FBI attorney at the Minneapolis office who alerted FBI Director Robert Mueller to the fact that the FBI had brushed off pleas to investigate Zacarias Moussaoui, now indicted as a September 11 co-conspirator. Cynthia Cooper informed the board at WorldCom about phony bookkeeping and the attempt to cover up $3.8 billion losses. According to *Time*, "Democratic capitalism requires that people trust in the integrity of public and private institutions alike. As whistle-blowers, these three became fail-safe systems that did not fail. For believing— really believing—that the truth is one thing that must not be moved off the books, and for stepping in to make sure that it wasn't, they have been chosen by *Time* as its Persons of the Year for 2002." In its attempt to identify characteristics these three women shared, *Time* noted that all three grew up in small towns and all were firstborns. All are married and serve as chief breadwinners in their families. None of this explains why they were willing to risk so much in order to reveal the truth. As of the end of 2002, Watkins had left Enron voluntarily to start her own consulting firm. The other two were still employed by their organizations. That doesn't mean that they haven't paid a price. They claim to be hated by some colleagues, and they laughed when asked if executives at their organizations had thanked them. *Time* quoted Ibsen's play *An Enemy of the People* in its tribute to the three women. "A community is like a ship. Everyone ought to be prepared to take the helm." These women "stepped up to the wheel."[23]

CONCLUSION

This chapter has highlighted some of the most common ethical problems you might encounter during your career, and provided some advice on raising issues if you feel the need. Although ethical problems can be very difficult to evaluate, it can be easier to decide what to do when you've spent some time thinking about them ahead of time—before they happen. In the next two chapters, we'll examine tools you can use to help you evaluate dilemmas and decide what to do.

DISCUSSION QUESTIONS

1. Have antidiscrimination laws helped or hurt the fair treatment of workers?
2. Is diversity management an ethical issue?
3. Is sexual harassment as important an issue for men as it is for women?
4. What conditions would make accepting a gift from a vendor or a client acceptable?
5. Describe the conditions under which you could hire a college friend.
6. Why do certain professionals—bankers, accountants, lawyers, physicians, clergy—have fiduciary responsibilities?
7. What would you do if a former subordinate asked you to write him/her a letter of reference on corporate letterhead?
8. Do employers have a responsibility to alert other employers to an employee's wrongdoing by supplying an unfavorable reference? Why or why not? Discuss the conflict between community responsibility and self-protection.
9. What conditions would have to be present for you to blow the whistle about unethical conduct you observed at work? How would you go about it?
10. If Sherron Watkins had blown the whistle to the *Houston Chronicle* and not to Enron's CEO Ken Lay, do you think she would have kept her job at Enron?
11. Research a story of whistle-blowing. Relate what "your" whistle-blower did with the seven steps recommended in the chapter. What have you learned from the comparison?

CHAPTER 3 COMMON ETHICAL PROBLEMS **85**

SHORT CASES

For each of the ethical dilemmas below, describe at least two courses of action you might take and the pros and cons of each.

HUMAN RESOURCES ISSUE

Your division has formed a committee of employees to examine suggestions and create a strategy for how to reward good employee ideas. The committee has five members, but you are the only one who is a member of a minority group. You're pleased to be part of this effort since appointments to committees such as this one are viewed generally as a positive reflection on job performance. At the first meeting, tasks are assigned and all the other committee members think you should survey minority members for their input. During the weeks that follow, you discover that several committee meetings have been held without your knowledge. When you ask why you weren't notified, two committee members tell you that survey information wasn't needed at the meetings and you'd be notified when a general meeting was scheduled. When you visit one committee member in his office, you spot a report on the suggestion program that you've never seen before. When you ask about it, he says it's just a draft he and two others have produced.

CONFLICT OF INTEREST ISSUE

You've just cemented a deal between a $100 million pension fund and Green Company, a large regional money manager. You and your staff put in long hours and a lot of effort to close the deal and are feeling very good about it. You and three of your direct reports are having lunch in a fancy restaurant to celebrate a promotion, when the waiter brings you a phone. A senior account executive from Green is on the phone and wants to buy you lunch in gratitude for all your efforts. "I'll leave my credit card number with the restaurant owner," he says. "You and your team have a great time on me."

CUSTOMER CONFIDENCE ISSUE

You're working the breakfast shift at a fast-food restaurant when a delivery of milk, eggs, and other dairy products arrives. There's a story in the local newspaper about contaminated milk distributed by the dairy that delivers to your restaurant. When you read the article more closely, you discover that there's a problem with only a small portion of the dairy's milk, and the newspaper lists the serial numbers of the containers that are affected. When you point out the article to your manager, he tells you to forget it. "If you think we've got time to go through every carton of milk to check serial numbers, you're crazy," he says. "The article says right here that the chances are minuscule that anyone has a contaminated carton." He also explains that not only doesn't he have the workers to check the milk, but also destroying the milk would require him to buy emergency milk supplies at the retail price. So, he tells you to get back to work and forget about the milk. He says, "I don't have the time or the money to worry about such minor details."

USE OF CORPORATE RESOURCES ISSUE

You work for Red Co. You and a colleague, Pat Brown, are asked by your manager to attend a week-long conference in Los Angeles. At least 25 other employees from Red Co. are attending, as well as many customers and competitors from other institutions. At the conference, you attend every session and see many of the Red Co. people, but you never run into Pat. Although you've left several phone messages for her, her schedule doesn't appear to allow room for a meeting. However, when you get back to the office, the department secretary, who is coordinating expense reports, mentions to you that your dinner in L.A. must have been quite the affair. When you ask, "What dinner?" she describes a dinner with 20 customers and Red Co. employees that Pat paid for at a posh L.A. restaurant. When you explain that you didn't attend, she shows you the expense report with your name listed as one of the attendees.

NOTES

1. Toffler, B. 1986. *Tough choices: Managers talk ethics.* New York: John Wiley & Sons, 12.
2. Fishman, C. 1998. The war for talent, *Fast Company,* August.
3. Wilson, J. Q. 1993. *The moral sense.* New York: The Free Press, 55–78.
4. Rice, F. 1994. How to make diversity pay. *Fortune,* August 8: 79.
5. Sheppard, B., Lewicki, R., and Minton, J. W. 1992. *Organizational justice: The search for fairness in the workplace.* New York: Lexington Books.
6. Goldstein, M. 2002. The Enron papers, *Smart Money,* January 18.
7. Benac, N. 2002. Enron and Phil and Wendy Gramm, *North County (San Diego) Times* (Associated Press), January 24.
8. Zellner, W. 2002. A wedding—if not bliss—for Skilling, *Business Week,* March 5.
9. Morgenson, G. 2002. Settlement is a good deal for Merrill. How about investors? *The New York Times,* May 22.
10. Byrne, J.A. 2002. No excuses for Enron's board. *Business Week,* July 29: 50.
11. Dugan, I. J. 2002. Auditing old-timers recall when prestige was the bottom line. *The Wall Street Journal,* July 15.
12. Wee, H. 2002. Corporate ethics: Right makes might, *Business Week,* April 11.
13. Webber, R. 1989. Whistle blowing. *Executive Excellence,* July: 9–10.
14. Ibid.
15. Dunkin, A. 1991. Blowing the whistle without paying the piper. *Business Week,* June 3: 138–139.
16. Hoffman, W. M., and Moore, J. M. 1984. *Business ethics: Reading and cases in corporate morality.* New York: McGraw-Hill, 257.
17. Pellegrini, F. 2002. Person of the week: "Enron Whistleblower" Sherron Watkins. *Time,* January 18.
18. Rothracker, Rick. 1997. Whistle-blower law reap big payoffs for U.S. Treasury. *Legi-Slate,* August 29: 1.
19. Dryer, P., and Carney, D. 2002. Year of the Whistleblower. *Business Week,* December 16: 107–110.

20. Soeken, K. L., and Soeken, D. R. 1987. A survey of whistleblowers: Their stressors and coping strategies. *Proceedings of the Hearing on H.R. 25* (pp. 156–166). Washington, D.C.: U.S. Government Printing Office. Miceli, M., and Near, J. 1992. *Blowing the whistle.* New York: Lexington Books, p. 303.
21. Dryer, P., and Carney, D. 2002. Year of the Whistleblower. *Business Week*, December 16 :107–110.
22. Ibid.
23. Lacayo, R., and Ripley, A. 2002. Persons of the Year 2002: Cynthia Cooper, Coleen Rowley, and Sherron Watkins. *Time,* December 22. www.time.com/time/personoftheyear/2002/.

# APPROACHES TO ETHICAL DECISION MAKING

CHAPTER 4

DECIDING WHAT'S RIGHT: A PRESCRIPTIVE APPROACH

INTRODUCTION

There are two ways to think about individual ethical decision making—the prescriptive approach and the descriptive approach. The prescriptive approach, derived from philosophy, offers decision-making tools (ways of thinking about ethical choices) that prescribe what decision you *should* make as a "conscientious moral agent" who thinks carefully about moral choices.[1] They're designed to help you make the best possible ethical decision. In this chapter we'll introduce some of these tools and explain how you can integrate them and use them in a practical way.

We know, however, that people don't always make the best decision. Prescriptions aren't always followed. So it's helpful to understand how people's minds really work—how people really make decisions. The descriptive approach, discussed in the next chapter, relies on psychological research and describes how people actually make ethical decisions. It focuses in particular on the cognitive biases and limitations that often keep us from making the best possible decisions. Hopefully, if we understand both approaches, we can improve our ethical decision making.

Many ethical choices are clear-cut enough for us to be able to decide what to do rather quickly because they pit "right" against "wrong." Is deciding whether to embezzle corporate funds a tough ethical dilemma? Not really, because embezzling is stealing and it's wrong, period. There's not much of a "dilemma" there. But things can get pretty murky in situations where two or more important values, rights, or obligations conflict and we have to choose between equally unpleasant alternatives. Consider the following ethical dilemma.

The Layoff

> You're the plant manager in one of ABC Company's five plants. You've worked for the company for 15 years, working your way up from the factory floor after the company sent you to college. Your boss just told you in complete confidence that the company will have to lay off 200 workers. Luckily, your job won't be affected. But a rumor is now circulating in the plant, and one of your workers (an old friend who now works for you) asks the question, "Well, Pat, what's the word? Is the plant closing? Am I going to lose my job? The

closing on our new house is scheduled for next week. I need to know!" What should you say? What will you say?

This is a true ethical dilemma because two values are in conflict. Two "right" values that can create significant conflict are truth and loyalty. As illustrated in the case, telling the truth to your friend would mean being disloyal to the company that has treated you so well. In this chapter, we'll introduce conceptual tools that are designed to help you think through ethical dilemmas from multiple perspectives. None of the approaches is perfect. In fact, they may lead to different conclusions. The point of using them is to get you to think carefully and avoid falling into a solution by accident. At the very least, you can feel good about the fact that you've thought about the issue from every angle.

PRESCRIPTIVE APPROACHES TO ETHICAL DECISION MAKING IN BUSINESS

Philosophers have been wrestling with ethical decision making for centuries. We certainly don't intend to provide a philosophy course here, but we can distill some important principles that can guide you in your ethical decision making. In this section, we'll outline some of the major contemporary approaches that we think can provide you with the most practical assistance.[2] We'll then incorporate them into a series of steps that you can use to evaluate ethical dilemmas, and we'll apply these steps to the short layoff case.

Focus on Consequences (Consequentialist Theories)

One set of philosophical theories is categorized as consequentialist (sometimes referred to as teleological, from the Greek *telos*). When you're attempting to decide what's right or wrong, consequentialist theories focus attention on the results or consequences of the decision or action.

Utilitarianism is probably the best known consequentialist theory. According to the principle of utility, an ethical decision should maximize benefits to society and minimize harms. What matters is the net balance of good consequences over bad.

A utilitarian would approach an ethical dilemma by identifying the alternative actions and their consequences (harms and/or benefits) for all stakeholders. For example, what would be the consequences (societal harms and benefits) of my telling my friend what I know about the layoff? What would be the consequences (societal harms and benefits) of not sharing what I know? This would be followed by a mental calculation of all the costs and benefits of these consequences, stakeholder by stakeholder. For example, one cost of telling my friend would be that he or she might tell others and send the plant into chaos. Perhaps more people would lose their jobs as a result. Another cost might be that I could lose the trust of my boss who provided information to me in confidence. I might even lose my job. A potential benefit might be that I would retain the trust of a valued friend. Another potential benefit might be that my friend could use the information to make a decision about going through with the decision to buy the new house. The "best" ethical decision would be the one that yielded the greatest net benefits for society, and the "worst" decision would be the one that yielded the greatest net harms for society. So, if more people would be ultimately hurt than helped if Pat informs her friend of the impending layoff, a utilitarian would conclude that Pat shouldn't tell. Keep in mind that this perspective requires you to think broadly about the consequences for "society," not just for you and those close to you. When thinking about consequences, our inclination is to think too narrowly and to focus too much on the consequences for ourselves, our friends, or our organizations.

The utilitarian approach can be extremely practical and helpful in thinking through an ethical dilemma. Don't we generally look at the consequences of our own and others' actions in trying to decide what's right? And don't we consider who will benefit and who will be harmed? When the state decides to build a new highway through your property, aren't they using a utilitarian rationale when they argue that the benefits to the community (increased development and jobs, reduced traffic, fewer accidents, etc.) outweigh the harm to the few property holders who will be inconvenienced by an eyesore in their back yard?

But a challenge involved in using a strictly consequentialist approach is that it is often difficult to obtain the information required to evaluate all of the consequences for all stakeholders who may be directly or indirectly affected by an action or decision. When, in business, do you have *all* of the facts? And even if you have all of the information, it can be extremely cumbersome to have to calculate all of the harm and benefits every time you encounter a new ethical dilemma. Try it. Can you list all of the potential harms and benefits for all of those who may be directly or indirectly involved in the layoff situation described above? It's relatively easy to list the potential harm and benefits to yourself and those close to you. But can you envision all of the potential harm and benefits to all of the other people who may be involved? Remember, according to utilitarianism, the most ethical decision maximizes benefits and minimizes harm to society. The challenge of making the best ethical decision is to get outside of yourself and think as broadly as possible about all of the consequences for all of those affected.

Another difficulty with this type of approach is that the rights of a minority group can easily be sacrificed for the benefit of the majority. For example, slaveholders in the old South argued that the greatest good for the greatest number would be served by maintaining the system of slavery.

Nevertheless, the utilitarian approach remains particularly important to ethical decision making in business for a variety of reasons. First, utilitarian thinking—through its descendant, utility theory—underlies much of the business and economics literature. Second, on the face of it, most of us would admit that considering the consequences of one's decisions or actions is extremely important to good ethical decision making. In fact, studies of ethical decision making in business have found that business managers generally rely on a utilitarian approach.[3] The remaining question is whether other kinds of considerations are also important.

Focus on Duties, Obligations, and Principles (Deontological Theories)

The word *deontological* comes from the Greek *deon,* "duty." Rather than focusing on consequences, a deontological approach would ask, "What is Pat's duty now that she knows about the layoff?" Deontologists base their decisions about what's right on broad, abstract universal principles or values such as honesty, promise keeping, fairness, loyalty, rights (to safety, privacy, etc.), justice, compassion, and respect for persons and property. According to some deontological approaches, certain moral principles are binding, regardless of the consequences. Therefore, some actions would be considered wrong even if the consequences of the actions were good. In other words, a deontologist focuses on doing what is "right" (based on moral principles such as honesty), whereas a utilitarian focuses on doing what will maximize societal welfare. An auditor taking a deontological approach would insist on telling the truth about a company's financial difficulties even if doing so might risk putting the company out of business and many people out of work. A utilitarian auditor would weigh the societal harms and benefits before deciding what to do.

Some deontological theories focus on rights rather than duties or principles. The concept of rights goes back to classical Greek notions of "natural rights" that emerge from "natural law." Rights can be thought of as "negative rights," such as the limits on government interference with citizens' right to privacy or the pursuit of happiness. Or rights can be thought of in more positive terms, such as the individual's rights to health and safety. The rights of one party can conflict with the rights of another party, as when the rights of a company to seek profits for its shareholders conflict with the rights of a community to clean air or water. Furthermore, the rights of one party are generally related to the duties of another. So, if we agreed that communities have the right to clean water, businesses would have the duty to protect that right.

How does a deontologist determine what rule, principle, or right to follow? Some rely on Western biblical tradition or moral intuition for guidance. For example, the Golden Rule, familiar to many of us, provides an important deontological guide: "Do unto others as you would have them do unto you." In our layoff situation, the Golden Rule would suggest that Pat should tell her friend what she knows because she would want her friend to do the same for her if the situation were reversed. But note that the Golden Rule leads you to the best decision only if you're highly ethical. For example, do you think that the Golden Rule would expect you to lie for a friend who has broken the law because you would want the friend to do that for you? No, a highly ethical person wouldn't ask a friend to lie. The ethical person would accept the consequences of his or her actions.

The German philosopher Emmanuel Kant provided a particular mode of deontological thinking about ethical choices through his "categorical imperative": "Act as if the maxim of thy action were to become by thy will a universal law of nature." This mode of thinking asks whether the rationale for your action is suitable to become a universal law or principle for everyone to follow. For example, if you break a promise, the categorical imperative asks, "Is promise breaking a principle everyone should follow?" No, if everyone did this, promises would become meaningless. In fact, they would cease to exist.

A practical deontological question to ask yourself might be, "What kind of world would this be if everyone behaved this way or made this kind of decision in this type of situation?" What kind of world would this be if everyone broke promises at will? Consider the following example:

> A number of physicians are recruited to participate in a large-scale multicenter study to investigate the survival rates of breast cancer victims who are being treated with a new drug. Strict rules are developed regarding inclusion of patients in the study. Only those who have had surgery within the last three months can be included. Dr. Smith has a patient who hears about the study and wants very much to participate. Because Dr. Smith thinks the drug could really help this patient, he agrees to include her even though her surgery took place six months ago. He changes the dates on her charts to conform with the study requirements and reasons that this one little change shouldn't affect the study results.

According to the categorical imperative, we must ask whether the rationale for Dr. Smith's action (helping his patient by breaking the study rules) is suitable to become a principle for all to follow. The answer is no. What if a number of other doctors did the same thing as Dr. Smith? What if those involved in medical research followed their own preferences or motives rather than the rules guiding the study? Society would be unable to rely on the results of medical research. What kind of a world would it be if researchers were routinely dishonest? It would be one where we simply couldn't rely on the integrity of scientific research, and most of us would deem that kind of world unacceptable.

A major challenge of deontological approaches is deciding which duty, obligation, right, or principle takes precedence, because, as we said earlier, ethical dilemmas often pit these against each other. What does the deontologist do if one binding moral rule clashes with another? Can it be determined which is the more important right or principle? Because the U.S. Constitution is based on a rights approach, many U.S. public policy debates revolve around questions such as these. For example, the abortion debate rests on the question of whether the rights of the mother or the fetus should take precedence.

Another difficulty of deontological approaches involves the difficulty of arguing for a rule or principle that, if followed in a particular situation, will have devastating consequences. That's where consequentialist and deontological approaches conflict. For example, in World War II Germany, telling the truth to Nazis about whether Jews were hiding in your attic would have had devastating consequences—they would have been taken and killed. In our case, what if Pat determines that telling her friend what she knows (in accordance with the principles of honesty and respect for her friend as a person) could have devastating consequences for the company as a whole? In response to this concern, some philosophers argue that deontological principles (i.e., truth telling, promise keeping) don't have to be regarded as absolute. For example, one could violate a rule or principle for a good reason (according to Kant, a reason that you would be willing to accept for anyone in the same position).[4]

Focus on Integrity (Virtue Ethics)

The virtue ethics approach focuses more on the integrity of the moral actor than on the moral act itself. Although virtue ethics as a philosophical tradition began with Aristotle, a number of contemporary ethicists (including business ethicists) have brought it back to the forefront of ethical thinking.[5]

A virtue ethics perspective considers primarily the actor's character, motivations, and intentions. This doesn't mean that principles, rules, or consequences aren't considered at all, but they're considered in the context of assessing the actor's character and integrity. For example, one's character may be assessed in terms of principles such as honesty, in terms of rule following (did this actor follow his profession's ethics code?) or in terms of consequences (as in the physician's agreement to, above all, do no harm).

In virtue ethics, character is very much defined by one's community. Therefore, it's important to think about the community or communities within which business people operate. Think about yourself. What community or communities would you look to for help in deciding whether you were a business person of integrity? Your professional association? Your religious community? Your family? Your peers within your company? Would the communities you identify be different if you were evaluating your nonwork self? Choose the community that you think would hold you to the highest standards given the particular ethical dilemma situation.

Virtue ethics may be particularly useful in determining the ethics of an individual who works within a professional community that has well-developed norms and standards of conduct. For example, the accounting profession has developed a code of conduct for professional accountants. Being a virtuous accountant would mean abiding by that code of professional responsibility. The same goes for certified financial consultants or engineers who agree to abide by specific professional rules and standards.

A virtue ethics approach allows the decision maker to rely on such relevant community standards without going through the complex process of trying to decide what's right in every situation using deontological or consequentialist approaches. The assumption is that the community has already done this type of thinking. However, what if the community hasn't done this type of thinking? Or what if the community is just wrong? The usefulness of virtue ethics in business may be limited because in many areas of business there is limited agreement about what the standards are. There is no universal code of conduct for all business managers to follow. Furthermore, many students make the mistake of considering their work group, or even their organization as the relevant community. But sometimes these immediate communities are not the best communities for guidance in ethical dilemma situations. In such cases, it's better to look to the broader community or society for guidance.

A shortcut approach to ethical decision making, based upon the virtue ethics approach and the broader community as a guide, is known as "the disclosure rule." The disclosure rule asks, "How would you feel if your behavior appeared on _____? You fill in the blank of what media outlet, person, or set of persons would be your "harshest moral critic"—is it the front page of *The New York Times, The Wall Street Journal,* your hometown newspaper, *60 Minutes,* CNN, your family? The assumption behind the disclosure rule is that community standards exist, and at a gut level, most of us know what those are. If our gut tells us it wouldn't look good to have our behavior appear in one of these media outlets, or we wouldn't be happy to have our family (or other harshest moral critic) learn about what we did, we simply shouldn't be doing it because it means that we wouldn't be considered a person of integrity. A useful exercise is to think of who our harshest moral critic would be and what he or she would think of the behavior we're contemplating. Most of us have someone in our lives whose integrity we respect and whose moral judgment of us would be important.

These are just a few of the philosophical approaches that may be applied in ethical dilemma situations. We've introduced the ones we feel have the most practical benefit to business managers, and, admittedly, we've introduced them in a rather general way, without many of the nuances developed by philosophers over the years. We've suggested that all of the approaches have limitations. No one of them, by itself, provides perfect guidance in every situation. Obviously, if all of the approaches lead to the same solution, the decision is a relatively easy one. The tough ones arise when the approaches conflict. When that happens, it will be up to you to decide what is most important to you. That's why it's important to think about your values now and prioritize them. Stuart Youngblood, professor of management at Texas Christian University in Fort Worth, suggested the following example that he has used in his business ethics class: Assume you approach a burning building and hear voices coming from both ends, each seeking help. Assume you can only go to one or the other end of the building. Initially, you hear multiple voices at one end and a sole voice at the other end. Which way do you go? Why? Now add some additional information. The sole voice is that of your daughter (father, mother, etc). Do you still choose to go to the end with multiple voices (to do the greatest good for the greatest number)? If not, why not? What has changed?

We certainly won't resolve the academic controversies over the "best" philosophical approach here. But we believe that the approaches we've presented suggest important factors to keep in mind in making business ethics decisions. Therefore, we offer the following eight steps that integrate the types of analysis just discussed.[6] Before presenting them, we'd like to offer a caveat. The eight steps suggest a linear decision-making process that is necessarily inaccurate. Ethical decision making is often not linear. But it will be helpful to cover all of these points, even if not in this particular sequence.

EIGHT STEPS TO SOUND ETHICAL DECISION MAKING IN BUSINESS

Step One: Gather the Facts

The philosophical approaches don't tell us explicitly to gather the facts. But they seem to assume that we'll complete this important step. You might be surprised at how many people jump to solutions without having the facts. Ask yourself, "How did the situation occur? Are there historical facts that I should know? Are there facts concerning the current situation that I should know?"[7]

Fact gathering is often easier said than done. Many ethical choices are particularly difficult because of the uncertainty involved in them. Facts may simply be unavailable. For example, in our layoff case, Pat may not have good information about the legal requirements on informing workers about layoffs. Also, she may not have enough information to determine how long it would take these 200 workers to find new jobs. But recognizing these limitations, you should attempt to assemble the facts that are available to you before proceeding.

Step Two: Define the Ethical Issues

Many of us have knee-jerk responses to ethical dilemmas. We jump to a solution without really thinking through the ethical issues and the reasons for our response (we'll talk more about why in Chapter 5). For example, in the layoff case, one person might say, "Oh, that's easy, promise keeping is the ethical issue. Pat has to keep her promise to her boss and protect her job." Another person might say that honesty is the key ethical issue: "Pat just has to tell the truth to her friend."

Don't jump to solutions without first identifying the ethical issues or points of values conflict in the dilemma. There are generally multiple ethical issues that go back to the deontological, or principle-based, theories we just discussed. For example, in the case above, one ethical issue has to do with the rights of both the workers and the company. How would you define the workers' right to know about the plant closing in advance? How much advance notice is appropriate? What does the law say? Another ethical issue has to do with the company's right to keep the information private. Furthermore, what is the company's obligation to its workers in this regard? At a more personal level, there are the ethical issues related to principles such as honesty, loyalty, and promise keeping. Is it more important to be honest with a friend or to keep a promise to one's boss? Who is owed more loyalty? Think about the situation from a justice or fairness perspective: What would be fair to the company and to those who would be laid off?

Points of ethical conflict may go back to the conflict between consequentialist and deontological approaches. For example, if I tell the truth (consistent with the principle of promise keeping), bad things will happen (negative consequences). A consequentialist would think about the ethical issues in terms of harms or benefits. Who is likely to be harmed? Who is likely to benefit from a particular decision or action? A virtue ethics approach would suggest thinking about the ethical issues in terms of community standards. Does your relevant community identify a particular action as wrong? Why or why not?

Our inclination is to stop with the first ethical issue that comes to mind. For example, in our layoff case, we might be inclined to stop with the issue of loyalty to a friend. Challenge yourself to think of as many issues as you possibly can. Here's where talking about the problem with others can help. Present the dilemma to coworkers, to your spouse, or to friends you respect. Ask them whether they see other issues that you may have missed.

Step Three: Identify the Affected Parties (the Stakeholders)

Both consequentialist and deontological thinking involve the ability to identify the parties affected by the decision. The consequentialist will want to identify all those stakeholders who are going to experience harm and benefits. The deontologist might want to know whose rights are involved and who has a duty to act in the situation.

Being able to see the situation through others' eyes is a key moral reasoning skill. Lawrence Kohlberg, developer of a key theory of moral reasoning, called this skill "role taking." Frequently, you have to think beyond the facts provided in a case in order to identify all affected parties. It often helps to begin with the individuals in the case who are immediately affected (e.g., Pat, the worker, Pat's boss) and then to progressively broaden your thinking to incorporate larger groups. For example, in this case, you might include the other workers, the rest of the company, the local community, and society in general. As you think of more and more affected parties, additional issues will probably come to mind. For example, think about the local community. If this is a small town with few other employers, fairness to the entire community becomes an important issue. Shouldn't they have as much time as possible to plan for the impact of this plant closing? Try to put yourself in their shoes. How would they argue their case? How would they feel?

In Chapter 1, we introduced the concept of stakeholders, all of those who have a stake in what an organization does and how it performs. Stakeholders can include owners, managers, customers, employees, suppliers, financial institutions, the community, the government, the natural environment and, of course, stockholders. In the context of ethical decision making in business, we should identify the stakeholders affected by the decision and ask how they are affected. Try to make your thinking as broad as possible here. Some of the stakeholders affected by the decision may not even be born yet. The best concrete example of unborn stakeholders might be "DES daughters." In the 1940s, DES, a synthetic estrogen, was prescribed for pregnant women who seemed to be in danger of miscarrying. By 1971, it became clear that DES produced a birth defect in the daughters of these women. Because of the birth defect, DES daughters were more likely to develop vaginal cancer, especially between the ages of 15 and 22. They also had a higher than normal rate of cervical cancer.[8]

Once stakeholders are identified, role-playing can help you to see the issue from different stakeholder perspectives. In your classroom or your department, get individuals to seriously play the relevant roles. You may be surprised at how perspectives change based on this simple exercise. What decision would you reach if you were someone else in the situation? This step incorporates the Golden Rule: Treat others as you would like others to treat you. Imagine yourself as each of the players in a decision situation. What decision would they reach and why?

Another consideration may be to ask whether you can "test" a potential decision with affected parties before your prospective course of action is made final. The objective is to gauge how various audiences will react, and to be able to adjust or fine-tune a decision along the way.[9] One question you could ask yourself is, how would this or that stakeholder react if this decision were made public? For example, imagine that ABC Co. (in our layoff case) had another thriving plant in another location. However, in the decision-making process, it was assumed that employees wouldn't want to relocate because of their ties to the local community. Wouldn't it be best to ask them their preferences than to assume what they would want to do?

Step Four: Identify the Consequences

After identifying the affected parties, think about the potential consequences for each of these parties. This step is obviously derived from the consequentialist approaches. It isn't necessary to identify every possible consequence. But you should try to identify consequences that have a relatively high probability of occurring and those that would have particularly negative consequences if they did occur (even if the probability of occurrence is low). Who would be harmed by a particular decision or action? For example, in our case, telling the truth to the worker might cause Pat to lose her job, which would have negative consequences for her entire family (especially if she's a single mother). However, it would give her worker (and presumably others who would be told) the benefit of more time to look for a new job, perhaps saving many families from negative financial consequences. Can you determine which solution would accomplish the most net good? A popular version of utilitarianism asks the question, "Which decision or action will produce the greatest good for the greatest number of people?" Would telling a lie to your friend benefit the most people? Or would it be better for all affected parties if you were to tell the truth?

Think about the drug thalidomide. It was prescribed to women in the late 1950s to treat morning sickness and produced devastating birth defects in 12,000 babies in Europe, Canada, Australia, and Japan (the Food and Drug Administration never approved it for use in the United States). Many of the babies died, but others were left to live with severe deformities. Randy Warren, a Canadian born in 1961, is the founder of the Thalidomide Victims Association of Canada. His mother took just two doses of thalidomide, but Warren is only a little over 3 feet tall and has no thumbs, arms that are 2 inches too short, and stumps for legs. The consequences of this drug when prescribed to pregnant women are obviously devastating, and shortly after Warren was born, the drug was banned in most places. But continued research produced renewed interest in thalidomide as an effective treatment for Hansen's disease, a painful skin condition associated with leprosy, "wasting" disease in AIDS patients, arthritis, blindness, leukemia, and other forms of cancer. This drug that had such terrible consequences for so many had to be considered for approval because it also had the potential to help many people who were dealing with other devastating illnesses. As Warren put it, "When I heard…that thalidomide takes people out of wheelchairs and I think of myself and others that were put in wheelchairs…tell me we don't have the moral quandary of the century." In the end, Warren was consulted and became involved in the decision to return the drug to the marketplace. In 1998, the FDA approved the drug to treat Hansen's disease under the highest level of restriction ever given to a drug. Doctors, pharmacists, and patients all must be registered with the manufacturer, Celgene. Two forms of birth control are required in order to prevent the possibility of pregnancy and resulting birth defects. Male patients are required to use condoms. No automatic refills of the drug are allowed. And Warren has become "something of a company conscience." Although extremely difficult, the decision to market thalidomide in the United States was made with input from those most familiar with its potential for both devastating consequences and remarkable benefits. Regulators at the FDA and company officials got to know Randy Warren as a real person who continues to suffer consequences that they might not have been able to imagine from just reading reports and statistics.[10]

LONG-TERM VERSUS SHORT-TERM CONSEQUENCES In business decisions, it's particularly important to think in terms of short-term *and* long-term consequences. Are you confident that your position will be as valid over a long period of time, even if circumstances or people change? In this case, is the long-term health of the company and the people who will remain employed more important than the short-term consequences to the 200 workers who will be laid off?

SYMBOLIC CONSEQUENCES In business, it's also extremely important to think about the potential symbolic consequences of an action. Every decision and action sends a message; it stands for something. What message will a particular decision or action send? What will it mean if it is misunderstood? For example, if Pat doesn't tell her worker the truth, and he finds out later that she knew, what will the symbolic message be to this worker and the others who work for Pat—that she's more interested in saving her own hide than in taking care of them?

CONSEQUENCES OF SECRECY If a decision is made in private in order to avoid some negative reaction, think about the potential consequences if the decision were to become public. For example, the public has been outraged by the fact that tobacco companies may have hidden their knowledge of the negative health effects of cigarette smoking.[11]

Step Five: Identify the Obligations

Identify the obligations involved and the reasons for each. For example, consider Pat's obligations toward the affected parties. When identifying Pat's various obligations, be sure to state the reasons why she has this duty or obligation. Think in terms of values, principles, character, or outcomes. For example, if you're considering Pat's obligation to keep her promise to her boss, your reasoning might go like this: "Pat shouldn't break her promise to her boss. If she does, the trust between them will be broken. Promise keeping and trust are important values in superior/subordinate relationships."

The obligations you identify will vary depending on the people involved and the roles they play. For example, our faith in our financial system depends in part on auditors' obligation to tell the truth about a company's financial difficulties. Similarly, our faith in science as an institution depends on the integrity of the scientific data and how scientists report it. The auditor and the scientist have a particularly strong obligation to tell the truth.

Step Six: Consider Your Character and Integrity

In thinking about what you should do in an ethical dilemma, it can be useful to consider what your relevant community would consider to be the kind of decision that an individual of integrity would make in the situation. Begin by identifying the relevant community. Then, determine how community members would evaluate the decision or action you're considering.

Remember the disclosure rule. It asks whether you would feel comfortable if your activities were disclosed in the light of day in a public forum like *The New York Times* or some other medium. In general, if you don't want to read about it in *The New York Times*, you shouldn't be doing it. If you would be uncomfortable telling your parents, children, spouse, or clergy about your decision, you should rethink it.

Boris Yavitz, the former dean of Columbia University's Graduate School of Business, offered another version of the test for New Yorkers: "Unless you would do it in Macy's department store window at high noon, don't do it." And Thomas Jefferson expressed it like this: "Never suffer a thought to be harbored in your mind which you would not avow openly. When tempted to do anything in secret, ask yourself if you would do it in public. If you would not, be sure it is wrong."

This kind of approach can be especially valuable when a decision needs to be made quickly. Suppose someone in your organization asks you to misrepresent the effectiveness of one of your company's products to a customer. You can immediately imagine how a story reporting the details of your conversation with the customer would appear in tomorrow's paper. Would you be comfortable having others read the details of that conversation? The ideal is to conduct business in such a way that your activities and conversations could be disclosed without your feeling embarrassed.

Another method might be to ask a question asked by the Seneca people (one of the five original nations of the great Iroquois Confederacy located in the northeastern United States and southeastern Canada) in their guidelines for self-discipline: "How will I be remembered when I'm gone?"[12] Many people don't often think about this question, but it's a good one. Will you be remembered as an individual of integrity or not?

Step Seven: Think Creatively about Potential Actions

Before making any decision, be sure that you haven't unnecessarily forced yourself into a corner. Are you assuming that you have only two choices, either "a" or "b"? It's important to look for creative alternatives. Perhaps if you've been focusing on "a" or "b," there's another answer "c." For example, what if you received an extravagant gift from a foreign supplier. This situation could easily be conceptualized as an "a" or "b" quandary. Should you accept the gift (which is against company policy), or should you refuse it (which could be interpreted as a slap in the face by this important supplier from a culture where gift giving is a valued part of business relationships)? A potential "c" solution might be to accept the item as a gift to the company that would be displayed in the headquarters entrance, explaining that large personal gifts are against company policy. Obviously, you would have to check with your company about the acceptability of this "c" solution. But the idea is to think "outside the box."

Here is another example. In an overseas location, Cummins Engine Company was having difficulty with local children cutting through a wire fence and stealing valuable electronic components. The "a" or "b" solution was to arrest or not arrest these young children when they were caught. After involving the community, the managers were able to arrive at a "c" solution. They discovered that the children were stealing because there weren't enough classrooms at the local school, leaving the children with little to do but get into trouble. Cummins made classrooms available on their site. The mayor provided accreditation, books, and teachers. This "c" solution cost the company very little and accomplished a great deal. Three hundred and fifty students were accommodated, the stealing problem disappeared, and Cummins became a valued corporate citizen.

Step Eight: Check Your Gut

The emphasis in these steps has been on a highly rational fact-gathering and evaluation process once you know that you're faced with an ethical dilemma. But don't forget your gut. Empathy is an important emotion that can signal awareness that someone might be harmed. And intuition is gaining credibility as a source for good business decision making. We can't always say exactly why we're uncomfortable in a situation. But years of socialization have likely made us sensitive to situations where something isn't quite right. So if your gut is bothering you, give the situation more thought. In fact, this may be your only clue that you're facing an ethical dilemma to begin with. Pay attention to your gut. But don't let it make your decision for you. Once you know you're facing an ethical dilemma, use the rational decision-making tools developed here to help guide your decision making.

PRACTICAL PREVENTIVE MEDICINE

Doing Your Homework

There's no doubt that you'll encounter ethical dilemmas—every employee probably encounters hundreds of them during a career—the only thing in doubt is when. Your mission is to be as prepared as much as possible before you run into a problem. The more informed you are, the more effective you'll be in protecting yourself and your employer. The best way to do that is to learn the rules of your organization and your profession, and to develop relationships that can help you if and when the need arises.

You can learn the rules in various ways. First, read your company's code of ethics (if it has one) and policy manual. Since most policy manuals are huge, you obviously can't memorize one. But if you skim the contents, some of the rules will sink in—you may not remember the exact policy, but you'll probably remember at least that one exists and where to find it.

Second, ask questions. Managers, executives, and peers will admire your initiative when you ask what they think is "important around here." Since many organizational standards are unwritten and they differ from company to company, the best way to find out about them is by asking. Query your coworkers (including management) about what kinds of ethical situations are most common in your organization and how your organization generally handles those issues. Ask your manager how to raise ethical issues within your organization. Since he or she will certainly tell you to raise an issue with him or her first, be sure to find out how you raise an issue in your manager's absence. This not only gives you a road map for raising issues, but it also sends a signal to your manager that ethics are important to you.

Finally, develop relationships with people who are outside of your chain of command. Get to know people in human resources, legal, audit, and other departments who might be able to provide information, help you raise an issue or determine if something even is an issue, or vouch for your credibility in a crisis. You might also want to join a professional group or association. Many professions have developed ethical standards apart from those that may exist in your company, and it can be very helpful to know other people in your profession who can advise you if a crisis arises in your company. Some may say that this is being political, but we think it's just plain smart to network with people outside of your immediate job and company. It's the difference between being a victim of circumstance and having the power, the knowledge, and the network to help manage circumstances.

It's possible that after you've done your homework and learned about your company's standards and values, you find that your values and your employer's values are in conflict. If the conflict is substantial, you may have no choice but to look for work in another organization.

When You're Asked to Make a Snap Decision

Many business people place value on the ability to make decisions quickly, and, as a result, many of us can feel pressure to make up our minds in a hurry. This can be a particular issue when people are inexperienced for whatever reason—this may be their first job or a new company or industry—and they may feel a need to prove their competence by making decisions quickly. Obviously, that can be dangerous. The ethical decision-making tools described earlier in the chapter assume that you'll have some time to devote to the decision—to consider multiple sides of the issue and the inherent conflicts with any one course of action. Do your best to get the time to assess, think through, and gather more information and consider the following guidelines when a quick decision seems called for:

1. Don't underestimate the importance of a hunch to alert you that you're facing an ethical dilemma. As we said earlier, your gut is your internal warning system. As one senior executive at a multinational computer company

said, "The gut never lies." When your gut tells you something's wrong, consider it a warning siren.
2. Ask for time to think it over. Most snap decisions don't have to be that way. Say something like, "Let me think about it and I'll get back to you soon." Bargaining for time is a smart way to give yourself a break—then you can really think about the decision and consult with others. It's better to take the time to make a good decision than it is to make a bad decision quickly and have lots of time to regret it. Would you rather be known as cautious or reckless?
3. Find out quickly if your organization has a policy that applies to your decision.
4. Ask your manager or your peers for advice. You should consider your manager the first line of defense when you encounter an ethical dilemma. Regardless of your level within the organization, you should never hesitate to ask for another opinion. This is where the network comes in handy. If you have friends in human resources or the legal department, you can float the issue with them on a casual basis to see if there even is an issue.
5. Use the quick-check *New York Times* test (the disclosure rule). If you'd be embarrassed to have your decision disclosed in the media or to your family, don't do it.

> You're upgrading your department's data processing capabilities and have just placed an order for four personal computers and two laser printers with a computer company representative. When you mention that you wish you had a printer at home like the ones you just ordered, the representative tells you that because of your large order, she can give you a 50 percent discount on a printer for your home. You feel that this is not quite right, but you're not sure why and would like some time to think about her offer.

In this case, the employee could have real doubt about whether or not to accept a 50 percent discount on a printer for his home. Even though he feels funny about the offer, he might be thinking that he does a lot of work at home, so accepting a discount on a personal printer could be justified. And since the computer representative made the offer after the order was placed, there's no conflict of interest—the employee's decision to purchase obviously wasn't influenced by the offer of a discount.

But he should listen to his gut, which is feeling that this isn't quite right. He can first stall the computer representative by telling her he'll get back to her later in the day or tomorrow. He can find out what his company policy says about making purchases. (Many companies would equate the discount with a gift and forbid accepting it unless it's available to all employees.)

Suppose he finds nothing in the policy manual to prohibit the discount, and other workers have said "go for it." Then he can use the *New York Times* test. How would the public react to his decision? Some people would probably think that his order was influenced by the offer of a discount. He knows that's not true, but it might be difficult to convince other people of that. This is called an appearance of a conflict of interest, and as discussed in Chapter 3, an appearance can be as damaging as an actual conflict. If someone could think your judgment has been affected by a relationship or, in this case a discount, it could be viewed as the appearance of a conflict and should be avoided. Appearances are extremely important in business and may not be accounted for by the philosophical tools provided earlier in the chapter. Whether you appear to be fair may be as important as whether you're really fair.

The bottom line is: If you think that your decision could be misinterpreted or if someone could think the objectivity of your decision has been compromised, rethink the decision. The representative's offer can be refused politely by saying something like, "My company doesn't allow personal discounts," or "I just don't feel right about it."

If you ever feel that accepting a favor from a vendor will place you under an obligation to the vendor in the future, be very careful. For example, a public relations manager, Mary, described an incident with a printing company (we'll call it Type Co.) sales representative who was trying to get her business. Type Co. already did business with a number of departments within her company, but Mary was satisfied with her current printer and saw no reason to switch. Just before the holidays, Type Co. sent a miniature television to Mary and to all of its customers in her company. Mary immediately felt that the gift was inappropriate, but to check out her judgment, she called one of Type Co.'s other customers in her company. Mary's colleague assured her that there was nothing wrong with accepting the gift and that it was simply a token of good will. (If Mary had been friendly with one of her company's lawyers or human resources managers, she would probably have received very different advice.) Mary listened to her internal warning system, despite what her colleague said. She sent the television back.

When asked why she returned the gift, Mary said, "I felt like I was being bribed to do business with Type Co." A reader of *The New York Times* would probably agree.

CONCLUSION

This chapter has presented a prescriptive approach to individual ethical decision making. When you're confronted with an ethical dilemma, you should find it helpful to inform your choice by considering the ideas and steps offered in this chapter. The end-of-chapter questions and case should give you some practice in applying these ideas and steps to real ethical dilemmas.

However, the prescriptive approach needs to be complemented by the descriptive approach offered in Chapter 5. In the next chapter, you'll learn about psychological research that can help you understand how people actually make ethical decisions—the individual characteristics and cognitive processes that affect the decisions people make.

DISCUSSION QUESTIONS

1. If you had to choose just one of the philosophical approaches discussed in this chapter to guide your decision making, which would you choose? Why?

2. Some of the steps in the 8-step model might suggest very different courses of action for resolving your dilemma. How would you choose among these distinct courses of action? Why?
3. Think about an ethical dilemma situation that you've faced. Apply the 8 steps recommended in this chapter. Does it change your thinking about the situation? Would it change your action?
4. Some corporations and other organizations have designed ethical decision-making tests that incorporate some of the principles and systems described in this chapter. For example, Carl Skooglund, former vice president and ethics director at Texas Instruments, outlined the following Ethics Quick Test recommended for use by Texas Instrument employees:[13]

- Is the action legal?
- Does it comply with your best understanding of our values and principles?
- If you do it, will you feel bad?
- How will it look in the newspaper?
- If you know it's wrong, don't do it, period!
- If you're not sure, ask.
- Keep asking until you get an answer.

Think about this list in terms of the decision-making guides discussed in the chapter. Which ones are being used here? Which are not? What recommendations, if any, would you make to alter this list? If you had to make up a list for your company, what would be on it? Why?

Do the same with the Rotary International Four-Way Test:

- Is it the truth?
- Is it fair to all concerned?
- Will it build good will and better relationships?
- Will it be beneficial to all concerned?

The Seneca people's guidelines for self-discipline also include these questions:[14]

- Am I happy in what I'm doing?
- Is what I'm doing adding to the confusion?
- What am I doing to bring about peace and contentment?
- How will I be remembered when I am gone?

Could they serve as guides for ethical decision making in business? Why or why not?

5. The last question leads us to a useful exercise. If you had to write your own epitaph, what would it say? How would you like to be remembered? What kind of life do you hope to lead?
6. What limitations, if any, can you think of to the prescriptions provided in this chapter? Can you think of reasons why they might not work?

CASE

PINTO FIRES

by Dennis A. Gioia

On August 10, 1978, three teenage girls died horribly in an automobile accident. Driving a 1973 Ford Pinto to their church volleyball practice in Goshen, Indiana, they were struck from behind by a Chevrolet van. The Pinto's fuel tank ruptured and the car exploded in flames. Two passengers, Lynn Marie Ulrich, 16, and her cousin, Donna Ulrich, 18, were trapped inside the inferno and burned to death. After three attempts, Lynn Marie's sister, 18-year-old Judy Ann, was dragged out alive from the driver's seat, but died in agony hours later in the hospital.

They were merely the latest in a long list of people to burn to death in accidents involving the Pinto, which Ford had begun selling in 1970. By the time of the accident, the car had been the subject of a great deal of public outcry and debate about its safety, especially its susceptibility to fire in low-speed rear-end collisions. This particular accident, however, resulted in more media attention than any other auto accident in U.S. history. Why? Because it led to an unprecedented court case in which the prosecution brought charges of reckless homicide against the Ford Motor Co.—the first time that a corporation had been charged with criminal conduct, and the charge was not negligence but murder. At stake was much more than the maximum penalty of $30,000 in fines. Of immediate concern, a guilty verdict could have affected 40 pending civil cases nationwide and resulted in hundreds of millions of dollars in punitive damage awards. Of perhaps greater concern, however, were larger issues involving corporate social responsibility, ethical decision making by individuals within corporations, and ultimately, the proper conduct of business in the modern era.

How did Ford get into this situation? The chronology begins in early 1968 when the decision was made to battle the foreign competition in the small car market, specifically the Germans, but also the growing threat from the Japanese. This decision came after a hard-fought, two-year internal struggle between then-president Semon "Bunky" Knudsen and Lee Iacocca, who had risen quickly within the company because of his success with the Mustang. Iacocca strongly supported fighting the competition at their own game, while Knudsen argued instead for letting them have the small car market so Ford could concentrate on the more profitable medium and large models. The final decision ultimately was in the hands of then-CEO Henry Ford II, who not only agreed with Iacocca but also promoted him to president after Knudsen's subsequent forced resignation.

Iacocca wanted the Pinto in the showrooms by the 1971 model introductions, which would require the shortest production planning period in automotive history to that time. The typical time span from conception to production of a new car was more than three and a half years; Iacocca, however, wanted to launch the Pinto in just over 2 years. Under normal conditions, chassis design, styling, product planning, advance engineering, component testing, and so on were all either completed or nearly completed prior to tooling of the production factories. Yet, because tooling had a fixed time frame of about 18 months, some of these other processes were done more or less concurrently. As a consequence, when it was discovered through crash testing that the Pinto's fuel tank often ruptured during rear-end impact, it was too late (in other words, too costly) to do much about it in terms of redesign.

A closer look at the crash-test reports reveals that Ford was aware of faulty fuel tank design. Eleven Pintos were subjected to rear-end collisions with a barrier at average speeds of 31 miles per hour to determine if any fuel would be lost after impact. All eight of the Pintos equipped with the standard fuel tank failed. The three remaining cars, however, survived the test because special measures had been taken to prevent tank rupture or fuel leakage. These measures included a plastic baffle placed between the axle housing and the gas tank, a steel plate between the tank and the rear bumper, and a rubber lining in the gas tank.

It should be noted that these tests were done under guidelines established by Federal Motor Vehicle Safety Standard 301, which was proposed in 1968 by the National Highway Traffic Safety Administration (NHTSA), but not officially adopted until the 1977 model year. Therefore, at the time of the tests, the Pinto met the required standards. Standard 301 had been strenuously opposed by the auto industry, and specifically Ford Motor Co. In fact, the lobbying efforts were so strong that negotiations continued until 1976, despite studies showing that hundreds of thousands of cars burned every year, taking 3,000 lives annually; the adoption of the standard was projected to reduce the death rate by 40 percent. Upon approval of Standard 301 in 1977, all Pintos were provided with a rupture-proof fuel tank design.

But for the Pinto's 1971 debut, Ford decided to go with its original gas tank design despite the crash-test results. Because the typical Pinto buyer was assumed to be extremely price conscious, Iacocca set an important goal known as "the limits of 2,000": the Pinto could not cost more than $2,000 and could not weigh more than 2,000 pounds. Thus, to be competitive with foreign manufacturers, Ford felt it could not spend any money on improving the gas tank. Besides, during the late 1960s and early 1970s, American consumers demonstrated little concern for safety, so it was not considered good business sense to promote it. Iacocca echoed these sentiments when he said time and time again "Safety doesn't sell," a lesson he had learned after a failed attempt to add costly safety features to 1950s Fords.

Ford had experimented with placing the gas tank in different locations, but all alternatives reduced usable trunk space. A design similar to that of the Ford Capri was successful in many crash tests at speeds over 50 miles per hour, but Ford felt that lost trunk space would hurt sales too much. One Ford engineer, when asked about the dangerous gas tank said, "Safety isn't the issue, trunk space is. You have no idea how stiff the competition is over trunk space. Do you realize that if we put a Capri-type tank in the Pinto, you could only get one set of golf clubs in the trunk?"

The last of Ford's reasons for not making adjustments to the fuel tank design, however, was unquestionably the most controversial. After strong lobbying efforts, Ford and the auto industry in general convinced NHTSA regulators that cost/benefit analysis would be an appropriate basis for determining the feasibility of safety design standards. Such an analysis, however, required the assignment of a value for a human life. A prior study had concluded that every time someone died in an auto accident there was an estimated "cost to society" of $200,725 (detailed in Table 4.1: What's Your Life Worth?).[15]

Having this value in hand, Ford calculated the cost of adding an $11 gas tank improvement versus the benefits of the projected 180 lives that would be saved (via

Table 4.1 What's Your Life Worth

The chart below, from a 1971 study by the National Highway Traffic Safety Administration, is a breakdown of the estimated cost to society every time someone is killed in a car accident. The Ford Motor Company used the $200,725 total figure in its own cost-benefit analysis.

Component	1971 Costs
Component	
Future productivity losses	
Direct	$132,300
Indirect	41,000
Medical costs	
Hospital	700
Other	425
Property damage	1,500
Insurance administration	4,700
Legal and court	3,000
Employer losses	1,000
Victim's pain and suffering	10,000
Funeral	900
Assets (lost consumption)	5,000
Miscellaneous accident cost	200
Total per fatality	$200,725

an internal memo entitled "Fatalities Associated with Crash-Induced Fuel Leakage and Fires"). This is presented in Table 4.2: The Cost of Dying in a Pinto.[16] As is demonstrated, the costs outweigh the benefits by almost three times. Thus, the cost/benefit analysis indicated that no improvements to the gas tanks were warranted.

Ford decided to go ahead with normal production plans, but the Pinto's problems soon surfaced. By early 1973, Ford's recall coordinator received field reports suggesting that Pintos were susceptible to "exploding" in rear-end collisions at very low speeds (under 25 miles per hour). Reports continued to indicate a similar trend in subsequent years, but no recall was initiated despite the mounting evidence. At every internal review, those responsible decided not to recall the Pinto.

Prior to the Indiana accident, the most publicized case concerning the Pinto's gas tank was that of Richard Grimshaw. In 1972, Richard, then 13, was riding with a neighbor on a road near San Bernardino, California, when they were hit from the rear. The Pinto's gas tank ruptured, causing the car to burst into flames. The neighbor was burned to death in a crash that would have been survivable if there had been no fire. Richard suffered third-degree burns over 90 percent of his body and subsequently underwent more than 60 operations, with only limited success. A civil suit was settled in February 1978, when a jury awarded a judgment of over $125 million against Ford, most of which consisted of punitive damages (later reduced to $6 million by a

Table 4.2 The Cost of Dying in a Pinto

These figures are from a Ford Motor Co. internal memorandum on the benefits and costs of an $11 safety improvement (applicable to all vehicles with similar gas tank designs) that would have made the Pinto less likely to burn.

Benefits
Savings: 180 burn deaths, 180 serious burn injuries, 2,100 burned vehicles.
Unit Cost: $200,000 per death, $67,000 per injury, $700 per vehicle.
Total Benefit: (180 × $200,000) + (180 × $67,000) + (2,100 × $700) = $49.5 million.

Costs
Sales: 11 million cars, 1.5 million light trucks.
Unit Cost: $11 per car, $11 per truck.
Total Cost: (11,000,000 × $11) + (1,500,000 × $11) = $137.5 million.

---

judge who nonetheless accused Ford of "callous indifference to human life"). This judgment was based on convincing evidence that Ford chose not to spend the $11 per car to correct the faults in the Pinto gas tanks that its own crash testing had revealed.

The Pinto sold well until the media called special attention to the Pinto fuel tank story. As a consequence, in June 1978, in the face of pressure from the media, the government, pending court cases, and the potential loss of future sales, Ford ordered a complete recall of all 1.5 million Pintos built between 1970 and 1976. During the 1980 Indiana trial that resulted from the fatal accident of 1978, differing views continued to be expressed about the Pinto fires case. Ford representatives argued that companies must make cost/benefit decisions all the time. They claimed that it is an essential part of business, and even though everyone knows that some people will die in auto accidents, buyers want costs held down; therefore, people implicitly accept risks when buying cars.

In a scathing article accusing Ford of criminally mismanaging the Pinto problem, investigative reporter Mark Dowie framed the case in a different and rather more sensational way, with this often-quoted speculation: "One wonders how long the Ford Motor Company would continue to market lethal cars were Henry Ford II and Lee Iacocca serving twenty-year terms in Leavenworth for consumer homicide."[17]

Case Questions

1. Put yourself in the role of the recall coordinator for Ford Motor Co. It's 1973 and field reports have been coming in about rear-end collisions, fires, and fatalities. You must decide whether to recall the automobile.
   a. Identify the relevant facts.
   b. Identify the pertinent ethical issues/points of ethical conflict.
   c. Identify the relevant affected parties.
   d. Identify the possible consequences of alternative courses of action.
   e. Identify relevant obligations.
   f. Identify your relevant community standards that should guide you as a person of integrity.

g. Check your gut.

What will you decide?

SHORT CASE

As a counselor in an outplacement firm, you've been working with Irwin for six months to find him a new position. During that time, he has completed extensive assessment work to determine if he's in an appropriate profession or if he might benefit from a career change. The results of the assessment indicate that Irwin has low self-esteem, probably could benefit from psychotherapy, and is most likely ill-suited for his current profession. Irwin has been actively interviewing for a position that's very similar to two others he has held and lost. He desperately wants and needs this job. The company where he's interviewing happens to be one of your most important clients. You receive a call from the head of human resources at the company, who tells you that Irwin suggested she call you for information about his abilities, interests, and personality style as measured by the assessment process. She also asks you for a reference for Irwin. Since he has, in effect asked that you share information with this woman, is it okay for you to give her an honest assessment of Irwin? What are your obligations to Irwin, who is your client in this case? Is there a way for you to be honest, yet not hurt Irwin's chances to obtain this job? Or is that important? What will you do?

NOTES

1. Rachels, J. 1983. *The elements of moral philosophy.* New York: McGraw-Hill.
2. Peach, L. 1994. An introduction to ethical theory. In *Research ethics: Cases and materials,* edited by R. L. Penslar. Bloomington: Indiana University Press.
3. Fritsche, D. J., and Becke, H. 1984. Linking management behavior to ethical philosophy: An empirical investigation. *Academy of Management Journal* 27: 166–175.
4. Rachels, *The elements of moral philosophy.*
5. Solomon, R. C. 1988. *Ethics and excellence.* New York: Oxford University Press.
6. Bebeau, M. 1994. Developing a well-reasoned moral response to a moral problem in scientific research ethics. Paper distributed at the Teaching Research Ethics conference, Poynter Research Center for the Study of Ethics and American Institutions. Bloomington: Indiana University, May.
7. Nash, L. 1989. Ethics without the sermon. In *Ethics in Practice,* edited by K. R. Andres. Boston: Harvard Business School Press.
8. Larson, D. E. 1990. *Mayo Clinic family health book.* New York: William Morrow.
9. Nash, Ethics without the sermon.
10. Stolberg, S. G. 1998. Their devil's advocates: Thalidomide returns with an unlikely ally: a group of its original victims. *The New York Times Magazine,* January 25: 20–25.
11. Messick, D. M., and Bazerman, B. 1994. Ethics for the 21st century: A decision making perspective. Unpublished manuscript.
12. Steiger, B. 1984. *Indian medicine power.* Atglen, PA: Whitford Press, 92.
13. Skooglund, C. 1992. Ethics in the face of competitive pressures. *Business Ethics Resource,* Fall: 4.
14. Steiger, *Indian medicine power.*
15. Dowie, M. 1977. How Ford put two million fire traps on wheels. *Business and Society Review* 23: 51–55.
16. Ibid.
17. Ibid.

CHAPTER **5**

DECIDING WHAT'S RIGHT: A PSYCHOLOGICAL APPROACH

INTRODUCTION

Chapter 4 introduced prescriptive ethical theories. These theories, developed by philosophers, have been designed to help individuals decide what they should do in response to ethical dilemmas. But people don't always even recognize the ethical dimensions of the issue or situation they face. When they do, they don't always make the best decisions. And even when they identify the best decision, they may not have the will to follow through. Research in psychology points to some reasons why. This chapter focuses on the psychology of individual ethical decision making. As opposed to discussing what individuals should do, it describes what people actually do by introducing the psychological factors—the individual differences and cognitive processes that influence how people think and how they behave in response to ethical dilemmas. It also discusses some of the cognitive barriers that can keep well-intentioned people from making good ethical decisions and suggests some ways to overcome these barriers.

MORAL AWARENESS AND MORAL JUDGMENT

If a decision maker is to engage in moral judgment processes (like those discussed in Chapter 4), she or he must first recognize the ethical nature of the situation at hand.

Moral Awareness → Moral Judgment

We refer to this initial step in the ethical decision-making process as moral awareness. With moral awareness, a situation or issue is recognized to be an issue that raises ethical concerns and must be thought about in moral terms. It is an important step that shouldn't be taken for granted, because awareness of the ethical nature of the situation is far from automatic. Sometimes people are simply unaware that they are facing an issue with ethical overtones. And, if they don't recognize the issue as an ethical issue, moral judgment processes are not likely to be engaged. Consider the following example from your life as a student.

Students are doing more research for classroom assignments on the Internet. The technology makes it easy to find up-to-date information, download it, and cut and paste it right into a paper that then gets submitted to a professor for a grade. You may have

CHAPTER 5   DECIDING WHAT'S RIGHT: A PSYCHOLOGICAL APPROACH   **111**

done this yourself without thinking too much about it. However, in this process, students often overlook the fact that they may be plagiarizing—"stealing" someone else's intellectual property. Intellectual property is protected by copyright and patent laws in the United States. These laws are important because there would simply be no incentive to write a book, publish a magazine, or develop a new product if anyone could simply reproduce it freely without any attention to the rights of the person or company that invested time and resources to create it. (That's why the entertainment industry is so concerned about downloading music and video from the Internet.) The education community has adopted norms that guide how students can fairly use intellectual property. In keeping with those norms, students are expected to paraphrase and then carefully reference the sources of their information. And, when quoting someone else's words, these words must be put in quotation marks, and the exact citation must be provided. In pre-Internet days, this kind of research meant going to the library, searching for information in reference books and magazine articles, copying pertinent information by hand, making careful notes about the sources, and then organizing the information into a paper that had to be typed from scratch. Plagiarism actually required some conscious effort in those days. Now, information is so accessible and it's so easy to simply cut and paste that it can be harder to recognize the ethical issues involved. On the other hand, if your professor takes the time to explain the importance of academic integrity, the role of intellectual property in our society, the definition of plagiarism, and your responsibilities as a member of the higher education community, you should be more aware of the ethical issues. Under those circumstances, when you're tempted to just cut and paste, you'll be more likely to think about the ethical dimensions of your actions—the rights of the intellectual property owner, and whether your actions would be considered plagiarism by your professor and others in the community.

Now for a work-related example.

> You've just started a new job in the financial services industry. One afternoon, your manager tells you that he has to leave early to attend his son's softball game, and he asks you to be on the lookout for an important check that his boss wants signed before the end of the day. He tells you to do him a favor—simply sign his name and forward the check to his boss.
>
> To a naive employee, this may seem like a straightforward and easily accommodated request. But if the company trained you well, you would immediately be aware of the ethical nature of the situation. Your manager has asked you to engage in forgery, a serious ethical lapse, especially in the financial services industry. Recognizing the moral nature of the situation would likely lead to some very different thinking about how to respond.

A recent study found that people are more likely to recognize the moral nature of an issue or decision if they believe that their peers will consider it to be ethically problematic, if moral language is used to present the situation to the decision maker, and if the decision is seen as having the potential to produce serious harm to others.[1]

Let's take these factors one at a time. First, if you believe that your coworkers are likely to see a decision as ethically problematic, it probably means that the issue has been discussed, perhaps in a company-sponsored ethics training program or informally among coworkers. Such discussions prime you to think about situations in a particular way. When a similar situation arises, it triggers memories of the previous ethics-related discussion, and you are more likely to categorize and think about the situation in those terms.[2] Using the forgery example, perhaps a company training program actually presented a similar problem to your work group and you all agreed that signing the check would be inappropriate. Having participated in such a discussion, you would recognize that your peers believe that signing the check would be ethically problematic and you would be more likely to see your boss's request as a request to do something unethical—an ethical problem.

Second, situations can be represented or "framed" in different ways—using moral language or more neutral language. Using moral language (words like integrity, honesty, fairness, propriety, or lying, cheating, stealing) will more likely trigger moral thinking because these terms are attached to existing cognitive categories that have moral content. For example, if the manager in the example above had asked you to forge the check for him, the word "forge" would be more likely to trigger legal or ethics-related concerns than if he simply asked you to sign the check (more neutral language). In response to the term *forgery,* you would more likely wonder if signing the check was wrong, if anyone was being hurt, and what the consequences would be if you did or didn't do it. The term "plagiarism" would likely trigger similar thinking.

Finally, an issue or situation that has the potential to produce serious harm to others is likely to be seen as an ethical issue. In the forgery example, if forging the check would result in serious harm to customers, you would more likely see it as a serious issue than if no one would be harmed. Thomas Jones proposed that individuals are more likely to recognize the ethical nature of issues that are morally intense.[3] The moral intensity of an issue is higher when the consequences for others are potentially large, these consequences are relatively immediate and likely to occur, and the potential victims are psychologically or physically close to the decision maker. For example, a decision to leak toxic chemicals into the local water supply is highly likely to harm many people in one's own community. Such a decision is "morally intense," and therefore the decision maker is likely to see it as an ethical issue. In contrast, a decision that might require laying off a few individuals in a foreign subsidiary would be less likely to trigger moral awareness. Only a few people would be affected, the consequences will occur in the future, and these individuals are both psychologically and physically distant from the decision maker.

This research suggests that managers can encourage employees to be morally aware by providing training and by talking with employees about the types of ethical issues they're likely to face and why these issues are ethically problematic, by encouraging employees to have these discussions themselves, by using moral language in these interactions, and by encouraging employees to think about the consequences of their actions and to take responsibility for the consequences of the decisions they make. By doing these things, managers can help their employees to be more morally aware and more able to recognize ethical issues when they arise.

INDIVIDUAL DIFFERENCES, MORAL JUDGMENT, AND ETHICAL BEHAVIOR

Once people are aware of the ethical dimensions of a situation or decision, they engage in moral judgment processes that can contribute to ethical conduct. Much of this book focuses on the situational pushes and pulls that influence thought and action. For example, people follow leaders or their peers. They tend to do what's rewarded. Yet, despite these powerful pushes and pulls, people do bring something of themselves to situations. Heroes emerge when you least expect it. People blow the whistle despite fear of retaliation. Others embezzle funds or lie to customers despite all of management's efforts to support good conduct. How can we explain these ethical and unethical behaviors? Very simply, ethical conduct is influenced by both situational pushes and pulls *and* characteristics of the individual that we'll call individual differences.

When people are hired, they come with personalities—individual predispositions to think and behave in certain ways. Research has uncovered a number of individual traits that influence the way people think and behave in response to ethical dilemmas.

Cognitive Moral Development

The best explanation for moral judgment and action based on individual characteristics comes from the moral reasoning research of Lawrence Kohlberg.[4] When people behave morally, they must, among other things, decide what course of action is morally right (as we discussed in Chapter 4), and they must choose the morally right path over others.[5] In other words, if they decide that blowing the whistle is the morally right path, they must follow through and do it.

Kohlberg's moral reasoning theory is a cognitive developmental theory that focuses primarily on how people decide what course of action is morally right. His research began by following 58 American boys ranging in age from 10 to 16 years old. He interviewed them every three years over a 12-year period, asking for their open-ended responses to hypothetical moral dilemmas. Their responses were analyzed and resulted in new understanding of how moral reasoning gradually changes from middle childhood to adulthood.

The resulting cognitive moral development theory proposes that moral reasoning develops sequentially through three broad levels, each composed of two stages. As individuals move forward through the sequence of stages, they can comprehend all reasoning at stages below their own but cannot comprehend reasoning more than one stage above their own. Development through the stages results from the cognitive disequilibrium that occurs when an individual perceives a contradiction between his or her own reasoning level and the next higher one. This can occur through training but generally occurs through interaction with peers and life situations that challenge the individual's current way of thinking. According to Kohlberg, the actual moral decision isn't as important as the reasoning process used to arrive at it. However, he argued that the higher the reasoning stage, the more ethical the decision because the higher stages are more consistent with prescriptive ethical principles of justice and rights (like those discussed in the deontological approach, in Chapter 4).

Kohlberg's theory has been successfully applied to studies of adults in business settings.[6] For example, James Weber interviewed business managers about their responses to the following hypothetical dilemma:[7]

> Evelyn worked for an automotive steel casting company. She was part of a small group asked to investigate the cause of an operating problem that had developed in the wheel castings of a new luxury automobile and to make recommendations for its improvement. The problem did not directly create an unsafe condition, but it did lead to irritating sounds. The vice-president of engineering told the group that he was certain that the problem was due to tensile stress in the castings. Evelyn and a lab technician conducted tests and found conclusive evidence that the problem was not tensile stress. As Evelyn began work on other possible explanations of the problem, she was told that the problem had been solved. A report prepared by Evelyn's boss strongly supported the tensile stress hypothesis. All of the data points from Evelyn's experiments have been changed to fit the curves, and some of the points that were far from where the theory would predict have been omitted. The report "proved" that tensile stress was responsible for the problem.

A number of questions were presented to the interviewees. For example, they were asked whether Evelyn should contradict her boss's report and why. We will use this hypothetical dilemma to understand the theory and how responses to the above question (along with others) help to identify an individual's placement in Kohlberg's moral reasoning stage framework. Table 5.1 outlines the levels and stages involved.

LEVEL I: PRECONVENTIONAL At level I (labeled the preconventional level and including stages 1 and 2), a person views rules as imposed and external to the self. The decision about what's right is explained in terms of rewards and punishments and the exchange of favors. Stage 1 individuals are guided by obedience for its own sake. Avoiding punishment is the key consideration. It's easy to imagine a small child thinking, I should share my toy with my brother because if I don't Mom will yell at me (i.e., I'll be punished). A stage 1 response to the Evelyn situation might argue that it would be wrong to contradict her boss because she must obey her superiors and she would certainly be punished if she disobeyed.

At stage 2, concern for personal reward, satisfaction, and a sense of duty to oneself become important. In addition, a kind of market reciprocity is considered. What is right may be judged in terms of a "you scratch my back, I'll scratch yours" reciprocity. A stage 2 child might think, "If I share my toy with my brother, he might share his with me later." A stage 2 response in the Evelyn situation might argue that Evelyn should support her boss because he is responsible for her performance appraisals, and if she lets this one go, he might overlook some of her problems from the past. Also, if her boss has been kind or helpful to her in the past, she may consider her obligation to repay the favor.

Table 5.1 Levels of Cognitive Moral Development According to Kohlberg

Stage	What is considered to be right
Level I: Preconventional	
Stage 1: Obedience and Punishment Orientation	Sticking to rules to avoid physical punishment. Obedience for its own sake.
Stage 2: Instrumental Purpose and Exchange	Following rules only when it is in one's immediate interest. Right is an equal exchange, a fair deal.
Level II: Conventional	
Stage 3: Interpersonal Accord, Conformity, Mutual Expectations	Stereotypical "good" behavior. Living up to what is expected by peers and people close to you.
Stage 4: Social Accord and System Maintenance	Fulfilling duties and obligations of the social system. Upholding laws except in extreme cases where they conflict with fixed social duties. Contributing to the society or group.
Level III: Postconventional or Principled	
Stage 5: Social Contract and Individual Rights	Being aware that people hold a variety of values; that rules are relative to the group. Upholding rules because they are the social contract. Upholding nonrelative values and rights regardless of the majority opinion.
Stage 6: Universal Ethical Principles	Following self-chosen ethical principles of justice and rights. When laws violate principles, act in accord with principles.

Source: Adapted from Kohlberg, L. (1976) "Moral Stages and Moralization: The Cognitive-Developmental Approach." In *Moral Development and Behavior: Theory, Research, and Social Issues,* edited by T. Lickona. New York: Holt, Rinehart and Winston, pp. 34–35.

LEVEL II: CONVENTIONAL At level II (labeled the conventional level and including stages 3 and 4), the individual has internalized the shared moral norms of society or some segment like a family or work group. What's morally right is explained in terms of living up to roles and the expectations of relevant others, fulfilling duties and obligations, and following rules and laws. Kohlberg's research placed most American adults at this level, and Weber's research found that most managers' responses to the Evelyn dilemma were at level II, stages 3 and 4.

At stage 3, what's morally right is thought to be that which pleases or helps others or is approved by those close to you. Interpersonal trust and social approval are important. For example, a stage 3 response to the Evelyn dilemma might say that Evelyn shouldn't contradict her boss because she would be perceived as disloyal by her boss and might lose the social approval and trust of her boss and peers. On the other hand, what if Evelyn shares her dilemma with close family members whose opinions are important to her, and they feel strongly that she must contradict her boss? In this case, she would likely reason that she should contradict her boss because the people she trusts most believe it's the right thing to do.

At stage 4, the perspective broadens to consider society. The individual is concerned about fulfilling agreed-upon duties and following rules or laws that are designed to promote the common good. Therefore, a stage 4 response might say that Evelyn should contradict her boss because of her duty to society. What if the noises do represent a safety problem? She has a responsibility as a good member of society to report it. She would feel particularly strongly about this if she were aware of product safety laws that required her to report the problem.

LEVEL III: POSTCONVENTIONAL Finally, we come to level III (postconventional, sometimes called principled reasoning—stages 5 and 6). The principled individual has gone beyond identification with others' expectations, rules, and laws to make decisions more autonomously and consistent with principles of justice and rights. It's important to remember that very few adults in our society actually reach stage 5 and that stage 6 is thought to be a theoretical stage only.

At stage 5, the emphasis is still on rules and laws because these represent the social contract, but stage 5 thinking considers the possibility of changing the law for socially useful purposes. And a stage 5 individual would take into account moral laws above society's laws, such as considering what decision would create the greatest societal good. A stage 5 Evelyn might reason that she should contradict her boss because doing so would be consistent with the ethical principle of the greatest societal good, particularly if she considered safety of the automobiles to be a potential problem. Her responsibility goes beyond that of a good law-abiding member of society. A stage 5 Evelyn is also responsible to principles of justice and rights. So, even if there is no law requiring her to report what she knows, a stage 5 Evelyn would consider the rights to safety of the potential automobile consumers as an important reason for her to tell.

Adherence to *any* principle does not qualify as "principled" thinking in Kohlberg's theory. Kohlberg is quite precise about the kinds of principles that qualify as "principled" thinking, and he specifies how a researcher would score an interview to determine an individual's moral reasoning stage. Broadly defined, level III principles are principles of justice and rights generally consistent with the kind of principles introduced in Chapter 4 under deontological theories. Adherence to other principles simply does not qualify as "principled" thinking. For example, someone might take "looking out for myself first and foremost" as a guiding principle. This principle is not considered principled-level thinking because it is inconsistent with theories of justice that require the decision maker to take into account all of those affected in a situation. Similarly, the principle "I always do what my religion tells me to do because God will punish me if I don't" would not qualify. In Kohlberg's model, this type of thinking actually represents a low level of cognitive moral development because it is based upon unquestioning obedience to authority and fear of punishment. Often religious prescriptions are consistent with theories of justice and rights. But, in order to be considered a principled decision maker, an individual would have to think through the ethical situation on his or her own (reasoning according to principles of justice and rights), and not just take on faith what a particular religion requires.

To understand Kohlberg's theory, you must remember that it is a cognitive theory. What counts is the reasoning processes involved in a decision, not just the decision made. A stage 1 individual and a stage 5 individual may make the same decision, but their reasons for making it will be very different.

ARE WOMEN AND MEN DIFFERENT? In 1982, psychologist Carol Gilligan published *In a Different Voice,* a book about women's cognitive moral development. Gilligan, who had been Kohlberg's student, claimed that Kohlberg's theory was flawed because he had studied only boys and then had simply applied the same theory to girls. Her own research led Gilligan to question the exclusive focus on justice in Kohlberg's higher moral reasoning stages. She found that interviewees raised both justice and care concerns when describing moral conflicts. But, she also found that males focused almost exclusively on justice considerations and that a care focus was almost exclusively a female phenomenon. Females were more likely to use a "morality of care" that emphasized relationships—raising issues related to caring for others, responsibility to others, and the continuity of interdependent relationships.[8]

Gilligan's claims have received a great deal of attention, particularly in the child and adolescent development fields. But their applicability to adults working in business organizations is limited. Gilligan's own research comparing the moral reasoning of male and female medical students found no significant difference between the genders, suggesting that both men and women are strongly influenced by the powerful cultural norms of medical practice.[9] Similarly, an interview study of business managers based on Gilligan's theory found no gender differences.[10] All but one of the managers (male and female) who described a moral conflict at work based their moral reasoning on rights, not care. Finally, many cognitive moral development studies based on Kohlberg's theory and conducted by many researchers over the years have found only trivial, if any, gender differences. When differences have been found, females generally have scored higher than men in justice-based reasoning.[11] Business ethics researchers now agree that additional research on the question of gender differences is unnecessary and likely to be fruitless.[12]

We can now begin to address the second requirement for ethical behavior: doing what's right. Recall that to behave morally, people must first decide what course of action is morally right (probably depending to a large degree on their moral awareness and stage of moral development), and then they must choose the morally right path over others.[13]

LOOKING UP AND LOOKING AROUND We've already learned that most adults are at the conventional level of cognitive moral development (level II), meaning that they're highly susceptible to external influences. Their decision about what's morally right, and therefore their likely action, is inextricably linked with what others think, say, and do. We call this looking up and looking around for ethical guidance.[14]

These individuals aren't autonomous decision makers who strictly follow an internal moral compass. They look up and around to see what their superiors and their peers are doing and saying, and they use these cues as a guide to action. Therefore, most people are highly likely to do what's expected of them as a result of the reward system, role expectations, authority figure demands, and group norms. That's why the remainder of this book focuses so heavily on these external influences and why it's so important that managers structure the work environment to support ethical conduct. The large majority of employees will be looking for guidance and they'll do what's right if guided and supported along those lines.

AUTONOMOUS PRINCIPLED THINKING AND ACTION Higher stage thinking is more independent of these external influences. The postconventional principled thinker (level III, representing a minority of people) has developed his or her own justice and rights-based principles that guide ethical decision making. Research has demonstrated that these people are also more likely to behave consistently with their own principle-based decisions—they'll carry through and do what they think is right. More-principled individuals also have been found to be less likely to cheat, more likely to resist pressure from authority figures, more likely to help someone in need, and more likely to blow the whistle on misconduct.[15] But it's important for managers to remember that level III individuals are rare. Autonomous decision making based on principles of justice and rights is the exception rather than the rule.

The bottom line for managers is this: Cognitive moral development theory and research tell us that most of the people you manage are going to be strongly influenced by what you do, say, and reward. They are looking up and looking around for guidance from you and their peers, and they're likely to follow what they see around them. Therefore, it's your responsibility to structure the work environment in a way that supports ethical conduct. If you avoid this responsibility, these people will look elsewhere for guidance, and the guidance they receive may not support ethical conduct at all.

Those few individuals who have reached principled levels of moral reasoning should be singled out to lead key decision-making groups. They can be identified with the use of instruments that have been developed by cognitive moral development researchers. Research on ethical decision making in groups suggests that when less principled individuals lead a group, the group's ethical decision-making performance decreases. On the other hand, groups with leaders higher in moral reasoning either improve or stay the same.[16]

Moral reasoning can also be increased through training. Over the years, Kohlberg and his students and colleagues have designed training approaches based on cognitive moral development theory. In this type of training, facilitators give participants hypothetical ethical dilemmas for discussion. The facilitator promotes movement through moral reasoning stages by challenging participants' thinking and by exposing individuals to reasoning higher than their own. This creates cognitive conflict, leading the participant to question and eventually revise his or her own reasoning. Research has supported the effectiveness of this type of training with adults in dental, medical, and business schools.[17] Managers may want to consider incorporating these ideas into their firms' ethics training.

Locus of Control

Another individual characteristic that has been found to influence ethical conduct is locus of control.[18] Locus of control refers to an individual's perception of how much control he or she exerts over life events. Locus of control can be thought of as a single continuum from a high internal locus of control to a high external locus of control. An individual with a high internal locus of control believes that outcomes are primarily the result of his or her own efforts, whereas an individual with a high external locus of control believes that life events are determined primarily by fate, luck, or powerful others. Locus of control is not something a person is born with. It develops over time through interaction with other people and the social environment. Therefore, although it is thought to be relatively stable, one's locus of control can shift. For example, if someone with a very high internal locus of control became a prisoner of war with little chance of escape, he or she would likely develop a more external focus over time.

RELATIONSHIP TO ETHICAL CONDUCT How is locus of control related to ethics? First, individuals with a high internal locus of control see the relationship between their behavior and its outcomes more clearly than do those with an external locus of control. Internals see themselves as being in control of things that happen. Therefore, they're more likely to take responsibility for the consequences of their actions. It would be more difficult for such an individual to say, "Well, it's not my responsibility. I just work here" or "I'm just following orders." Studies have found that internals are more likely to help another person, even if there's a penalty for doing so.[19]

Internals see themselves as in charge of their own fates. Therefore, they should also be less willing to be pressured by others to do things they believe to be wrong. One interesting study asked subjects to complete a story in which the main character was pressured to violate a social norm.[20] The more internal the subject's locus of control, the more likely the story completion had the hero resisting the pressure. In an obedience-to-authority experiment (explained in more detail in Chapter 7), externals were more likely to give apparently (but not really) harmful electric shocks to someone if told to do so by the experimenter.[21]

For managers, it may be helpful to know where your workers fit on the locus of control continuum. It can help you understand how they think and how they might react in a variety of situations, including ethical situations. For example, workers who constantly blame bad luck and other external factors for performance failures or ethical lapses may be doing so because of an external locus of control—that's the way they view the world. You can work with such individuals to help them see the relationship between their actions and the outcomes by consistently holding them responsible and accountable for what they do. As a result, their locus of control may shift over time and they will take more responsibility for the consequences of their actions.

COGNITIVE BARRIERS TO GOOD ETHICAL JUDGMENT

Individual differences aside, all human beings share certain ways of thinking about the world. The steps offered in Chapter 4 assume a rational ethical decision-making process, prescribing how an ethical decision should be made. However, studies have found that actual human decision making falls short of this rational ideal. Although people intend to be rational in their decision making, for a variety of reasons they're not. In recent years, psychologists have discovered a number of weaknesses and biases in how people make decisions.[22] Some of these have direct implications for ethical decision making in organizations and for the advice given in Chapter 4.[23] Think of this part of the chapter as a kind of "reality check." If you're going to manage your own and others' ethical behavior, you need to understand how people really think in addition to how they should think.

As a backdrop for your thinking, recognize that the cognitive weaknesses and biases we will be discussing operate primarily because people try to reduce uncertainty and simplify their world. Although uncertainty is a fact of organizational life, business people want very much to deny the uncertainty they face. Therefore, they tend to act as if the world is rational and they're in control. Being "in charge" and able to predict events is a highly valued characteristic, especially in business. But this focus on being in charge is an illusion that can get managers into trouble. What if you really don't know all of the facts—what the risks are—who the potential affected parties are—what all the consequences of your decisions are? You'll see in this chapter that the best way to avoid decision-making weaknesses and biases is to become aware of them and to incorporate steps into your decision making that are explicitly aimed at reducing their impact.

Script Processing: The Pinto Fires Case

Dennis A. Gioia, management scholar and expert on social cognition in organizations, has provided us with a rare opportunity to look inside the head of someone who was involved in a widely publicized business ethics situation. He has analyzed his own thoughts and behavior as vehicle recall coordinator at Ford Motor Company shortly after the Ford Pinto was introduced in both an article in the *Journal of Business Ethics*[24] and in his "Reflections," accompanying this chapter.

In the summer of 1972, Gioia graduated with an MBA. His value system included opposition to the Vietnam War and deep concerns about the ethical conduct of business. "I cultivated my social awareness; I held my principles high; I espoused my intention to help a troubled world; and I wore my hair long. By any measure I was a prototypical 'Child of the '60s.'"[25] A car enthusiast, Gioia was hired by the Ford Motor Company as a "problem analyst." Within 2 years he became Ford's field recall coordinator, in charge of organizing current recall campaigns and identifying developing problems.

In analyzing his participation in the decision *not* to recall the Pinto, Gioia suggests that his behavior was highly influenced by script processing. Scripts are cognitive frameworks that guide human thought and action. Although they are generally not written down, scripts contain information about the appropriate sequence of events in routine situations. For example, most of us have a fairly complex script for how to behave in a fancy restaurant, from approaching the maître d', to tasting the wine, to choosing a fork to use, to leaving the appropriate tip. Information processing is made much more efficient because a cognitive script allows the individual to call on an established behavior pattern and act automatically without contemplating every decision or action in great detail. Active thinking is not required because the situation fits the mental prototype, which triggers the script and the prescribed behaviors. According to Gioia, this is something like "cruising on automatic pilot." Many of us discover that we have been cruising on automatic pilot when we drive to a familiar destination, but we can't recall how we got there. We were following an established behavior pattern. The route was so familiar that we didn't have to think about it anymore. Somehow we were magically there. Similar things happen at work. Behaviors become routine or "scripted" and we do them pretty much without thinking.

Given the huge information load expected of someone who was simultaneously managing hundreds of files on potential safety problems, scripts provided a great information processing advantage. Rather than treating every potential problem situation as unique, Gioia could save time and mental energy by making quick and efficient decisions about problems as they arose. As early reports about the Pinto began to trickle in, they didn't raise any red flags because they fit the scripted criteria for a "normal" accident and they didn't fit the scripted criteria for a recall. Among other criteria, Gioia was taught to look for a large number of cases, a pattern of component failure, and a traceable cause to a design or manufacturing problem before proposing a recall. Therefore, he filed the claims automatically and gave seemingly more important problems his active attention.

In addition to its contribution to information processing efficiency, however, script processing clearly has disadvantages. Gioia admittedly "looked right past" potential problems because he had seen similar information patterns hundreds of times before. The scripted definition of a crisis case was not met by the information he received, so the Pinto wasn't singled out for attention. Consistent with research on script processing, he selectively perceived information that was consistent with the script and ignored information that didn't fit the pattern.

Muffled emotions can also become part of a script. Many jobs require the control of emotions, particularly negative emotions. The recall coordinator's job fit this category. In order for Gioia to function in his job every day, his emotions had to be squelched to some degree. Even when one event penetrated his script, it didn't lead to recall of the Pinto. He had received a photograph of a burned Pinto and subsequently saw in person the burned hulk of an actual automobile. These powerful visual images moved him to bring the case before members of the field recall office. However, at the meeting, it became clear that the characteristics of the Pinto problem didn't meet the group's shared scripted criteria for a recall. For example, only a few field reports had come in about the Pinto, much fewer than the number that would generally support a recall decision. All members, including Gioia, voted not to recall.

Script processing can be particularly problematic for ethical decision making. First, ethical decision making requires active consideration of the moral dimensions of the situation and a "custom" decision, tailored to the complexities of that particular case. Yet, Gioia argues, in many situations organizational members are not even aware that they are dealing with an ethical dilemma. In terms of our previous discussion, they are morally unaware. They handle situations by following scripts that are likely to exclude ethical considerations. In other words, ethical dilemmas do not lend themselves to "automatic pilot" decisions. But the realities of our hectic work lives make this sort of default decision making very common.

Cost/Benefit Analysis

Frequently, in addition to the cognitive processing limitations of individual decision makers, institutionalized decision-making processes can powerfully influence the decisions that are made by individuals or groups. In the Pinto fires case, a controversial decision-making process was used to justify the decision not to change the gas tank design. The National Traffic Safety Association had approved the use of cost/benefit analysis to establish automotive safety design standards. This involved the assignment of a dollar value for a human life, deemed to be approximately $200,000 in 1970. As an internal memo revealed, Ford had tabulated the costs of altering the tank design (for all similarly designed vehicles) to be $137 million, or $11 per vehicle. The benefits were calculated to be $49,530,000. These included the savings to society that would be accrued by preventing 180 deaths at $200,000 each, plus 180 projected burn injuries at $67,000 per injury and 2,100 burned cars at $700 per car. Using the cost/benefit analysis made the decision seem straightforward. The costs of redesign outweighed the benefits and would therefore not be undertaken. Moral considerations didn't figure into the equation.

Attempts to reduce complex decision making to quantitative terms aren't uncommon, especially in a highly competitive business environment. In this way, complex decisions can be simplified, an apparent advantage. Assigning a value to human life is also still done by many government agencies as they attempt to calculate the costs and benefits of new regulations. And those managing relief efforts after the World Trade Center terrorist attack had to decide how much money should be given to families who lost loved ones. What is a life worth? Are some people's lives "worth" more than others because they would have had more earning potential had they lived? Unfortunately, this kind of decision making is a part of our modern lives. But the potential disadvantages of reducing the value of human life to quantitative terms should be clear. Such simplification can remove moral criteria from the decision-making process.

The Pinto fires example also points to the importance of multiple selves and role behavior that will be discussed more in Chapter 7. Gioia was an idealistic young student, but he admittedly dropped his idealism at the corporation door, picking it up on his way out each day. In performing his job of recall coordinator, the role expectations and guiding scripts were more influential. As he says:

> The recall coordinator's job was serious business. The scripts associated with it influenced me more than I influenced [them]. Before I went to Ford I would have argued strongly that Ford had an ethical obligation to recall. After I left Ford, I now argue and teach that Ford had an ethical obligation to recall. But, while I was there, I perceived no obligation to recall and I remember no strong ethical overtones to the case whatsoever. It was a very straightforward decision, driven by dominant scripts for the time, place, and context.

Clearly, these processes that individuals and organizations use to simplify complex decisions can have significant implications for the ethical decisions managers make. Although script processing and quantitative decision-making criteria clearly help us to do our jobs more efficiently, they can also strip ethical considerations from the decision-making process.

One way to address this problem is to make ethical considerations part of the script. Gioia suggests that this may be possible, although he warns that "it will take substantial concentration on the ethical dimension of the corporate culture (see Chapter 9), as well as overt attempts to emphasize ethics in education, training, and decision making before typical organizational scripts are likely to be modified to include the crucial ethical component."[26] You can help your subordinates by working with them to make the scripts explicit and to analyze them for their ethical components.

You can also require decision-making groups to analyze the ethical aspects of their decisions and to include this analysis in their report(s). Just as environmental impact statements are now a routine part of many business decisions, an ethical analysis could require that managers focus on the influence of a particular decision on stakeholders' rights and consequences for the community or communities affected by the decision. You can also require groups to justify their decision-making process (e.g., decision-making criteria and weighting) in moral as well as quantitative terms.

Thinking about Fact Gathering

In Chapter 4, we advised you to "get the facts" as an important first step in good ethical decision making. But be aware that your thinking about the facts is likely to be biased. Research evidence suggests that you may look for the wrong ones or stop looking too soon because you think you already have all the facts you need.

We know that most people, including business students and business executives, are overconfident about their knowledge of the facts. For example, in research studies, people were asked factual questions. Then they were asked to judge the probable truth of their answers. In response to the question "Is Rome or New York farther north?" most people chose New York, and they believed that the probability was about 90 percent that they were right. Actually, they were wrong. Rome is slightly north of New York. Being overconfident can make you fail to search for additional facts or for support for the facts you have.[27]

Even if you gather additional facts or support, another cognitive bias termed the confirmation trap may influence your choice of which facts to gather and where to look.[28] All of us have the tendency to look for information that will confirm our preferred answer or choice and to neglect to search for evidence that might prove us wrong. If you're a pharmaceutical executive who wants to believe that a new product is safe, you're more likely to ask your managers something like, "Does it meet all FDA regulations?" In this case, the executive expects and will probably get a confirming response, and a quick decision to go ahead with the drug can be made. However, the meeting might take a very different turn if the executive asks, "What health and safety problems are still possible with this drug?"[29]

In an attempt to overcome these limitations and biases, it's important that you consciously try to think of ways you could be wrong. Incorporate questions in your individual and group decision-making processes such as, "How could I/we be wrong?" "What facts are still missing?" and "What facts exist that might prove me/us to be wrong?" You may still miss some important facts, but you'll miss less of them than if you didn't ask these questions at all.

Thinking about Consequences

In Chapter 4, we also introduced consequentialist theories, and we advised you to think about all the potential consequences of your decision for a wide variety of stakeholders. Who can argue with such sage advice? But psychologists have found a number of problems with how people think about consequences.

REDUCED NUMBER OF CONSEQUENCES One way people simplify their decisions and make them more manageable is to reduce the number of consequences they consider. They're especially likely to ignore consequences that are thought to affect only a few people. But consequences that affect only a few people can be serious. For example, a highly beneficial drug may have beneficial consequences for many and adverse consequences for only a few people. But what if those few people could die from side effects of the drug?[30] Obviously, you wouldn't want to ignore such serious consequences no matter how few people are affected. In attempting to consciously deal with this situation, it helps to consult a broad range of people who have a stake in the decision you're making. Invite input from all interested parties, especially those who disagree with you and those with the most to lose. Ask them what consequences they're concerned about and why. Then, incorporate these consequences in your decision making.

CONSEQUENCES FOR THE SELF VERSUS CONSEQUENCES FOR OTHERS
Consequentialist theories require us to think about costs and benefits for society—for multiple stakeholders. But psychological research suggests people tend to make decisions in a self-interested manner. For example, they're inclined to give more weight to the consequences of a decision or action for themselves (or those close to them) than for others. That may be because consequences to the self are more immediate or more imminent. In addition, when the consequences of multiple alternatives are ambiguous, people tend to choose the alternative that they personally prefer rather than the one that is more just. To make matters worse (from an ethics perspective), people underestimate the extent to which they are self-interested and the extent to which they rationalize their own behavior. They just aren't aware of their own cognitive biases. Again, it can help to consciously consider those outside of yourself who are going to be affected by a decision or action. As a manager, you can ask your people to make a list of those individuals or groups who might be affected and seek their input or try to imagine themselves in the shoes of those stakeholders. How would they react?[31]

CONSEQUENCES AS RISK One way to think about consequences is to think in terms of decision making about risk. Research suggests that people tend to underestimate potential risks because of an illusion of optimism. They overestimate the likelihood of good future events and underestimate the bad. People also generally believe that they're less susceptible to risks than others. This belief is supported by the illusion of control, the general belief that we really are in charge of what happens. And if we think we can control events, we also think bad things are less likely to happen. This illusion of control has been demonstrated to exist in MBA students from top U.S. business schools, suggesting that managers are certainly vulnerable.[32] Managers whose judgment is influenced by these cognitive biases are likely to underestimate the risk facing the firm as a result of a particular decision. But if managers ignore risks, they're also ignoring important consequences. So it's important to recognize this tendency to ignore risk, and design risk analysis into your decision-making processes.

Even if we attend to risks, we still have difficulty thinking about them in a completely rational way. One tendency that can contribute to downplaying risk was already discussed—the tendency to attend to information that will help to confirm the decision we would prefer to make (confirmation bias). In the famous space shuttle *Challenger* disaster, everyone knew that there was risk. The question was how much, and was it too much? Many economic and political factors were pushing NASA to launch this shuttle. The media were paying more attention to the launch than they usually would because a schoolteacher was on board. Researchers now believe that confirmation bias may have influenced decision makers to focus on the information that confirmed their preference, which was to launch, and to discount available information about risks that would have supported a delay.[33]

CONSEQUENCES OVER TIME: ESCALATION OF COMMITMENT The prescription to think about consequences also fails to take into account the fact that decisions are not isolated choices, but often become part of a series of choices within the context of a larger decision or project. Consider the following scenario:

> You finally graduated from college and landed a great job, and you invested most of your savings in the car of your dreams—a used BMW. But in a short time, the car began having mechanical problems. Every time you bring it to the mechanic, he claims that it is fixed for good, but the problems continue and your bank account is being drained. Should you quit trying to fix the car?

Because you've already made the decision to buy the car and you've already invested a lot of money in it, your tendency will be to continue to be committed to this previously selected course of action. This tendency has been called "escalation of commitment to a losing course of action" or "throwing good money after bad."[34] A perfectly rational decision maker would consider the time and expenses already invested as "sunk costs." They aren't recoverable and shouldn't be considered in a decision about what to do. Only future costs and benefits should be considered. But this is difficult. Norms in our society and in our organizations support trying, persisting, and sticking with a course of action. Also, if others are involved, we're likely to feel the need to justify our original decision—whether it was to buy a car, a piece of equipment, or land.

One way to overcome escalation of commitment is, as with many biases, to recognize that it exists and try to adjust for it. Ask yourself explicit questions about whether you're committed to a decision just because failure would make your original decision look bad. Ask yourself, "If I took over the project today, with no personal investment, would I support the project?" Another approach is to bring in outsiders and ask for their opinions or turn the project over to them completely. That gets your own ego out of the decision-making process.

Thinking about Integrity

In Chapter 4, you were also advised to think about your own integrity—to ask yourself what a person of integrity in your moral community would do in the particular situation. But cognitive biases can get in the way here too. First, if your thoughts about yourself are controlled by illusion rather than reality, how can you make a good decision about your integrity? The basic idea here is that individuals prefer to think positively about themselves. They're likely to unconsciously filter and distort information in order to maintain the positive self image they prefer. Psychologists know that people have an illusion of superiority. Surveys have found that people tend to think of themselves as more ethical, fair, and honest than most other people.[35] It's obviously an illusion when the large majority of individuals claim to be more honest than the average person, or more ethical than their peers. It's a little like Garrison Keillor's mythical Lake Wobegon, where all the children are above average. There isn't a whole lot you can do here except to try to be honest with yourself.

Second, the virtue ethics approach suggests that you rely upon the ethics of your profession (or other relevant moral community) to guide you. But consider the accounting professionals in recent cases in which Arthur Andersen auditors signed off on audits that misrepresented the finances of companies such as Waste Management, Enron, and Adelphia Communications. Certified public accountants are supposed to be guided by the AICPA code of professional ethics. That code says that, as professionals, auditors have a responsibility to act in the public interest—be free of conflicts of interest, not misrepresent facts, or subordinate professional judgment to others. Given human cognitive limitations, however, this expectation is probably unrealistic. Consider what is likely to go through an auditor's mind when deciding whether to provide a negative audit opinion on the financial statements of a big client. Auditors work closely with their audit clients, often over a long period of time. By contrast, auditors have no personal relationship with the "public" they are supposed to represent. Therefore, as biased information processors, their thinking is likely to emphasize the potential negative consequences of a qualified (or negative) audit opinion for themselves and the client—not for the public. The negative consequences for themselves and the client are more clear and immediate. The auditor who offers a qualified audit may very well lose the client (and the money associated with that client) as well as the personal relationships forged over time. On the other hand, the consequences for the public of a qualified audit opinion are more ambiguous and likely spread over more people and time. It isn't clear how much specific members of the public will gain or lose, especially if the misrepresentation is deemed to be small or unclear. So auditors can easily rationalize a decision that is consistent with their own and their company's self-interest and downplay the potential consequences to an ambiguous, unknown public.[36]

What is a professional organization to do? It is important to recognize that auditors (and other professionals) are human beings who are affected by cognitive limitations and biases. Given what we know about these biases, here are some potential solutions. First, auditors should be discouraged from developing personal relationships or socializing with their clients. As some have proposed, companies should probably change auditors every few years to avoid forging such personal ties. Second, audit firms should work hard to sensitize auditors to the likely negative consequences of financial misrepresentation for their own firms and the public. The Enron bankruptcy contributed to huge financial losses to its employees and investors and to the ultimate demise of Arthur Andersen. Regular attention to the importance of maintaining the integrity and long-term reputation of the audit firm is key. The reward system (discussed more in Chapters 7 and 9) can be used to send important signals along these lines. For example, auditors who turn down client business or risk losing a client by providing a negative audit opinion should be supported and reinforced for doing so. Those auditors who risk the reputation of the firm should be disciplined.

Thinking about Your Gut

Our last piece of advice in Chapter 4 was to listen to your gut. But in this chapter, we've spent a great deal of time telling you that your gut may well be wrong—led by cognitive limitations and biased thinking.

Your gut can still be useful in alerting you that something might be wrong—that you're facing an ethical dilemma—in the first place. But once that decision is made, you should temper your gut with careful analysis guided by the knowledge gained in this chapter and the rest of the book. Hopefully, the combination of your gut and an informed brain will help you to make better decisions.

EMOTIONS IN ETHICAL DECISION MAKING

Finally, we should acknowledge the importance of emotions in ethical decision making.[37] People often decide to take action because they feel empathy, guilt, or anger, not because they have rationally decided on the best course of action. For example, consider how General Motors managers handled a four-year legal battle with VW over their allegation that a 56-year-old GM executive, Jose Lopez, took 20 boxes of GM proprietary documents when he left GM to join Volkswagen in 1993. In 1992, Lopez was GM's worldwide purchasing czar, known for his ability to cut costs ruthlessly. The missing documents included information about GM's suppliers and their prices for auto parts, as well as information about upcoming Opel car models in the GM Europe division. *Fortune* magazine referred to the four-year legal battle that ensued as a tale of "betrayal" and "revenge." Lou Hughes, head of GM Europe, was furious that Lopez would take proprietary documents to its fiercest competitor. He insisted that there would be no settlement with VW as long as Lopez remained there. When asked what he hoped to gain from the litigation, Hughes replied, "Look, this is not a question of business. This is a question of ethics."[38] Years of investigation yielded no hard evidence to suggest that anyone at VW had actually used the secret GM information. *Fortune* suggested that at the time, "one might have expected GM to act pragmatically, find some face-saving exit, and return its attention to the car business."[39] That might have been the "rational," cool-headed thing to do. Instead, GM escalated the fight, bringing a racketeering suit that was expected to drag on for years and cost tens of millions of dollars. When pragmatic board members questioned the action, the board chairman insisted that the company had to pursue the suit because it "had been terribly wronged." "Some things aren't measured in time and money. They're just who we are."[40] Finally, in January 1997, the two companies settled the case. Lopez, who had already resigned from Volkswagen, was barred from doing any work for VW through the year 2000. Volkswagen paid GM $100 million and agreed to buy $1 billion worth of GM parts over seven years. *Fortune* asked, "But what, in the end did the long, bitter, and costly struggle accomplish? In the cold light of day, the answer seems simple and shocking: not much."[41] A huge company devoted years of attention and spent millions of dollars because its managers were morally outraged that their former friend had betrayed them.

Clearly, anger and other emotions can influence thoughts and actions. Whether that is good or bad depends on whether the emotion leads to "right" or "wrong" action. If empathy or guilt lead you to think about the consequences of your actions for others, that's a good thing. If moral outrage leads you to seek justice, that's good as well. But moral outrage can also lead to a desire for revenge, and that may be the time to bring cooler heads to the decision. Those who are not as emotionally involved should be able to offer a more rational and more balanced assessment of the situation at hand. In the GM–Volkswagen case, those pragmatic board members may have been right to support a quick settlement of the case.

REFLECTIONS ON THE PINTO FIRES CASE

Dennis A. Gioia

The last chapter ended with a provocative case highlighting some of the sordid events in the history of the Pinto fires problem. As the authors have indicated in this chapter, I was involved with this infamous case in the early 1970s. They have asked me to reflect on lessons learned from my experience.

I take this case very personally, even though my name seldom comes up in its many recountings. I was one of those "faceless bureaucrats" who is often portrayed as making decisions without accountability and then walking away from them—even decisions with life-and-death implications. That characterization is, of course, far too stark and superficial. I certainly don't consider myself faceless, and I have always chafed at the label of bureaucrat as applied to me, even though I have found myself unfairly applying it to others. Furthermore, I have been unable to walk away from my decisions in this case. They have a tendency to haunt—especially when they have such public airings as those involved in the Pinto fires debacle have had.

But why revisit 20-year-old decisions, and why take them so personally? Here's why: because I was in a position to do something about a serious problem—and didn't. That simple observation gives me pause for personal reflection and also makes me think about the many difficulties people face in trying to be ethical decision makers in organizations. It also helps me to keep in mind the features of modern business and organizational life that would influence someone like me (me, of all people, who purposefully set out to be an ethical decision maker) to overlook basic moral issues in arriving at decisions that, when viewed retrospectively, look absurdly easy to make. But they are not easy to make, and that is perhaps the most important lesson of all.

The Personal Aspect

I would like to reflect on my own experience mainly to emphasize the personal dimensions involved in ethical decision making. Although I recognize that there are strong organizational influences at work as well, I would like to keep the critical lens focused for a moment on me (and you) as individuals. I believe that there are insights and lessons from my experience that can help you think about your own likely involvement in issues with ethical overtones.

First, however, a little personal background. In the late 1960s and early 1970s, I was an engineering/MBA student; I also was an "activist," engaged in protests of social injustice and the social irresponsibility of business, among other things. I held some pretty strong values that I thought would stand up to virtually any challenge and enable me to "do the right thing" when I took a career job. I suspect that most of you feel that you also have developed a strongly held value system that will enable you to resist organizational inducements to do something unethical. Perhaps. Unfortunately, the challenges do not often come in overt forms that shout the need for resistance or ethical righteousness. They are much more subtle than that, and thus doubly difficult to deal with because they do not make it easy to see that a situation you are confronting might actually involve an ethical dilemma.

After school, I got the job of my dreams with Ford and, predictably enough, ended up on the fast track to promotion. That fast track enabled me to progress quickly into positions of some notable responsibility. Within two years I became Ford's vehicle recall coordinator, with first-level responsibility for tracking field safety problems. It was the most intense, information-overloaded job you can imagine, frequently dealing with some of the most serious problems in the company. Disasters were a phone call away, and action was the hallmark of the office where I worked. We all knew we were engaged in serious business, and we all took the job seriously. There were no irresponsible bureaucratic ogres there, contrary to popular portrayal.

In this context, I first encountered the neophyte Pinto fires problem in the form of infrequent reports of cars erupting into horrendous fireballs in very low-speed crashes and the shuddering personal experience of inspecting a car that had burned, killing its trapped occupants. Over the space of a year, I had two distinct opportunities to initiate recall activities concerning the fuel tank problems, but on both occasions I voted not to recall, despite my activist history and advocacy of business social responsibility.

The key question is how, in the space of two short years, could I have engaged in a decision process that appeared to violate my own strong values—a decision process whose subsequent manifestations continue to be cited by many observers as a supposedly definitive study of corporate unethical behavior? I tend to discount the obvious accusations: that my values weren't really strongly held; that I had turned my back on my values in the interest of loyalty to Ford; that I was somehow intimidated into making decisions in the best interests of the company; that despite my principled statements I had not actually achieved a high stage of moral development, and so on. Instead, I believe a more plausible explanation for my own actions looks to the foibles of normal human information processing.

I would argue that the complexity and intensity of the recall coordinator's job required that I develop cognitive strategies for simplifying the overwhelming amount of information I had to deal with. The best way to do that is to structure the information into cognitive "schemas," or more specifically "script schemas," that guide understanding and action when facing common or repetitive situations. Scripts offer marvelous cognitive shortcuts because they allow you to act virtually unconsciously and automatically, and thus permit handling complicated situations without being paralyzed by needing to think consciously about every little thing. Such scripts enabled me to discern the characteristic hallmarks of problem cases likely to result in recall and to execute a complicated series of steps required to initiate a recall.

All of us structure information all of the time; we could hardly get through the workday without doing so. But there is a penalty to be paid for this wonderful cognitive efficiency: We do not give sufficient attention to important information that requires special treatment, because the general information pattern has surface appearances that indicate that automatic processing will suffice. That, I think, is what happened to me. The beginning stages of the Pinto case looked for all the world like a normal sort of problem. Lurking beneath the cognitive veneer, however, was a nasty set of circumstances waiting to conspire into a dangerous situation. Despite the awful nature of the accidents, the Pinto problem did not fit an existing script; the accidents were relatively rare by recall standards, and the accidents were not initially traceable to a specific component failure. Even when a failure mode suggesting a design flaw was identified, the cars did not perform significantly worse in crash tests than competitor vehicles. One might easily argue that I should have been jolted out of my script by the unusual nature of the accidents (very low speed, otherwise unharmed passengers trapped in a horrific fire), but those facts did not penetrate a script cued for other features. (It also is difficult to convey to the layperson that bad accidents are not a particularly unusual feature of the recall coordinator's information field. Accident severity is not necessarily a recall cue; frequently repeated patterns and identifiable causes are.)

The Corporate Milieu

In addition to the personalized scripting of information processing, there is another important influence on the decisions that led to the Pinto fires mess: the fact that decisions are made by individuals working within a corporate context. It has escaped almost no one's notice that the decisions made by corporate employees tend to be in the best interest of the corporation, even by people who mean to do better. Why? Because socialization processes and the overriding influence of organizational culture provide a strong, if generally subtle, context for defining appropriate ways of seeing and understanding. Because organizational culture can be viewed as a collection of scripts, scripted information processing relates even to organizational-level considerations. Scripts are context bound; they are not free-floating general cognitive structures that apply universally. They are tailored to specific contexts. And there are few more potent contexts than organizational settings.

There is no question that my perspective changed after joining Ford. In retrospect, I would be very surprised if it hadn't. In my former incarnation as a social activist, I had internalized values for doing what was right, as I understood rightness in grand terms; but I had not internalized a script for applying my values in a pragmatic business context. Ford and the recall coordinator role provided a powerful context for developing scripts—scripts that were inevitably and undeniably oriented toward ways of making sense that were influenced by the corporate and industry culture.

I wanted to do a good job, and I wanted to do what was right. Those are not mutually exclusive desires, but the corporate context affects their synthesis. I came to accept the idea that it was not feasible to fix everything that someone might construe as a problem. I therefore shifted to a value of wanting to do the greatest good for the greatest number (an ethical value tempered by the practical constraints of an economic enterprise). Doing the greatest good for the greatest number meant working with intensity and responsibility on those problems that would spare the most people from injury. It also meant developing scripts that responded to typical problems, not odd patterns like those presented by the Pinto.

Another way of noting how the organizational context so strongly affects individuals is to recognize that one's personal identity becomes heavily influenced by corporate identity. As a student, my identity centered on being a "good person" (with a certain dose of moral righteousness associated with it). As recall coordinator, my identity shifted to a more corporate definition. This is an extraordinarily important point, especially for students who have not yet held a permanent job role, and I would like to emphasize it. Before assuming your career role, identity derives mainly from social relationships. Upon putting on the mantle of a profession or a responsible position, identity begins to align with your role. And information processing perspective follows from that identity.

I remember accepting the portrayal of the auto industry and Ford as "under attack" from many quarters (oil crises, burgeoning government regulation, inflation, litigious customers, etc). As we know, groups under assault develop into more cohesive communities that emphasize commonalities and shared identities. I was by then an insider in the industry and the company, sharing some of their beleaguered perceptions that there were significant forces arrayed against us and that the well being of the company might be threatened.

What happened to the original perception that Ford was a socially irresponsible giant that needed a comeuppance? Well, it looks different from the inside. Over time, a reasonable value for action against corporate dominance became tempered by another reasonable value that corporations serve social needs and are not automatically the villains of society. I saw a need for balance among multiple values, and, as a result, my identity shifted in degrees toward a more corporate identity.

The Torch Passes to You

So, given my experiences, what would I recommend to you, as a budding organizational decision maker? I have some strong opinions. First, develop your ethical base now! Too many people do not give serious attention to assessing and articulating their own values. People simply do not know what they stand for because they haven't thought about it seriously. Even the ethical scenarios presented in classes or executive programs are treated as interesting little games without apparent implications for deciding how you intend to think or act. These exercises should be used to develop a principled, personal code that you will try to live by. Consciously decide your values. If you don't decide your values now, you are easy prey for others who will gladly decide them for you or influence you implicitly to accept theirs.

Second, recognize that everyone, including you, is an unwitting victim of his or her own cognitive structuring. Many people are surprised and fascinated to learn that they use schemas and scripts to understand and act in the organizational world. The idea that we automatically process so much information so much of the time intrigues us. Indeed, we would all turn into blithering idiots if we did not structure information and expectations, but that very structuring hides information that might be important—information that could require you to confront your values. We get lulled into thinking that automatic information processing is great stuff that obviates the necessity for trying to resolve so many frustrating decisional dilemmas.

Actually, I think too much ethical training focuses on supplying standards for contemplating dilemmas. The far greater problem, as I see it, is recognizing that a dilemma exists in the first place. The insidious problem of people not being aware that they are dealing with a situation that might have ethical overtones is another consequence of schema usage. I would venture that scripted routines seldom include ethical dimensions. Is a person behaving unethically if the situation is not even construed as having ethical implications? People are not necessarily stupid, ill-intentioned, or Machiavellian, but they are often unaware. They do indeed spend much of their time cruising on automatic, but the true hallmark of human information processing is the ability to switch from automatic to controlled information processing. What we really need to do is to encourage people to recognize cues that build a "Now Think!" step into their scripts—waving red flags at yourself, so to speak—even though you are engaged in essentially automatic cognition and action.

Third, because scripts are context-bound and organizations are potent contexts, be aware of how strongly, yet how subtly, your job role and your organizational culture affect the ways you interpret and make sense of information (and thus affect the ways you develop the scripts that will guide you in unguarded moments). Organizational culture has a much greater effect on individual cognition than you would ever suspect (see Chapter 9).

Last, be prepared to face critical responsibility at a relatively young age, as I did. You need to know what your values are and you need to know how you think so that you can know how to make a good decision. Before you can do that, you need to articulate and affirm your values now, before you enter the fray. I wasn't really ready. Are you?

For a more thorough description and analysis of Dennis Gioia's experiences, see his 1992 article "Pinto fires and personal ethics: A script analysis of missed opportunities," *Journal of Business Ethics* 11(5,6): 379–389.

CONCLUSION

This chapter has introduced you to individual differences that can influence ethical decision making. The chapter has also outlined the cognitive limitations and biases that can interfere with good ethical decision making. Hopefully, knowing about these and how they can be overcome will help you to be a better individual decision maker. Much of the remainder of the book will move beyond this individual focus to look at the group and organizational influences that can have a profound influence on your decisions and actions.

DISCUSSION QUESTIONS

(Note that these questions apply to Gioia's "Reflections" as well as the rest of the chapter.)

1. Steven F. Goldstone,[42] chairman and CEO of RJR Nabisco (one of the four biggest U.S. cigarette manufacturers), said in a magazine interview, "I have no moral view of this business … I viewed it as a legal business. You shouldn't be drawing a moral judgment about a business our country says is perfectly legal and is taxed like crazy by it."[43] Think about Goldstone's statement in terms of moral awareness. What might happen if he began thinking about his business in moral, and not just legal, terms?
2. Evaluate yourself in terms of cognitive moral development and locus of control. What does this tell you about your own ethical decision making? Do the same for someone you know well.
3. Identify a situation in which you have used script processing in a work or other life situation.
4. What does it mean to say that everyone is a victim of his or her cognitive structures? Think about cognitive moral development, locus of control, and Gioia's actions in the Pinto fires case.
5. Do you believe that scripts can override one's value system?
6. Answer the question posed in Gioia's Reflections: Is a person behaving unethically if the situation was not even construed in ethical terms—if there was no moral awareness?
7. What does it mean to say that organizational culture is a collection of scripts?
8. Who should make the decision about taking risks with others' lives in designing products?
9. Should a person be permitted to place a value on a human life? Should a company? Should the government? If not, how would decisions be made about whether to market certain products (that might be risky for some, but helpful for others), how much those who have lost family members in disasters should be compensated, and so on?
10. How do you feel about the use of cost/benefit analysis where human life is part of the cost calculation? Might the infusion of moral language have changed the decision makers' thinking? For example, what if decision makers had talked about their responsibility for killing 180 human beings?
11. Given that all automobiles are unsafe to some degree, where do you draw the line on product safety? How safe is safe enough—and who decides?

SHORT CASE

Mary, the director of nursing at a regional blood bank, is concerned about the declining number of blood donors. It's May, and Mary knows that the approaching summer will mean increased demands for blood and decreased supplies, especially of rare blood types. She is excited, therefore, when a large corporation offers to host a series of blood drives at all of its locations, beginning at corporate headquarters. Soon after Mary and her staff arrive at the corporate site, Mary hears a disturbance. Apparently, a nurse named Peggy was drawing blood from a male donor with a very rare blood type when the donor fondled her breast. Peggy jumped back and began to cry. Joe, a male colleague, sprang to Peggy's defense and told the donor to leave the premises. To Mary's horror, the male donor was a senior manager with the corporation. What is the ethical dilemma in this case, and what values are in conflict? How should Mary deal with Peggy, Joe, the donor, and representatives of the corporation?

NOTES

1. Butterfield, K., Treviño, L. K., and Weaver, G. R. 2000. Moral awareness in business organizations: Influences of issue-related and social context factors. *Human Relations* 53(7): 981–1018.
2. Fiske, S. T., and Taylor, S. E. 1991. *Social cognition.* 2nd ed. New York: McGraw-Hill.
3. Jones, T. M. 1991. Ethical decision making by individuals in organizations: An issue-contingent model. *Academy of Management Review* 16: 366–395.
4. Kohlberg, L. 1969. Stage and sequence: The cognitive-developmental approach to socialization. In *Handbook of socialization theory and research,* edited by D. A. Goslin. New York: Rand McNally, 347–380.
5. Rest, M. 1986. *Moral development: Advances in research and theory.* New York: Praeger.
6. Treviño, L. K., and Youngblood, S. A. 1990. Bad apples in bad barrels: A causal analysis of ethical decision-making behavior. *Journal of Applied Psychology* 75 (4): 378–385.
7. Weber, J. 1988. The relationship between managerial value orientations and stages of moral development: Theory development and empirical investigation with behavioral implications. Unpublished dissertation, The University of Pittsburgh.
8. Gilligan, C. 1982. *In a different voice.* Cambridge: Harvard University Press.
9. Gilligan, C., and Attanuci, J. 1988. Two moral orientations. In *Mapping the moral domain,* edited by C. Gilligan, J. V. Ward, and J. M. Taylor. Cambridge: Harvard University Press, 73–86.
10. Derry, R. 1987. Moral reasoning in work-related conflicts. *Research in Corporate Social Performance and Policy* 9: 25–50.
11. Rest, M. 1986. *Moral development; Advances in research and theory.* New York: Praeger.
12. Ambrose, M.L. and Schminke, M. 1999. Sex differences in business ethics: The importance of perceptions. *Journal of Managerial Issues,* 11(4): 454–474.
13. Ibid.
14. This phrase was used with different meaning by R. Jackall in *Moral Mazes* (Oxford University Press).
15. Treviño, L. K. 1992. Moral reasoning and business ethics. *Journal of Business Ethics* 11: 445–459.
16. Dukerich, J., Nichols, M. L., Elm, D. R., and Vollrath, D. A. 1990. Moral reasoning in groups: Leaders make a difference. *Human Relations* 43: 473–493.
17. Treviño, L. K. 1992. Moral reasoning and business ethics. *Journal of Business Ethics* 11: 445–459.
18. Rotter, J. B. 1966. Generalized expectancies for internal versus external control of reinforcement. *Psychological Monographs: General and Applied* 80:1–28.
19. Midlarski, E. 1971. Aiding under stress: the effects of competence, dependency, visibility, and fatalism. *Journal of Personality* 39: 132–149. Midlarski, E., and Midlarski, M. 1973. Some determinants of aiding under experimentally induced stress. *Journal of Personality* 41: 305–327. Ubbink,

E. M., and Sadava, S. W. 1974. Rotter's generalized expectancies as predictors of helping behavior. *Psychological Reports* 35: 865–866.
20. Johnson, R. C., Ackerman, J. M., Frank, H., and Fionda, A. J. 1968. Resistance to temptation and guilt following yielding and psychotherapy. *Journal of Consulting and Clinical Psychology* 32: 169–175.
21. Propst, L. R. 1979. Efforts of personality and loss of anonymity on aggression: A re-evaluation of deindividuation. *Journal of Personality* 47: 531–545.
22. Bazerman, M. H. 1994. *Judgment in managerial decision making.* New York: John Wiley & Sons.
23. Messick, D. M., and Bazerman, M. 1994. Ethics for the 21st century: A decision-making perspective. Unpublished manuscript. The International Consortium for Executive Development Research.
24. Gioia, D. 1992. Pinto fires and personal ethics: A script analysis of missed opportunities. *Journal of Business Ethics* 11(5,6): 379–389.
25. Ibid.
26. Ibid.
27. Messick and Bazerman, Ethics for the 21st century.
28. Bazerman, *Judgment in managerial decision making.*
29. Messick and Bazerman, Ethics for the 21st century.
30. Ibid.
31. Loewenstein, G. 1996. Behavioral decision theory and business ethics: Skewed trade-offs between self and other. In *Codes of conduct: Behavioral research into business ethics,* edited by D. M. Messick and A. E. Tenbrunsel. NY: Russell Sage Foundation.
32. Messick and Bazerman, Ethics for the 21st century.
33. Ibid.
34. Staw, B. M., and Ross, I. 1987. Understanding escalation situations. In *Research in Organizational Behavior,* Vol. 9, edited by B. M. Staw and L. L. Cummings. Greenwich, CT: JAI Press.
35. Messick and Bazerman, Ethics for the 21st century.
36. Loewenstein, G. 1996. Behavioral decision theory and business ethics: Skewed trade-offs between self and other. In *Codes of conduct: Behavioral research into business ethics,* edited by D. M. Messick and A. E. Tenbrunsel. NY: Russell Sage Foundation.
37. Eisenberg, N. Emotion, regulation, and moral development. 2000. *Annual Review of Psychology* 51: 665–697. Gaudine, A. and Thorne, L. 2001. Emotion and ethical decision making in organizations. *Journal of Business Ethics* 31(2): 175–187.
38. Elkind, P. 1997. Blood feud. *Fortune,* April 14: 90–102.
39. Ibid.
40. Ibid.
41. Ibid.
42. Goldberg, J. 1998. Big tobacco's endgame. *New York Times Magazine,* June 21: 36–42, 58–60.
43. Ibid.

ETHICAL RESPONSIBILITIES OF MANAGERS I

CHAPTER **6**

ETHICAL PROBLEMS OF MANAGERS

INTRODUCTION

Ethical issues for individual employees and managers are very different, since managers are responsible for the entire range of human resources activities such as hiring, firing, disciplining, and evaluating performance. Also, since managers are responsible for employee supervision, the courts can hold them accountable for the activities and behavior of the people who report to them. Finally, because managers are role models for the workers in their department, it's critical that managers be able to discuss the ethical implications of decision making and provide advice to employees who find themselves in an ethical quandary. These facts of corporate life have frustrated many managers. "How can I possibly manage the ethics or morality of the people I manage? Is it even possible to manage ethics? Where are the special pitfalls for me as a manager?" In this chapter, we're going to examine what responsibilities managers have and how you as a manager can influence your direct reports to make ethical decisions.

MANAGING THE "BASICS"

A manager brings new people into the organization and determines employee work assignments once employees are on the job. The new people may be permanent employees or they may be part-time employees, temporary workers, or consultants. Perhaps there's never been more competition to hire and retain qualified workers than in today's marketplace. The result: Managers need to be proficient at hiring the best people, evaluating their performance, disciplining them, and even terminating a worker who is an unsatisfactory performer.

Hiring and Work Assignments

> **HIRING CASE #1**
>
> After two years of complex negotiations and hand-holding, your bank has finally signed Big Holding Co. as a client. Big Holding has three main divisions: a chemicals business in Louisiana, a heavy-equipment division outside

of Cleveland, and an agricultural business in Iowa. Since the business is so enormous, you assign three junior employees to the company—one employee per division. Jim Patterson, a talented chemical engineer, will head the effort for the chemicals business. When you and your three employees meet with the senior management team from Big Holding to plot long-term strategy, the chief financial officer pulls you aside to chat. "You shouldn't send Jim to Louisiana," he says. "There have been numerous violent incidents there involving people of his race, and I would be afraid for his safety. Why don't you assign him to one of the other divisions and send someone else down South?"

HIRING CASE #2

You're planning to hire a new sales manager and the most promising candidate is really homely. You are concerned about how your customers—and even his colleagues—would react to him. The specific job he's applying for requires extensive customer contact, and his appearance is frankly disconcerting. On the other hand, his credentials are excellent and he's certainly qualified for the job.

Federal law prohibits discrimination based on race, religion, sex, color, ethnic background, and age, and it protects those who are pregnant or handicapped. In the first example above, which involves an African-American male, the correct answer is not as clear-cut as it may appear. The worker is certainly qualified for the job—and he should be given the opportunity to be assigned to the part of the business he seems most qualified to manage. Although federal legislation supposedly protects him from discrimination, the element of danger in this case caused at least one company to reassign an employee in a very similar case; and the young man, one of the organization's brightest stars, left in a matter of weeks.

Another solution might have been to give the employee the choice of whether to go or accept another assignment. Many senior managers who have reviewed this case have suggested that one way to handle this situation may be to say, "Here are the facts as I know them—and it's your decision. I'll support whatever you decide." Other managers have suggested doing some research to determine whether your customer is honestly relating a troublesome situation or is actually discriminating against one of your employees. Or perhaps there is another agenda of which you are unaware. Whatever your customer's reasons, some prudent research might give you a better understanding of his motivations.

In the second example, which involves a homely candidate, the solution is even more ambiguous. He is certainly qualified for the job, and unattractive looks are not included in protectionist handicapped legislation. But the larger issue is, what qualities should determine whether or not an individual should be hired?

All protectionist legislation points to the answer, as does the concept of fairness. Hiring, promotions, and terminations should be based on ability, period. However, it's one thing to ignore someone because of your own prejudice and quite another to hesitate to put someone in a situation where he or she might suffer discrimination from an external audience, such as your customers, that's out of your control. It's difficult to say whether you're doing someone a favor by setting him or her up for possible failure in an environment that's hostile.

Prejudice is difficult to overcome. Everyone has biases: Some people don't like very tall people, or very short people, or fat ones, or skinny ones, or old ones, or young ones. Others have biases against brown eyes, or blue eyes, or eyes with wrinkles, or big noses, or aquiline noses, or balding heads, or hair that appears to be too long. Some people like individuals from certain schools or from particular parts of the country. What if someone interviews for a job and, as in this case, he is just plain unattractive, or she's deaf, or he had cancer three years ago, or she speaks English with an accent? Do those qualities have anything to do with an ability to do the job, or with talent?

Some employers have a "corporate profile" in mind when they hire, especially when they're trying to fill positions with "extensive public contact." Some large *Fortune* 100 companies are well known for their penchant for hiring certain types of employees. They look for healthy, young people with regular features, moderate height, a medium build, and no discernible accent. Do employers with a conscious or subconscious "corporate profile" think that the public or their customers are somehow homogeneous? If history had used a "corporate profile" as a yardstick, Abraham Lincoln, Benjamin Franklin, Marian Anderson, Albert Einstein, Sammy Davis, Jr., and Franklin Roosevelt may have been relegated to positions with "no public contact."

Talent and ability come in a variety of packages. When managers use anything other than those two factors to evaluate qualifications for hiring, promotions, or work assignments, they shortchange not only the individual but also their employer. They also help to perpetuate stereotypes, instead of trying to build a workforce that reflects real life.

Performance Evaluation

> You were recently promoted to manager of a department with five professionals and two clerical staff. One of the professionals, Joe, is a nice guy, but he simply hasn't been able to match the performance of the others in the department. When he tells you he has been interviewing for another job in a different part of your company, you pull his personnel file and see that your predecessor had rated Joe's performance as "good to excellent." You frankly disagree. Joe has asked you for a recommendation. Based on the written appraisals, you could give him a good one—but your personal observation is at odds with the written evaluations. Joe's prospective manager—your peer in another department—asks for your opinion. What do you say?

When we talk about performance evaluation, we're really talking about two things. First, there's a written assessment of an employee's performance. Most large companies have a formal performance management system, with forms to standardize the process, and a mandate to complete a written evaluation on every employee usually once each year. These written appraisals usually have some influence on any salary adjustments, and they usually become part of the employee's permanent personnel file. Second, there's the informal process of performance evaluation that ideally is an ongoing process throughout the year. When a manager gives continuous feedback—when objectives are stated and then performance against those objectives is measured—employees generally aren't surprised by the annual written performance appraisal.

Why is continuous evaluation important? A training manager in New York City tells a story about the importance of accurately and continuously appraising performance. "Imagine you're bowling," he says. "A bed sheet is stretched across the lane and you can't see what you're doing. Your manager is the only person who can tell you how you're doing. What would happen if your manager told you how you were doing only occasionally or once a year? How would your performance be affected if he or she told you about your performance only when you got gutter balls? What would happen if he or she commented just when you did well?" It's only when your manager gives you consistent feedback—reflecting the complete range of your behavior—that you can improve your performance.

The problem with performance evaluation is that most managers hate to do it. It's certainly easier to recognize an employee's achievements than his or her shortcomings, but many managers are so busy that they forget to recognize either. Pointing out an employee's deficient performance is extremely difficult for most managers. It's such a thorny issue that in a survey of 4,000 *Fortune* 500 executives, five out of seven executives said that they would rather lie to employees about performance than confront them about performance problems.[1]

In the last example, you as the manager think Joe has been inaccurately (and perhaps even dishonestly) evaluated in the past. Since most employers require a rating of "good" or "satisfactory" before an employee can transfer to another job, you will probably feel pressure to supply such a recommendation so Joe can qualify for the transfer. This is a common problem. Many organizations have employees like Joe, who are less than stellar performers but who are never confronted with their poor performance. In Joe's company, no manager has been brave enough to bite the bullet and either try to get Joe to improve his performance or initiate the termination process. It's easier to pass Joe along to someone else—to turn him into a Ping-Pong ball, bouncing from department to department, never really improving his performance because no one will confront him with the truth. And because his written appraisals have been less than honest, prospective managers get buffaloed into thinking Joe's performance is adequate. It's a vicious cycle and a real disservice to the employee, his or her coworkers, and the organization. Coworkers who are doing a good job can get discouraged if someone like Joe is getting a rating similar to theirs for inferior work. And perhaps the party most disadvantaged by this kind of problem is the organization. Joe's manager has sent the message that "not very good" is good enough. And that's a message that erodes organizational efforts around quality, and integrity, and ethics.

One good way to ensure continuous performance evaluation is to establish a formal system with the employees who report to you, whether or not your company requires it, and certainly more often than once each year. Meet with every employee and jointly agree to job objectives and how to measure success for each objective.

Make sure that the goals for your department goals are directly linked to corporate goals and that the individual goals of the people who report to you are directly linked to your department goals. Establish a clear line of sight between the goals of individuals and the organization and between the results of the organization and the individual. Then meet monthly with each employee and discuss how the employee is meeting his or her objectives. When objectives and measurement standards are established in advance and progress is tracked, it's much easier for employees to perform. They know what the target looks like, how to get there, and how they'll know when they've met it. They will understand and internalize what it means to create value. An ongoing process eliminates the need to blast a nonperformer once a year and can greatly reduce misunderstanding, resentment, and charges of discrimination or bias.

Probably the best way to handle the situation with Joe is to be honest with him. "I can't write you the kind of letter you want for the following reasons. [Spell out the performance problems.] We can either wait until you get your performance on track, or I can write you a letter that reflects my honest evaluation of your work at this time. It's your decision."

Discipline

> Steven is a salesman who reports to you, the regional director of sales for an office supply company. He has a great track record and has consistently surpassed his sales targets, but he has one terrible flaw: He's not on time for anything. He's late both for meetings with you and for lunches with clients, and the problem extends to his paperwork. His expense reports, sales reports—everything is handed in a week late. As his manager, you've counseled him about his tardiness, and he has improved. Now instead of being 15 minutes late for a meeting, he's only five minutes late. And instead of submitting his expenses a week late, they're only two days late. His lateness seems minor in view of his achievements, but it's driving you and his coworkers crazy.

Most managers view disciplining employees as something to be postponed for as long as possible. Many people in a work environment try to ignore a worker's shortcomings in the hope that the situation will improve. Discipline, however, is important for a number of reasons: not only to ensure worker productivity, but also to set the standard that certain behaviors are expected from all employees, and to meet the requirements of the U.S. Sentencing Guidelines. As we discussed in Chapter 2, the Sentencing Guidelines specify that all employees in an organization must receive consistent discipline for similar infractions. For example, in the case of employee theft, a secretary and a senior vice president must be treated in the same way. The guidelines are violated if people in different job classifications are treated differently—if one receives a slap on the wrist and the other is suspended or fired.

In the case of Steven, the salesman who is always late, you as a manager could be tempted to view disciplining his lateness as nit-picking. He's a star after all, right? However, to expect promptness from all of your other employees and not from Steven is unrealistic and unfair.

Research has given us clues about the most effective ways to discipline employees. First, the discipline must be constructive and done in a professional manner. For example, although you might be tempted to scream at Steven and call him a jerk, that's not going to change his behavior. It's much more effective to meet with him, explain the consequences of his lateness, and focus the discussion on his behavior, not on him personally.

Second, the discipline should be done privately. Employees should never be criticized in front of other employees. It's just as embarrassing as being criticized in public by your parent or your spouse, and it encourages nothing but hard feelings. Those discussions should always be held behind closed doors.

Third, employees should have input into the process and be encouraged to explain their side of the story. The entire idea of "team" management revolves around individuals being encouraged to share their view of a situation. The real problem may not be with the particular employee you want to discipline. Steven, for example, may be late with reports because people are late in submitting data to him. To solve problems at the simplest point, it's wise to ask for an employee's explanation.

Finally, discipline should be appropriately harsh and consistent with what other employees have received for similar offenses. This aspect of discipline is perhaps the most important in terms of ensuring good performance in the future.[2]

For example, a highly respected financial professional (let's call her Beth) was fired from her position at a large financial services company for providing an inaccurate calculation in a report to senior management. The director of human resources had given Beth an almost-impossible assignment: to use a new formula to calculate the company's pension obligations on all current employees. The assignment was given at 6:00 P.M. on a Tuesday, and the report needed to be written, typed, and copied for a senior management meeting the next morning at 9:00 A.M. Beth and her secretary stayed at the office all night long, doing calculations, writing the report, and finally preparing it for the meeting the next morning. When one of the senior managers discovered an error in one of the complex calculations, Beth was summarily fired by the human resources director. It sent a huge message, not only to Beth, but to the entire human resources department. Other mistakes had been made—even by the director—and if those errors had been punished, it had been with a reprimand, certainly not a firing. And, of course, the impossible deadline constituted an extenuating circumstance in everyone's opinion except the director. The effects of unreasonable discipline are far reaching, and that's why discipline needs to be appropriate to the offense and consistent with what others have received. In the case of Steven, the tardy salesman, unless you're willing to be consistent and accept tardiness in all other employees, his behavior needs to be addressed. Just don't follow the example of the human resources director—she had been placed in the role as part of her company's grooming process of high-potential executives. If she had succeeded, she surely would have moved on to bigger and better things. However, the executive team viewed her behavior with Beth and others as erratic and ill advised. She left human resources after a few years and ended up in a senior marketing role somewhere in one of the company's subsidiaries—not in the enterprise-wide role she had been on track for before the debacle.

Terminations

> You're a manager in a large commercial bank. You discover that Patricia, a loan officer who reports to you, has forged an approval signature on a customer loan, which requires signatures from two loan officers. When you confront Pat with the forgery, she apologizes profusely and says that her husband has been very ill. The day she forged the signature, he was going into surgery and she just didn't have time to find another loan officer to sign the authorization for the loan. Pat has been with your bank for 15 years and has a spotless record.

Terminations come in many varieties, none of them pleasant. There are terminations for cause—meaning that an individual has committed an offense that can result in instant firing. "Cause" can represent different things to different companies, but generally theft, assault, cheating on expense reports, forgery, fraud, and gross insubordination (including lying about a business matter) are considered to be "cause" in most organizations. Many companies define "cause" in their employee handbooks.

In the case above, Patricia will most likely be fired for cause. In banking, there are few things as sacred as a signature, and a professional with 15 years of banking experience would certainly be expected to know this. Forgery of any kind cannot be tolerated in a financial institution. It's a sad case and any manager would feel compassion for Patricia. However, some offenses are unpardonable in a financial institution, and this is probably one of them.

There are also terminations for poor performance. This type of firing is most often based on written documentation such as performance appraisals and attendance records. Many employers have a formal system of warnings that will occur before someone is actually terminated for poor performance. A verbal warning is usually the first step in the process, followed by a written warning, and then termination. The process can differ from company to company.

Then there's downsizing or layoffs. Layoffs can result from many kinds of reorganizations such as mergers, acquisitions, and relocations, or they can be the result of economic reasons or changes in business strategy. A layoff can result from a decision to trim staff in one department or from a decision to reduce head count across the company. Whatever the reason, layoffs are painful, not only for the person losing his or her job but also for the coworkers who'll be left behind. Coworkers tend to display several reactions: They exhibit low morale; they become less productive; they distrust management; and they become extremely cautious.[3]

In addition, layoff survivors are generally very concerned about the fairness of the layoff. They need to feel that the downsizing was necessary for legitimate business reasons; that it was conducted in a way that was consistent with the corporate culture; that layoff victims received ample notice; and that the victims were treated with dignity and respect. If management provided "a clear and adequate explanation of the reasons for the layoffs," survivors will be more likely to view the layoffs as being fair.[4] These are just a few reasons why layoffs have to be handled well.

Whatever the reason for a termination, you can take certain steps as a manager to make it easier for the employee being terminated and for yourself.[5] Again, the main goals are to be fair and to allow the employee to maintain personal dignity.

1. Do your homework before you meet with the employee. Prepare a brief explanation of why this termination is necessary and have ready an explanation of the severance package being offered to this employee, including financial and benefits arrangements. It's also helpful to check the calendar and consult with your company's public relations department to ensure you're not firing someone on his birthday or on the day she receives recognition from an industry group or professional association.
2. If at all possible, you should arrange to have an outplacement counselor or human resources professional on hand to meet with the employee after you have spoken to him or her. Most outplacement counselors advise managers to give the bad news to terminated employees early in the day and early in the week, if possible. This gives the employee time to meet with a counselor if necessary. (Obviously, this advice doesn't apply to employees who are fired for cause.)
3. It's generally a good idea to terminate someone on neutral ground, in a conference room for example, rather than in your office. In that way, you can leave if the situation becomes confrontational. If possible, try to assess what the employee's reaction might be. If you're about to fire a violent person for cause (like assaulting a coworker), you might want to have security nearby when you deliver the news.
4. Speak privately with each individual and deliver the news face-to-face, not by e-mail, telephone, or in a meeting or other kind of public forum. When you deliver the news, be objective, don't be in any way abusive, be compassionate, do it quickly (if possible), and never, never get personal.
5. Finally, keep all information about the termination private. Never discuss the reasons for a firing with anyone who doesn't have a need to know. The exception to this advice is when numerous layoffs occur. Survivors—coworkers who are left behind—will require some explanation of why layoffs were needed. In this case, you might want to speak about the business reasons for why the layoff was necessary. Never explain why particular individuals were involved and others weren't. (For more information on downsizing, see Chapter 8.)

Terminations for cause don't go unnoticed, and the employee grapevine will assuredly carry the news of a termination around your organization. That's a good thing because it's important for employees to understand that bad acts get punished. However, it's generally improper to publicly explain why an individual has been punished; the primary objective is to protect the dignity and privacy of the person who has been punished.

WHY ARE THESE ETHICAL PROBLEMS? Hiring, performance evaluation, discipline, and terminations can be ethical issues because they all involve honesty, fairness, and the dignity of the individual. Rice and Dreilinger[6] say that the desire for justice is a "fundamental human characteristic. People want to believe that the world operates on the principles of fairness; they react strongly when that belief is violated."

In fact, the majority of calls to corporate ethics hotlines (discussed more fully in Chapter 10) relate to precisely these types of issues.

COSTS Much federal legislation exists to protect the rights of individuals in situations that involve hiring, performance evaluation, discipline, and terminations. There are myriad legal remedies for employees who feel they have suffered discrimination. (See Discrimination Costs in Chapter 3 for more details.) In response to increased litigation, employment practice liability insurance is a hot product among corporations. This insurance covers organizations that are sued by employees over charges such as harassment, discrimination, or wrongful discharge. The insurance, which was virtually unheard of ten years ago, has been purchased by many *Fortune* 500 companies. This is surely the result of the huge increase in litigation and in settlements. The Equal Employment Opportunity Commission received 15,475 sexual harassment complaints in 2002, up from 6,883 in 1991. Also, the monetary benefits—excluding such benefits that resulted from litigation—jumped from under $12 million in 1991 to more than $53 million in 2001. As of 1998, the record amount paid in an EEOC case was $10 million, up from $1.3 million just two years earlier.[7]

In addition to perhaps paying legal costs and fines, organizations that have been charged with discrimination can also expect to pay a price in terms of employee morale and organizational reputation. Research evidence indicates that employees who perceive that they have been unfairly treated are less satisfied, less likely to go the extra mile, and more likely to steal from the organization.[8]

MANAGING A DIVERSE WORKFORCE

Experts predict that the workforce is becoming more diverse and that the key to many managers' success will be how well they can persuade diverse groups to sing together as a well-tuned chorus. Companies that best address the needs of a diverse population will probably be in a better position to succeed than companies that ignore this new reality. The result: Managers need to be able to deal with individuals of both sexes and all ages, races, religions, and ethnic groups. Managers need not only to have this ability themselves, but also to encourage this ability in team members. Managers must become "conductors" who orchestrate team performance—sometimes teaching, sometimes coaching, always communicating with employees and empowering them to learn and make good decisions.

The second skill set required of the new manager involves positively influencing the relationships among other team members and creating an ethical work environment that enhances individual productivity. Everyone we work with has a range of issues that could affect the ability to perform well. Many people are responsible for children, parents, or other relatives. Many workers have chronic illnesses or conditions or allergies; and those workers who are lucky not to have a chronic condition can suddenly become ill or injured. Other employees have chemical dependencies, such as an addiction to drugs or alcohol. Managers need to be able to accomplish tasks and the mission of a department or team in spite of the often painful events and conditions that can distract team members.

Since a bias-free person hasn't been born yet, managers also have to be able to counsel team members in their relationships with one another. Because every team will include a wide range of personalities, a manager frequently needs to be a referee: mediating and resolving disputes, assigning tasks to the workers who can best accomplish them, and ensuring that fairness is built into the working relationships of team members.

The examples that follow are similar to those in Chapter 3, but are presented from the perspective of the manager rather than the individual. And, as we said earlier in this chapter, managers have a different level of responsibility.

Diversity

> One of your best customers is a very conservative organization—a real "white-shirt' company. Reporting to you is David, a very talented African American who could benefit greatly from working with this customer account—and the customer account would benefit greatly from David's expertise and creativity. The issue is that David dresses in vibrant colors and wears a *kufi,* an African skullcap. Your company long ago recognized David's brilliance, and his dress within the company isn't an issue. But you know your customer would react to David's attire with raised eyebrows.

WHAT IS IT? A diverse workforce consists of individuals of both sexes and myriad races, ethnic groups, and religions. The role of a manager is to create an environment in which the contribution of each individual can be maximized. Since the population of the United States is remarkably diverse, it makes perfect sense to believe that products and services offered to this population should be developed, produced, and marketed by a diverse workforce.

The danger of ignoring this diversity was illustrated during an interview with a chemical company executive. One of the company's products is wallpaper. Even though the wallpaper was of a very high quality and priced competitively, sales were down. This was even more of a mystery since home repairs and renovations, especially by do-it-yourself decorators, were at record numbers.

Baffled by the problem, several senior marketing managers conducted customer surveys and found that the patterns of the company's wallpaper were the problem. Consumers viewed the patterns and styles as being outdated and old-fashioned. The managers then investigated the process the company used to select patterns and styles. What kind of market research was performed before patterns were selected for the next season?

They discovered that even though female consumers made more than 90 percent of all wallpaper purchases, there were no women on the team of chemical company employees who selected patterns for production. All style decisions were made by male employees. The marketing managers and other executives insisted that women and other diverse voices be included on the selection committee. The results were immediate. As soon as the new styles of wallpaper appeared in stores, sales increased substantially.

In the example at the beginning of this section, David's attire could be viewed as problematic by some managers. In this case, and others like it, honesty is the best policy. You may want to tell David frankly that you want him to work on this account because his ability would benefit the customer. You may perhaps say that the customer is conservative and that his attire may distract the customer from his ability. Let David decide how he wants to dress when meeting with the customer.

You may also be frank with your customer: Tell him or her that David is extraordinarily talented and is the best person to add value to your relationship. To lessen the surprise of the initial meeting mention in advance that David often wears ethnic garb. This approach lets David know how the client might interpret his clothing, but it doesn't force him into some narrow corporate box. It also prepares the client to deal with diversity. The point is to balance your interpretation of what a customer might appreciate with David's individuality and diverse voice.

Dress codes tend to raise some people's hackles. The intention of most dress codes is not to restrict individuality, but to ensure a professional appearance in the workplace. Ethnic garb shouldn't really be an issue, as long as it's modest. The aim of most dress codes is to eliminate clothing that could be viewed as immodest or too casual to a customer.

Harassment

> Your profession has been traditionally a male-dominated one, and Marcia is the only woman in your department. Whenever Sam, your senior engineer, holds staff meetings, he and the other males in the department compliment Marcia profusely. They say things like, "It's hard for us to concentrate with a gorgeous woman like you in the room," or "You've got to stop batting your eyelashes at us or the temperature in this room will trigger the air conditioning." They compliment her apparel, her figure, her legs, and her manner of speaking. Although flattering, their remarks make her feel uncomfortable. She has mentioned her discomfort to you on several occasions, and you've told Sam and the others to cut it out. They just laughed and told you that Marcia was too sensitive. You think that while Marcia was being sensitive, she did have justification for being upset about her coworkers' remarks. (For a review of the legal definitions of sexual harassment, see Chapter 3.)

Do compliments constitute harassment? They do when they embarrass someone and serve to undermine an individual's professional standing in front of coworkers. If Marcia is disturbed by the remarks of her coworkers, it's your responsibility as her manager to do something about it. In cases like these, it's sometimes helpful to reverse the situation. Imagine that your department was predominantly female and that the women continually said to the lone male, "You're just a hunk." "We all get aroused when you bat your eyelashes at us." "That's a great suit you're wearing; those slacks really show off your gorgeous thighs." How ridiculous does that banter sound?

In this case, Marcia's discomfort is the issue, and it's irrelevant whether or not you or others think she's being a "little too sensitive." She has already taken the appropriate steps, first by telling her coworkers to stop and then approaching you when they didn't. You should meet immediately with the members of your department, individually or as a group. You could reverse the situation as in the previous paragraph and show the men how ridiculous their comments would sound if the sex of the players was reversed. Explain to them that inappropriate compliments are not acceptable and that anyone who behaves inappropriately in the future will be disciplined. Make it clear that every member of the team has the right to feel comfortable on the team and to be treated with respect. If you don't act swiftly and firmly, and then back up future offenses with disciplinary action, you may be inviting a lawsuit.

Here's another kind of harassment:

> One of your direct reports, Robert, belongs to a fundamentalist church. Although you have no problems with anyone's religious beliefs, Robert is so vocal about his religion that it's becoming a problem with other employees in your department. He not only preaches to his fellow employees, but he also has criticized the attire of some of his female coworkers and continually quotes the Bible in staff meetings. You've received complaints about his behavior from several employees. A few weeks ago, you suggested to Robert that he tone down his preaching, and he reacted as if you were a heathen about to persecute him for his beliefs. His behavior has since escalated.

The job of a manager is to try to maintain a balance between the rights of the individual and the rights of the group, in this case, the attempt by one individual to impose his or her opinions or behavior on other team members. The objectives are fairness and respect for each individual.

In the case of Robert, it appears that he has crossed the line from expressing diverse views to harassment. Although it's important to recognize the value of diverse backgrounds, it's just as important to have an environment where one individual can't constantly attempt to impose his beliefs on other team members. Robert has ignored your requests and those of his coworkers, and has continued his preaching. This kind of behavior will no doubt disrupt the performance of the team and the relationships among team members. In this case, it's probably reasonable to begin documenting Robert's performance since you've already verbally warned him. His hostility and his refusal to respect the opinions of his coworkers and his manager can be viewed as insubordination. In organizations that have a due process approach to discipline, the next step might be a written warning to curb his attempts to influence the religion of his coworkers, or termination will result. Then, if Robert's harassment of his coworkers doesn't stop, he could be fired.

Family and Personal Issues

> One of your direct reports is Ellen, who just returned from maternity leave. She now has two children; her infant is four months old and her older child is three years old. Ellen is not only a talented worker, but she's also a wonderful person.

> Before the birth of her second child, she had no problem handling the workload and the demands on her time; she had a live-in nanny who could care for her child regardless of when she returned home. Recently, however, her live-in left, and Ellen is now sending her children to a day care facility with strict opening and closing times. Although Ellen is very productive when she's in the office, her schedule no longer has any flexibility—she must leave the office no later than 5:00 pm. This has caused a hardship for all of her peers who must complete team assignments whether or not she's present. Although you don't want to cause problems for her, the situation doesn't seem fair to her coworkers.

Family and personal issues are those situations and conditions that, though not directly related to work, can affect someone's ability to perform. People simply can't leave their personal and family problems at home. The difficulty in situations like these is achieving a balance between maintaining a worker's job commitment, performance, and attendance with his or her right to privacy and with fairness to coworkers. The yardstick is that if someone is performing well, and his or her attendance is satisfactory, there's probably no cause for action on the part of the manager, beyond offering assistance if the worker wants it.

In Ellen's case, she has a temporary inability to match her coworkers' schedules. Sooner or later, every worker must deal with situations that place limitations on the ability to maintain certain working hours. Similar situations could result from a variety of other causes including illness, family responsibilities, home construction, and commuting schedules. The issue here is fairness in attendance, not performance or productivity. The ideal solution may be to build more flexibility into the working hours, not just for Ellen but also for the entire team. The ideal solution would involve confronting the problem head-on by asking the people in your area to collaborate and find a solution. For example, you could make an attempt to hold all team meetings in the middle of the day, when everyone can attend. Individual activities could be relegated to the afternoon, so that it would not be essential that Ellen—or anyone else—stay late to work as a group. If your organization has flexible work hours, you could talk to your manager about the possibility of your area incorporating flexible work schedules, where people could arrive and leave at varying times, but where the office and department would always be covered. The objective is to make life easier for individual employees and fair for the entire group, and as a result enhance the team's overall productivity.

Personal illnesses and chemical dependencies of employees present a different set of issues. These situations can affect not only work schedules but also an individual's ability to perform. Most corporations have explicit policies for managing employee illness. Generally, employees are guaranteed a specific number of sick days and then go on some sort of disability program. If an employee, however, hasn't received a formal diagnosis and is simply taking sick days, acting erratically, or showing a change in his or her performance, you might suspect a physical or mental illness. Encourage the employee to see a doctor, and consult with the company medical department (if you have one) if you continue to be concerned about an employee's health. It's important to remember that illnesses of any kind—depression, cancer, AIDS—are private and should be kept confidential. These conditions do not cause any danger to co-workers, and many people who suffer from them can resume normal or modified work schedules. Managers can help these employees by protecting the employee's privacy and by being fair and compassionate.

Drug or alcohol abuse is a different matter. Most corporations have policies that prohibit any kind of drug or alcohol use on company premises, and many companies have severe penalties for employees who are caught working under the influence of alcohol or drugs. Both alcoholism and drug addiction are costly in terms of the abuser's health, and they can both cause extreme danger in the workplace. A corporate bond trader who's high on cocaine can wreak havoc on himself, his employer, and his customers. A pilot who's drunk poses obvious risks to an airline and its passengers. Would you like to ride with a railroad engineer who just smoked a few joints, or have the sale of your home negotiated by a real estate broker who's inebriated, or have your child's broken leg set by a doctor who's on amphetamines?

If you suspect that one of your employees is abusing drugs on or off the job, keep track of any changes in behavior and performance, in writing. (Even if an employee uses drugs or alcohol only off company premises, the residual effects of the substance may affect job performance.) This is an important step because some medications smell like alcohol on the breath, so it's important to be sure that you're dealing with abuse and not a medical condition. Once you're fairly certain that you're dealing with abuse, contact your human resources department. Substance abuse is considered an illness (and generally not an offense that will get the employee fired—at least in many large corporations), and the employee usually will be counseled by human resources. If abuse is present, most large employers offer substance abuse programs for employees and will probably insist that your employee participate in such a program. In most large companies, employees are given one or two chances to get clean. If the problem recurs, substance abusers can be terminated. The important issue here is to get fast help for the employee—for the sake of the employee, the company, and your customers.

WHY ARE THESE ETHICAL PROBLEMS? These are all ethical issues because they concern fairness and respect for the individual. A large percentage of the ethical issues that arise in business are related to human resources, and they can usually be addressed by local managers who act quickly, fairly, and with compassion.

COSTS The personal, professional, and corporate costs of discrimination and sexual harassment are described earlier in this chapter and in Chapter 3. The costs for mishandling most issues connected to diversity are not clear-cut, and they're often difficult to quantify.

To glimpse how costly the publicity associated with such cases can be, we have to look no further than the now infamous Texaco case, which is described in detail at the end of Chapter 9. Texaco executives were heard on tape complaining about Hanukkah and Kwanzaa interfering with the celebration of Christmas, and recounting the destruction of documents connected to a pending discrimination case.[9] In the wake of a firestorm of bad publicity, Texaco was forced to settle the case for $176 million. Obviously, the costs to Texaco—both financially and in damaged reputation—were significant. Yet those costs are just the tip of a giant iceberg. If we could combine all of the fairness issues—performance evaluation systems, harassment, subtle and not-so-subtle discrimination, and how managers handle family, substance, and illness issues—and figure out how much it costs businesses when employees are treated unfairly, the result would probably be astronomical, and not just in terms of financial costs and damaged reputations. How many people leave a job because of unresolved problems with a coworker? How many people choose not to go the extra mile because the organization doesn't treat its employees fairly? How many of the best performers choose to work for a company that allows them flexible hours to care for a child or an aging parent? How many people are depressed and frustrated because they're picking up the slack for a coworker who's a chronic alcoholic? The toll in human suffering, morale, loyalty, productivity, and lost opportunity is inestimable.

THE MANAGER AS A LENS

Managers perform a crucial role in organizations because they interpret company policy, execute corporate directives, fulfill all of the people management needs in their particular area of responsibility, cascade senior management messages down the chain of command, and communicate employee feedback up the chain. They are probably the most important ingredient in an organization's success and they are frequently the most overlooked. But make no mistake about it—managers are the lens through which employees view the company, as well as the filter through which senior executives view employees. In many respects, to many employees, managers *are* the company. Managers can be the inspiration behind why someone stays with an organization or the impetus behind why someone leaves. As a result, no one employee group needs more senior management attention, more training, and more communication skills than managers.

The Buck Stops with Managers

If we could take a peek at the innermost thoughts of managers, they might very well contain the following sentiment: "I hope we do good work and get recognized for it. But most of all, I hope there's nothing going on that I don't know about that could hit the fan."

As a manager, you'll soon discover that your employees can bring you glory and they can get you into big trouble. But the good news is that you can make investments over time to help ensure that nothing hits the fan, or if it does, you find out about it before it mushrooms out of control. As a manager, you can design your own little insurance policy to help protect you and your organization from employees who might cause problems.

You can begin to protect yourself by understanding and internalizing the fact that the people who report to you are looking to you for guidance and approval. That means that you need to actively manage ethics. Your employees want to know what your rules are, so you need to think carefully about your stan[dards and make a con]scious effort to communicate and enforce them. Most impor[tant, under]stand that you are a role model and your employees will fol[low your lead. We'll talk] more about the importance of ethical leadership in Chapter [7.]

Boris Yavitz, former dean of Columbia University's Graduate Sch[ool of Business] and a member of several large corporate boards, had sage advice for managers. [First,] communicate your expectations and standards publicly and privately. Employees are much less likely to disregard a personal challenge—"Are we doing it right?"—than they are if they have only seen that expectation expressed in a policy manual. Second, managers should prove their commitment through personal example. They need to "walk the talk" or no one will take their expectations seriously. Finally, since employees are naturally inclined to protect managers from bad news, managers need to explicitly tell employees that they don't want that kind of protection. "Tell me everything." The best policy is to communicate loudly and clearly that you don't want protection. Of course, that also means that you can't shoot the messenger who brings you bad news, or it will be the last time you ever hear from a messenger.

BEGIN WITH CLEAR STANDARDS All organizations have standards and many organizations even have written standards. Written standards—usually in the form of a mission statement or guiding principles—can be a double-edged sword. It's great if an organization has written standards that actually guide how it does business. It's a huge problem if those written standards are just window dressing and the real standards have nothing to do with the ones that are printed up and hanging on the wall. The disconnect between written standards and reality (referred to as cultural misalignment in Chapter 9) destroys credibility, and a company can't be effective over the long term without credibility.

The same is true for managers. Any employee can tell you what the rules are for working for a particular manager. "You must tell the truth here or you'll be fired," might be a rule, or "Don't rock the boat," or "Don't tell me how you do it, just do it." The very best way for managers to gain credibility among employees (as well as their respect) is to set clear standards, live by those standards, very deliberately communicate them, and insist on adherence to those standards by everyone.

The truth is that employees are always trying to figure out if managers mean what they say. Think about this case: The manager of a food processing plant consistently talks about the importance of quality. "The consumer should always come first," he says. Then one day a shipment of food is delivered for processing. The factory equipment is ready to go, the employees have been waiting for this huge delivery, and the food is just on the wrong side of spoiled. "It's good enough," the manager says. "The processing will kill any contaminants and the consumer will never know the difference because this will be flash-frozen after the processing. We'll lose a lot of money if we don't process something now." What message has he just sent too his employees? Suppose that a month later, an employee finds a few rodent droppings in a food processing unit. It'll cost a lot of money to stop the machinery and clean it, plus the food already in the hopper would have to be destroyed. What do you think employee would do? Would he or she believe that the consumer comes first? Or would the employee decide that it's OK to cut a corner to save money?

It's important to understand that, as a manager, you are setting standards all the time. In fact, failing to deliberately set ethical standards is a standard in itself since your employees may very well interpret it as meaning you have *no* standards. In this era of teams and empowered employees, managers need to be very deliberate in spelling out what they stand for and "how things are going to be done around here." Those ethical standards have to be demonstrated by the manager and enforced or people won't believe them. It's what "walking the talk" really means.

DESIGN A PLAN TO CONTINUALLY COMMUNICATE YOUR STANDARDS

Good communication skills are at the very heart of effective ethics management. Without them, it's virtually impossible to encourage ethical behavior. Regardless of where you are in the management hierarchy, if you haven't made effective communication your top priority, you had better get ready for some big surprises. Here's a Big Truth: If you don't communicate with your employees, they won't communicate with you. You won't know what's going on; you'll be out of the loop; you'll be ignorant; you'll be inviting ethical transgressions. And in business, ignorance is definitely not bliss.

Communicating with one group of employees is not enough because you'll know what's going on only with them. You'll see information about other employee groups only through the filter of that one group. That's why "management by walking around" always gets such high marks from management experts. Managers can be knowledgeable only when they regularly interact with and listen to many different people on many different levels. (You may think this is simplistic, but think about how many top executives think they are communicating when they do it just with the executives who report to them.)

Consider this example: A young, newly named CEO decided to create an executive floor and bring all of his most senior people together on one floor to improve communication within the group and make it easy to work together. It happens all the time in companies around the world. Is it a good idea? Probably not, since he effectively isolated not only himself but also the rest of the executive team. He also created an atmosphere of elitism within the organization.

You can improve the communication within your department by holding regular staff meetings where you discuss the company mission, business results, and the way you want things done. Talk about what you stand for and what you want your department to stand for. Use ethical language—for example, when employees are designing a new program or product, ask them in a staff meeting if they have considered everyone who could be affected by their plans. Ask them if they think they're doing the right thing. Framing business decisions in ethical terms goes a long way in increasing moral awareness, communicating your standards and the importance of ethical behavior.

Once you have deliberately articulated and communicated your standards both privately to individuals and publicly in front of your team, you need to think about how approachable you are. You need to think long and hard about how you react when people raise issues or ask questions or deliver criticism. If you kill the messenger or react with hostility if someone asks a question or seem too busy to clarify directions, you are asking for trouble. Your people may well consider you unapproachable, and managers who can't be approached have laid the groundwork for being blindsided. The first time they may hear about a problem is not from an employee, but from a lawyer, a newspaper reporter, or a regulator.

Managers Are Role Models

Professional basketball player Charles Barkley made sports headlines when he proclaimed, "I'm not paid to be a role model."[10] A colleague on the courts, Karl Malone, responded in an issue of *Sports Illustrated,* "Charles, you can deny being a role model all you want, but I don't think it's your decision to make. We don't *choose* to be to be role models, we're *chosen*. Our only choice is whether to be a good role model or a bad one." Like Barkley, some managers may not want to be role models. But Barkley and managers are indeed role models, not because they want to be, but because of the positions they hold. Being a manager and a good role model means more than just doing the right thing; it also means helping your employees do the right thing. A manager who is a good role model inspires employees, helps them define gray areas, and respects their concerns.

Managers can provide guidance to employees who encounter ethical dilemmas by encouraging them to gather all of the facts and then evaluate the situation using some of the advice detailed in Chapter 4. And after that, they need to go further. What happens if one of your employees raises an issue with you and you don't see where there is a problem? The employee goes away, satisfied for the moment with your response that there's nothing wrong. But soon she is back because she still doesn't feel right about the situation. What do you do now? Probably the most responsible thing you can do at that point is to offer to pursue it with her to make sure there is no problem. This sends a huge message to the employee and to her colleagues. First, you're saying that you're glad that she brought this to your attention. Second, you're taking her seriously even if you don't particularly agree with her. Third, you're saying that you trust her instincts and that she should, too. Fourth, you're declaring that ethics are important to you; so important that you're willing to pursue this with her even though you don't agree with her in an effort to make her feel more comfortable. These are all critical messages to send to employees. (You also may find that she is right in her suspicions.)

The most important thing for managers to remember about their job as role model is that what they do is infinitely more important than what they say. They can preach ethics all they want, but unless they live that message, their people won't. As a manager, all eyes are upon you and what you're doing. Your actions will speak much louder than your words and if there is a disconnect, you will have no credibility.

MANAGING UP AND ACROSS

Gone are the days when a person could advance in an organization by impressing only the next level of management. The new team structures mandate that workers treat everyone well. An example of how some corporations are institutionalizing this approach is an increasingly popular method of performance appraisal that some companies call 360-degree feedback. This means that when reviewing an employee's performance, a manager asks for input from the employee's coworkers and subordinates. Feedback of this sort, which comes from all directions, is probably a much more effective barometer of performance than old methods that measure only how well people manage up. Of course, it means that workers need to carefully consider all of their work relationships: up, down, and across. It's also an indicator of what astute workers have always known: Since you never know who you might end up reporting to, or who is going to be crucial to your success in the future, it's critical to effectively manage all of your work relationships.

In team situations, managers can still have a profound impact on your future. They sign off on or approve performance appraisals, pay raises, transfers, and generally are a primary influence on your career mobility and trajectory. It can be difficult to overcome a poor relationship with a manager unless you have solid relationships with individuals on or above your manager's level. That's why it's important for you to cultivate your manager's respect.

Although it may appear that your peers don't have as direct an impact on your career as your manager does, they nevertheless can have a profound effect on your future success. Since you generally "get as good as you give," if you don't cooperate with your peers, they'll probably refuse to cooperate with you—perhaps even sabotage you behind the scenes—and that lack of cooperation could cripple you. In addition, peers can be promoted to management positions, which can prove to be truly unfortunate if you haven't developed good relationships with them.

Honesty Is Rule One

> Michael is a lawyer who reports to Paula, the corporate counsel for a chemical company. During one particularly busy period, Paula asks Michael to prepare a summary of all pending lawsuits and other legal activity for the company's senior management. Since Michael has several court appearances and depositions cluttering his schedule, he assigns the report to one of his paralegals, who completes the report in several days. Since he's so busy, Michael simply submits the report to Paula without reviewing it. When Paula asks him what he thinks of the report, he assures her that it's fine. The next day, Paula asks Michael into her office and says that she has found a major omission in the report. Michael has no choice but to admit that he didn't have time to review it.

There's probably nothing that trips up more people than the temptation to lie or stretch the truth. There's also probably nothing that will trip up your career faster than a lie or an exaggeration. In business, your reputation is everything, and lying or exaggerating can quickly undermine it.

Michael has basically lied to his manager. Even if he can weasel his way out of the hot seat by saying he didn't have time to thoroughly review the report, he has created an indelible impression on Paula. She may question not only his future reports, but also his activities in general. Michael could have told Paula up front that he didn't have time to prepare a report. He could have suggested that one of the paralegals prepare it. He could have asked for more time so that he could carefully review it. Paula may not have been thrilled with his analysis of the situation, but she probably would have understood and helped him look for another solution. However, by implying that he had completed and reviewed the report when in fact he hadn't looked at it, Michael has severely damaged his reputation with his manager. A worker's responsibility includes identifying a problem and then proposing a solution. If you provide a solution when you report a concern, you stand a good chance of having your idea implemented. If you just report an issue with no solution, you'll probably have a solution imposed on you.

Managers and peers rely on the information they receive from the people who report to them and who work with them. Obviously, that information must be truthful and accurate, or someone else's work will be skewed. Once someone has reason to doubt your veracity, it may be impossible for you to recover. As one executive said, "Lying will end someone's relationship with me, period." The caveat: Be completely honest about all aspects of your work, including your ability, the information you provide, and your ability to meet deadlines. Keep your promises.

Standards Go Both Ways

> It began when Bruce asked Andy to lie to his wife about his whereabouts. "If Marcia calls, tell her I'm in Phoenix on a business trip," he told Andy. Of course, he had also confided to Andy that in case of an office emergency, he could be reached at a local golf tournament or at a nearby hotel where he was staying with another woman. Since Bruce was senior to Andy and was a powerful contributor in the department, Andy went along with his request. When Marcia called, Andy told the lie about Bruce being in Phoenix. Bruce asked several more "favors" of Andy, and Andy complied. Then Bruce asked for a big favor: He instructed Andy to inflate monthly sales figures for a report going to senior management. When Andy objected, Bruce said, "Oh, come on, Andy, we all know how high your standards are."

Just as it's important for managers to set standards within their departments, it's equally important that workers set ethical standards with their managers and peers. The best way to ensure that you're not going to be asked to compromise your values is to clearly communicate what people can expect from you.

In Andy's case, he made his first mistake by going along with Bruce's lie to his wife. Although it's tempting to help out a colleague—especially one who's powerful and senior to you—you're sliding down a slippery slope when it involves a lie. And the chances are excellent that Bruce would not have asked Andy to lie about the monthly sales figures if he hadn't already known that he could manipulate Andy. If Andy had refused to lie for Bruce on that first occasion, Bruce would probably have vastly different expectations of him. When Bruce asked Andy to lie to his wife, Andy could have replied, "Hey, Bruce, don't drag me into that one! I'll tell her you're not in the office, but I'm not going to outright lie to her." Andy could have said it in a nonthreatening way and Bruce probably would have understood. Bruce might even have been embarrassed. But once Andy got caught up in Bruce's conspiracy, Bruce felt he would probably go along with other untruths. The caveat: Say it politely but say it firmly and unequivocally. If a coworker or manager asks you to betray your standards—even in the tiniest of ways—refuse to compromise your standards or you'll end up being confronted with increasingly thorny dilemmas.

CONCLUSION

Employees are strongly influenced by the conduct of management. That's why it's so critical that individual managers understand how they, and their influence on decisions, are viewed by employees. It's also critical that managers understand that if they set high standards, foster good communications, and act as role models, they will have the power to create an environment that encourages employees to behave ethically. It's equally important that workers appreciate the importance of managing their relationships with the manager and their peers, and know how to alert the company's senior executives to wrongdoing in the safest way possible.

DISCUSSION QUESTIONS

1. Why should performance be measured as an ongoing process, and not just as a once-a-year event?
2. Should high performers be allowed to work by rules that are different from those that apply to other workers? Why or why not?
3. Imagine that you're the manager of a facility where 200 layoffs are scheduled. Design an action plan for how the layoffs would occur. How would you handle those being laid off and the survivors?
4. Are there ways in which managers can avoid harassment issues among employees who report to them? What would your strategy be?
5. Imagine that someone who reports to you is on a prescription medication that makes his breath smell like alcohol. How would you handle this situation?
6. Imagine that one of your employees complained that a coworker was harassing him or her. Also imagine that you suspect the motives of the person who is complaining to you. How would you handle this situation? Is there a way you could discern motivation, or does it matter? When would you involve your company's human resources department?
7. As a manager, how would you respond when a worker's performance has declined and you suspect a problem at home is the cause?
8. List ways you can communicate your ethical standards to your employees and to your peers.

SHORT CASES

EMPLOYMENT BASICS

You've recently been promoted to a supervisory position and are now responsible for coordinating the work of four other employees. Two of these workers are more than 20 years older than you are, and both have been with the company much longer than you have. Although you've tried to be supportive of them and have gone out of your way to praise their work, whenever there is some kind of disagreement, they go to your boss with the problem. You've asked them repeatedly to come to you with whatever issues they have; they just ignore you and complain to other workers about reporting to someone your age. Design a strategy for dealing with these workers and your manager.

MANAGING A DIVERSE WORKFORCE

After two years of sales calls and persuasion, a large, multinational petroleum company—Big Oil Ltd.—decides to sign with your employer, Secure Bank. Since Big Oil is headquartered in Saudi Arabia and most of the meetings with the client have been in the Middle East, Secure Bank's senior executive in charge of oil and oil products companies, Julie, has not attended. Although the Secure Bank employees who have met with the company have told the Big Oil executives that the lead on their account will be a woman, the news must not have registered, perhaps because of language difficulties. Today, the Big Oil reps are in Chicago to sign on the dotted line and meet with Secure Bank's senior managers, and of course, they've met with Julie. A member of your sales team calls you to say that Big Oil's senior team member has told him he does not want Julie to work on their account, period. Because of cultural issues, Big Oil execs are uncomfortable dealing with women from any country. As Julie's manager, what do you do?

MANAGING UP AND ACROSS

As an operations professional, you need to be able to interact effectively with many internal customers—from corporate managers to field representatives. One of your peers is Jessica, who is a talented operations professional but who is downright rude to her internal customers. Her attitude is so bad that people around your company ask specifically to deal with you instead of Jessica. You've heard many tales about her sarcasm and her unwillingness to deliver anything other than the absolute minimum to other employees. You've thought about talking to Bruce, the manager to whom both you and Jessica report, but you and everyone else knows that they're dating. In the meantime, your workload is increasing because of Jessica's reputation. How do you handle Jessica and Bruce?

NOTES

1. Halper, J. 1988. *Quiet desperation: The truth about successful men.* New York: Warner Books.
2. Ball, G., Treo, L., and Sims, H. P., Jr. 1994. Just and unjust punishment incidents: Influence on subordinate performance and citizenship. *Academy of Management Journal* 37: 299–332.
3. Rice, D., and Dreilinger, C. 1991. After downsizing. *Training and Development Journal* (May): 41–44.
4. Brockner, J. 1992. Managing the effects of layoffs on survivors. *California Management Review* (Winter): 928.
5. Labich, Kenneth. 1996. How to fire people and still sleep at night. *Fortune,* June 10: 65–71.
6. Rice and Dreilinger, After downsizing.
7. Solomon, J. 1998. Fire, flood, and now ... sexual-harassment insurance. *Newsweek,* March 16, online edition.
8. Greenberg, J. 1990. Employee theft as a reaction to underpayment inequity: The hidden cost of pay cuts. *Journal of Applied Psychology* 75: 56—64.
9. Leo, J. 1997. Jellybean: The sequel. *U.S. News & World Report,* February 10: 20.
10. Gelman, D.1993. I'm not a role model. *Newsweek,* June 28: 56.

ETHICAL RESPONSIBILITIES OF MANAGERS II

CHAPTER 7

MANAGING FOR ETHICAL CONDUCT

INTRODUCTION

Managers need simple and practical tools for managing ethical conduct. Therefore, this chapter introduces some basic management concepts that provide a foundation for understanding how to manage for ethical conduct in organizations. These principles can be applied at the department level or at the level of the entire organization. Consistent with the focus of the book, each section concludes with practical implications for managers. Underlying our recommendations to managers are several key assumptions:

1. That managers want to be ethical
2. That managers can and should work to develop their own ethical decision-making skills (see Chapters 4 and 5)
3. That, based on their experience, managers will have insight into the unique ethical requirements of the job
4. That managers will want their subordinates to be ethical as well

IN BUSINESS, ETHICS IS ABOUT BEHAVIOR

In business, when people talk about ethics, they're talking about behavior. In this context, ethics isn't mysterious or unusual, nor does it depend on the individual's innate goodness, religious conviction, or understanding (or lack thereof) of philosophy. People find themselves in work situations every day where they're faced with ethical dilemmas—questions of right and wrong where values are in conflict. Should I hire, fire, promote, or demote this individual? Should I offer or accept a gift in this or that situation? How should I respond when my supervisor asks me to act against my own beliefs?[1]

The study of ethical behavior in business involves understanding the factors that influence how people behave in these situations. Although we've seen that internal factors such as individual moral development are important, ethical conduct depends, to a large extent, on such external factors as the rules of the work context, the reward system, what peers are doing, what authority figures expect, the roles people are asked to play, and more. In this chapter, we're going to focus on these external factors because they're the ones that managers can influence the most. Once managers understand how management principles apply to ethical conduct, they can manage ethical behavior more proactively and effectively. On the other hand, if managers fool themselves into thinking that ethical conduct is determined exclusively by some mysterious character trait, they'll throw up their hands and walk away from situations that they could proactively manage. Or they'll think that by simply getting rid of a "bad apple," unethical conduct won't recur. This kind of thinking is a cop-out. Unethical behavior is rarely as simple as a bad apple. It's often something about the work environment that allows the bad apple to behave badly. And the work environment is managers' responsibility. Top managers are responsible for the broad organizational culture (as we'll see in Chapter 9). But, in most cases, lower-level managers can do a lot to influence the subordinates in their own departments.

Practical Advice for Managers about Ethical Behavior

What are the practical implications for managers? First, think of ethics in concrete behavioral terms. Specifically, what kind of behavior are you looking for in your subordinates, and how can you create a context that will support that behavior? Specifying concrete goals for ethical behavior means going beyond abstract statements, such as "integrity is important here" to more concrete statements, such as "I expect sales representatives to be absolutely honest with our customers about such things as the characteristics of our products and our ability to deliver by a certain date." Finally, it's the manager's responsibility to create a work environment that supports ethical behavior and discourages unethical behavior just as much as it's the manager's responsibility to manage for productivity or quality. Don't just set ethical behavior goals. Follow up to make sure that they're achievable and that they're being met, and model ethical conduct yourself. Your people will pay more attention to what you do than to what you say. Take advantage of opportunities to demonstrate the ethical conduct you expect.

OUR MULTIPLE ETHICAL SELVES

To understand ethics at work, we must understand that people are socialized to accept different behavior depending on the context. Cultural anthropologists have known for years that we have multiple selves and that we behave differently depending on the situation we confront.[2] Children in our society are taught very early that it's all right to be loud and boisterous on the playground, but they must be reverent at the church, synagogue, temple, or mosque. Table manners are important when visiting, but eating with one's fingers may be acceptable at home. As adults, we play highly differentiated roles, and we assume that each social context presents different behavioral expectations. Football players are expected to tackle each other deliberately and aggressively on the playing field, a behavior that they would be arrested for on the street. Business people are expected to be aggressive against competitors but gentle with their spouses and children. Game jargon is often applied to business dealings— like the term *playing field*—which makes the business dealings less subject to moral scrutiny. One "bluffs" and conceals information in business negotiations the same way one "bluffs" in a poker game. "Bluffing" sounds a lot better than lying (the word lying would raise "moral awareness," as discussed in Chapter 5), and the game analogy helps to distinguish business behavior from morality in other situations. Although we might prefer to think that we take a single ethical self from situation to situation, reality suggests that most people accept different rules for different contexts. This means that we can and do have multiple ethical selves.

The Kenneth Lay Example

Kenneth Lay, chairman of Enron Corporation (until he was forced out by the firm's creditors in 2002), exemplifies the concept of multiple ethical selves. A *Newsweek* article, written after Enron's bankruptcy, described the paradox that was Ken Lay.[3] First, we see the affable leader who was loved and admired by Enron employees. Even Sherron Watkins, the Enron whistleblower who brought Lay her concerns about the accounting problems and was rebuffed, described Lay as a man of integrity. He grew up a poor preacher's son who pulled himself up by his bootstraps, eventually winning the Horatio Alger Award (designed to foster entrepreneurship and honor the American dream of success through hard work). At the University of Missouri, he was president of a dry fraternity and went on to earn a Ph.D. in economics. He created Enron, and by 2000 it was the seventh largest company in the United States in terms of revenue. Despite becoming quite rich, he never flaunted his wealth. He drove an old Cadillac and used rental cars rather than limos when traveling. He was highly philanthropic in the Houston community, as was his company. He talked about making Houston a world-class city and worked to make that happen, spreading his largesse to the ballet, symphony, museums, the United Way, the NAACP—you name it. He was even discussed as a possible mayoral candidate.

But Lay had another side. He has been described as an arrogant gambler who valued risk taking and boosting the firm's stock price above all. He transformed Enron from the 1980s merger of two old-fashioned pipeline companies into a huge energy trader. Enron "became a giant casino, taking positions, hedging, betting on winners and losers."[4] Interestingly, the merger deal was financed by Michael Milliken, 1980s junk-bond trader and one of Lay's heroes (despite the fact that Milliken had done jail time for financial fraud). Lay fired Enron's conservative accounting firm, Deloitte Haskins Sells, early on because they were "not as creative and imaginative" as he wished, and he replaced them with Arthur Andersen. He created a corporate culture that was described by insiders as "cutthroat" and "vicious," and hired Ivy League "hot shot risk takers" like Jeff Skilling (CEO) and Andrew Fastow (CFO) to run it. People who didn't make their numbers were quickly fired, and a large internal security force came to be feared by employees. Lay was also a political pro. He gave generously to political candidates and received favors in return, including exemptions from a variety of local and state regulations. He was also the largest single contributor to George W. Bush's presidential campaign.

When Jeff Skilling resigned in August 2001, Lay told employees that the company's upcoming financials looked fine and he encouraged them to "talk up the stock and talk positively about Enron to your family and friends." Those who heeded his suggestion saw their retirement plans wiped out and were furious when they learned had been unloading his own stock for years. According to *Newsweek,* Lay knew about Enron's "elaborate schemes to hide losses and debts"—the off-the-books partnerships that no one, including stock analysts, really understood.

Is Kenneth Lay ethical or unethical? The answer is that, like many people, he has multiple selves. In some areas of his life, he did good things, including his many philanthropic efforts. But philanthropy shouldn't be equated with ethical conduct in daily business dealings. In this case, hubris and an inclination toward risk taking apparently combined in a business leader who created a Darwinian corporate culture that brought out some of the worst inclinations in himself and others.

A prominent victim of the Enron bankruptcy was Cliff Baxter, Enron's 43-year-old former vice chairman, who committed suicide following Enron's collapse. We can only speculate about the reason, but the clash of his multiple ethical selves may have been involved. Those who knew him described Baxter as a family man who balanced his home and work lives. He was certainly instrumental in helping to create the massive Enron fortune in the 1990s. But, over time, he clashed with Andrew Fastow, openly criticizing the firm's involvement in financial deals he considered to be questionable and inappropriate. Unable to influence what was happening, he left the company in May 2001 (citing a desire to spend more time with his family). We will likely never know for sure why Baxter committed suicide. Friends said that he was "devastated by the company's demise." He may have felt responsible for the many employees who lost their life savings in the collapse that could have been prevented. It's possible that the ethical self who cared about those employees could no longer live with the self who contributed to their pain.[5]

The Dennis Levine Example

Now for an example of someone lower in the organizational hierarchy. Dennis Levine's personal account of his insider-trading activities, which resulted in his arrest and imprisonment in the 1980s, also suggests multiple ethical selves. He describes himself as a good son, husband, and father, and a man who had been encouraged by his parents to "play straight." "I come from a strong, old-fashioned family ... [my father] taught me to work hard, believe in myself, and persevere ... as a kid I always worked."[6] Levine's wife, Laurie, had no idea that he had been secretly and illegally trading in stocks for years. In fact, the family lived in a cramped one-bedroom apartment for nearly three years after their son was born despite Levine's huge insider trading profits. That someone is "from a good family" or is "a family man or woman" is no guarantee of ethical behavior in the office. At the office, the manager is dealing with the "office self," who may be very different from the "family self" or the "religious self."

Levine was a good son, husband, and father. But he separated his family self from his insider trading self. Why was his insider trading self allowed to exist? We can only speculate that this office self fit into an environment where peers were crossing the ethical line and not getting caught. Most important, his continuing huge profits led him into a downward spiral of unethical behavior that he found difficult to stop despite his recognition that it was illegal.

Practical Advice for Managers about Multiple Ethical Selves

So what should managers do? First, it's important to evaluate the organizational environment. As a lower or middle-level manager, you can do only so much to influence that environment, and if senior executives are creating a cut-throat Darwinian culture where only bottom-line results count, it's probably time to look elsewhere for a job. Chapter 9 provides information about how to conduct an "ethical culture audit" that can help you make that tough decision. But let's assume that senior management is supportive. Then, it will be up to you to contribute to the larger organizational culture by creating a work environment that supports ethical conduct and integrity for the people you manage. Integrity is defined as that quality or state of being complete, whole, or undivided. The ultimate goal is to bring these multiple ethical selves together—to support the idea that an individual can be as ethical at the office as at home. But managers should pursue that goal with the practical understanding that many people find it quite possible to divide themselves into multiple ethical selves.

Begin by analyzing yourself. Get to know your own office ethical self. Is it consistent with your personal ethical self? If not, what will be required to bring the two together? Again, you're an important role model for your subordinates. If you're clearly a "whole" person of integrity, they're more likely to aspire to "wholeness" themselves.

Next, think about your subordinates. Make no assumptions about ethics at work based on a person's background, religious affiliation, family life, or good deeds in the community. Instead, find out what norms and expectations guide their office selves and make sure that they support ethical behavior. You can learn a great deal simply by keeping your eyes and ears wide open. Of course, the best way to find out how your people think about these issues is to ask them, either in person or in survey form. You may be surprised what they'll tell you. And you're sending an important symbolic message about what concerns you just by asking. Do they feel, as many surveys have suggested, that they must compromise their personal ethics to get ahead in your organization? If so, what do they think can be done about it?

Find out what influences their thoughts and behavior in ethical dilemma situations. Find out what inhibits them from being the best they can be—from doing the right thing. You can base your questions on real or hypothetical situations. Most supervisors have never bothered to ask the question. Is it any wonder then that most subordinates end up believing that their managers don't really care about ethics? Once you've had this type of discussion, it's essential that the organization follow up in ways that support ethical conduct. A number of practical ideas for how to do that follow.

REWARD SYSTEMS

People Do What's Rewarded and Avoid Doing What's Punished

Reward systems are probably the single most important formal influence on people's behavior at work. Ask any manager about reward systems, and he or she can probably recite a few basics recalled from a college psychology or management class. For example, most of us remember something about reinforcement theory—people are more likely to behave in ways that are rewarded, and they're less likely to do what's punished. That seems simple enough. But we often fail to recognize the power of these simple concepts. People in work organizations are constantly on the lookout for information about rewards and punishments—especially if this information isn't explicit. In fact, the more ambiguous the situation, the more people search for clues. They know that to be successful at work, they'll have to determine what's rewarded and do those things while avoiding behaviors that are punished.

How Reward Systems Can Encourage Unethical Behavior

THE ELECTRONICS APPLIANCE SALES EXAMPLE How does this simple idea apply to the management of ethical and unethical behavior? Imagine an employee in an electronic appliance store who works on a modest salary plus commission basis. In other words, the salespeople are paid a percentage on the items they sell. The company frequently advertises specials on certain television models in the local newspaper and, of course, people come into the store asking about those models. But because of the lower profit margin on these sale items, the company also lowers the commission that sales personnel receive on these models. The higher rewards (higher commissions) come with sales of models that aren't on special. The company prefers to sell the higher-priced models but advertises the lower-priced ones to get customers into the store. The company has set sales goals for each salesperson, with higher goals for the higher-priced models. The company offers little sales training. New salespeople spend a day or so working with the store manager, and then they're pretty much on their own. The manager doesn't seem to care how sales are made—just that they are made. The manager's own commissions are based on store sales.

If the salespeople value money (and their jobs), and the assumption is that they do, they'll be motivated to sell the higher-priced models. They can do this in a variety of ways. For example, they might point out that some of these models have features that the sale models don't have. Some customers will probably listen to the advice and buy the more expensive models. As buyers listen and go along, the connection between selling higher-priced items and positive outcomes (commissions, praise from the manager) becomes stronger, and the motivation to sell more of these items grows.

But there are still probably lots of folks who insist on buying the sale models. To sell more of the higher-priced models, the salesperson might try stressing the advantages of the high-priced model's features, whether or not the customer needs those features. The salesperson may find that a good number of people go along. There are more rewards—higher commissions, more praise from the manager—and no obvious negative outcomes. This behavior can even be justified, or at least rationalized. These customers are getting features they wouldn't otherwise get, right? And the salesperson doesn't know much about their finances or personal life, so there would be no way to know (without asking) if spending more money really had negative consequences for the customer.

Things are going so well that the salesperson might now be tempted to go a bit farther—perhaps playing with the controls to make it look as if the picture on the sale TV is a bit fuzzier than the picture on the more expensive models. That makes it even easier to sell the more expensive models.

Explained this way, the connection between rewards and unethical behavior seems pretty clear. Although no one was explicitly telling salespeople to be unethical, the opportunity was there: Management set higher sales goals for higher-priced models and rewarded the sale of these models with higher commissions. The store manager didn't seem to care how the sales got made and didn't object to the salesperson playing with the controls to deceive customers.

The goal was to sell higher-priced models. But the exclusive focus on goals frequently obscures the means to the goal—how you get there. If managers are concerned about ethical conduct, it's essential that they also focus on how the goal is being achieved. They must let their subordinates know that they're interested in ethical means as well as ends. If individuals are rewarded for meeting goals no matter what methods are used, they're much more likely to try methods that cross over the ethical/unethical line.

Many people have told us of their experience with managers who make a statement something like the following, "I don't care how you do it, just do it." Or, "I don't want to know how you meet the goal, just meet it." These statements are clearly giving permission to use any means necessary (ethical or unethical) to meet the goal. Managers who have uttered these words shouldn't be surprised to find that unethical behavior is often the result. Goal setting is one of the most effective motivational methods available to managers. Set challenging and achievable goals, and people will do their best to meet them. That's why responsible managers need to be clear about the importance of using only ethical means to achieve the goals they have set for their employees.

Practical Advice for Managers about Reward Systems

First, remember that people do what's rewarded. And these rewards don't have to be explicit. The electronics store in our example would probably never have dreamed of saying that it was rewarding salespersons for being unethical. In fact, they weren't doing this explicitly. But if the designers of the motivational plan had thought carefully about the plan's potential effects (and it's their responsibility to do so), they might very well have identified its fatal flaw—it focuses on ends only and leaves it to the salespeople to figure out the means (how to accomplish the goals). Managers are more likely to identify these flaws in advance if they put themselves in their employees' shoes. Think about what an individual would be likely to do given the reward system that's in place or being considered. What kinds of attitudes and behaviors are being rewarded explicitly or implicitly? How can you find out? Ask your staff. If you have good open communication with them, they'll tell you.

Second, think carefully about the goals you've set for your employees. Combining specific, challenging, and achievable goals with rewards for goal achievement is a powerful motivational tool. People set their sights on those goals and work hard to achieve them. It's up to the manager to think about the likely behavioral outcomes. Ask yourself whether you have set goals for ethical conduct (e.g., honesty with customers) as well as for bottom-line performance (e.g., number of TVs sold)—for means (how we get there) as well as ends. We believe in an ethical "Pygmalion effect." In tests of the more general Pygmalion effect, researchers have found that people in school and work settings generally live up to the expectations that are set for them, whether high or low.[7] Students and workers perform better in response to a teacher's or supervisor's high expectation, but they fall behind if they're expected to fail. With the ethical Pygmalion effect, expectations for ethical behavior (as well as performance) are set high, and people are expected to fulfill them. This ethical Pygmalion effect appeals to people's desire to do what's right. It is also likely to get people to think about how they achieve their goals, not just whether they've achieved them.

Recognize the Power of Indirect Rewards and Punishments

It's important to recognize that workers don't have to be individually rewarded for the message to have an impact. A powerful extension of reinforcement theory is social learning theory.[8] According to social learning theory, people learn a great deal from observing the rewards and punishments of others. Recall that we said that workers are constantly on the lookout for information about rewards and punishments. But they don't have to experience the reward or punishment themselves in order for these to influence behavior. If they see that others get away with lying, cheating, or stealing, or worse yet, if they see those individuals promoted or getting the big bonuses, they're much more likely to try these behaviors themselves. On the other hand, if they see someone quickly dismissed for lying to a customer, they learn that such behavior is unacceptable.

THE TAILHOOK EXAMPLE As an example of how people learn about rewards and punishments from observing others, consider the 1991 Tailhook scandal. The Tailhook Association is a nonprofit organization of naval aviators, and in 1991, the organization had formal ties with the U.S. Navy. According to many insiders, the type of sexual harassment (of some 90 women) that occurred at the annual Tailhook Association meeting held in the Las Vegas Hilton in 1991 had been implicitly rewarded (or at least not punished) in the Navy for some time. These sexual harassment rituals were regular events that the male participants experienced as fun (rewarding). The Navy brass was known to turn a blind eye to reports, responding with a "boys will be boys" attitude. Investigations were torturously slow and resulted in little, if any, punishment. The reward system became well known, and therefore the men continued to engage in these "rewarding" behaviors that weren't punished.

Many people (especially women) looked to the Navy's reaction to the Tailhook scandal as an opportunity to change the messages being sent to all about the acceptability or unacceptability of such conduct. Some early signs were encouraging, but the longer-term results were disappointing to many women. The Secretary of the Navy resigned his post at the outset of the scandal, and the Navy severed ties with the Tailhook Association in late 1991. Investigations of potential criminal misconduct were also launched. However, the Navy's discussions with 1,500 men resulted in only two suspects. When the Pentagon took over, 140 aviators were accused of indecent exposure, assault, or lying under oath. However, only 80 of these individuals were ever fined or even moderately disciplined. None of those involved in the assault of the 90 women was court-martialed or seriously disciplined. Perhaps most significant, in early 1994 the young woman who filed the first complaint, Lt. Paula Coughlin, resigned from the Navy, explaining that Tailhook "and the covert attacks on me that followed have stripped me of my ability to serve."[9] Lt. Coughlin left amid "rumor mongering by officers trying to impugn her credibility" and with a "stack of hate mail." However, also in 1994, a federal jury awarded Lieutenant Coughlin $1.7 million in compensatory damages and $5 million in punitive damages, holding the Hilton Hotel responsible.[10] The Navy's top admiral, Frank B. Kelso, retired two months early "with a flowery note from the Defense Secretary praising him 'as a man of the highest honor and integrity.'" The Tailhook Association continues to hold an annual convention, but it is now a much tamer affair. In 1999, after an investigation of the Tailhook Association and its 1999 convention in Reno, the Navy restored its ties with the organization. Secretary of the Navy Richard Danzig said, "The shameful events of the Tailhook Convention in 1991 led to a withdrawal of our support for the Association. Over the past eight years, however, the Association took a number of constructive steps that warranted a review of its status ... [and] we've concluded that the time is right to restore ties." The association has committed itself to prevent the type of misconduct that occurred in 1991. (See www.tailhook.org for more information on the association.)

The message to Navy men (and women) has clearly been mixed. Yes, the event caused a lot of turmoil, probably enough to suggest to Navy men that assaulting their female colleagues was not going to be as "rewarding" as it used to be. In fact, membership in the Tailhook Association dropped dramatically after the incident, especially among younger members.[11] And several admirals have been discharged for inappropriate sexual behavior committed since Tailhook. Sexual-harassment sensitivity training is now required in the Navy. But in 1996 *Newsweek* reported that in the four years after Tailhook, the Navy received more than 1,000 harassment complaints and more than 3,500 charges of indecent assault. Women still complained that they faced reprisals for filing complaints.[12] So what's the message that's being sent today? We don't know. But the Navy should be aware of the powerful messages being sent to all Navy personnel every time a decision is made to respond to a sexual harassment complaint.

Managers, take note of the messages you're implicitly sending to all of your workers by what you reward and punish (or fail to punish). Employees are constantly on the lookout for these cues. They want to know what's OK and not OK in your work environment. If they observe that people advance by stepping on others, by lying to customers, and by falsifying reports, they'll be more inclined to do so themselves. If they see sexual harassment go undisciplined, they may feel free to engage in it themselves. So if you become aware of unethical behavior in your group, chances are that it is being rewarded somehow. Ask yourself how the reward system might be intentionally or unintentionally rewarding the undesired behavior, and take responsibility for changing it. On the other hand, if unethical individuals are dismissed, and persons of integrity advance, the ethical lesson is also clear. Integrity is valued and unethical behavior won't be tolerated.

Can You Really Reward Ethical Behavior?

Reward systems assume the use of rewards and punishments. However, for years, management writers have preached that managers should use rewards whenever possible—that punishment is inherently a bad management practice. This idea, good as it sounds, may be impractical when the goal is to encourage ethical behavior and discourage unethical behavior. Relying on rewards means rewarding ethical behavior. So, let's think about how a manager might reward ethical behavior. Perhaps he or she could give awards or bonuses to those whose expense reports were honest and accurate or to those managers who didn't harass their secretaries. Ridiculous? Of course. Workers don't expect to be rewarded for behaviors that are expected of everyone—for simply doing the right thing. So in the short term, it's quite difficult to reward ethical behavior.

IN THE LONG TERM, YES. If we switch to longer-term thinking, there should be rewards for doing the right thing. For example, in most organizations people are aware of how one gets ahead. Do people get promoted despite ethical lapses? If so, the message is clear. If you want to get ahead around here, you have to do whatever it takes. People who make it are likely the ones who have decided to go along to get along or, worse yet, the ones who stepped on others to get ahead. Or, are those who have advanced to the highest levels known for their integrity? If so, a general message about the importance of integrity is being sent. Rewards are a limited tool for influencing specific behaviors today or tomorrow, but they should be used to set the tone for what's expected and rewarded in the long term.

What About Punishment?

As for punishment, we all know that managers sometimes have to discipline their subordinates, just as responsible parents are expected to discipline their children. It's part of the manager's job to step in when an employee is headed down the wrong path. We also know that discipline works. If people expect their misconduct to be detected and punished, they're less likely to engage in it. So, if it works, why not use it? Well, it turns out that punishment works best when it's carried out in a particular way—when workers perceive it as fair.

If we examine the idea that punishment should be avoided, we find that it's based on old psychological research that was conducted on rats and small children. It has little to do with adults in work settings who can distinguish punishment that's fair (i.e., punishment that is deserved and fairly administered) from punishment that's unfair. Have you ever heard an adult say, "I had it coming, I deserved it"? As Dennis Levine said of his arrest and imprisonment for insider trading, "I've gained an abiding respect for the fairness of our system of justice. ... When I broke the law, I was punished. The system works." He also said, "My former life was destroyed because I figured the odds were a thousand to one against my getting caught."[13] If he had thought he would be caught and punished, the odds would have been reversed, and he may never have cut an insider trading deal. Once caught and punished, he acknowledged that the punishment was just.

Punishment should be administered fairly. Research evidence suggests that punishment results in more positive outcomes (e.g., the behavior improves and the employee becomes a better corporate citizen) if the recipient perceives it to be fair.[14] As we said in Chapter 6, these positive outcomes are linked primarily to the appropriate severity of the punishment and employee input. The punishment should "fit the crime," and it should be consistent with what others have received for similar infractions. It's also important that you give the employee an opportunity for input—to explain his or her side of the story. Also, the disciplined worker is more likely to respond positively to the punishment if you approach it in a constructive fashion and carefully explain the reasons for the punishment. Finally, if you punish, do it in private. Punishment can be a humiliating experience, and public punishment adds insult to injury.

Recognize punishment's indirect effects. The punished employee should not be the manager's only concern. Social learning theory suggests that other workers will be powerfully affected as well. Remember, we learn a great deal from observing the rewards and punishments of others. But if the punishment occurs in private, how will others know about it? Anyone who has worked in a real organization knows about the "grapevine," the communication network that flashes organizational news throughout a department or company. Good managers are aware of the power of the grapevine and rely on it to transmit important information. And research has discovered that when people are aware that unethical behavior has taken place, they want the violators to be punished.[15] The idea here is that people want to believe that the workplace is "just"— that good guys are rewarded and bad guys are punished. They also want to feel that they aren't suckers who, in a sense, are being punished for following the rules when others get away with breaking them. This is an important reason why managers must discipline unethical behavior when it occurs. There must be no exceptions. High-level rule violators must be held to the same standards. By clearly disciplining all rule violators, managers not only send an unequivocal message to the violator and all observers that this behavior won't be tolerated, but they support the notion that this is a just place to work where the rules are enforced fairly and consistently.

THE THOMAS J. WATSON, JR./IBM EXAMPLE In *Father Son & Co.; My Life at IBM and Beyond,* Thomas Watson, Jr., the son of IBM's founder, ran the company for almost 20 years at a time when IBM dominated the computer industry. In his book, he discussed the importance of swift, severe punishment for breaches of integrity and the indirect effects of punishing or not punishing. Watson said, "If a manager does something unethical, he should be fired just as surely as a factory worker. This is the wholesome use of the boss's power." But, as he explains in the following excerpt, his managers didn't always follow his advice.

> On one occasion some managers in one of our plants started a chain letter involving U.S. savings bonds. The idea was that one manager would write to five other managers, and each of those would write to five more, who

would each send some bonds back to the first guy and write to five more, and so on. Pretty soon they ran out of managers and got down to employees. It ended up that the employees felt pressure to join the chain letter and pay off the managers. I got a complaint about this and brought it to the attention of the head of the division. I expected him to say, at a minimum, "We've got to fire a couple of guys, I'll handle it." Instead, he simply said, "Well, it was a mistake." I couldn't convince him to fire anybody. Now, you could admire him for defending the team, but I think there is a time when integrity should take the rudder from team loyalty. All the same, I didn't pursue the matter any further, and my failure to act came back to haunt me.

A couple of years later in that same division, a manager fired a low-level employee who had been stealing engineering diagrams and selling them to a competitor. Firing him would have been fine, except that the manager handled it in a brutal way. The employee in question had one thing in his life that he was proud of—his commission in the U.S. Army Reserve, where he held the rank of major. Instead of simply going to the man's house and telling him, "You swiped the drawings and we're going to fire you," the manager picked a week when the fellow was in military camp to lower the boom. Somehow the military authorities got involved as well, and the man was stripped of his commission. The humiliation caused him to become insanely angry, and for the next few years he devoted himself to making me uncomfortable. He sent pictures of Tom Watson Jr. behind bars to his senators and his congressman and to every justice of the Supreme Court. And he kept harking back to that chain letter, because he knew we had tolerated the men responsible for it. Eventually he simmered down, but the incident really taught me a lesson. After that I simply fired managers when they broke rules of integrity. I did it in perhaps a dozen cases, including a couple involving senior executives. I had to overrule a lot of people each time, who would argue that we should merely demote the man, or transfer him, or that the business would fall apart without him. But the company was invariably better off for the decision and the example.[16]

Sometimes employees are punished for trying to do the right thing. For example, Owen Cheevers was an experienced researcher at the Bank of Montreal who wrote an honest report expressing his concerns about the radio industry. Investment bankers at the firm asked him to make his report more positive. When he refused to write a more glowing report, Cheevers was fired. Obviously, such punishment sends a powerful message to all other employees who are aware of it—go along or be fired.[17]

Practical Advice for Managers about Punishment

Tom Watson learned the hard way what can happen when breaches of integrity aren't disciplined swiftly and severely. Workers have long memories about incidents such as the chain letter and how management handles them. They tuck that sort of information away for later use. When the employee who stole the engineering drawings was fired in a particularly humiliating way, he was outraged. His severe and public punishment seemed particularly unfair when compared with the way others had been treated. And he reacted in ways that managers are told to expect from punished employees. He was angry at the punisher and the organization.

The important point about punishment is that adults differentiate between fair and unfair punishment. If you use punishment consistently to enforce the rules, employees will expect to be punished when they break them. However, they expect punishment that fits the crime and that is consistent with how others have been treated. In most cases, if you impose discipline fairly, the problem behavior improves and the subordinate goes on to be a productive organizational citizen.

Remember that you should be concerned about observers who pay a great deal of attention to how rule violations are handled. When the chain letter offenders weren't severely punished, an implicit message was sent to all who were aware of the scheme, and expectations were set up for how management would respond to future breaches of integrity. A "just" organization is one that punishes rule violations fairly and consistently and doesn't punish people who try to do the right thing. Workers expect managers to discipline fairly, and they're morally outraged when management doesn't do its job.

"EVERYONE'S DOING IT"

People Follow Group Norms

"Everyone's doing it" is the refrain so frequently used to encourage (and rationalize or justify) unethical behavior. We've all heard it. From fraternity brothers who are expected to advise their peers about the content of exams, to college football players who accept booster money, to waiters and waitresses who don't claim all of their tip income for tax purposes, to auditors who sign off on financial statements that haven't been thoroughly checked, to insider traders who share secrets about upcoming financial deals, individuals are much more likely to engage in unethical behavior if they're convinced that others are doing it too. It lets them off the hook by providing an acceptable justification and rationale for the behavior. Also, recall what you learned about moral awareness in Chapter 5. People are more likely to recognize issues as "ethical issues" if there is social consensus in the group that the issue raises ethical concerns. But if "everyone is doing it," social consensus is low (everyone seems to agree that the behavior is not a problem) and it's more likely that ethical concerns just won't come up.

Rationalizing Unethical Behavior

For some behaviors, the refrain "everyone is doing it" is used primarily as a rationalization. The employee who inflates his or her expense reports believes that it's justified first because everyone else is doing it (and getting away with it, too). A group may also develop other reasons to bolster the rationalization process. For example, inflating expenses may be explained in the group as a way of compensating for the extra hours spent away from home, to pay for the drink at the bar or a movie, and other expenses that aren't deductible under the organization's formal travel cost reimbursement policy. These rationalizations are often explicitly or implicitly supported by the boss, who suggests the behavior or who engages in it himself or herself. Either way, the manager sends a powerful message that it's okay to bend the rules, a message that can easily be generalized to other rules in the organization.

A better way to manage the process is to state the rules clearly and then enforce them. In other words, if it seems reasonable to reimburse a traveling employee for a drink at the bar, a movie, or a telephone call home, then change the rules so that these expenses can be legally reimbursed under the organization's formal travel policy. Then abuses of the system can be disciplined.

Pressure to Go Along

For other behaviors, the "everyone is doing it" refrain represents not just a rationalization but actual pressure to go along with the crowd. The argument is used to encourage those who are reluctant. "Aw, c'mon, everybody does it!" Not going along puts the individual in the uncomfortable spot of being perceived as some sort of goody-goody who is highly ethical but also unlikable, and certainly not someone who can be trusted. The result can be ostracism from the group, and most of us would rather go along than be ostracized.[18] Many individuals will go along with unethical behaviors because of the strong need they have to be accepted. If left to their own devices, they might very well follow the rules. But, in the group situation, they feel that they have no choice but to comply, or at least remain silent about what others are doing.

Practical Advice for Managers about Group Norms

So what does this mean for the manager? Above all, you must be acutely aware of the power of group norms (informal standards of behavior) that may be consistent or inconsistent with the formal, written rules. Group norms represent what's really happening in the group, and you must be in touch with this reality. Any new employee will be quickly schooled in "the way we do things in this group" and will be expected to go along. Loyalty to the group may be the most powerful norm, and one that's extremely difficult to counteract. If the group norms support ethical behavior, you have no problem, but if they don't, you face a particularly tough situation. If the group is strong and cohesive, one approach you can use is to identify the informal group leader and attempt to influence that individual, hoping she or he will influence the others. It's also important to consider the reward system. Norms often arise to support behaviors that are implicitly rewarded. If people are doing something, it's usually because they find it rewarding and the system somehow encourages it. Changes in the reward system can lead to changes in group norms.

THE SLADE COMPANY CASE EXAMPLE A classic Harvard Business School case explains how a highly productive manufacturing work group with a strong informal leader has created a problematic group norm for punching in and out. After the foreman leaves, all but one of the group members goes home. The one person remaining behind punches out all of the other group members. The result is that group members are paid for more hours than they actually work. On occasion, when a group member is delayed in the morning, the group punches him in. But this is carefully controlled, and the group has developed norms so that this practice is not abused. Although the punch-out system seems to be clearly wrong, the case is complicated by the fact that management admits that although pay is low, productivity in the group is high. Furthermore, the group is highly cohesive and very willing to work hard when necessary to fulfill last-minute orders or to solve unusual production problems. The workers also value the ability to have some control over the workday. Finally, management has known about the practice for some time and has ignored it.

The solution to the case isn't clear-cut. The case writers have suggested that management might be better off leaving well enough alone. "If it ain't broke, don't fix it." However, we believe that this is impossible if the ethical dimensions of the case are brought into focus. Leaving it alone implies tacit acceptance and approval of rule breaking and sends that message not only to this work group but to all of the others as well. Other groups that, for some reason, can't manage to do the same (perhaps because of less cohesion or because their supervisor stays later) will no doubt resent the injustice. Management must also accept some responsibility for tacitly approving this over a long period of time.

Remembering that people do what's rewarded, we believe that the norm is most likely to change via adjustments in the reward system. For example, moving to a five-day salary (somewhat higher than their current average take home pay) rather than hourly pay would reward people for getting the job done rather than staying a certain number of hours on weekdays. Group members could still be paid extra for weekend overtime work when it's available. If the late-arrival norm isn't being abused, it could be institutionalized. If someone must be late, a new rule could state that he or she must inform someone in the work group by a certain time. Like absences, a certain number of late arrivals would be allowed within a specified time period. The informal group leader should be involved in devising the solution with an appeal to his or her concern for fairness to other workers in the organization.

PEOPLE FULFILL ASSIGNED ROLES

Roles are strong forces for guiding behavior, and workers are assigned roles that can powerfully influence their behavior in ethical dilemma situations. Roles can reduce a person's sense of his or her individuality by focusing attention on the role and the expectations that accompany it. It doesn't really matter who fills the role. It's the role requirements that are important. This focus on the role reduces the individual's awareness of the self as an independent individual who is personally responsible for an outcome. This psychological process is called deindividuation.[19]

So, the individual acts "in role" and does what's expected. This is fine when behaving "in role" means doing the right thing. But what happens when "in role" behavior involves behaving illegally or unethically? For example, aggression is part of the police officer's role. But sometimes, police officers step over the ethical/legal line when they become overly aggressive, assaulting suspects without cause. Several such incidents have been recorded by bystanders on videotape in recent years. Another important part of the police officer role is loyalty to other police officers and protection of one's peers. Police officers often travel in pairs and must rely on each other in difficult, life-threatening situations. Therefore, loyalty, protection, and trust within the ranks serve an important, positive purpose. But loyalty can also end up supporting unethical behavior when, for example, a fellow police officer is overly aggressive and a peer who observes the conduct doesn't report it.

Consider this example from an old television series. Two female police detectives were part of a stakeout to catch one of their fellow police officers stealing heroin. They realized that they faced a complex moral dilemma when he told them that he was stealing the heroin for his mother who was dying of cancer and in severe pain. He had clearly broken the law, and the rules clearly said that they must turn him in. But loyalty and protection were important parts of their police role. Their colleague had good intentions—to help his dying mother. After much discussion and individual soul searching, they decided to protect their colleague and keep silent about what they knew. Although we may disagree about whether they made the right decision, the point here is that the peer protection and loyalty aspects of the police officer role were an important part of that decision.

The Zimbardo Prison Experiment

A powerful and widely cited social-psychological study illustrates the power of roles to influence behavior.[20] The researchers created a prison environment in the basement of the psychology building at Stanford University. Twenty-four psychologically healthy subjects (people like us) were recruited and randomly assigned to play the roles of prisoners or guards. General rules were provided regarding how to fulfill the role, but subjects were left free to interact within those general guidelines. With the cooperation of the local police, the guards were actually sent out to arrest the prisoners, book them, and transport them to their simulated cells. The prisoners were given uniforms and were referred to by identification numbers. The guards were given comfortable quarters and a recreation area. The guards wore uniforms and mirrored sunglasses, and worked standard eight-hour shifts where they were given a great deal of control over the prisoners, short of physical abuse. With rare exceptions, the guards enjoyed the social power and status of the guard role. Some "guards" were exhilarated by the experience, reinforcing their guard role with aggression, threats, and insults. The "prisoners" quickly began to show dramatic signs of emotional change, including acute anxiety, helplessness, and passivity verging on complete servility. Some became severely distressed and physically ill.

Although the experiment was originally scheduled to last two weeks, it was halted after only six days due to concern about the prisoners' well-being. "At the end of only six days ... it was no longer apparent to most of the subjects (or to us) where reality ended and their roles began. The majority had indeed become prisoners or guards, no longer able to clearly differentiate between role playing and the real self. There were dramatic changes in virtually every aspect of their behavior, thinking, and feeling."[21]

After the experiment was concluded, guards expressed a combination of excitement and dismay at the darker side of themselves that had emerged. The simulated situation had become real very quickly, and both sides readily assumed the roles expected of them as members of their respective groups (prisoner or guard). This occurred despite the other roles these individuals may have played in their "normal" lives just days before. Finally, when individuals attempted to deviate from the role behavior, the deviation was quickly suppressed by pressure to conform expressed by other group members. The experimental results were used to support the "situational" explanation for prison behavior. In other words, perfectly normal people behaved cruelly and aggressively when placed in a role where these behaviors were either expected or allowed.

Roles at Work

But prisons aren't your average work setting. How do the results of this experiment apply to work organizations? People enter work organizations in a state of "role readiness."[22] In this state, they're likely to engage in behaviors that are consistent with their organizationally prescribed role, even if those behaviors violate other values they hold (another example of multiple ethical selves). A particularly interesting example is provided by corporate professionals such as lawyers, physicians, and accountants. Professionals are thought to adhere most closely to their professional roles. In fact, this is part of the definition of a professional. Although there's little research evidence, much anecdotal evidence suggests that many corporate physicians, lawyers, and accountants identify more closely with their organizational role. For example, Johns Manville medical personnel conformed to corporate policy and remained silent about asbestos exposure, despite the known medical dangers.[23] In their dual roles of physician and organizational member, the latter took precedence. The same can be said of auditors who are supposed to adhere to the ethical guidelines of their professional organization, the AICPA. They are supposed to protect the public interest and report financial irregularities they find. But, as we have learned from recent auditing scandals, the corporate organizational role seems to take over for many.

Conflicting Roles Can Lead to Unethical Behavior

In their jobs, people are sometimes expected to play different roles that may make competing demands on them, causing internal conflict and stress that may be resolved via unethical behavior such as lying. For example, professional nurses are taught that patient education and patient advocacy are important aspects of the nursing role. Yet these nursing role expectations may conflict with physicians' orders, or they may be difficult to implement because of time pressures and paperwork that take nurses away from patients. In a research study, nurses responded to scenarios, some of which placed them in role conflict situations.[24] Those nurses who were in role-conflict situations said that they would be more likely to lie by misreporting their behavior on the patient's chart.

Managers must be aware that conflicting role demands can pressure workers to be dishonest. The best way to avoid this type of dishonesty is to minimize conflicting role demands. Ask your staff to analyze their jobs and to identify sources of conflict that could cause them to feel that they have to lie to you or someone else in order to successfully accomplish some aspect of their job. Then, see if the job can be redesigned to minimize these conflicts.

Roles Can Support Ethical Behavior

Roles can also work to support ethical behavior. For example, whistle-blowing (reporting the misconduct of others) is sometimes prescribed for individuals in certain jobs. This makes a difficult behavior easier to carry out. A survey of internal auditors found that whistle-blowing was more likely when the auditors saw reporting as a prescribed job requirement.[25] Therefore, managers should consider the extent to which organizational roles encourage either ethical or unethical behavior. Obviously, those that support and encourage unethical behavior should be changed. Those that encourage ethical behavior (e.g., whistle-blowing) should be bolstered. For example, research has found that although reporting a peer's misconduct is a distasteful and difficult act, people are more likely to report a peer if doing so is explicitly made a part of their role via an honor code or code of conduct.[26] In other words, if their role requires them to report misconduct when they see it, they're more likely to do so. Many colleges and universities have honor codes that require students to report cheating that they observe. The requirement makes it easier for the reporter because the behavior becomes a duty, a role responsibility rather than a voluntary ethical act.

Practical Advice for Managers about Roles

The key for managers is that roles influence behavior. Think about the roles people play in your department or organization. What are the implications of their role expectations for ethical and unethical behavior? Do some individuals experience conflicts between their roles? For example, are professionals torn between their organizational and professional roles? Or do employees experience conflicts within a role, like nurses who are supposed to play the conflicting roles of patient advocate and subordinate to the physician? Again, the individuals who hold the jobs are probably the best source of information about their role expectations and potential conflicts. Once you've analyzed roles and role conflicts, determine whether jobs need to be altered to reduce conflict. If change isn't possible, at least you can anticipate the problems that are likely to arise for people in these jobs.

PEOPLE DO WHAT THEY'RE TOLD

In a *60 Minutes* segment, Americans working for a Japanese company in the United States reported that their supervisor told them to unpack machine tools manufactured in and shipped from Japan, remove the "Manufactured in Japan" label, change a few things, replace the label with a "Manufactured in the U.S." label, and recrate the machine tools for shipping. These products were then shipped as if they had been manufactured in the United States to, of all places, the American military (where U.S. manufacture of machine tools was a requirement). An American accountant at the firm finally blew the whistle, but when the workers who had been doing the unpacking and recrating were asked why they did it, they replied that they were doing what their supervisor had told them to do. One of the men who had attempted to protest was told that he could find another job if he didn't like it. So, he continued doing what he was told to do.

This is just one of many examples we could cite of workers at all levels doing what they're told by managers. Participants in the famous 1972 Watergate break-in referred to their unquestioning obedience to superior orders in testimony before the Senate investigating committee, as did Nazi SS officers in war crimes trials and participants in the Iran–Contra affair.[27] Organizations (corporate, political, or military) are authority structures whose members accept the idea that, to be members in good standing, they must give up a certain amount of independence and autonomy. They expect that managers will tell them what to do. That's the managerial role. They also assume that they should do what's expected of them. That's the subordinate role. These assumptions and expectations allow organizations to avoid chaos and function in an orderly fashion. Also, individuals often feel that they owe the organization and their manager their loyalty, further reinforcing the pressure to comply.

The Milgram Experiments

Classic social-psychological studies conducted by Stanley Milgram provide uncomfortable insights into how normal adults behave in authority situations.[28] Most adults will carry out the authority figure's orders even if these orders are contrary to their personal beliefs about what's right.

In a number of laboratory experiments, Milgram paid subjects recruited from the New Haven, Connecticut, area to participate in a one-hour study on the effects of punishment on learning. The subject was asked to play "teacher" in a learning experiment; the "learner," unbeknownst to the teacher/subject, was a member of the research team. The learner was strapped into a chair with an electrode attached to his or her wrist. The teacher/subject was seated at a shock generator and was told to pose questions to the learner. Each time the learner provided an incorrect response to a question, the teacher/subject was told to turn a dial to administer an increasingly severe shock—though in fact no shocks were actually given. As the apparent "shocks" intensified, the learner verbally expressed increasing discomfort, finally screaming and then going silent. During the experiments, many teacher/subjects would question the experimenter and express the desire to stop. The experimenter, dressed in a white lab coat, would provide the following scripted response, "Although the shocks may be painful, there is no permanent tissue damage, so please go on." If the teacher/subject continued to resist, the experimenter would respond with three successive prods: "The experiment requires that you continue"; "It is absolutely essential that you continue"; "You have no choice, you must go on." If the teacher continued to resist, the experiment was finally terminated.

To the surprise of Milgram and other observers, about 60 percent of the teacher/subjects in these experiments continued to the end, obeying the authority figure's instructions despite the conflict they felt and expressed. It's not that they felt OK about what they were doing. In fact, their emotional appeals to the experimenter suggested that they very much wanted to stop. But most of them didn't. They may have felt that refusing to continue would challenge the experimenter's authority, the legitimacy of the experiment, and that they would risk embarrassing themselves.[29] They acted as if they were constrained to do as they were told by the authority figure, rather than as independent adults who could end the experiment at any time. We should also note that teacher/subjects who were at the principled level of cognitive moral development (see Chapter 5) were more likely to challenge the experimenter's authority and that they were more likely to stop giving the electric shocks.

Obedience to Authority at Work

The obedient behavior seen in the Milgram experiments is similar to behavior observed over and over again in work organizations. The notion of legitimate authority is an accepted tenet of organizational life. In 1968, American military men massacred hundreds of innocent civilians at My Lai, Vietnam. They didn't ask questions. They did what they were told to do. Twenty years later, Colonel Oliver North, who was tried for arranging the illegal sale of arms to the Nicaraguan contra forces, claimed that he was only following the orders of his superiors. Individuals who testified to the U.S. Congress about price-fixing practices in the electrical industry were asked why they didn't report these practices to higher authorities. They responded that they felt they couldn't because they reported to a prescribed superior only.[30] And Roger Boisjoly, who questioned the safety of the O-rings and who attempted to convince managers to cancel the launch of the space shuttle *Challenger,* never went outside the chain of command to protest.[31]

Practical Advice for Managers about Obedience to Authority

Managers must realize the power they hold as legitimate authority figures in work organizations. Old concepts die hard. And even today in team-oriented organizations, most people will do as they're told. Therefore, authority figures must exhibit ethical behavior, and they must send powerful signals that high ethical standards are expected of everyone. This message should begin at the top of the organization and work its way down through every level. Moreover, when unethical behavior is uncovered, the investigation must consider the explicit or implicit messages being sent by authority figures. Don't assume that the individual acted alone and without influence. Our tendency is to try to isolate the problem, find the one "culprit" (bad apple), and get on with our lives. But the culprit may have been explicitly or implicitly encouraged by a superior, and this possibility should be taken into account.

RESPONSIBILITY IS DIFFUSED IN ORGANIZATIONS

In order for a relationship to exist between what people think is right and what they do, they must feel responsible for the consequences of their actions.[32] Therefore, the sense of personal responsibility is a prerequisite for moral action. If you believe that a decision you yourself made to market a particular product might hurt small children or the environment, you are much more likely to seriously consider the moral implications of the decision. But in organizations, the individual often becomes disconnected from the consequences of his or her actions and doesn't feel personally responsible for them. Responsibility becomes diffused. No individual feels the need to take responsibility, so in the end, no one does, and unethical behavior is more likely.

There are at least four reasons why individuals may not feel personally responsible for their organizational actions. Responsibility is diffused because it is taken away, shared with others in decision-making groups, obscured by the organizational hierarchy, or diluted by psychological distance to potential victims.

"Don't Worry—We're Taking Care of Everything"

First, at work, individuals are often encouraged to turn responsibility over to those at higher levels. This is related to our earlier discussion of obedience to authority. But in this case, the individual is simply told not to worry—that the problem or decision is someone else's responsibility. For example, an individual who expresses concern about a safety or environmental problem may be told, "We appreciate your concern, but you don't need to worry about it. We're taking care of everything." This type of response absolves the subordinate of feelings of responsibility for the consequences of the organization's action. Someone, particularly someone at a higher level, has taken the responsibility.

However, even if the superiors are highly responsible and highly ethical, the act of absolving subordinates of responsibility may have significant implications for their subsequent ethical behavior. Because of the feeling that they must do as they're told by authority figures, most people feel that they have no choice but to follow superiors' orders. In this case, the orders are to hand over responsibility for decision making and the individual feels that she or he has no choice but to give it up. If this sort of response becomes routine, individuals will come to believe that it isn't their responsibility to be on the lookout for ethical violations, and that they may stop bringing potential problems to the attention of superiors.

Diffusing Responsibility in Groups

Second, important organizational decisions are often made in groups. Therefore, responsibility for the decision becomes diffused among all group members. No single individual feels responsible. Diffusion of responsibility in groups is used to explain the results of classic research on the likelihood that bystanders will help a seizure victim.[33] This research suggests that when others are present, responsibility is diffused among all of the bystanders and individuals are less likely to help.

Diffusion of responsibility also operates in group decision making through processes such as "groupthink."[34] Groupthink can occur in cohesive groups where group members have a commitment to the group and a strong desire to remain a group member. A major characteristic of groupthink is the conformity of individual group members to the decision they think the majority of group members prefer. Individual group members may find it very difficult to express disagreement and tend to censor themselves even if they disagree with the group decision.

One important symptom of groupthink is the group's "illusion of morality," the sense that the group simply wouldn't do anything wrong. In a classic instructional film on groupthink, a group of managers makes a decision to market a new drug despite disturbing evidence that it may cause dangerous side effects. The illusion of morality is expressed by a group member who states that the company has a well-earned good reputation and would never do anything to hurt its customers.

Clearly, decisions with ethical overtones that are made in a group setting require special attention. The manager must make sure that the ethical implications are identified and carefully analyzed. The group leader should be careful not to state his or her preference up front, because group members will tend to censor their own beliefs to conform with those of the leader. Other techniques can be used to make sure that alternative points of view are aired. For example, an individual can be appointed to the role of devil's advocate, or multiple individuals can be appointed to voice multiple alternative perspectives. It's easier for these individuals to take an alternative stance when it's their role to do so. Another alternative is to open the group to outside stakeholders who would come in to present their concerns and perspectives.

Diffusing Responsibility by Dividing Responsibility

Third, responsibility in organizations is often so divided that individuals see themselves as only a small cog in a large machine. Or they simply don't have vital information that would be required to make a good decision. Division of responsibility is essential for the kind of specialization required in modern jobs. But this means that organizational members often do their jobs with blinders on; they see only what's directly ahead of them, and no one sees (or takes responsibility for) the whole picture.

With regard to information, think about September 11, 2001, and the discussions about whether the government should have been able to "connect the dots" and anticipate the terrorist attacks. Different people in different government agencies had extremely relevant information (about specific terrorists, their activities in the U.S. such as flight training, and plans to fly planes into other key structures such as the Eiffel Tower). But these agencies were not set up to communicate with each other on a regular basis. In fact, some of them (the CIA and FBI) were explicitly designed to operate independently because of concerns about the power of an integrated agency. So the design of an organization (and decisions about who communicates with whom) influences the nature of information individuals receive in organizations and whether they can be held responsible.

Regarding the Pinto Fires case (Chapters 4 and 5), students often assume that the recall coordinator knew about the crash tests that were conducted while the car was being designed. But, according to Dennis Gioia, recall coordinator at the time, he had no information about those. That information was buried in engineering reports and didn't surface until much later. So, as recall coordinator, he couldn't make a decision (whether or not to make the $11 fix) that he knew nothing about.

Scott Peck is a psychiatrist and author of the bestseller *The Road Less Traveled*. He was part of a group dispatched to study the 1968 My Lai massacre in South Vietnam. At My Lai, American troops slaughtered a village of unarmed women, children, and elderly men. The killing took all morning, and only one person, an observant helicopter pilot, tried to stop it. Peck's interviews with military people revealed a bureaucratic organizational structure that allowed individuals to see only their own narrow part of the problem, thereby allowing them to avoid feelings of responsibility. When he wandered the halls of the Pentagon, questioning those involved in directing the manufacture of napalm and its transportation to Vietnam as bombs, the replies he received were something like the following: "We appreciate your problem and your concerns, but we are not the department you want. We are in ordnance. We supply the weapons, but we don't determine how they're used." Down the hall, another group suggested that the broad issues were also beyond their purview. "We simply determine how the war will be conducted—not whether it will be conducted."[35] Peck termed this process "the fragmentation of conscience." "Any group will remain inevitably potentially conscienceless and evil until such time as each and every individual holds himself or herself directly responsible for the behavior of the whole group—the organism of which he or she is a part. We have not yet begun to arrive at that point."[36]

Research has documented the diffusion of responsibility process. In a variation on the Milgram obedience-to-authority experiments discussed earlier, the diffusion of responsibility was simulated by dividing the teacher's role between two people, a "transmitter" and an "executant." The transmitter would inform the executant when a shock had to be administered and at what level. The experiment found that transmitters were significantly more likely to obey than executants.[37] One can imagine that it was easier for the transmitter to rationalize his or her actions. "I didn't actually do the harm—someone else did." This rationalization should become easier and easier, the greater the distance between the individual decision maker and the actual outcome.

Diffusing Responsibility by Creating Psychological Distance

Finally, responsibility can be diffused because of the psychological distance between the decision maker and potential victims.[38] When potential victims are psychologically distant or out of sight, it's more difficult to see oneself as responsible for any negative outcomes. This was exemplified in further variations on the obedience to authority studies in which Milgram varied the closeness of the learner "victim" to the teacher.[39] For example, when the learner was placed in the same room with the teacher, the level of obedience dropped more than 20 percent (to 40 percent). In another variation, when the teacher was asked to physically force the learner's hand onto the shock plate, the obedience level dropped another 10 percent. In these situations, as psychological distance decreased, the teacher felt personal responsibility more strongly and was less likely to comply with the authority figure's demands to harm the learner.

This research suggests that personal responsibility for the outcomes of our organizational decisions will be less clear in situations where the potential harm is far removed. For example, when the plant is not in our community, but in Mexico or somewhere in Asia, potential negative consequences are more distant; we may feel less personal responsibility and we may be more willing to make decisions that would harm people.

Practical Advice for Managers about Personal Responsibility

People are much more likely to act ethically if they perceive themselves as responsible for the outcomes of their decisions and actions. That means that they also need to have the relevant information. As a manager, you should make individual responsibility a highly salient issue. Spell out the responsibilities associated with specific positions and hold individuals to those expectations. Also, when a worker brings up an ethical concern, don't take it completely off his or her hands. And don't say that it's someone else's responsibility. If it becomes necessary to do so, be sure to keep the concerned individual informed of the progress and outcome of the decision.

When it comes to groups, make it clear that every group member will be held personally responsible for the outcome of group decisions. Ask groups to present minority reports or recommendations so that a communication mechanism exists for those who don't agree with the group. Appoint a devil's advocate or multiple advocates to question the assumptions of the group and the group's decision.

Don't forget to think about the design of your organization. How is the work divided up? Does the division of labor contribute to diffusion of responsibility by keeping people in the dark about relevant facts? Does the organizational structure make people feel like they're just cogs in a bigger wheel? Encourage information and responsibility sharing across bureaucratic divides.

The current movement to decrease levels in the organizational hierarchy may have a positive side benefit. People find that they have to communicate more laterally—

across the organization. Also, with fewer levels, it should become more difficult for organizational members to rationalize that higher ups were responsible. Finally, personal visits to geographically distant work sites and personal contact with customers should decrease psychological distance and increase the manager's felt responsibility for the outcomes of any decisions or actions that impact people in these locations.

CONCLUSION

You now have some important management concepts that can be applied to the management of ethical and unethical conduct. The remaining challenge is to analyze yourself (or your manager) in relation to these ideas. A common phrase used by today's managers is "walking the talk." If your intention is to be an ethical manager, here are some questions to ask yourself to see if you're "walking your ethical talk."

AM I "WALKING MY ETHICAL TALK?"

1. Do I talk about the ethical implications of decisions with the people who report to me and with job candidates I'm interested in hiring? With my peers? With my manager?
2. Have I made it clear to the people who report to me that I don't want to be protected from bad news? Do they understand that they can tell me anything without fear of retribution? Do my reports come to me with ethical concerns?
3. Do I provide guidance on ethical decision making, and have I participated in the ethics training of those who report to me?
4. When evaluating the performance of my staff, do I consider ethical goals as well as performance and quality goals? Do I focus on the means as well as the ends in decision making and performance appraisals?
5. Do I reward ethical conduct and discipline unethical conduct?
6. Do I require my people to take responsibility for their decisions?
7. What are the informal norms in my department? If my employees were asked to list the "rules" of working for me, what would they say? Are any of these problematic if ethical conduct is the goal?
8. If I were to die tomorrow, would the people who report to me say that I had integrity? How would my peers describe me? And what would my manager say?

The answers to these questions should form a sound beginning for understanding and managing ethical behavior in your work group. We'll discuss the important broader issue of organizational culture in Chapter 9.

DISCUSSION QUESTIONS

For the following questions, if you don't have work experience, interview someone who does.

1. Have you ever been in a situation, especially a work situation, where the norms supported a particular behavior, ethical or unethical, where you felt pressured to go along? Explain.
2. Have you ever been in a situation where the rewards explicitly or implicitly supported unethical conduct? Explain.
3. Can you think of situations in which unethical behavior was dealt with appropriately (punished justly) or inappropriately? What were the reactions of others in the organization?
4. What do you think would be appropriate punishment for those found guilty of assault or indecent exposure in the Tailhook situation? Why?
5. Have you ever felt obligated to do something you felt was wrong because a person in a position of authority told you to do it?
6. Think about how you might design work to maximize workers' taking responsibility for the consequences of their actions.
7. Evaluate yourself or a manager you know using the "do you walk your talk" questions above.

CASE

SEARS, ROEBUCK, AND CO.: THE AUTO CENTER SCANDAL

Sears, Roebuck, and Co. began in the late 1800s as a mail-order company that sold farm supplies and other consumer items. Its first retail store opened in the mid-1920s. Responding to changes in American society, such as the move from farms to factories and the presence of the automobile in many homes, hundreds of retail stores opened over the years. The company expanded rapidly, and eventually it diversified to include other businesses: insurance (Allstate Insurance), real estate (Coldwell Banker), securities (Dean Witter Reynolds), and credit cards (Discover). Each of these other businesses became its own division, in addition to the merchandising group which included retail stores, appliances, and auto service centers. By the early 1990s, the company was reporting revenues and earnings in the billions of dollars.[40]

Despite its long history of high earnings and its penetration into the U.S. market, Sears' retail business began to experience serious financial difficulties in the 1980s. Discount retailers such as Wal-Mart were pulling ahead in market share, leaving Sears lagging. Sears responded by adding non-Sears name brands and an "everyday low price" policy. But despite these efforts, in 1990 Sears reported a 40 percent decline in earnings, with the merchandising group dropping a whopping 60 percent! Cost-cutting measures were planned, including the elimination of jobs and a focus on profits at every level.[41]

In 1991, Sears unveiled a productivity incentive plan to increase profits in its auto centers nationwide. Auto mechanics had traditionally been paid an hourly wage and were expected to meet production quotas. In 1991, the compensation plan was changed to include a commission component. Mechanics were paid a base salary plus a fixed dollar amount for meeting hourly production quotas. Auto service advisors (the counter people who take orders, consult with mechanics, and advise customers) had traditionally been paid a salary. In order to increase sales, however, commissions and product-specific sales quotas were introduced for them as well. For example, a service advisor might be given the goal of selling a certain number of front-end alignments or brake repairs during each shift.[42]

In June 1992, the California Department of Consumer Affairs accused Sears, Roebuck, and Co. of violating the state's Auto Repair Act and sought to revoke the licenses of all Sears auto centers in California. The allegation resulted from an increasing number of consumer complaints and an undercover investigation of brake repairs. Other states quickly followed suit. Essentially, the charges alleged that Sears Auto Centers had been systematically misleading customers and charging them for unnecessary repairs. The California investigation attributed the problems to Sears Auto Centers' compensation system.[43]

In response to the charges, Sears CEO and Chairman Edward A. Brennan called a news conference to deny that any fraud had occurred, and he defended Sears' focus on preventive maintenance for older cars. He admitted to isolated errors, accepted personal responsibility for creating an environment where "mistakes" had occurred, and outlined the actions the company planned to take to resolve the issue. These included:

- Eliminating the incentive compensation program for service advisors
- Substituting commissions based on customer satisfaction
- Eliminating sales quotas for specific parts and repairs
- Substituting sales volume quotas

According to Brennan, "We have to have some way to measure performance."[44]

Sears also introduced "shopping audits" of its auto centers in which employees would pose as customers, and Brennan published a letter of explanation to the company's customers in *The Wall Street Journal* and *USA Today* on June 25, 1992.

Note that the compensation system for mechanics, based on number of tasks performed and parts replaced, was maintained. In the summer of 1992, Chuck Fabbri, a Sears mechanic from California, sent a letter about Sears' wage policy for mechanics to U.S. Senator Richard Bryan. Fabbri said:

> It is my understanding that Sears is attempting to convince your committee that all inspections in their auto centers are now performed by employees who are paid hourly and not on commission. This is not the case. The truth is that the majority of employees performing inspections are still on commission....
>
> The Service Advisors ... sell the repair work to the customer.... The repairs that they sell are not only based on their inspections, but to a larger degree based on the recommendations of mechanics who are on commission....
>
> On January 1, 1991, the mechanics, installers and tire changers had their hourly wages cut to what Sears termed a fixed dollar amount, or FDA per hour which varied depending on the classification. At present

the mechanic's FDA amount is $3.25 which, based on current Sears minimum production quotas, is 17% of my earnings. What this means is that for every hour of work, as defined by Sears, that I complete, I receive $3.25 plus my hourly base pay. If I do two hours worth of work in one hour I receive an additional $3.25 therefore increasing my earnings.

Sears calls this type of compensation incentive pay or piecework; however, a rose by any other name is still a rose. This is commission plain and simple. The faster I get the work done the more money I make, and as intended, Sears' profits increase. It is therefore obvious to increase his earnings, a mechanic might cut corners on, or eliminate altogether, procedures required to complete the repair correction. In addition to this, since the mechanic often inspects or performs the diagnosis, he has the ideal opportunity to oversell or recommend more repair work than is needed. This would be especially tempting if it has been a slow day or week. In part greed may create this less than ethical situation, but high pressure to meet quotas by Sears' management also presents a significant contribution. I have recently been threatened with termination if my production didn't at least equal Sears' minimum quotas. I might add that prior to this new wage policy, management had only positive response to my production, and my record proves this....

There is no doubt in my mind that before their auto center employees were put on commission Sears enjoyed the trust of its customers. Today presents a different story. The solution is obvious not only for Sears, but for the industry.[45]

Sears agreed to a multimillion-dollar settlement with the state of California and the 41 other states that had filed similar charges. The company was placed on three-year probation in California. It also settled a number of consumer class-action suits. In July 1992, the U.S. Congress held hearings on fraud in the auto repair industry.

The long-term impact of the scandal is unclear. Sears has now sold off its securities firm, the Discover card, most of its real estate and mortgage business, and 20 percent of Allstate Insurance. At the end of 1992, auto center sales lagged behind prior levels.[46] Also in 1992, *Business Week* reported that employees in other areas of Sears' business, such as insurance and appliance sales, were feeling the same kinds of pressures from sales quotas.[47]

Case Questions

1. Identify the ethical issues involved in the case from a consequentialist and deontological perspective (refer to Chapter 4).
2. Identify the management issues involved in the case. For example, think about the case in terms of multiple ethical selves, norms, reward systems, diffusion of responsibility, obedience to authority. What factors contributed the most to the alleged unethical conduct on the part of service advisors and mechanics?

3. How would you evaluate Sears' response to the allegations and the changes they made? Has Sears resolved its problem? Why or why not?
4. What do you think is the impact of the scandal on Sears' reputation for quality and service?
5. Respond to Brennan's comment, "We have to have some way to measure performance." What can management do to prevent "overselling?" Propose a management plan (including a compensation system) that allows management to measure performance and encourages auto center employees to behave ethically. Be specific.
6. Should anyone be disciplined? If so, who, and when? What should the discipline be?
7. Think more generally about Sears management's response to the firm's financial problems. How else could they have increased auto center sales without providing incentives to employees to sell specific products?

SHORT CASE

You've recently been promoted into the position of marketing manager in the communications division of your company. Your new job involves managing a staff and creating the publications and marketing materials for insurance sales professionals in three regions.

You have met the directors of the three regional sales forces before, and now you ask each one for a meeting to discuss in depth how your team can best meet their needs. Two of the sales directors were very cordial, and each explained what the technical demands of their areas are and how your department can best meet their needs.

However, during your meeting with Bill—the sales director of the third region and one of your firm's biggest moneymakers—he lays down the law. He says that his area is the largest of the three regions, and it produces significantly more revenue for your company than the other two regions combined. "You and your people need to know that when I say, 'Jump,'" he says, "they need to ask, 'How high?'"

In return, he says, he'll recommend you and your people for every award the company has to offer. In addition, he says he'll personally give you a monetary bonus, based on your team's performance, at the end of the year. Although you have never heard of a manager giving someone a bonus out of his own pocket, you suspect that your company would frown on such a practice.

Case Questions
1. What are the ethical issues in this case?
2. What are some reasons the decision maker in this case might be inclined to go along? Not go along?
3. If you were the decision maker, how would you handle the situation?
4. Would you report the conversation to your manager? Why or why not?

NOTES

1. Toffler, B. 1986. *Tough choices.* New York: John Wiley & Sons.
2. Barrett, R. A. 1984. *Culture and conduct: An excursion in anthropology.* Belmont, CA: Wadsworth.
3. Thomas, E., and Murr, T. & A. 2002. The gambler who blew it all. *Newsweek,* February 4: 18–24.
4. Ibid.
5. Gesalman, A. B. 2002. Cliff was climbing the walls. *Newsweek,* February 4: 24.
6. Levine, D. B. 1990. The inside story of an inside trader. *Fortune,* May 21: 80–89.
7. Eden, D. 1984. Self-fulfilling prophecy as a management tool: Harnessing Pygmalion. *Academy of Management Review* 9: 64–73.
8. Bandura, A. 1986. *Social foundations of thought and action: A social-cognitive theory.* Englewood Cliffs, NJ: Prentice-Hall.
9. Goodman, E. 1994. Nobody deemed accountable for Tailhook. *Centre Daily Times,* February 15: 6A.
10. Waller, D. C. 1994. Tailhook's lightning rod. *Newsweek,* February 28: 31.
11. Marshall, A. 2000. Knowing what's ahead can prevent looking back with regret. *Hotel and Motel Management,* March 6: 10.
12. Vistica, G. L. 1996. Anchors aweigh. *Newsweek,* February 5: 69–71.
13. Levine, D. B. 1990. The inside story of an inside trader. *Fortune,* May 21: 80–89.
14. Ball, G., Treviño, L. K., & Sims, H. P., Jr. 1994. Just and unjust punishment incidents. *Academy of Management Journal,* 37: 299–322.
15. Treviño, L. K., & Ball, G. A. 1992. The social implications of punishing unethical behavior: Observers' cognitive and affective reactions. *Journal of Management* 18: 751–768.
16. Watson, Thomas J., Jr. 1990. *Father son & co.: My life at IBM and beyond.* New York: Bantam.
17. Morgenson, G. 2002. The enforcers of Wall St.? Then again, maybe not. *New York Times* online, June 20.
18. Treviño, L. K., & Victor, B. 1992. Peer reporting of unethical behavior: A social context perspective. *Academy of Management Journal* 353: 38–64.
19. Zimbardo, P. G. 1970. The human choice: Individuation, reason, and order versus deindividuation, impulse, and chaos. In *Nebraska Symposium on Motivation,* 1969. W. J. Arnold & D. Levine, eds. Lincoln: University of Nebraska Press, 237–307.
20. Haney, C. C., Banks, & Zimbardo, P. 1973. Interpersonal dynamics in a simulated prison. *International Journal of Criminology and Penology* 1: 69–97.
21. Zimbardo, P. 1982. Pathology of imprisonment. In *Readings in social psychology: Contemporary perspectives,* 2nd ed. D. Krebs, ed. New York: Harper & Row.
22. Katz, D., & Kahn, R. 1978. *The social psychology of organizations,* 2nd ed. New York: John Wiley & Sons.
23. Brady, F. N., & Logdson, J. M. 1988. Zimbardo's "Stanford prison experiment" and the relevance of social psychology for teaching business ethics. *Journal of Business Ethics,* 7: 703–710. Brodeur, P. 1985. Outrageous misconduct: The asbestos industry on trial. New York: Pantheon.
24. Grover, S. 1993. Why professionals lie: The impact of professional role conflict on reporting accuracy. *Organizational Behavior and Human Decision Processes.* 55: 251–272.
25. Miceli, M. P., & Near, J. P. 1984. The relationships among beliefs, organizational position, and whistle-blowing status: A discriminant analysis. *Academy of Management Journal* 27: 687–705.
26. Treviño, L. K., & Victor, B. 1992. Peer reporting of unethical behavior: A social context perspective. *Academy of Management Journal* 353: 38–64.
27. Kelman, H. C., & Hamilton, V. L. 1989. *Crimes of obedience.* New Haven, CT: Yale University Press.
28. Milgram, S. 1974. *Obedience to authority; An experimental view.* New York: Harper & Row.
29. Kelman & Hamilton, *Crimes of obedience.*
30. Waters, J. A. 1978. Catch 20.5: corporate morality as an organizational phenomenon. *Organizational Dynamics,* Spring: 319.
31. Kelman & Hamilton, *Crimes of obedience.*
32. Schwartz, S. H. 1968a. Words, deeds, and the perception of consequences and responsibility in action situations. *Journal of Personality and Social Psychology* 10: 232–242. Schwartz, S. H.

33. 1968b. Awareness of consequences and the influence of moral norms on interpersonal behavior. Sociometry 31: 355–369.
33. Darley, J. M., & Latane, B. 1968. Bystanders' intervention in emergencies: Diffusion of responsibility. *Journal of Personality and Social Psychology* 8: 373–383.
34. Janis, I. 1982. *Group Think,* 2nd ed. Boston: Houghton Mifflin.
35. Peck, S.M.D., & Scott, M. D. 1983. *People of the lie: The hope for healing human evil.* New York: Simon & Schuster.
36. Ibid.
37. Kilham, W., & Mann, L. 1974. Level of destructive obedience as a function of transmitter and executant roles in the Milgram obedience paradigm. *Journal of Personality and Social Psychology* 29: 696–702.
38. Kelman & Hamilton, *Crimes of obedience.*
39. Milgram, S. 1974. *Obedience to authority: An experimental view.* New York: Harper & Row.
40. Santoro, M. A. 1993. *Sears auto centers.* Boston: Harvard Business School.
41. Ibid.; Kelly, K. 1992. How did Sears blow this gasket? *Business Week,* June 29: 38.
42. Santoro, *Sears auto centers.*
43. Kelly, How did Sears blow this gasket?
44. Gellene, D. 1992. New state probe of Sears could lead to suit. *Los Angeles Times,* June 12, part D: 1.
45. Hearing before Subcommittee on Consumer of the Senate Committee on Commerce, Science, and Transportation, 102nd Congress, 2nd Sess., July 21, 1992 (Sen. Hearing 102972), p. 83.
46. Santoro, *Sears auto centers.*
47. Flynn, J. 1992. Did Sears take other customers for a ride? *Business Week,* August 3: 24–25.

ETHICAL PROBLEMS FACING ORGANIZATIONS

CHAPTER 8

ETHICAL PROBLEMS OF ORGANIZATIONS

INTRODUCTION

In the third quarter of 2002, the Brookings Institution, a Washington, D.C., think tank, estimated that the corporate scandals that began with the Enron debacle in late 2000 would cost the U.S. economy $35 billion. That is the equivalent of a $10 increase per barrel of oil.[1] It is, in a word, staggering. And we may not have seen the end of it.

Long before Enron's collapse, a number of business ethicists and business professionals watched with concern as Wall Street analysts demanded increasingly strong corporate financial performance to support rising corporate stock prices. At the same time, the gargantuan compensation packages (including stock options) of the top executives running these companies became inextricably linked to their companies' stock prices. (A generation ago, average CEO pay at major corporations was 40 times the pay of the average worker. Today it is 500 times the pay of the average employee.[2] It was an "accident" waiting to happen, although everyone was making so much money in the market that no one wanted to admit that something could be fundamentally wrong. Experts warned of a bubble—even Alan Greenspan, head of the Federal Reserve, cautioned against "irrational exuberance" in the markets.[3] But no one could have predicted how bad things would get.

In a June 2002 interview on PBS's *Frontline,* Arthur Levitt, former head of the Securities and Exchange Commission, explained how stock prices influence executives and their ethical decision making (or lack thereof): "There is an obsession with short-term earnings and short-term results, and our stock markets reflect that obsession. A drop of one or two pennies in quarterly earnings that vary from expectations can result in a 30 percent decline in the price of the stock, virtually overnight. We've developed a short-term culture in American business, where executives have become obsessed with the selling price of their stock. They drive earnings in whatever way they possibly can to meet the expectations of analysts, rather than presenting a picture that is totally accurate."[4]

With news of unfathomable greed and misdeeds at Enron, Arthur Andersen, WorldCom, Adelphia, Merrill Lynch, Citigroup, Tyco, and others flooding the media, it's easy to wonder if any organization is doing the right thing. Well, wonder no more. There are thousands of organizations that work every day to uphold ethical standards and train employees in what those standards mean. If you try to imagine the hundreds of thousands of transactions that occur every day and then think about how many you hear about as being illegal or unethical—even with all of the bad news in 2001 and 2002—the real proportion of wrongdoers is probably quite small.

In this chapter, we're going to look at a series of business ethics cases within the framework of stakeholders—those individuals or groups who have a stake in what the organization does or how it performs. Many of the cases you'll read about here are well known as major business disasters. You might wonder why we're focusing on disasters instead of typical ethical issues within corporations. Here's why: If you read these cases carefully, you'll discover that many of them started as small issues until mismanagement, denial, or other more malevolent motives caused these seemingly minor situations to mushroom into huge legal, ethical, and public relations nightmares.

Some of the issues we look at in this chapter are similar to the issues we explored in Chapters 3 and 6. But now we're looking at the organizational level, where the stakes are much higher and events can escalate into a debacle much faster. In addition to the business ethics nightmares, we'll also look at some of the positive programs businesses are promoting and at some hypothetical cases that we hope will get you thinking.

MANAGING STAKEHOLDERS

Business wasn't always as complex as it is today. At the end of the nineteenth century, many of the country's largest corporations were privately held, and consequently, their owners had very few constituencies to answer to. The magnates and robber barons of a century ago ruled their companies with an iron hand. There were no unions or laws to protect workers, and the sporadic media attention of the era left the public largely unaware of most corporate abuses. Of course, all of that has changed.

As we've explained in earlier chapters, modern corporations have multiple stakeholders with myriad and often conflicting interests and expectations. Few corporations today are run unilaterally by one individual, as they well might have been 100 years ago. Even in the handful of companies where an individual founder or owner has a looming presence—like Bill Gates at Microsoft—there are boards of directors, regulatory agencies, and consumer groups that dramatically influence how an organization is managed. Corporations are frequently traded on the various stock exchanges and have numerous taskmasters—institutional and individual—in the investor community. In addition, because individuals have invested in money market funds and the stock market in numbers unprecedented even a decade ago, the press is vigilant in its coverage of corporate misdeeds or any other factor that could influence corporate earnings.

What exactly is a stakeholder? To fully understand what a stakeholder is, we first must have some idea of what a stake is. A stake is an interest or a share in some effort or undertaking.[5] For example, any couple who has ever planned a wedding understands that there are multiple stakeholders in the grand event, including the bride and groom, their parents and siblings, friends, business associates, extended families, and all of the vendors who are being paid to make the event happen. The couple will discover that many people feel as if they should be part of the planning process for the event. Various stakeholders will have opinions on the formality of the wedding, the food, dresses, tuxedos, music, flowers, and especially who is to be invited and how much is to be spent. There are many stakeholders in the couple's wedding plans. Similarly, in business, neighbors living near a manufacturing plant will feel as if they should have some say in new plant construction, customers will feel as if they should be consulted when a product is being redesigned, and employees will no doubt think that they should have some input when it comes to revising corporate policy.

A stake can also be a claim, or a right to something. A claim is a demand for something due or something perceived to be due. In the wedding example, the parents of the bride will have more than an interest in the marriage plans; if they are paying for the event, they will surely feel as if they have the right to invite some of their relatives, friends, and business associates. In business, employees will probably feel they have a right to privacy, customers will feel they have a right to receive quality goods and services for their money, and shareholders will feel they have a right to a healthy return on their investment because they have assumed a financial risk.

A stakeholder is any individual or group that has one or more stakes in an organization. In other words, a stakeholder is an individual or group that can affect or be affected by business decisions or undertakings.[6]

What do businesses owe their stakeholders? Once we have determined who the stakeholders in a situation are, how do we determine our organization's obligations to them? And if those obligations conflict, how does an organization resolve those conflicts?

Perhaps the easiest way to think about this is to divide stakeholders into primary and secondary groups.[7] Primary stakeholders are those groups or individuals with whom the organization has a formal, contractual relationship: In most cases this means customers, employees, shareholders or owners, suppliers, and perhaps even the government. Secondary stakeholders are other individuals or groups to whom the organization has obligations, but who are not formal, contractual partners. Obviously, organizations should strive to satisfy their obligations to their primary stakeholders while also trying to keep their secondary stakeholders happy. It's a difficult balancing act, but a helpful exercise if companies are to be fair to the people and groups they can affect.

This approach is so useful that David Abrahams, a managing consultant with Marsh Ltd. in London, recently designed a similar stakeholder model to help his corporate clients identify and quantify risk to their brand. As one of the largest insurers in the world, Marsh has great interest in developing tools to help companies mitigate reputational and other kinds of risk. Abrahams's model identifies three primary stakeholders—business partners, customers, and employees—and three secondary stakeholders—opinion formers, community, and authorities. He maintains that by analyzing a company and its business using those six groups as a guide, one can begin to identify how a variety of calamities might affect a company's reputation and the value of its brand, and how much those calamities might cost.[8]

The cases that follow are divided into categories representing four of the major stakeholder groups in many business decisions: consumers or customers, employees, shareholders, and the community. In all the cases, more than one stakeholder group is affected; we have categorized the cases under headings that represent the stakeholder group that we feel is most affected. However, as you read through the cases, we urge you to identify all of the stakeholders in each case and to try to discern each organization's obligations to all of its various stakeholders.

ETHICS AND CONSUMERS

It might surprise many people to learn that there were few laws protecting consumers before the 1960s. At the turn of the last century, consumers didn't even have the right to sue a manufacturer for defective equipment. The first real consumer law took effect early in the twentieth century when, in *McPherson v. General Motors,* a consumer was given the right to sue the auto manufacturer for a defective vehicle. Until then, the only recourse for the owner of an auto was to go after the dealer who sold the vehicle to him or her. Another landmark law was the Pure Food and Drug Act, which was passed in 1906 to prohibit adulteration in food and drugs.[9]

Although more consumer laws were passed in the first half of this century, consumers had to wait until the early 1960s for any real protectionist legislation that positioned consumers as a major stakeholder group. The framework of consumer protection as we know it today was constructed during the Kennedy administration. In his speech to Congress on consumers in 1962, President John F. Kennedy outlined four consumer "rights": the right to safety, the right to be heard, the right to choose, and the right to be informed.[10] This message and the legislation that resulted laid the groundwork for today's consumer movement.

Exactly what do companies and organizations owe their customers? According to some observers, products and services should be produced and delivered according to the "due care" theory.[11] This theory stipulates that due care involves:

- Design—products and services should meet all government regulations and specifications and be safe under all foreseeable conditions, including misuse by the consumer.
- Materials—materials should meet government regulations and be durable enough to withstand reasonable use.
- Production—products should be made without defects.
- Quality control—products should be inspected regularly for quality.
- Packaging, labeling, and warnings—products should be safely packaged, should include clear, easily understood directions for use, and should clearly describe any hazards.
- Notification—manufacturers should have a system in place to recall products that prove to be dangerous at some time after manufacture and distribution.

Although we've certainly alluded to some organizational responsibilities in earlier chapters, we're going to concentrate on three duties in this chapter: to respect the customer and not engage in activities that conflict with the interests of an established customer base, to produce a safe product that is free from any known defects, and to honestly advertise a product or service.

Conflicts of Interest

Although we usually think of conflicts of interest as situations involving individuals, they can also involve organizations. As we've seen over the last few years, conflicts involving organizations are even more damaging than those that involve individuals. Many people think that the poster child for corporate conflicts is Arthur Andersen and other large accounting firms who offer both auditing and consulting services to clients. It's hard to believe that gargantuan consulting fees wouldn't color the judgment of auditors. However damaging those accounting firm conflicts were, they are dwarfed by what happened at Enron. (Please note that, while this case appears under "Ethics and Consumers," it could just as easily appear under "Ethics and Employees" or "Ethics and Shareholders" because its effects were so far reaching. But evidence is mounting to suggest that Enron's manipulation of the energy markets harmed energy consumers in California.)

> **COMPANY:** Enron
> **INDUSTRY:** Energy
>
> **SITUATION**
> In 2002, *Fortune* magazine still ranked Enron as the fifth-largest company in the United States, although by the time the magazine was published, Enron had already filed for Chapter 11 bankruptcy protection.[12] It was quite a ride: from a regional gas pipeline trader to the largest energy trader in the world, and then back down the hill into bankruptcy and disgrace. Since the company and its executives were still involved in litigation when this book went to press, many of the facts were not known. We do know that the company, with the help of its investment bankers, accountants, and others, constructed a series of off-the-books partnerships that were used to hide Enron's massive debt and inflate its stock price. These partnerships were managed by Enron executives—a clear conflict of interest—who stood to benefit financially from the deals. Enron also used very aggressive accounting practices to bolster the bottom line. A particularly sad aspect of this debacle was how much Enron employees lost in their 401(k) plans as the stock price plummeted. In the fall of 2000, Enron changed administrators for its 401(k) plan and, as is typical, the plan was "closed" while that transfer took place. When a plan is closed, no one can buy, sell, or trade in his or her 401(k) until the moratorium is over. Sadly, this moratorium began just as the stock really began to tank, and by the time Enron employees could once again make changes in their 401(k) elections, the stock price had dramatically decreased and the retirement savings of many average employees were wiped out.

HOW THE COMPANY HANDLED IT

Executives denied there was trouble for as long as they could, but the fall from grace was swift and dramatic. Top executives resigned in disgrace and one committed suicide. The company filed for Chapter 11 bankruptcy in December 2001 and later sold its primary energy trading unit.[13]

RESULTS

The results are evolving as this book goes to press. Andrew Fastow, Enron's former CFO, has been indicted on 78 counts of fraud, money-laundering, and conspiracy. Fastow pleaded not guilty, but the prosecutors claimed that the funds were obtained illegally and tried to seize $37 million from Fastow, his family, and his associates. Former CEO Kenneth Lay and former president Jeffrey Skilling, claimed ignorance of Fastow's schemes. Matthew Kopper, a former managing director, pleaded guilty to money laundering and conspiracy to commit wire fraud and he forfeited $8 million to settle an SEC civil fraud case. The accounting firm, Arthur Andersen, was convicted in a federal court of obstruction of justice and relinquished its license to practice public accountancy.[14]

COMMENTS

Once again, former SEC chairman Levitt aptly described the scope of the problems at Enron:[15]

> I think the Enron story was a story, not just of the failure of the firm but also the traditional gatekeepers: the board, the audit committee, the lawyers, the investment bankers, the rating agencies. All of them had a part in this.
>
> Take the rating agencies, for instance. They deferred downgrading Enron, pending a merger which they knew very well might never have taken place.
>
> Take the investment bankers, who developed the elaborate scheme that Enron used to hide the obligations of the parent company in subsidiaries. That didn't come out of the blue; that was a scheme concocted between the investment bankers and the chief financial officer of Enron.
>
> Take the accounting firm.... Enron was the most important audit client that they had, and Enron was also the largest consulting client that they had—a client that paid them over a million dollars a week in fees. In my judgment, that accounting firm was compromised. Their audit was compromised. Putting aside any fraudulent activity that may have been part of this, they were clearly compromised by the nexus of consulting with auditing.
>
> Take the lawyers that were paid vast fees. I think here you have a very interesting case where the American Bar Association

> prevents lawyers from revealing financial fraud of clients to regulators. And here we had a case in point where a major client of the law firm was obviously involved in practices that may well prove to have been fraudulent, and they didn't blow the whistle.
>
> And [take] the analysts, who were claiming that Enron was a buy even after this story had broken and Enron had declared bankruptcy. These are analysts that were being paid by investment bankers that were receiving large fees from Enron for performing a variety of services. How independent could their research have been? And what could an investor have expected from an analyst who was recommending the purchase of Enron, while at the same time his employer was receiving millions of dollars in fees from that company? How likely was it that the analysts would tell it as it was? Very unlikely, in my judgment.

It appears Enron had plenty of help in constructing its massive fraud. Its true financial performance was shrouded in partnerships that hid debt from its books and, as a result, from investors and from rank and file employees.

However, Enron was not alone in its involvement in corporate conflicts of interest. The investment banking community has also been embroiled in myriad conflicts in recent years. In fact, investment banking firms—by their very nature—face a huge potential conflict of interest. They are in the business of helping corporations raise money in the markets and are consequently focused on keeping a client company's stock price as high as possible. Yet these same investment banks also serve investors, who are interested in buying stocks at as low a price as they can.[16] Talk about tension! And that tension spilled over for several big firms in the late 1990s and early 2000s. Merrill Lynch was fined $100 million when its analysts—in e-mails to one another—privately trashed the stocks of the companies they were publicly touting to investors.[17] That case and others like it were later parodied in a television commercial by investment firm Charles Schwab & Co. In the commercial, a Wall Street manager is seen urging his brokers to push an unfavorable stock. He tells them, "Let's put some lipstick on this pig." (Schwab does not underwrite stocks and consequently does not face the same conflict that other brokerage firms do.) James P. Gorman, a Merrill Lynch executive, called Schwab's commercial a "cheap shot" for "kicking someone when they're down".[18] We wonder whether investors thought Schwab's commercial was a cheap shot or a pretty accurate portrayal of some Wall Street bankers.

Investment bankers were investigated for another major conflict—how much they knew about the alleged frauds committed at Enron, WorldCom, Adelphia, and other companies. At Enron, for example, banks such as Credit Suisse First Boston, Citigroup, and JP Morgan Chase helped Enron structure the secret partnerships that hid Enron's debt and kept Enron's stock price high. Then these investment banks not only received fees for helping to structure debt, they also made money from their investments in Enron stock.[19]

But perhaps no conflict in investment banking is as egregious as what happened in a series of initial public offerings (IPOs) for dot.com companies before the bottom of that market fell out in late 2000. According to some observers, many dot.com IPOs in the late 1990s were nothing less than high-stakes poker games—with stacked decks—in which the young companies going public eventually got shafted and the investment bankers and their cronies made out like bandits. Traditionally, the objective of an IPO is to raise money for fledgling companies—money that is used to grow the business, for marketing, to expand into new markets, and to invest in new technology. In the late 1990s and into 2000, investment banks began to aggressively underprice the stock in IPOs—instead of selling the shares to the investors who would pay the most for them, they handed them out to favored cronies or clients (in an effort to gain favor) at a much reduced price. These cronies and clients—generally large, institutional investors—would flip the shares when the stock reached its full market price on the first day of trading. The money that should have gone to the issuers went to the clients of the investment banks. Things got so bad that in 1999 and 2000, investment banking fees and forgone proceeds accounted for 57 cents of every dollar raised for IPO corporations.[20] Those dot.com companies might have done better by going to mob loan sharks.

The results of these very public conflicts of interest will be felt for years. Various regulators and attorneys general from a number of states are investigating the banks and their business practices. The companies that have acted unethically will be fined, their corporate brands will be severely damaged, and some of their executives will no doubt be jailed. However, all of that "justice" won't completely restore the faith of the public in the markets, nor will it help the hundreds of thousands of individual investors who have lost their shirts because of these shenanigans.

In Chapter 3, we defined a conflict of interest as occurring when someone could think that your judgment might be clouded because of a relationship you have. The definition is the same for organizations: If an organization's customers or other stakeholder group think that an organization's judgment is biased because of a relationship it has with another company or firm, a conflict exists. Corporate or organizational conflicts are just as risky as those that exist between individuals and should be avoided at all costs.

Product Safety

Obviously, a major ethical obligation of any organization is to produce a quality product or service. Just as obviously, nothing will put a company out of business faster than offering a product that is dangerous, poorly produced, or of inferior quality. The competition in the marketplace generally helps to ensure that goods and services will be of a quality that is acceptable to consumers. However, sometimes a company will become the victim of external sabotage (like Johnson & Johnson), and sometimes a company will make a foolhardy decision (like A.H. Robins), and the result is a product that is not safe. Let's look at these classic cases.

COMPANY: Johnson & Johnson
INDUSTRY: Pharmaceuticals

SITUATION
In September 1982, seven people in the Chicago area were killed when they ingested Tylenol, a painkiller produced by McNeil Labs, a division of Johnson & Johnson. The Tylenol in question was found to have been laced with cyanide, and it was not known for several weeks whether the contamination was the result of internal or external sabotage. A thorough investigation later proved that the poisonings were the result of external sabotage.

HOW THE COMPANY HANDLED IT
First, the company pulled all Tylenol from shelves in the Chicago area. That was quickly followed by a nationwide recall of all Tylenol—31 million bottles with a retail value of over $100 million. Johnson & Johnson sent Mailgram messages explaining the situation and the recall to over 500,000 doctors, hospitals, and distributors of Tylenol. It also established a toll-free crisis phone line where consumers could ask questions about the product. In addition, its CEO, James Burke, and other executives were accessible to the press and were interviewed by a variety of media.

Since Tylenol had captured over a third of the painkiller market before the poisoning, Johnson & Johnson decided to try to rebuild the brand and its franchise. That wasn't going to be easy since consumer fear ran high immediately after the poisoning. In one survey conducted a month after the incident, 87 percent of the respondents understood that Johnson & Johnson was not to blame for the Tylenol deaths, yet 61 percent declared they would be unlikely to buy Tylenol in the future. So even though most consumers knew the poisonings were not the fault of Johnson & Johnson, a majority wouldn't buy the product again. Johnson & Johnson tackled this problem head-on by offering coupons to entice consumers back to Tylenol and, ultimately, by redesigning Tylenol's packaging to be tamper resistant.

RESULTS
Johnson & Johnson's reaction to the Tylenol poisoning has been hailed as the benchmark for how organizations should react to a crisis. As we've mentioned in other chapters, Johnson & Johnson's reaction to the Tylenol crisis proved that its famous credo, in which it outlines its responsibilities to its consumers, employees, community, and stockholders, wasn't hollow. It was that concern for the customer—its primary stakeholder—that drove its response to the crisis. By being accessible to the press, Johnson & Johnson's executives displayed concern for the consumer by refusing to dodge responsibility or blame any other party for their difficulties.

The results of the crisis have been far reaching. The tamper-resistant packaging pioneered by Johnson & Johnson has become commonplace in a wide variety of products, from food to pharmaceuticals. Johnson & Johnson's reputation as a quality producer of pharmaceuticals and as a company that cares about its customers is still strong, two decades after the crisis. Its former chairman, James Burke, is renowned for his concern about ethical issues and is a sought-after speaker on a wide variety of topics related to ethics. Also, by the mid-1980s, Tylenol had regained almost all of its market share.

COMMENTS

The background of former Johnson & Johnson CEO James Burke was critical to the company's behavior during the Tylenol crisis. Burke was a marketing man, who knew and understood the value of timely, accurate communication. Not many executives are comfortable with open communication, and their natural reticence can be enormously harmful to their organizations when a crisis strikes.[21]

UPDATE

While Johnson & Johnson has long been admired for its handling of the Tylenol crisis, in recent years it has stumbled. For example, J&J's LifeScan division pleaded guilty to criminal charges in 2000 and paid $60 million in fines for selling defective glucose-monitoring devices to diabetics and for later submitting false information about the problem to federal regulators. Lawyers who filed the class-action suit against LifeScan estimated that at least three diabetics had died because of the faulty readings they obtained from LifeScan's SureStep monitoring device. LifeScan, in court documents, admitted that it had not adequately described the product's defects to the Food and Drug Administration, failed to disclose the problem to patients, and then failed to notify the FDA once problems began to occur. It's very difficult to reconcile this image of Johnson & Johnson with the Tylenol one. The chairman of Johnson & Johnson, Ralph S. Larsen, wrote in a statement, "Mistakes and misjudgments were made. We fully acknowledge those errors and sincerely apologize for them. We are committed to learning from this experience."[22]

COMPANY: A. H. Robins

INDUSTRY: Pharmaceuticals

SITUATION

In 1970, A. H. Robins, a small, family-owned pharmaceutical company best known as the manufacturers of Chap Stick and Robitussin cough syrup, purchased ownership of the Dalkon Shield, a new intrauterine device (IUD) at the time. Interest in birth control measures had dramatically increased in the 1960s, and big profits were being made from contraceptives. This was a new market for Robins; in fact, it had no obstetrician or gynecologist on its staff. The problems with the Dalkon Shield were present from the very beginning, although A. H. Robins was initially ignorant of the time bomb it had just purchased. Because it was a medical device, the Dalkon Shield wasn't required to undergo the rigorous testing the government required of new drugs. And the

Dalkon Shield had had precious little testing before Robins purchased the rights to it. Robins aggressively marketed it anyway. By 1975, there were more than four million Dalkon Shields in use all over the world, and more than half of those were in use in the United States.

The major problem with the Dalkon Shield was the "tail" that allowed for its removal by a physician. Other IUDs had monofilament tails—the tails were one solid piece of plastic. By contrast, the Dalkon Shield had a multifilament tail—it was made up of hundreds of pieces of plastic that proved to be an efficient breeding ground for bacteria. This tail could introduce bacteria into the user's uterus, and the result could be severe sepsis that could cause massive infection, sterility, miscarriage, or death.

HOW THE COMPANY HANDLED IT

A. H. Robins stonewalled at every opportunity. Its executives falsified medical data, lost or destroyed key company files and records related to the IUD, and completely denied knowledge of the danger under oath. The company finally alerted 120,000 doctors to the danger in 1975. However, it didn't recall the IUD until 1984, when it conducted a massive press campaign to encourage women to have the device removed at Robins' expense.

RESULTS

The results of A. H. Robins's inaction were tragic. Fifteen women died as a result of severe pelvic inflammatory disease, and over 60,000 women suffered miscarriages. Hundreds more women gave birth to children with severe handicaps such as blindness, cerebral palsy, and mental retardation. In 1984, Robins established a fund of $615 million to deal with claims from the Dalkon Shield. Shortly thereafter, it became apparent that with hundreds of thousands of claims against the company, the fund would prove inadequate, and the company declared Chapter 11 bankruptcy in late 1985. In 1988, the company was acquired by American Home Products.[23]

COMMENTS

Part of the tragedy in this case is that A. H. Robbins began thinking about stakeholders in 1975, when it alerted physicians across the country that there was a problem with the Dalkon Shield. However, the company didn't take action to prevent harm to its primary stakeholders—the women into whom the IUDs were inserted—for another nine years! Think of how different the outcome of this case would have been if A. H. Robbins had protected its consumers in the same way Johnson & Johnson had.

As we saw in Chapter 4, one of the most common faults in ethical decision making is to ignore the long-term consequences of a decision. Although most organizations try hard to produce a product or service of high quality (to stay in business, if for no other reason), many don't take the time to identify all stakeholders and think long-term about the consequences of their decisions. In issues that involve product safety and possible harm to consumers, thinking long-term is critical. Is this product going to harm someone? How serious is the potential harm? Even if it might harm only one person, is there a way that can be avoided? Is there a way we can warn against possible harm? What can we do to ensure this product's safety? If the product is sabotaged by angry insiders or outsiders, or if we discover problems with this product or service at a later date, how can we protect the public, consumers, and ourselves? Do we have a crisis management plan? How closely did the companies involved in the classic cases adhere to the due care theory described earlier?

Advertising

The subject of ethics in advertising is a murky one, simply because there are varying opinions of exactly what "truth" is, and furthermore, what "responsible" is. Does a certain moisturizer really make skin look younger, or is it the 20-year-old model who has a young, dewy complexion? How would that moisturizer work for a 50-year-old? Do automakers and beer makers really need young women in skimpy bathing suits to sell their products? Do companies have a responsibility to respect all consumers? Are certain segments of the population fair game when it comes to the art of selling? Should we protect children from sugary cereal ads or teenagers from ads for expensive athletic shoes? How truthful, or responsible, does advertising have to be to qualify as ethical? Let's take a look at a few recent cases that point out a number of ethical issues in the marketing of pharmaceuticals to consumers:

> **INDUSTRY:** Pharmaceuticals
>
> **SITUATION #1**
> Novartis, the large Swiss drug company, recently paid actress Lauren Bacall to mention one of its products, Visudyne, during an interview with Matt Lauer on NBC's *Today* show. Visudyne is a drug used to treat macular degeneration, an eye condition that strikes many people beginning in middle age. Bacall described how macular degeneration had caused a friend to go blind, urged viewers to get tested for the condition, and then plugged Visudyne.[24] What's the problem? Remember, this was not a commercial, but an interview. The viewing public had no idea that Bacall was a paid Novartis spokesperson. Bacall is not alone, nor is Novartis. Actors Kathleen Turner and Rob Lowe have also pitched drugs, and other drugs have been mentioned by name on shows such as *Law and Order, West Wing, ER,* and on the other morning shows such as *Good Morning America* by drug firms such as Amgen, Schering Plough, and Pfizer. Is marketing drugs the same as marketing breakfast cereal or deodorant? Should there be a higher standard for health care products in general? Should television viewers be informed when a celebrity or a sitcom is being paid by a drug company to talk about or display its products?
>
> **SITUATION #2**
> Recently, investigators for the U.S. Government's General Accounting Office (GAO) claimed that several drug companies had repeatedly made misleading claims about prescription drugs in their advertising on TV and in print, even after being cited for violations. The reason is not surprising: Advertising

results in significant increases in the use of prescription drugs and in higher drug spending. The GAO study estimates that 8.5 million Americans each year ask their doctors for specific drugs that they have seen advertised, and their doctors prescribe the desired drugs. While some lawmakers claim that the drug companies spend more per year on advertising than on research and development, the GAO found evidence that the drug companies in 2002 spent $30 billion on research and development and $19 billion on advertising.[25] The cost and use of prescription drugs is one of the engines that has driven the astronomical increases in health care costs in recent years. Why have pharmaceutical companies spent so much money marketing to patients as well as to physicians? What are the advantages of direct marketing to consumers? What are the disadvantages?

SITUATION #3
In 2002, drugstore chain Walgreens and pharmaceutical company Eli Lilly were sued after a Florida consumer received an unsolicited free sample of the antidepressant drug Prozac Weekly in the mail. The recipient had kept her depression secret for many years—from her employers, family, and friends—fearing that she would suffer repercussions if her mental condition was known. Imagine her surprise when she received Prozac Weekly in the mail, along with a letter from Walgreens and her doctors. The sample itself was supplied free by the manufacturer, Eli Lilly. She filed a class-action suit alleging invasion of privacy, unfair trade practices, and commercial exploitation of confidential medical information by all parties.[26] Is it acceptable for drug makers to market products directly to drugstore customers, using past patient records as indicators of the drugs they might need? Are patients helped by this practice? Are they harmed? What about their rights to privacy? What are the dangers of drug companies being closely aligned with drug store chains?

SITUATION #4
Dentists who perused the *Journal of the American Dental Association* in May 2001 might have read about a study lauding the benefits of a new pain drug, Bextra, produced by Pharmacia and Pfizer. The article described a new study indicating that Bextra often relieved patients from the acute pain that sometimes follows dental surgery. This article helped spur sales of Bextra—in fact, sales of the drug increased 60 percent in the three months after the article appeared. What the dentists didn't know, however, was that the investigators who led the new scientific study of the drug were from a little company called Scirex, owned partly by advertising giant Omnicom. Historically, drug companies have used universities to conduct drug studies, but now that approach is considered too time-consuming. Drug companies want their drugs to become blockbusters in a hurry. But federal law does not allow drugs to be marketed before they go through clinical trials and receive FDA approval. To speed things up, advertising companies like Omnicom, Interpublic, and WPP are spending millions to get into the business of buying or investing in companies

that do clinical trials of drugs.[27] What's wrong with this picture? Would you have any problem buying a drug that had been clinically tested by the advertising company hawking it? Is there an inherent conflict of interest here? Could science be corrupted in an effort to speed a drug to market?

HOW THE COMPANIES HANDLED IT
The pharmaceutical companies argue persuasively that their marketing tactics do nothing but help to educate the consumer.

RESULTS
If you look at the lawsuits that have been filed against drug companies over the last five-to-ten years, the majority deal with advertising and marketing issues. It's clear that how drugs are advertised and brought to market poses huge ethical issues for the drug companies, which traditionally have been admired for their ethical reputations. However, the lawsuits around their marketing tactics continue to pile up and eventually they may tarnish some of the most sterling corporate reputations in the world.

In advertising, there's a thin line between enthusiasm for a product and high-pressure sales tactics, between optimism and truth, and between focusing on a target market and perhaps tempting that market into unfortunate activities. A classic example of a company tempting consumers into unhealthy activities is, of course, the tobacco industry. Although the hazards of smoking have been well documented for over two decades, tobacco companies spent most of that time denying the health risks of smoking and used "benign" advertising devices such as Joe Camel to market their very dangerous products. Another example could be gambling casinos, where consumers are urged to have a good time playing roulette, blackjack, or slot machines. Are there ethical obligations for casinos, which know that they may be tempting compulsive gamblers into a binge? Who are the stakeholders for the tobacco industry and the casino industry? And what are the companies' ethical responsibilities? Does the fact that most people begin smoking as children change our expectations of the tobacco industry?

Another case involves various brands of bottled water, which most consumers believe come from fresh water springs in Maine, Minnesota, or some other location with a reputation for a clean environment. In fact, despite the picture of the mountain on the label, some bottlers package filtered water from the municipal water supplies of several American cities. Is it up to consumers to read labels closely, or are companies obligated to represent their products honestly on all labels and in advertisements?

Can you think of any products where outrageous claims have been made? Is it fair to appeal to the emotions of a particular market segment? Why not? Can you think of particular advertising devices or symbols that are used to appeal to a specific group of consumers? How far is "too far" in advertising?

ETHICS AND EMPLOYEES

Certainly, one of the key stakeholder groups in any corporate situation should be the employees of the organization(s) involved in the case. Organizations have myriad ethical obligations to their employees. Some of these could include the right to privacy, the right not to be fired without just cause, the right to a safe workplace, the right to due process and fair treatment, the right to freedom of speech (whistleblowing), and the right to work in an environment that is free of bias.[28] We've addressed a number of these rights in other chapters. In this section, we're going to focus on two specific rights: a safe workplace and the right to keep a job unless just cause can be found for a firing.

Employee Safety

The most basic of employee rights is the right to work without being maimed or even killed on the job. In 1970, the Occupational Safety and Health Administration (OSHA) was created in an attempt to protect workers from hazards in the workplace. OSHA's mission is not only to protect workers against possible harm, but also to ensure that employees are informed of the hazards of their particular industry and job.

Let's look at a classic employee safety case.

> **COMPANY:** Johns Manville
> **INDUSTRY:** Asbestos
>
> **SITUATION**
> For decades, asbestos was the favorite insulator in myriad construction products. Some estimate that over 3,000 products contained some kind of asbestos component. Millions of homes, schools, and other buildings contained asbestos insulation; thousands of ship workers in World War II installed asbestos in battleships and other watercraft; and thousands of auto mechanics had fixed innumerable automobile brakes lined with asbestos. The danger of inhaling even minute amounts of asbestos was not publicly known until the 1970s, mainly because the incubation period for many of the asbestos-related lung diseases and cancers is anywhere from 10 to 40 years. However, by the mid-1970s tens of thousands of people who worked with asbestos were beginning to suffer from the fatal diseases we now know are characteristic of asbestos exposure.
>
> **HOW THE COMPANY HANDLED IT**
> According to company documents, Johns Manville became aware of the adverse health effects of asbestos exposure as early as the mid-1930s. (In fact, Prudential Insurance stopped insuring asbestos workers' lives in 1928.) Although some executives were disturbed by the connection between their product and workers' illnesses, the sentiments of the stonewallers prevailed. Warning labels were not placed on asbestos packaging until 1964. In addition, company doctors lied to asbestos workers at Manville facilities and told them they had no health problems. Johns Manville executives hid scientific data; lied to the public, the government, and their employees; and kept quiet about the danger to which tens of thousands of workers were being exposed. The only stakeholder groups considered by Johns Manville during this period

seem to be the senior executives and the shareholders. The company appeared to totally ignore the obligations it had to other stakeholder groups.

RESULTS

By 1982, more than 17,000 lawsuits had been filed against Johns Manville. That was the tip of the iceberg. Many more thousands are expected to be filed as more workers develop fatal diseases that were the result of exposure during World War II. Many of these deaths are lingering ones, in which the quality of life is greatly diminished over many years. As a result of the massive litigation, Johns Manville established a fund containing hundreds of millions of dollars to settle claims. The company filed for Chapter 11 bankruptcy protection in 1982, has been reorganized, and has been renamed the Manville Corporation. The new corporation has a strong commitment to funding the costs of the claims filed against its former self, and Manville executives have voiced what appears to be a real commitment to ethics within the corporation in an effort to prevent what happened from happening again.[29]

COMMENTS

One of the real mysteries surrounding this case is how so many senior executives over so many years could manage to live with themselves while keeping the awful secret of asbestos-related illness. It's one thing to hide something for a few years. But to keep this devastating secret for more than 40 years, throughout many changes in management, is a staggering notion to contemplate. Bill Sells, a manager with Johns Manville and the Manville Corporation for more than 30 years, wrote a *Harvard Business Review* article in which he analyzed what happened.[30] He contends that management was in denial. "Manville managers at every level were unwilling or unable to believe in the long-term consequences of these known hazards.... Had the company responded to the dangers of asbestosis and lung cancer with extensive medical research, assiduous communication, insistent warnings, and a rigorous dust-reduction program, it could have saved lives and would probably have saved the stockholders, the industry, and, for that matter, the product.... But Manville and the rest of the asbestos industry did almost nothing of significance—some medical studies but no follow through, safety bulletins and dust-abatement policies but no enforcement, acknowledgment of hazards but no direct warnings to downstream customers—and their collective inaction was ruinous."[31]

According to Sells, the denial was fed by the conviction that asbestos was an essential product and that the world couldn't get along without it. Managers also believed that they were doing enough because Manville's air quality standards were higher than the allowable limit set by the American Conference of Governmental Industrial Hygienists. But how did the company know whether the standard was really safe? They did little to find out. And what about the need for standards to protect those working with asbestos products such as brake shoe installers? Nothing was being done to protect them. Another factor feeding the denial was the fact that asbestos workers who were also smokers were much more likely to get sick. Managers could blame the tobacco industry and avoid self-blame. In addition, short-term financial consequences took precedence in managerial decision making. And, finally, managers sent a "don't tell me what I don't want to hear" message. Top managers may have actually been unaware of some of the problems. As Sells points out, however, juries convict companies based on what they "should have known,"[32] not necessarily what they did know.

Can you think of examples in other industries where employee safety and health are major issues? Are there health and safety issues in service (nonmanufacturing) industries? Are employers responsible for conditions such as carpal tunnel syndrome, in which the wrist is injured as a result of repeated movements like entering data into a computer? What recourse do employers have in situations where the performance of a job, in itself, can cause injury? If a company discovers that its employees are at risk for injury, is it under any obligation to inform the public?

Employee Downsizings

Employee downsizings or layoffs can result from many business conditions including economic depressions, the desire to consolidate operations and decrease labor costs, increased competition and unmet corporate objectives, to list just a few causes.[33] However justifiable the reason may be, the result always involves human misery. Organizations may not have an ethical obligation to keep labor forces at a specific number. They do, however, have an obligation to hire and fire responsibly. One major *Fortune* 500 company, with recent memories of a painful layoff, sent a directive to all of its managers when conditions began to improve in 1992. The directive stated that no unnecessary hirings were to take place. In other words, "This upturn may be temporary. Don't hire people today whom we may have to lay off next year."

One of the most contentious downsizing cases in recent years involved a major employer in the Northeast.

COMPANY: Scott Paper Company

INDUSTRY: Consumer Paper Products

SITUATION
In late 1993, Scott Paper had tired product lines, some extraneous business ventures, and a lagging revenue stream and stock price. Scott's board of directors wanted to breathe some life into the slumbering giant. In April 1994, Albert J. Dunlap, a self-proclaimed "Rambo in pinstripes," was named CEO of Scott Paper, and he immediately created his very own crisis to get the company moving. It was as if he lobbed a fire bomb through the doors of corporate headquarters.

HOW THE COMPANY HANDLED IT
Dunlap began by quickly selling off $2 billion worth of nonessential businesses.[34] He also quickly terminated one-third of the total workforce of

Scott—over 11,000 workers lost their jobs. But perhaps the most painful blow to the Philadelphia area was Dunlap's decision to move Scott's corporate headquarters out of the city where it had been founded 116 years earlier to Boca Raton, Florida, where Dunlap had a home. According to some sources, the move was prompted by Philadelphia's climate, which Dunlap didn't like.

RESULTS

Scott's stock price increased 146 percent in 14 months, and its profits doubled after one year of Dunlap's management. The company was sold in mid-1995 to Kimberly-Clark Corporation for $6.8 billion in stock.[35] Some stakeholders were delirious. Scott shareholders made out like bandits. Wall Street financial types did a jig. But no one was more gleeful than Dunlap, who pocketed $100 million in salary, stock profits, and other perks. Not bad for 15 months of his time.

COMMENTS

There are many people who think of Dunlap as a hero, including Dunlap himself. Many others, however, think of him as the worst kind of villain, as "Chainsaw Al," as some of his detractors call him. Though measures of that sort are painful, many people can understand why they might be necessary to turn around a company that could no longer compete. What infuriated everyone in the Philadelphia area, however, was moving Scott's corporate headquarters because Dunlap didn't like the weather in Philadelphia. Certainly, it is a very capricious reason to move an organization that was an institution in the area for over a century. Scott was not just some company. Rather, it had been an exemplary corporate citizen, providing talent and financing for local cultural and civic organizations. In addition, Dunlap's manner was arrogant, and he showed little or no sympathy either toward the long-term employees who had been axed or to the area he gutted.

UPDATE

After selling Scott Paper Company, Al Dunlap went on to become CEO of Sunbeam (maker of electric blankets and outdoor grills) in 1996. In typical Al Dunlap fashion, he quickly announced the closing or sale of two-thirds of the company's factories and the firing of half of its 12,000 employees. The stock rose and Wall Street applauded. In March of 1997, Sunbeam bought three companies: Coleman (camping equipment), First Alert (smoke alarms) and Signature Brands (Mr. Coffee). A year later it became clear to Sunbeam's board that the acquisitions had not been well managed and that the company was in financial trouble. They also discovered that the company was using highly aggressive sales tactics and accounting practices that inflated revenues and profits.[36] In June 1998, Chainsaw Al got the ax himself. In 2002, Dunlap settled charges with the SEC, paid a fine of $500,000, and neither admitted nor denied that he presided over accounting practices that resulted in Sunbeam overstating its profits in 1997 and 1998. And his legal woes did not end there. The Justice Department began an investigation of Sunbeam for the period it was managed by Dunlap.[37] Even more interesting was the disclosure that, early in his career, Dunlap was fired twice—once with the company's board accusing him of overseeing a huge accounting fraud. Dunlap erased these two firings from his official employment history and news of them only recently surfaced. Another interesting tidbit: in one of those companies that fired him, his relationships with his colleagues were so fractured that the entire senior team below Dunlap threatened to resign as a group unless Dunlap was canned.[38]

Contrast what happened to Scott Paper with the philosophy of Lincoln Electric Company, in Cleveland, Ohio.

COMPANY: Lincoln Electric Company

INDUSTRY: Electrical Components

SITUATION

Lincoln Electric has had an unusual relationship with its employees since it was founded by John C. Lincoln in 1895.[39] The company has been on the cutting edge of worker-friendly efforts. In 1923 it was among the first companies to offer company-paid vacation; in 1925 it was among the first to offer employee stock ownership plans; the first employee suggestion program was implemented in 1929; and Lincoln employees received incentive bonuses beginning in 1934. Perhaps the most controversial of its programs, however, is its guaranteed employment plan: After three years of continuous employment with Lincoln Electric, workers are guaranteed their jobs. In the early 1980s, however, the company experienced tremendous hardship. As a result of inflation, higher energy costs, and a recession in the United States, Lincoln's sales plummeted 40 percent. Company managers didn't know if they would be able to keep their promise of guaranteed employment.

HOW THE COMPANY HANDLED IT

The company was severely tested. However, not one Lincoln employee was laid off for lack of work. In fact, Lincoln has not laid off employees in the United States since 1948. The company's loyalty to its employees was returned in 1993, when Lincoln urged its employees to attain record levels of sales and production. Employees voluntarily postponed 614 weeks of vacation in order to meet customer demands.

RESULTS

In 1994, Lincoln added 600 new employees and by 1995 had reached $1 billion in sales. Incentive management is a cornerstone of Lincoln's culture. Having developed one of the first pay-for-performance systems in the country, it is frequently a subject of research by academics and other companies. Lincoln also has an elected advisory board for direct and open communications between employees and senior managers. The board was established in 1914. So loyalty at Lincoln is nothing new.

As we mentioned in Chapter 6, employees have the right to be treated fairly, without bias, and on the basis of their ability to perform a specific job. If a layoff or downsizing is necessary—if it involves one person or many—the layoff should be done with respect, dignity, and compassion. In the two cases we just outlined, what do you imagine are the key differences in philosophy? How could companies become more like Lincoln Electric? What are the pitfalls of Lincoln's approach? What are the pitfalls of Dunlap's? If you had to lay off employees, what factors would you consider in structuring a plan that would be as fair as possible to all involved?

Suppose the country experiences a recession. Should companies begin to lay off employees in order to maintain expected growth rates? To satisfy Wall Street's profit and growth expectations? What other stakeholder groups are affected? Are companies in business only to make a profit for shareholders? Are employee stakeholder groups more expendable than customer stakeholders? How can a company reconcile long-term obligations to all stakeholders with short-term financial crises?

ETHICS AND SHAREHOLDERS

Organizations also have a clear ethical obligation to shareholders and other "owners." This ethical obligation includes serving the interests of owners and trying to perform well, not only in the short term, but also over the long term. It also means not engaging in activities that could put the organization out of business and not making short-term decisions that might jeopardize the company's health in the future. As Kotter and Heskett say in their book, *Corporate Culture and Performance,* ". . . only when managers care about the legitimate interests of stockholders do they strive to perform well economically over time, and in a competitive industry that is only possible when they take care of their customers, and in a competitive labor market, that is only possible when they take care of those who serve customers—employees."[40] Thus, taking care of shareholders also means ultimately taking care of other key stakeholder groups. Let's examine how the ethics of the investment banking giant Salomon Brothers affected its shareholders.

> **COMPANY:** Salomon Brothers
>
> **INDUSTRY:** Investment Banking
>
> **SITUATION**
> In December 1990, the head of Salomon's government bond trading desk, Paul Mozer, decided to test the regulatory resolve of the U.S. Treasury. Annoyed by the federal limits on the percentage of Treasury bonds any one firm could bid for in Treasury auctions—the ceiling was 35 percent—Mozer devised a plan to evade the regulation. He submitted a bid for Salomon Brothers, and he submitted an unauthorized bid in the name of one of his customers. The two bids combined represented 46 percent of the auction—a clear violation of the rules. Mozer got his bonds and repeated this maneuver in February, April, and May 1991.

HOW THE COMPANY HANDLED IT

In April, Mozer described the tactic to four Salomon executives: Chairman John Gutfreund, President Thomas W. Strauss, Vice Chairman John W. Meriwether, and General Counsel Donald M. Feuerstein. These executives told Mozer to stop his scheme but did not report Mozer's activities to the Securities and Exchange Commission at that time. (In May, Mozer rigged the bidding again.) In June, the SEC subpoenaed Salomon for its auction records. In August, Salomon finally alerted the SEC to Mozer's activities. Immediately following the disclosure to the SEC, Mozer was suspended from his job, and shortly afterward, the board of directors asked the four Salomon executives to resign from the firm and fired Salomon's outside law firm. The board named one of its own members, Warren Buffett, as interim chairman.

RESULTS

The publicity generated by the Salomon scandal was devastating to the firm and its shareholders. Its market value dropped by over one-third—$1.5 billion—in the week following the disclosure. Their debt was downgraded by various rating agencies, and major banks reevaluated Salomon's loan terms. Because of the firm's decreased liquidity, its ability to trade was dramatically reduced. In addition to the immediate financial debacle, teams of Salomon Brothers personnel left the firm. For a year after the crisis, the financial press was awash in reports of high-level Salomon employees joining other firms. The defections no doubt damaged the firm for many years. In addition, at a time when the profits of other investment banks were soaring by as much as 50 percent over previous years, Salomon's underwriting revenues were down 26 percent—a huge and humbling disparity. Their profits were off substantially, customers left, and they were barred from some kinds of transactions or were rendered ineffective because of their weakened financial position. It took years for the firm to recover.[41]

COMMENTS

In the investment banking industry, reputation is everything. It's the yardstick by which customers evaluate quality and a firm's ability to do business. There is nothing more devastating for a financial services firm than the loss of reputation. Salomon is lucky it survived. It very well could have gone the way of E. F. Hutton and Drexel Burnham Lambert. E. F. Hutton was acquired by another financial firm after it could not survive pleading guilty to 2,000 felony counts of fraud in a check-kiting case. Drexel closed its doors after charges of wrongdoing in the high-yield market effectively crippled its ability to do business. In all cases, the firms put their own interests ahead of the interests of their primary stakeholders: their customers.

UPDATE

Salomon Brothers is now part of Salomon Smith Barney, which is the investment banking arm of the banking behemoth Citigroup. As this book went to press, Salomon was under investigation by New York State Attorney General

Eliot Spitzer, and the company and its former star telecom analyst, Jack Grubman, had been named in approximately 62 class action lawsuits.[42] The plaintiffs accused Salomon and Grubman of issuing unreasonable research reports and of failing to disclose conflicts of interest with companies profiled in those research reports, including WorldCom, AT&T, Global Crossing, Winstar, and others.[43]

Shareholders—in particular, individual investors—have been abused in recent years, with numerous ethical lapses driving a collapse in the stock market. Several of the cases described earlier in the "Ethics and Consumers" section are also relevant here. The level of investor disgust with the activities of certain companies and investment banks over the last several years is unprecedented and is driving change. In a 2002 poll taken by *Shareholder Value* magazine, 46 percent of the corporate executives responding said that the recent plethora of scandals had negatively affected the way investors view their companies, and 43 percent of those executives were changing business practices as a result.[44]

ETHICS AND THE COMMUNITY

As many people have discovered, companies don't exist in a vacuum. Companies are citizens in their communities, just as individuals are, and because of their size they can have an outsized impact on the communities of which they are a part. Therefore, a major stakeholder in business must be the communities of which corporations and other organizations are a part. Perhaps the most obvious way in which a company can affect its community is its approach to the environment.

The public's concern with the effect of business on the environment began in earnest in 1962 with the publication of Rachel Carson's *Silent Spring*.[45] In her book, Carson outlined the hazards of pesticides, and DDT in particular, to the environment. The resulting public outcry resulted in the Environmental Protection Act in 1969 and the creation of the Environmental Protection Agency in 1970. The goal of both the act and the agency is to protect the environment—air, water, earth—from the activities of businesses and individuals. Of course, the ethical obligation implicit for all of us is to think long-term about the health of the planet and its environs for ourselves, our children, and other generations to follow. Let's look at some classic environmental cases.

> **COMPANY:** Union Carbide
> **INDUSTRY:** Chemicals
>
> **SITUATION**
> Late in 1984, Union Carbide's plant in Bhopal, India, experienced a catastrophe unparalleled in corporate history. Forty tons of methyl isocyanate (MIC), a lethal chemical used in pesticide production, leaked from a storage tank, formed a toxic cloud, and began heading for the unsuspecting people who lived near the plant. Experts estimate that 2,500 people died and more than 300,000 suffered injuries from exposure to the chemical cloud. In addition to the human

casualties, significant damage was done to the surrounding countryside and to the animals living nearby. A complicating factor in the disaster was that although Union Carbide was the majority stockholder in the Bhopal plant, the Indian government owned 49.1 percent of the operation, and all of the workers and managers in Bhopal were Indian nationals. The links between the Indian plant and Union Carbide's U.S. headquarters were tenuous. To complicate the situation, only two international telephone lines existed between Bhopal and the rest of the world at the time of the disaster.

HOW THE COMPANY HANDLED IT
Because of a dearth of accurate information about the disaster, Union Carbide had difficulty ascertaining the exact details of the accident. Even with sketchy information, however, the company's reaction was swift and compassionate, and it recognized its obligations to multiple stakeholder groups. It immediately shut down its other MIC-producing plant in West Virginia. It quickly sent medical supplies and a doctor who was an expert in dealing with the effects of the chemical to India. In addition, and even more impressive, Union Carbide's CEO, Warren Anderson, flew to India the day after the disaster to inspect the damage and lend support to the local Union Carbide management team. Anderson was arrested by Indian officials when he arrived, although he was later released. The company also sent a team of experts to Bhopal to investigate the accident.

Meanwhile, Union Carbide's communications team in Danbury, Connecticut, was gearing up an enormous effort to communicate the company's position to all its stakeholders. In the year following the accident, "press requests increased from an average of 250 per year to more than 5,000; employee bulletins increased from annual levels of 40–50 to more than 200; and employee videotapes increased from 35 a year to 45."[46]

RESULTS
Wall Street investors reacted immediately to the Bhopal disaster, and Union Carbide lost almost $900 million in market value. In addition, the company image took a beating, with 47 percent of the public being able to identify Union Carbide as the company involved in the Bhopal tragedy. The disaster turned into a five-year nightmare for Union Carbide: Besides the negative publicity and a plummeting stock price, the company endured a two-year investigation, an attempted hostile takeover by GAF Corporation, and a gas leak at its West Virginia facility, as well as reorganizations, recapitalizations, and major divestitures. In February 1989, Union Carbide paid total damages of $470 million and $58 million in litigation costs. After the debacle, Union Carbide is still whole and profitable, albeit much wiser.[47]

COMMENTS
A long-term result of the accident is hopefully an increased awareness on the part of multinationals to keep closer tabs on their foreign operations,

especially those located in less-developed countries. Although Union Carbide handled the accident with incredible speed and compassion, its original mistake was to allow a foreign facility to operate with lax controls and poor links to the mother corporation.

COMPANY: Exxon

INDUSTRY: Petroleum

SITUATION

In 1989, the Exxon *Valdez,* an oil tanker bound for Long Beach, California, from the Port of Valdez in Alaska, ran aground in Prince William Sound. The *Valdez* contained 52 million gallons of crude oil, 10 million gallons of which began quickly to leak into the pristine Alaskan waters. The captain of the tanker, Joseph Hazelwood, was later tested for alcohol consumption and showed an increased blood alcohol level. Although it was never proven that Hazelwood was drunk at the time of the accident, he did violate company regulations by not being on the bridge of the tanker when navigating in those waters.

In addition, Alyeska, the consortium of seven oil companies that originally established Alaska as an oil capital with the construction of the Trans Alaska pipeline, was charged with safeguarding Alaska from just such an accident and with providing immediate help should such a catastrophe occur.

HOW THE COMPANY HANDLED THE CRISIS

Although Exxon immediately began cleanup efforts, critical equipment was either damaged and in the process of being repaired, or not on the scene. CEO Lawrence Rawls did place full-page apology ads in various newspapers one week after the accident, but he did not visit Alaska and was roundly criticized for that seeming insensitivity. In addition, Exxon appeared to blame everyone but itself for its problem. And Alyeska was not much help. Like Exxon, it was unprepared for a crisis of the magnitude of the Exxon *Valdez* spill. As a result, Exxon appeared as if it dropped the ball with this oil spill. It looked as if the firm denied responsibility.

RESULTS

Although over 800 miles of Alaskan beaches were initially covered with oil, by 1990, 85 percent of them had been cleaned. Wildlife in the area was not so lucky—more than 30,000 birds died, as well as at least 2,000 sea otters. In addition, the fish population was contaminated and may take years to recover. Exxon spent more than $2 billion on the cleanup and paid additional hundreds of millions to the city of Valdez and Alaskan fishermen. Captain Joseph Hazelwood was fired for not following the regulation about being on the bridge of the tanker.[48]

What really took a beating, however, was Exxon's image. Environmentalists publicly hammered the company, and some 40,000 consumers destroyed their Exxon credit cards in protest.

COMMENTS

The difference between the personality of Exxon CEO Lawrence Rawls and Johnson & Johnson CEO James Burke could be why Exxon received such poor marks on its handling of the *Valdez* crisis. Rawls was an engineer and uncomfortable with the media. His reaction appeared slow and seemingly dispassionate, and the lemon he was handed remained a lemon. Burke knew how to make lemonade.

UPDATE

In December 2002, a federal court in Alaska ordered ExxonMobil to pay $4 billion in punitive damages for the Valdez oil spill. An earlier judgment for $5 billion had been appealed and was reduced, although it was nowhere near the $40 million ExxonMobil thought it should pay in punitive damages. The company said it will appeal again.[49]

WHY ARE THESE ETHICAL ISSUES?

These are all ethical issues because they involve obligations to primary or key stakeholder groups. Consumers, shareholders, employees, and the community are probably the major constituencies of any organization that is not operating in a vacuum. What groups are more important to a company than the people who pay to have goods made, the people who make them, the people who buy them, and the place where the goods are made? These ethical obligations all involve fairness, safety, and honesty to the four main stakeholders of most organizations.

COSTS

As we've seen in the classic cases we've described in this chapter, the costs of bungling an ethical obligation to any of the four primary stakeholder groups can not only be crippling, they also can be fatal. Just as individuals who cross the line can short-circuit their careers or end up fired or prosecuted, organizations pay the same kind of price: Their ability to function can be severely limited, and they can even be forced out of business. At the very least, if a company's misdeeds are discovered, they will most certainly be excoriated in the press and by the public. Their reputation can suffer long-term damage that may be difficult to repair.

It's impossible to list here all of the regulatory bodies that watch over the rights of these four stakeholder groups. Certainly, as you enter a particular industry or company, you will need to know what laws apply to that sector and what regulatory bodies govern compliance. In general, federal, state, and local governments have agencies charged with protecting the rights of stakeholder groups. Regulatory bodies like the Securities and Exchange Commission, the Comptroller of the Currency, and the Federal Reserve Board guard rights of shareholders. The Food and Drug Administration, the Federal Trade Commission, and the Federal Communications Commission are federal watchdog agencies for consumer rights. Employee rights are protected by a wide range of agencies including the Equal Employment and Opportunity Commission, the Labor

Board, and the Occupational Safety and Health Administration. The Environmental Protection Agency is the primary protector of the environment.

CONCLUSION

The cases we've described in this chapter represent a few of the more memorable business ethics cases. No industry, and really no company, has been immune from ethical problems and unethical employees. Even Johnson & Johnson has taken its licks in recent years because of the LifeScan lawsuits, as well as alleged inflated prices for some medications prescribed for chronic medical conditions. The point of examining these cases is that truly smart managers should learn from the mistakes of others.

We hope it's obvious that all stakeholders are connected and their interests frequently overlap. For example, with the Enron debacle, not only consumers were harmed, but also employees, shareholders, and the communities where Enron had facilities. It's also obvious that some senior executives need a hefty injection of morality. A shocking reminder of that is contained in "What Went Wrong at Enron," a recent book on Enron's demise by Peter Fusaro and Ross Miller. They claim that while at Harvard Business School, Jeff Skilling, later president of Enron, was asked how he would handle a situation where his company was producing a product that might harm or even kill the consumers who used it. He allegedly replied, "I'd keep making and selling the product. My job as a businessman is to be a profit center and to maximize return to the shareholders. It's the government's job to step in if a product is dangerous".[50]

It's also clear that at the turn of the twenty-first century, business people are at a crossroads. We need to decide what kind of professionals we are going to be. Are we going to be honest and fair and deserving of the public's trust? Or are we going to push our own agendas and expect the government to make us behave, à la Jeff Skilling? According to a poll conducted by the Pew Research Center for the People and the Press, 66 percent of Americans thought that business executives had low business standards—that's a lower score than that of either journalists or politicians. That poll was conducted around the time the Enron case was unfolding. A more recent poll, in August 2002, showed that corporate chief executives ranked dead last on the "who do you trust scale"—below lawyers, brokers, and accountants.[51] It's a sorry state of affairs and it will take many business people many years to undo the damage that's been done and to restore the trust that has been eroded.

DISCUSSION QUESTIONS

1. What factors contributed to Johns Manville's long silence on the dangers of asbestos?
2. What role do you think the personality of a CEO plays in the handling of an ethical problem?
3. Imagine that you're the CEO of a large firm like any of the ones described in this chapter. What concrete steps would you take to restore your company's reputation?

4. How much testing is enough when launching a new product?
5. How can the interests of multiple stakeholders be balanced?

SHORT CASES

CONFLICT OF INTEREST

Big Company is a large manufacturer of health care products that is under fire from the government to lower costs. Big Company has an excellent reputation and is widely acknowledged as one of the best-managed companies in the country. In spite of its reputation, however, Wall Street has reacted negatively to government efforts to reform the health care industry as a whole, and Big Company's stock price has lost 30 percent of its value in the last year. To counter the effect of possible government intervention, Big Company has just purchased Little Company, a discount health care supplier. Wall Street has greeted the acquisition with enthusiasm, and Big Company's stock price has rebounded by more than 10 percent since news of the acquisition was made public.

While this acquisition could provide Big Company with a foothold in a growing part of the health care industry, a real problem lies in the mission of Little Company. Little has made its reputation by providing objective health care advice to its customers. Now that it's owned by Big Company, customers have expressed doubts about how objective Little can be in recommending health care products if it's owned by a health care giant. Will Little Company be pressured to recommend the products offered by Big Company, its parent? Or will Little Company's advice remain objective?

As the senior executive charged with bringing Little Company into the corporate fold, how do you proceed? What are your obligations to Big Company, Little Company, and the customers of both? What do you owe to shareholders and the financial community? Are there other stakeholders, and what do you owe to them? What provisions would you include in an ethics code for Little Company?

PRODUCT SAFETY

As a brand manager at a large food manufacturer, you're positioning a new product for entry into the highly competitive snack food market. This product is low fat and low calorie, and should prove to be unusually successful, especially against the rapidly growing pretzel market. You know that one of your leading competitors is preparing to launch a similar product at about the same time. Since market research suggests that the two products will be perceived as identical, the first product to be released should gain significant market share.

A research report from a small, independent lab—Green Lab—indicates that your product causes dizziness in a small group of individuals. Green has an impressive reputation and its research has always been reliable in the past. However, the research reports from two other independent labs don't support Green's conclusion. Your director of research assures you that any claims of adverse effects are unfounded and that the indication of dizziness is either extremely rare or the result of faulty research by Green Lab. Since your division has been losing revenue because of its emphasis on potato chips and other high-fat snack food, it desperately needs a low-fat moneymaker. Since you were brought into the division to turn it around, your career at the company could depend on the success of this product.

What are your alternatives? What is your obligation to consumers? Who are your other stakeholders, and what do you owe them? What is your obligation to your employer and to other employees at your company? What should your course of action be? How can you apply the due care theory to this case?

ADVERTISING

As a bottler of natural spring water, your advertising department has recently launched a campaign that emphasizes the purity of your product. The industry is highly competitive, and your organization has been badly hurt by a lengthy strike of unionized employees. The strike seriously disrupted production and distribution, and it caused your company to lose significant revenues and market share. Now that the strike is over, your company will have to struggle to recoup lost customers, and will have to pay for the increased wages and benefits called for in the new union contract. The company's financial situation is precarious to say the least.

You and the entire senior management team have high hopes for the new ad campaign, and initial consumer response has been positive. You are shocked then, when your head of operations reports to you that an angry worker has sabotaged one of your bottling plants. The worker introduced a chemical into one of the machines, which in turn contaminated 120,000 bottles of the spring water. Fortunately, the chemical is present in extremely minute amounts—no consumer could possibly suffer harm unless he or she drank in excess of 10 gallons of the water per day over a long period of time. Since the machine has already been sterilized, any risk of long-term exposure has been virtually eliminated. But, of course, the claims made by your new ad campaign could not be more false.

List all of the stakeholders involved in this situation. Do any stakeholder groups have more to gain or lose than others? Develop a strategy for dealing with the contamination. How much does a company's financial situation determine how ethical dilemmas are handled?

SHAREHOLDERS

You work for an investment bank that provides advice to corporate clients. The deal team you work on also includes Pat, a marketing manager, and Joe, who serves as the credit manager for the team, as well as several other professionals. Just before your team is scheduled to present details of a new deal to senior management, Pat suggests to Joe that the deal would have a better chance of being approved if he withheld certain financials. "If you can't leave out this information," Pat says, "at least put a positive spin on it so they don't trash the whole deal."

The other team members agree that the deal has tremendous potential, not only for the two clients, but also for your company. The financial information Pat objects to—though disturbing at first glance—would most likely not seriously jeopardize the interest of any party involved. Joe objects and says that full disclosure is the right way to proceed, but that if all team members agree to the "positive spin," he'll go along with the decision. Team members vote and all agree to go along with Pat's suggestion—you have the last vote. What do you do?

In this hypothetical case, what is your obligation to the shareholders of your organization and to the shareholders of the two organizations that are considering a deal? Are shareholders a consideration in this case? Are customers? Are employees? Could the survival of any of the three companies be at stake in this case? In a situation like this one, how could you best protect the interests of key stakeholder groups?

COMMUNITY

You have just been named CEO of a small chemical refinery in the Northeast. Shortly after you assume your new position, you discover that your three predecessors have kept a horrifying secret. Your headquarters location sits atop thirty 5,000-gallon tanks that have held a variety of chemicals—from simple oil to highly toxic chemicals. Although the tanks were drained over 20 years ago, there's ample evidence that the tanks themselves have begun to rust and leach sludge from the various chemicals into the ground. Because your company is located in an area that supplies water to a large city over 100 miles away, the leaching sludge could already be causing major problems. The costs involved in a cleanup are estimated to be astronomical. Because the tanks are under the four-story headquarters building, the structure will have to be demolished before cleanup can begin. Then, all 30 tanks will have to be dug up and disposed of, and all of the soil around the area cleaned.

You're frankly appalled that the last three CEOs didn't try to correct this situation when they were in charge. If the problem had been corrected 15 years ago before the building had been erected, the costs would be substantially less than they will be now. However, as frustrated as you are, you're also committed to rectifying the situation. After lengthy discussions with your technical and financial people, you decide that a cleanup can begin in two years. Obviously, the longer you wait to begin a cleanup, the riskier it becomes to the water supply. Before you begin the cleanup, it's imperative that you raise capital, and a stock offering seems to be the best way to do it. However, if you disclose news of the dump problem now, the offering will likely be jeopardized. But the prospect of holding a news conference and explaining your role in keeping the dump a secret keeps you up at night.

Who are the stakeholders in this situation? What strategy would you develop for dealing with the dump and its disclosure? Are you morally obligated to disclose the dump right away? How will Wall Street react to this news? Does your desire to correct the situation justify keeping it a secret for another two years?

Think about the due care theory presented earlier in this chapter. Can we draw parallels between due care for the consumer and due care for the environment? What if the oil tank dump mentioned in the hypothetical case was located in a foreign subsidiary of a U.S. company and the country in which it was located had no laws against such a dump? Would the CEO be under any obligation to clean it up? Should American companies uphold U.S. laws concerning the environment in non-U.S. locations? How much protection is enough?

NOTES

1. Beattle, Alan. 2002. Corporate scandals will cost the U.S $35bn, *The Financial Times*, September 5, p. 4.
2. Krugman, P. 2002. The outrage constraint. *New York Times*, August 23, www.nytimes.com.
3. Greenspan, A. 1996. Remarks by Chairman Alan Greenspan at the annual dinner and Francis Boyer Lecture of the American Enterprise Institute for Public Policy, Washington, D.C., December 5. www.federalreserve.gov.
4. Levitt, Arthur. 2002. *Frontline:* "Bigger than Enron." PBS, June 20, www.pbs.org.
5. Carroll, Archie B. 1989. *Business and society: Ethics and stakeholder management*. Cincinnati: Southwestern Publishing, 55–57.
6. Freeman, R.E. 1984. *Strategic Management: A Stakeholder Approach*. Boston: Pitman.
7. Ibid.
8. Association of British Insurers. 2001. Investing in social responsibility, risks and opportunities, p. 41.
9. Ferrell, O. C., & Fraedrich, J. 1994. *Business ethics: Ethical decision making and cases*. New York: Houghton Mifflin Co., 76.
10. Hay, R. D., Gary, E. R., & Smith, P. H. 1989. *Business & society: Perspectives on ethics & social responsibility*. Cincinnati: Southwestern Publishing Co., 288.
11. Boatright, J. R. 1993. *Ethics and the conduct of business*. Englewood Cliffs, NJ: Prentice-Hall, 332–335.
12. *Fortune*. 2002. *Fortune* 500 List. *Fortune* online, www.fortune.com.
13. Hoover's. 2002. Enron corporate profile. www.hoovers.com.
14. *Wall Street Journal*. 2002. Called to account: The Enron saga. Scandal Scorecard. www.wsj.com.
15. Levitt, Arthur. 2002. *Frontline:* "Bigger than Enron." PBS, June 20, www.pbs.org.
16. *Frontline*. 2002. "Who Dropped the Ball?" PBS, June 20, www.pbs.org.
17. Morgenson, G. 2002. Settlement is a good deal for Merrill. How about investors? *New York Times*, May 22, www.nytimes.com.
18. McGeehan, P. 2002. Washington insider, but Wall Street pariah. *New York Times*, November 24, www.nytimes.com.
19. *Frontline*. 2002. "Who Dropped the Ball?" PBS, June 20, www.pbs.org.
20. Tully, Shawn, 2001. Betrayal on Wall Street, *Fortune*, May 14, 2001. www.fortune.com.
21. Donaldson, T., & Werhane, P. H. 1988. Ethical issues in business: A philosophical approach. Englewood Cliffs, NJ: Prentice-Hall, 89–100, 414–424. Hartley, R. F. 1993. *Business ethics: Violations of the public trust*. New York: John Wiley & Sons, 295–305
22. Petersen, M. 2000. Guilty plea by division of drug giant. *New York Times*, December 12, sec C, p. 1.
23. Donaldson & Werhane, *Ethical issues in business*.
24. Petersen, M. 2002. Heartfelt advice, hefty fees, *New York Times*, August 11, www.nytimes.com.
25. Pear, R. 2002. Investigators find repeated deception in ads for drugs. *New York Times*, December 4, www.nytimes.com.
26. Elliott, V. S. 2002. Patient-focused drug campaigns may exploit data, invade privacy. *Amednews* (The Newspaper for America's Physicians) July 29, www.amednews.com.
27. Petersen, M. 2002. Madison Ave. plays growing role in drug research. *New York Times*, November 22, www.nytimes.com.
28. Carroll, *Business and society*.
29. Donaldson & Werhane, *Ethical issues in business*.

30. Sells, B. 1994. What asbestos taught me about risk. *Harvard Business Review,* March/April: 76–90.
31. Ibid., p. 76.
32. Ibid., p. 84.
33. Carroll, *Business and society.*
34. Knox, A. 1995. What will Albert Dunlap do next at Scott? *The Philadelphia Inquirer,* May 16, p. E4.
35. Gorenstein, N., & Mayer, C. 1995. Scott, Kimberly-Clark to merge. *The Philadelphia Inquirer,* July 18, p. C1.
36. Byrne, J. A. 1998. How Al Dunlap self-destructed. *Business Week,* July 6: p. 58–65.
37. Norris, F. 2002. Justice department starts inquiry at Sunbeam. *New York Times,* September 9, www.nytimes.com.
38. Norris, F. 2001. An executive's missing years: Papering over past problems. *New York Times,* July 16, www.nytimes.com.
39. Lincoln Electric Company Web site, www.lincolnelectric.com.
40. Kotter, J. P. and Heskett, J. L. 1992. *Corporate culture and performance.* New York: The Free Press, 46.
41. Smith, C. W. 1993. *Ethics and markets: Restructuring Japan's financial markets.* Homewood, IL: Business One Irwin, 335–345.
42. Gimein, M. 2002. The enforcer. *Fortune,* September 2, pp. 77–78
43. Dow Jones Newswire. 2002. Citigroup: Salomon, Grubman Face 62 Suits Over Research, November 13. *Wall Street Journal* online, www.wsj.com.
44. Useem, J. 2002. In corporate America, It's cleanup time, *Fortune,* September 2, p. 63.
45. Wood, D. J. 1994. *Business and society.* New York: HarperCollins, 664.
46. Smith, A. L. 1991. *Innovative employee communications.* Englewood Cliffs, NJ: Prentice-Hall, 41–44.
47. Hartley, *Business ethics.*
48. Ibid.
49. Reuters Newswire. 2002. Court puts Exxon Valdez damages at $4 billion. Reuters Newswire, December 6, www.reuters.com.
50. Plender, J. 2002. Inside track: Morals pay dividends. *Financial Times,* September 18, www.ft.com.
51. Gimein, M. 2002. The enforcer. *Fortune,* September 2, pp. 77–78.

CHAPTER 9
ETHICS AS ORGANIZATIONAL CULTURE

INTRODUCTION

"Culture" has become a common way of thinking about and describing an organization's internal world—a way of differentiating one organization's "personality" from another. In this chapter, we apply this culture concept to organizational ethics. We will propose that organizations can and should proactively develop an ethical organizational culture and that organizations with "ethics problems" should take a culture change approach to solving them. Given recent ethical scandals in the corporate world, we also propose that individuals should evaluate the ethical culture of an organization before joining it. Doing so can avoid stressful conflicts between personal values and organizational values and help ensure a satisfying work experience.

A "COOKIE CUTTER" APPROACH WON'T WORK

The theme of this chapter is that a "cookie cutter" or "one size fits all" approach to developing an ethical organization simply will not work. Ethics is an integral part of the organization's overall culture. Therefore, designing an ethical organization means systematically analyzing all aspects of the organization's ethical culture and aligning them so that they support ethical behavior and discourage unethical behavior. This kind of analysis and alignment requires a substantial and sustained effort over a long period of time and the full involvement of senior executives.

Organizations Don't Have Cookie-Cutter Ethical Problems

Standardized ethics programs are likely to be ineffective because organizations don't have cookie-cutter ethical problems. Although common ethical problems exist across virtually all organizations, organizations may vary in terms of the ethical problems that are most common or important for them. For example, a growing regional bank, a manufacturer involved in downsizing, and a defense contractor have different ethics program needs. Forgery or embezzlement may be key ethical issues at the bank. Conducting layoffs in a fair manner may be the hot ethical issue for the manufacturer, and accurately charging the government for contract work may be the major ethical concern for the defense contractor. Thus, each organization's approach must address the unique ethical problems that it faces.

Cookie-Cutter Programs Are Superficial

Second, no matter how well intentioned they are, cookie-cutter efforts are likely to be short lived or ineffective because they tend to be superficial, leaving deeper organizational systems unanalyzed and untouched. For example, a one-day training program that emphasizes "doing the right thing" won't have any impact if the organization's incentive system rewards unethical behavior. The reward system is still there, awaiting employees when they return to the job.

"Ethics for a Day" Breeds Cynicism

As interest in business ethics grew, more and more consultants offered packaged lectures and seminars. "The rule in ethics was spray and pray. Consultants sprayed some ethics over [big companies] and prayed that something happened."[1]

These spray and pray programs can breed cynicism because they raise employees' awareness of ethics problems while simultaneously suggesting, in many cases, how little the organization is doing about them. "We had our ethics-for-a-day training program. Now we're back to doing things the way we've always done them."

Many companies employ consultants to help them design their ethics initiatives. That may be appropriate, especially if the firm doesn't have the expertise in house. But in order for these initiatives to go beyond superficial cookie-cutter prescriptions, they need to be based on an in-depth analysis of the company and its current ethical culture. Many consultants provide this kind of service. Unfortunately, what firms sometimes receive is an off-the-shelf report with standard prescriptions that could apply to any firm. Companies that are looking for advice from consultants need a unique plan that is designed to fit their firm's needs and culture. Obviously, such a unique plan will take more time to develop than the off-the-shelf variety. It will require the consultants to get to know the firm, its people and operations. They will have to interview and survey employees, managers, and executives to learn about the current state of affairs. Such knowledge will allow them to propose a system that will address the firm's unique needs.

Proactively Develop an Ethical Organizational Culture

ALIGN MULTIPLE SYSTEMS TO SUPPORT ETHICAL BEHAVIOR Organizations that are serious about ethics must proactively develop an ethical culture that will guide employee actions and decisions. Cultures are complex combinations of formal and informal organizational systems. To create an ethical culture, these systems must be aligned (work together) to support ethical behavior. In other words, the formal and informal systems must be sending the same message. For example, if the formal ethics code tells people that honesty is highly valued in the organization, and high-level managers routinely tell customers the truth about the company's ability to meet their needs, employees receive a consistent message about the organization's commitment to honesty. The systems are aligned. On the other hand, if the same organization regularly deceives customers in order to land a sale, the organization is out of alignment. The formal code says one thing while its actions say quite another. Deceit is what the organization is really about, despite the ethics code.

DOW CORNING: AN ETHICAL CULTURE OUT OF ALIGNMENT? An organization may easily be lulled into thinking that its ethical house is soundly constructed (because it has an ethics code or program, for example), only to find that the roof has been leaking and it's about to cave in. This may be what happened to Dow Corning.

Dow Corning had been recognized as a corporate ethics pioneer. It was among the first, in 1976, to establish an elaborate ethics program. Then-chairman John S. Ludington set up a Business Conduct Committee comprised of six company executives, each of whom devoted up to six weeks a year to the committee's work and reported directly to the board of directors. Two of these members were given responsibility for auditing every business operation every three years. In addition, three-hour reviews were held with up to 35 employees who were encouraged to raise ethical issues. The results of these audits were reported to the Audit and Social Responsibility Committee of the board of directors. John Swanson, manager of corporate internal and management communication at the time, headed this effort and was quoted as saying that the audit approach "makes it virtually impossible for employees to consciously make an unethical decision."[2]

This apparently impressive program failed to help the organization avoid its problem with breast-implant safety, however, despite documented warnings from a company engineer in 1976 that suggested that the implants could rupture and cause severe medical problems. It isn't entirely clear why this well-intentioned ethics program failed. It's likely that, although it was designed to cultivate an overall environment of ethical conduct, aspects of the ethical culture were out of alignment—giving employees different messages.[3] "Layering in a bureaucracy is no substitute for a true corporate culture. Workers have a genius for discovering the real reason for a system and learn quickly how to satisfy its minimum requirements."[4] The system relied on managers to identify the key ethical issues covered by the auditors. Were these managers likely to alert the auditors to their most severe ethical problems? What would the consequences be? The system also relied on periodic planned audits. Did commitment to ethics peak during the planned audit sessions, only to disappear into the woodwork after the auditors left?[5] We don't know, but a comprehensive audit of the ethical culture might have provided the answer.

AUDIT OF THE ETHICAL CULTURE The only way to determine if the culture is aligned to support ethical behavior is to conduct a comprehensive audit of all relevant aspects of the ethical culture. This chapter provides guidelines for how to conduct such an audit. If the ethics audit determines that aspects of the current culture are not aligned to support ethical behavior, and the goal is to produce consistent ethical conduct, then the culture must change.

ORGANIZATIONAL ETHICS AS A CULTURAL PHENOMENON

What Is Culture?

Anthropologists define culture as a body of learned beliefs, traditions, and guides for behavior shared among members of a society or a group.[6] This idea of culture has been found to be particularly useful for understanding work organizations and the behavior of people in them.[7] The organizational culture expresses shared assumptions, values, and beliefs and is the social glue that holds the organization together.[8] Organizational culture is manifested in many ways, including norms, physical settings, modes of dress, special language, myths, rituals, heroes, and stories.[9]

Organizational cultures can vary widely, even within the same industry. For example, IBM has been known for its relatively formal culture, exemplified for years by a dress code that mandated dark suits, white shirts, and polished shoes. Apple Computer, on the other hand, was known for its informality. Particularly in its early days, T-shirts, jeans, and tennis shoes were the expected Apple "costume." *Fortune* magazine described IBM as "the sensible, wingtip, Armonk, New York, computer company, not part of that sneaker-wearing, tofu-eating Silicon Valley crowd."[10]

Strong versus Weak Cultures

Organizational cultures can be strong or weak.[11] In a strong culture, standards and guidelines are known and shared by all, providing common direction for day-to-day behavior. In the 1980s, Citicorp's culture was so strong that when Katherine Nelson, a co-author of this text and former vice president and head of human resources communications at Citicorp, traveled to the firm's offices in the Far East to deliver ethics training, she felt right at home (despite huge differences in national culture). "You could tell that you were in a Citicorp facility," she said, "whether you were in London, Tokyo, or New York." Nelson facilitated an ethics training session for Japanese managers. She presented them with a common ethical dilemma—what do you do if you have raised an important ethical issue with your manager and nothing is done? Moreover, the manager discourages you from pursuing the issue. The potential answers included do nothing, go around the manager to the next level, raise the issue in writing to the manager, or take the issue to a staff department such as human resources.

The Japanese managers unanimously gave the "correct" answer according to Citicorp's culture and policies at the time. They said that they would go around their manager and take the issue to the next level. Nelson was surprised at their response, thinking that it conflicted with the wider Japanese culture's attention to authority, seniority, and honor. So, she asked these managers, "Doesn't this conflict with Japanese culture?" To which they responded, "You forget—we are much more Citicorp than we are Japanese." Citicorp's culture proved to be so strong that standards and guidelines spanned continents and superseded national culture. This experience has since been verified by some of our international students who worked for U.S.-based multinationals before returning to school for their MBA degree. For example, one student worked for Baxter Healthcare in a country known for corruption and bribery. Baxter's strong ethical culture didn't allow such conduct, and employees were proud to be a part of such an organization.

In a weak organizational culture, subcultures within divisions or departments are more likely to guide behavior. Many large public universities can be thought of as having weak cultures. Departmental subcultures are often stronger than the overall university culture, with the romance languages department operating very differently from the accounting department, for example. Among students at a large state university, the fraternity/sorority subculture coexists with the political activist subculture, the devout Christian subculture, the jock subculture, and many other subcultures, and behavior is quite different within each. It's important to note that weak doesn't necessarily mean "bad." In some situations, weak cultures are desirable. They allow for strong subcultures, with diversity of thought and action. However, in a weak culture, behavioral consistency is difficult, if not impossible to achieve.

How Culture Influences Behavior: Socialization and Internalization

Employees are brought into and are taught the organization's culture through a process called enculturation, or socialization.[12] Through socialization, employees learn "the ropes." Socialization can occur through formal training or mentoring, or through more informal transmission of norms by peers and superiors. When effectively socialized, employees behave in ways that are consistent with cultural expectations. They know how to dress, what to say, and what to do.

With socialization, people behave in ways that are consistent with the culture because they feel that they are expected to do so. Their behavior may have nothing to do with their personal beliefs, but they behave as they are expected to behave in order to fit into the context and to be approved by people they care about.[13] An IBM employee whose personal preference is to work in jeans and a sweat shirt will nevertheless dress appropriately according to the more formal IBM culture because of socialization. Similarly, individuals who don't personally believe in giving kickbacks—but are taught that it's the organizational norm—feel that if they don't go along they'll risk disapproval or they won't fit in. Those who conform to expectations are retained and promoted. Those who don't fit into the culture are likely to leave. Obviously, socialization can support either ethical or unethical behavior.

Individuals may behave according to the culture for another reason—because they have internalized cultural expectations. With internalization, individuals have adopted the external cultural standards as their own. Their behavior, though consistent with the culture, also accords with their own beliefs about what's right. For example, an individual who prefers formal dress fits in with IBM's cultural expectations about attire. The standards are internalized and are therefore easily followed.

Organizational culture is created and maintained through a complex interplay of formal and informal organizational systems. Formally, executive leadership, structure, selection systems, orientation and training programs, rules and policies, reward systems, and decision-making processes all contribute to culture creation and maintenance.

Informally, the culture's norms, heroes, rituals, stories, and language keep the culture alive and indicate to both insiders and outsiders whether the formal systems represent fact or facade. The next section will describe and provide examples of each of these important ethics culture components. We will discuss them separately, although you will see that they are all interconnected.

FORMAL CULTURAL SYSTEMS

Executive Leadership

EXECUTIVE LEADERS CREATE CULTURE Leadership is a critical component of the organization's culture because senior leaders can create, maintain, or change culture.[14] The founder of a new organization is thought to play a particularly important culture-creating role.[15] Often, the founder has a vision for what the new organization should be. He or she may personify the culture's values, providing a role model for others to observe and follow, and guiding decision making at all organizational levels. For example, Thomas Jefferson founded the University of Virginia. Although he's long gone, it's said even today that when the governing board of the university is faced with a difficult decision, they're still guided by "what Mr. Jefferson would do."

The same has been said of Walt Disney. The question "What would Walt do?" has been asked for many years since Disney's death. Walt Disney's moral influence is represented in the introduction to the company's code of ethics. "Walt Disney believed that the right kind of entertainment would appeal to all people.... Walt believed that our audience would accept, above anything else, quality and good taste in entertainment. Time and time again throughout his career, he virtually bet his entire organization on this belief ... often in the face of skepticism and predicted failure by others. His philosophy rejected gimmicks and the fast buck, embracing instead a different and vastly more difficult philosophy ... to produce a quality family entertainment product. This philosophy has brought to the name 'Disney' a hard-earned public trust unparalleled anywhere else in the entertainment business."[16]

Herb Kelleher is the legendary founder and now chairman of the board of Southwest Airlines, generally cited as the best-run U.S. airline. The no-frills airline started in 1971 and has been flying high ever since. Southwest Airlines has never served a meal, and its planes are in and out of the gate in 20 minutes. During Kelleher's tenure, other airlines went bankrupt, suffered strikes, or disappeared. But Southwest continues to succeed even after the terrorist attacks of September 11, 2001, which sent the entire industry reeling. The secret is thought to be the company's culture, and an "esprit de corps" inspired by Kelleher. The culture combines efficiency, a family feeling, and an emphasis on fun. In support of efficiency, pilots have been known to load luggage or even clean planes if necessary. During a fuel crisis, Kelleher asked employees to help by saving $5 per day. The response was immediate and in only 6 weeks after Kelleher's request, employees had saved the company more than $2 million. In the area of fun, Kelleher is best known for his crazy antics, jokes, and pranks. He has settled business disputes by arm wrestling, and [when an air]line CEO criticized Southwest's promotion that featured Sham[u,] Kelleher sent him a huge bowl of chocolate pudding (meant to resemble [whale blubber]) with a note reading "With love, from Shamu."[17]

LEADERS MAINTAIN OR CHANGE ORGANIZATIONAL CULTURE Current leaders can also influence culture in a number of ways.[18] They can help to maintain the current culture, or they can change it by articulating a vision; by paying attention to, measuring, and controlling certain things; by making critical policy decisions; by recruiting and hiring personnel who fit their vision of the organization; and by holding people accountable for their actions.

We talked earlier about the importance of Walt Disney to the enduring culture of the company. In recent years, 59-year-old Michael Eisner, Disney's CEO since 1984, has come to "personify the company and its culture." "The man is The Mouse." He hosts *The Wonderful World of Disney* and pays fanatical attention to every detail of the business. For example, in the design of the Animal Kingdom Lodge at Disney World, he picked every piece of furniture! He considers himself the chief creative officer of the company and involves himself in script development and other details in a way that is unheard of at other entertainment giants. But he is also committed to the core values of Disney that go back to its founder. According to Eisner, "There are two ways to make money in entertainment, the high road and the low road. The low road is a road that I don't choose to be on... My value is in the area of making sure that everything we do is ethical, moral, and creatively of the highest quality."[19]

But sometimes new leaders change corporate culture. Jack Welch, recently retired CEO of General Electric Company, radically changed the formerly staid bureaucratic culture of GE into a lean and highly competitive organization. Welch began the culture change effort by clearly articulating his vision that the new GE would be number one or number two in the world in each of its businesses. Businesses that could not measure up would be sold.

Traditional GE employees had been attracted to the job security of the old GE. But Welch wanted to encourage competitiveness, risk taking, creativity, self-confidence, and dynamism. He recruited managers who were interested in doing a great job and then moving on, if GE no longer needed them. Many of the old-line GE employees found themselves out of sync and out of a job.

Welch also focused on identifying and eliminating unproductive work in the organization. He told managers to eliminate reports, reviews and forecasts, to speed decision cycles, and to move information more quickly through the organization by eliminating unnecessary bureaucratic layers. All of this has contributed to the "leaner and meaner" GE culture he created.

ETHICAL LEADERSHIP AND ETHICAL CULTURE Senior leadership represents an important component of an organization's ethical culture, as integrity (or the lack of it) flows from the top down and employees take their cues from the messages sent by those in formal leadership roles. But most employees don't know the senior executives of their organization personally. They only know what they can make sense of

ETHICAL PROBLEMS FACING ORGANIZATIONS

.rom afar. Senior executives must develop a "reputation" for ethical leadership by being visible on ethics issues. A recent study[20] found that such a reputation rests upon dual dimensions that work together: a moral person dimension and a moral manager dimension. (See Figure 9.1: Executive Ethical Leadership.) First, we will explain what each dimension represents and then we'll combine these dimensions into a matrix that shows how leaders can develop a reputation for ethical leadership, unethical leadership, hypocritical leadership, or ethically neutral leadership.

The moral person dimension represents the "ethical" part of the term ethical leadership and is key to developing a reputation for ethical leadership among employees. As a "moral person," the executive is seen first as demonstrating certain individual traits (integrity, honesty, and trustworthiness). For example, one executive described ethical leaders as "squeaky clean." But probably more important are visible behaviors. These include doing the right thing, showing concern for people and treating them with dignity and respect, being open/listening, and living a personally moral life. To some extent, senior executives live in glass houses. They are often public figures and active in their communities. So, they need to be particularly careful about their private behavior. Rumors can begin quickly and taint an otherwise solid reputation. Finally, contributing to one's perception as a moral person is making decisions in a particular

Executive Ethical Leadership Is about Reputation, Which Rests on These Two Pillars

Moral Person	Moral Manager
Tells followers how leader behaves	Tells followers how they should behave and holds them accountable
Traits: • Honesty • Integrity • Trust	Role Modeling Visible ethical action
Behaviors • Openness • Concern for people • Personal morality	Rewards/Discipline Hold people accountable for ethical conduct
Decision-making • Values-based • Fair	Communicating An "ethics and values" message

Executive Ethical Leadership Reputation Matrix

		Moral Person	
		Weak	Strong
Moral Manager	Strong	Hypocritical Leader	Ethical Leader
	Weak	Unethical Leader	?

←Ethically Neutral Leader→

FIGURE 9.1 Executive Ethical Leadership

way—decisions that are explicitly based upon values, fairness, concern for society, and other ethical decision rules.

But being a moral person, by itself, isn't enough to be perceived as an ethical leader. Being a moral person tells employees how the leader is likely to behave, but it doesn't tell them how the leader expects them to behave. Therefore, to complete the ethical leadership picture, executives must also act as "moral managers"—they must focus on the "leadership" part of the term "ethical leadership" by making ethics and values an important part of their leadership message and by shaping the firm's ethical culture. They do that by conveying the importance of ethical conduct in a variety of ways. The large majority of the messages employees receive in business are about bottom-line goals. Therefore, senior executives must make ethics a priority of their leadership if ethics is to get attention from employees. Moral managers do this by visibly role-modeling ethical conduct, by communicating openly and regularly with employees about ethics and values, and by using the reward system to hold everyone accountable to the standards. This "moral person/moral manager" approach is similar to what executive headhunters Thomas Neff and James Citrin list as their number one strategy (of six) of corporate stars: "Live with Integrity, Lead by Example." They say, "Integrity builds the trust in senior management that is critical for high-performing organizations."[21]

Kent Druyvesteyn, former staff vice president, ethics, General Dynamics Corporation, made an important point about leaders as ethical role models. "People in leadership need to ... set the tone by the example of their own conduct. We could have had all the workshops in the world. We could have even had Jesus and Moses and Mohammed and Buddha come and speak at our workshops. But, if after all of that, someone in a leadership position then behaved in a way which was contrary to the standards, that instance of misconduct by a person in a leadership position would teach more than all the experts in the world."

James Burke, former CEO of Johnson & Johnson, is probably the best-known example of a highly visible ethical leader. Soon after being appointed CEO in the late 1970s, he challenged his senior managers to revisit and update the company's age-old credo (discussed later in more detail). He wasn't willing to have it hanging on the wall unless his senior managers were committed to living it. After much disagreement, discussion, and input from J&J sites around the world, the credo was revised and its commitment to customers first and foremost was intact. Less than three years later, the Tylenol poisoning occurred (described in Chapter 8) and the credo guided corporate decision making successfully through the crisis. Following that crisis, Burke initiated a regular credo survey process in which employees were asked about the company's performance with regard to the credo—a process that continues to this day.[22] It was clear to employees that Burke really cared about the credo and the values it represented.

At Ruder Finn, a large public relations agency, the CEO chairs every ethics committee himself to make it clear how important ethics is to him and the organization. All staff members are invited to participate in the open forum. Ethical issues are discussed freely in the presence of an outside, objective adviser. The symbolic message of such high-level involvement is clear: Ethical issues are important enough to be handled by the most senior leaders, and the CEO really cares about it.[23] We talk elsewhere in this chapter about the importance of the reward system to the overall ethical culture and its alignment. Leaders set the tone for the reward system and make important decisions that affect everyone. Moral managers consistently reward ethical conduct and discipline unethical conduct at all levels in the organization. It's a way of demonstrating that the leader backs up words with actions.

Similar to business leaders, coaches of college sports are expected to set and enforce ethical standards. Joe Paterno, the legendary Penn State football coach, and Dean Smith, former coach of the University of North Carolina basketball team, are coaches who exemplify moral management. They set high expectations (for performance and ethics), create rules and policies for appropriate behavior, and enforce them.[24]

Coaches are also held responsible when ethical violations are discovered among players, assistants, and boosters. A number of coaches have lost their jobs or have resigned because of such violations.[25] When wrongdoing occurs in any type of organization, top managers are frequently held accountable even if they weren't personally involved. For example, the executives of Arthur Andersen, Enron, Worldcom, and Adelphia were all replaced soon after ethical scandals came to light.

UNETHICAL LEADERSHIP Unfortunately, unethical leaders can influence the development of an unethical culture. In terms of our matrix, unethical leaders have reputations as weak moral persons and weak moral managers. In interviews, senior executives cited Al Dunlap as a senior executive with a reputation for unethical leadership. John Byrne of *Business Week* wrote a book about Dunlap entitled *Mean Business* and published excerpts in the magazine. According to Byrne, Dunlap became famous for turning struggling companies around. But while at Sunbeam, he was also known for "emotional abuse" of employees—being "condescending, belligerent and disrespectful." "At his worst, he became viciously profane, even violent. Executives said he would throw papers or furniture, bang his hands on his desk, and shout so ferociously that a manager's hair would be blown back by the stream of air that rushed from Dunlap's mouth." Dunlap also demanded that employees make the numbers at all costs, and rewarded them handsomely for doing so. As a result, they felt pressure to use questionable accounting and sales techniques. Dunlap also lied to Wall Street, assuring them that the firm was making its projections and would continue to reach even higher. In the end, Dunlap couldn't cover up the real state of affairs and Sunbeam's board fired him in 1998. But he left the company crippled.[26] In 2002, Dunlap settled a civil suit filed by the SEC. He paid a $500,000 fine and agreed to never again be an officer or director of a public company. Whether federal prosecutors will pursue him remains an open question. Investigators have learned that allegations of accounting fraud on Dunlap's watch go back to the 1970s and follow him through a number of companies.

HYPOCRITICAL LEADERSHIP. There may be nothing that makes us more cynical than a leader who talks incessantly about integrity and ethical values but then engages in unethical conduct, encourages others to do so either explicitly or implicitly, rewards only bottom-line results, and fails to discipline misconduct. This leader is strong on the communication aspect of moral management but clearly isn't an ethical person—doesn't "walk the talk." It's a "do as I say, not as I do" approach. Al Dunlap made no pretense about ethics. All that mattered was the bottom line and he didn't pretend to be a nice guy. But hypocritical leadership is all about ethical pretense. The problem is that by putting the spotlight on integrity, the leader raises expectations and awareness of ethical issues. At the same time, employees realize that they can't trust anything the leader says. That leads to cynicism, and employees are likely to disregard ethical standards themselves if they see the leader doing so.

Jim Bakker remains the best public example of hypocritical leadership. In the late 1970s and early 1980s, Bakker built PTL into one of the world's biggest religious broadcasting empires. At its peak, Bakker's television ministry reached more than ten million homes and had 2,000 employees. Bakker, along with his wife, Tammy Faye, claimed to be doing "the Lord's work" as he raked in millions of dollars, convincing the faithful to purchase a limited number of lifetime memberships in two hotels he claimed would be built at the PTL's Heritage USA Christian theme park. The problem was that the 25,000 lifetime memberships (promising a free annual family stay for four days and three nights) in the Heritage Grand Hotel morphed into 66,683 memberships. And, instead of the limited 30,000 memberships at the proposed Heritage Towers, PTL sold 68,755 memberships. You do the math. It would be impossible to provide promised services to this many people. On top of that, the second hotel was never completed. The funds donated for these projects were being tapped to support PTL operating expenses, including huge salaries and bonuses for the Bakkers and other top PTL officials. When questioned at times about PTL's finances, Bakker referred to the organization's annual audits conducted by big auditing firms such as Deloitte and Laventhol. Unfortunately, PTL filed for bankruptcy in 1987, three months after Bakker resigned in disgrace. The IRS revoked PTL's tax-exempt status, and in 1989 Bakker was convicted on fraud and conspiracy charges. He spent 8 years in prison.[27]

ETHICALLY NEUTRAL LEADERSHIP Many top managers are neither strong ethical nor unethical leaders. They fall into what employees perceive to be an ethically "neutral" leadership zone. They simply don't provide leadership in the crucial area of ethics, and employees aren't sure what the leaders think about ethics, if anything. This may be because the leader doesn't realize how important executive ethical leadership is to the organization's ethical culture, or just doesn't care that much. On the moral person dimension, the ethically neutral leader is not clearly unethical, but is perceived to be more self-centered than people-oriented. On the moral manager dimension, the ethically neutral leader is thought to focus intently on the bottom line without setting complementary ethical goals. There is little or no ethics message coming from the top. But it turns out that silence represents an important message. In the context of all the other messages being sent in a highly competitive business environment, employees are likely to interpret silence to mean that the top executive really doesn't care how business goals are met (only that they are met), and they'll act on that message.[28]

Consider Sandy Weill, CEO of Citigroup. A *Fortune* magazine article recently described the firm as a "blockbuster money machine" that will "probably make

$16 billion dollars this year." But the article also recounted recent scandalous allegations about Citigroup and its Salomon Smith Barney unit. "Citi helped Enron hide debt; Salomon peddled worthless WorldCom debt; Star analyst Jack Grubman recommended Winstar as it was heading for bankruptcy; Salomon rewarded telecom execs with hot IPOs," and more.[29] The company is spending lots of time and money playing defense with the media, responding to ugly headlines on a regular basis. According to *Fortune,* Weill is contrite and has now "gotten religion," if a bit late. Weill has "told his board that he feels his most important job from now on is to be sure that Citigroup operates at the highest level of ethics and with the utmost integrity."[30] As a result, new procedures and business standards are being developed. However, the article also cites widespread cynicism about this recent turnabout, noting that Weill is often "tone deaf" on these issues and that it took a while for him to "get to the party."

At least from the perspective of public perception, Weill exemplifies "ethically neutral" leadership. Being "tone deaf" on these issues is exactly what ethically neutral leadership is about. Weill's public statement that the "company is too big to micromanage" applies to his approach to managing ethics. He says a CEO relies on "very competent people" and trusts them to do a good job. In the case of ethics management, that meant leaving it to the executives running Citi's various businesses. If the head of a division thought ethics was important, it got resources and attention. If the head didn't, it didn't. So, with a kind of benign neglect, Weill sat on the sidelines and provided little ethical leadership. And with corporate rewards focused primarily on the bottom line, there was little motivation for managers to attend to such issues. As a result, employees didn't know for sure where Weill stood. But the intense focus on the bottom line suggested that profits were most important and many employees probably acted accordingly. This approach to ethics is in sharp contrast to prior CEO John Reed's leadership on ethics issues. Reed spent almost his entire career at Citicorp and was its CEO when the huge American financial powerhouse merged with Weill's Travelers organization to form Citigroup. As a banker his entire life, Reed understood in his gut how important reputation is to a financial institution. As a result, Reed encouraged and supported the development of a strong, centralized corporate ethics program with global reach. Interestingly, the people associated with that program are all gone and much of the program itself has been dismantled since Weill took over.

Research has found that executive ethical leadership is critical to employees. In a recent study, unethical behavior was lower, and employees were more committed to their organization, more ethically aware, and more willing to report problems to management in firms that had an ethical culture characterized by top executives who represented high ethical standards, regularly showed that they cared about ethics, and were models of ethical behavior.[31] But, interestingly, senior executives are often not aware of how important their ethical leadership is. Many believe that being an ethical person who makes ethical decisions should be enough. But, it isn't enough. Executives must lead on this issue (be moral managers) if it is to register with employees. In a highly competitive environment of intense focus on the bottom line, employees need to know that the executive leaders in their organization care about ethics. An ethical leader makes it clear that strong bottom-line results are expected, but only if they can be delivered in a highly ethical manner.

Selection Systems

In general, selection systems are key to hiring people who fit the culture of the firm. For example, all employees at Southwest Airlines (including pilots) are selected based upon their personalities (traits that include cheerfulness, optimism, and team spirit) among other credentials. So it's not surprising to find pilots helping to clean the cabin when time is short, and flight attendants throwing gate parties on Halloween and telling jokes to passengers over the plane's loudspeakers.[32] Starbucks works to attract employees who know (or want to learn) about the company's specialized coffee products, are detail-oriented, and are eager to provide consistently excellent customer service.[33]

When considering the ethical culture, organizations can avoid ethical problems by recruiting the right people and by building a reputation that precedes the organization's representatives wherever they go. Although there are no foolproof integrity tests available, companies can certainly let prospective employees know about the importance of integrity in their organization and what happens to those who break the rules. Companies that are serious about integrity can include statements about their values and expectations in recruiting literature, in offer letters to candidates, and in new hire orientation programs. Coach Joe Paterno was outspoken on this topic in our interview with him. He claimed that the Penn State football program avoids lots of problems faced by other college sports organizations by being absolutely clear up front about its commitment to education for its athletes and to doing things "by the [NCAA] book":

> I think our reputation eliminates most problems before we start. Because we do have a reputation. If a kid is looking for some kind of a deal, he generally won't fool around with us. But, I remember one kid whose dad openly said, "He can't live on that. He's gotta have more money than that." I said, "That's all we can do." He said, "Well, somebody will give it to us." I wished the kid luck and walked out of the house.

Because the Penn State football program has a reputation for integrity, Coach Paterno and his staff rarely face such requests. Those who are looking for money under the table know to look elsewhere. And athletes who break the rules know in advance that they'll be disciplined.

These days, companies also need to be very selective when recruiting leaders who are being considered for important decision-making roles in the firm. Many recent business scandals have zeroed in on company CFOs (chief financial officers) who played with the numbers in order to make it look as if profit goals expected by Wall Street had been achieved when, in reality, they had not. Such individuals must display the strongest moral character in order to withstand marketplace pressures to make the numbers look good. Questions about how they would respond to such pressures and how they have handled them in the past can be useful in selecting these key players.

Organizational Structure

In Chapter 7, we learned that individuals should take responsibility for their own behavior and question orders to behave unethically. However, the organizational structure frequently reinforces, and sometimes creates, problems of authority and responsibility.

Most modern organizations are bureaucratic,[34] meaning that they have a hierarchy of authority, a division of labor or specialization, standardization of activities, and a stress on competence and efficiency. Bureaucracy provides many advantages, and large organizations require a certain amount of bureaucracy in order to function. However, certain characteristics of bureaucracy—such as specialization, division of labor, and hierarchy of authority—can present problems for the organization's ethical culture.

AUTHORITY, RESPONSIBILITY, AND ETHICAL CULTURE With bureaucracy comes the idea of legitimate authority. Look at any organizational chart. It will tell you who supervises whom—who has authority over whom. These authority figures serve important bureaucratic roles. They direct work, delegate responsibility, conduct performance appraisals, and make decisions about promotions and raises.[35]

But the idea of legitimate authority can present problems for the ethical culture. First, recall from Chapter 7 that people tend to obey authority figures no matter what they are ordered to do.[36] This natural tendency toward unquestioning obedience can be a real threat to the organization's attempt to build individual responsibility into its ethical culture. In attempting to control employee behavior, many firms expect loyalty and some demand unquestioning obedience to authority from their employees. You might think that's a good idea—that authority figures have more experience and should know what's right, and employees should follow their orders. But even the military expects soldiers to question unethical orders. Loyalty is generally a good thing, but you shouldn't be expected to be loyal or obedient to an unethical boss or organization. Unquestioning obedience to authority means that employees are not expected to think for themselves, to question bad orders, or to take personal responsibility for problems they observe. Therefore, a culture that expects unquestioning obedience from employees can result in serious ethical problems. A recent study found that the more a firm demands unquestioning obedience to authority, the higher the unethical conduct among employees, the lower their tendency to seek advice about ethical issues, and the lower the likelihood that employees would report ethical violations or deliver "bad news" to management.[37]

Some managers create a structure designed to help them avoid blame.[38] Their greatest fear is that when it comes time to blame someone, the finger will point their way, and their job will be at risk. By delegating responsibility to those at lower levels in the organization, the authority figure can often avoid blame for mistakes or ethical blunders. When it comes time to blame someone, the finger of blame frequently points down. Underlings, in particular, fear becoming the scapegoat for mistakes made at higher levels. CYA ("cover your ass") memos proliferate as managers look to blame someone in a relatively powerless position who is considered to be expendable.

The structure of an organization can also fragment jobs and r essarily that individuals don't want to take responsibility. But jo... divided up that they simply can't see the big picture.⁴⁰ We saw in Chapte. itary bureaucrats passed the buck for responsibility during an investigation of the Lai massacre. They saw themselves only as cogs in a machine. No one felt responsible for the larger outcomes of their actions.

The ethical culture must incorporate a structure that emphasizes and supports individual responsibility and accountability at every level. Each person must be encouraged to take responsibility for his or her actions and to question authority figures when they suspect problems. And individuals must be held accountable for negative consequences when they occur. However, tracking responsibility is difficult and time consuming and is rarely done well. Many organizations don't do this kind of record keeping at all, perhaps preferring to keep responsibility ambiguous and scapegoating a viable possibility.

NEW ORGANIZATIONAL STRUCTURES Organizations today are developing structures designed to remove bureaucratic layers, push responsibility down, and empower individuals to make decisions at every organizational level. Take the example of office furniture manufacturer Herman Miller, Inc. (HMI), which is committed to the values of "open communication," "the dignity of each individual," and "quality relationships based on mutual trust and integrity." Kevin Knowles, a crew leader for six years, said, "What always surprises me is that everyone in the company ... is free to talk with anyone in management about whatever they'd like to talk about." Managers at HMI cite workers' ability to go over their managers' heads as a major reason for the company's success. "There's no fear of retribution if you call someone three levels above." HMI touts a process its chairman calls "roving leadership" that allows anyone to be a leader on a particular issue.

Here is an example of how roving leadership was tested successfully. An employee with AIDS decided that he should let others know about his illness. A co-worker took the roving leader responsibility and informed the human resources manager. Quickly, the entire plant was informed, and a physician from headquarters flew in with a training videotape and a question and answer session. According to the "roving leader," what's important is that HMI's value system "allows us to act on our instincts and know the company will support us. Because the value of each individual is important to us, we were able to stop the manufacture of furniture for one day to take care of Peter."⁴¹ Such a culture likely contributes to the success of a company that was named in 2002 by *Forbes* magazine as among the 400 best-performing large American corporations. *Business Ethics* magazine also ranked Herman Miller, Inc., in the top ten among the "100 Best Corporate Citizens."

These recent structural changes have powerful implications for taking responsibility and for ethical decision making, and they increase the importance of having a strong ethical culture. When individuals are independently making decisions, with less direct supervision, they need a strong ethical culture to guide them. An important part of this strong ethical culture is a structure that supports taking individual responsibility for ethical action.

ETHICAL PROBLEMS FACING ORGANIZATIONS

Values and Mission Statements, Policies and Codes

Many organizations aim to guide employees' behavior through formal organizational value statements, mission statements, credos, policies, and formal codes of ethical conduct. Value and mission statements and credos are abstract, general statements of guiding beliefs. Most companies have them, but it's important that the mission statement be closely aligned with other dimensions of the culture. As evidence of the cynicism often associated with these mission statements, look at Dilbert's Web site (www.Dilbert.com), where Scott Adams includes a Mission Statements Generator (under games). Visitors can create their own lofty sounding mission statements from a selection of fancy verbs, adverbs, adjectives, and nouns. According to James Collins, co-author of *Built to Last: Successful Habits of Visionary Companies,* "the words matter far less than how they are brought to life. The mistake most companies make ... is not setting up procedures to make sure the mission is carried out."

In late 2000, Verizon's published core values were integrity, respect, imagination, passion, and service. But consider this. Customer service representatives were expected to finish each call with the following question to the customer, "Did I provide you with outstanding service today?" During a strike in the fall of 2000, workers cited this disconnect between values and operating procedures as a source of stress and cynicism. Asking customer service representatives to follow a specific "script" (that sometimes led to irate customers becoming even more irate) did not respect the individual customer service representative's ability to serve the customer in a more natural way, and it certainly didn't allow the employee to use imagination or passion in providing customer service. The script may have been well intentioned, but it conflicted with several of the core values professed by the company and appeared hypocritical to employees. Stated values that are inconsistent with management practice can quickly generate employee cynicism.[42]

Probably the most famous example of an effective mission and values statement is the Johnson & Johnson credo, which outlines the pharmaceutical company's commitments. On its Web site (www.jnj.com) the company says, "For more than 50 years, Our Credo has helped us in fulfilling our responsibilities to customers, employees, communities and stockholders. Our worldwide family of companies shares this value system in 36 languages spreading across Africa, Asia/Pacific, Eastern Europe, Europe, Latin America, Middle East and North America.... The Corporation has drawn heavily on the strength of the Credo for guidance through the years, and at no time was this more evident than during the TYLENOL® crises of 1982 and 1986, when the company's product was adulterated with cyanide and used as a murder weapon.... Company managers and employees made countless decisions that were inspired by the philosophy embodied in the Credo.... Today the Credo lives on in Johnson & Johnson stronger than ever. Company employees now participate in a periodic survey and evaluation of just how well the company performs its Credo responsibilities. These assessments are then fed back to the senior management, and where there are shortcomings, corrective action is promptly taken.... More than 50 years after it was first introduced, the Credo continues to guide the destiny of the world's largest and most diversified health care company."

Another good example comes from Starbucks. The senior management team at Starbucks developed the firm's mission statement in 1990. The mission statement outlines the company's commitment to being the "premier purveyor of the finest coffee in the world ... providing a great work environment, embracing diversity, developing enthusiastically satisfied customers, contributing positively to the company's communities and environment, and finally, recognizing that profitability is essential to the firm's future success." A "mission review" system asks employees to report concerns if they believe that management decisions are inconsistent with the mission statement. Comment cards for this purpose are given to new hires and are made available to all employees. Management promises to respond to all signed cards within just two weeks. The CEO, Howard Schultz, reviewed all of these cards in the beginning. With growth, regional groups were assembled to respond to employee concerns and senior managers met with interested employees in open forums that were held each quarter in every region.[43]

Formal ethics codes are longer and more detailed, providing guidance about behavior in specific situations. Policy manuals are even lengthier and include more detailed lists of rules covering a multitude of job situations. An extended discussion of policies and codes follows in Chapter 10. Most ethics codes were introduced within the past 25 years. In a mid-1990s study of the *Fortune* 1000, 98 percent of these large firms reported addressing ethics and conduct issues in formal documents. Of those 98 percent, 78 percent had codes of ethics.[44] In a 2000 Ethics Resource Center study, 78 percent of respondents reported that the companies they work for have ethics policy standards. This percentage is a bit lower because many employees of smaller firms were included in this study. When considering only those who work for firms with more than 500 employees, 89 percent reported that their employer has formal ethics standards.[45] So, it's fair to say that most companies of any size make an effort to provide some sort of formal guidance to their employees regarding ethical and legal conduct.

Research has found that employees working in organizations with codes of ethics report that they engage in less unethical behavior.[46] However, codes vary so much in content and implementation that it's difficult to generalize about their impact. We do know, however, that the existence of an ethics code alone will not solve all organizational ethics problems and can actually cause problems if it is implemented without attention to the rest of the ethical culture. A code can prescribe behavior. But if that behavior isn't followed, we end up with an organization out of alignment (an organization that says one thing and does another). We also have cynical workers who can cite one more instance of organizational hypocrisy. So, organizational follow-through is essential.

Most companies with codes now distribute them quite widely. In a survey of *Fortune* 1000 firms conducted in 1995, 75 percent of responding companies reported distributing their code or policy to at least 80 percent of their employees.[47] This may be a byproduct of the Sentencing Guidelines (discussed in Chapter 2), which specify communication of compliance standards to all employees as a guiding principle. Research has found that when employees are familiar with the code and refer to it for guidance, they are less likely to engage in unethical behavior, more likely to seek advice about ethical issues, and more likely to report ethical rule violations.[48] Some firms even distribute their codes beyond their own employees. For example, in 1993, Wakefern Food Corporation (Shop-Rite supermarkets) distributed its code to its suppliers along with a letter, signed by the president, that said:

> Dear Business Associate:
>
> As the holidays draw near, we are mindful of the mutually satisfying and mutually profitable relationship which exists between Wakefern and our suppliers. We look forward to many more years of successful growth together through our joint efforts to provide our customers with quality products, excellent service and low price.
>
> In recent years, we have found many of our staff members embarrassed by well-intentioned gifts from those with whom we do business. Our Board of Directors approved the enclosed Code of Ethics for Wakefern which clearly states our policy prohibiting Wakefern Associates from accepting gifts from our suppliers and customers. We feel that this policy should apply during the holidays as well as throughout the year.
>
> With so much attention being given to practices which bring the business community's ethics into question, we urge your support of our efforts to maintain the respect and confidence of the industry for the objectivity of our dealings with suppliers.
>
> Since failure to comply with our policy will result in disqualification from further business dealings with us, we request that you distribute this letter to those in your company who have business dealings with Wakefern Food Corporation and its subsidiaries.
>
> The most significant means of expressing your appreciation to Wakefern staff continues to be your efforts to help us grow together by anticipating and meeting the changing consumers' needs and wants.
>
> If you have any questions regarding this policy, please contact....
>
> With our best wishes for happy holidays and a healthy and prosperous 1994.

Research on honor codes in colleges and universities suggests that students cheat less in institutions with honor codes.[49] A recent study found, however, that students' perceptions of their peers' cheating had a more profound influence on their own cheating behavior than the existence of a code. In addition, the certainty of being reported and the severity of penalties were found to be important, supporting the idea that the code alone is not the most important influence.[50] A code must act in concert with other aspects of the ethical culture. The code must not only be distributed, but it must also be enforced and be consistent with other cultural systems. Otherwise, codes of conduct are more likely to be viewed as mere "window dressing" while being disregarded as guides for actual behavior.

Managers, especially middle managers, want to have a stated organizational policy or code when it comes to serious ethical matters. Remember, cognitive moral development research tells us that most people are looking outside themselves for guidance, and stated organizational policy can be an important source of that guidance. To determine where policy is needed, the organization can survey managers about areas of ethical concern and their perception of the need for policy in each area. In one study, managers made it clear that policy was needed in such areas as expense claims, gifts and bribes, and treatment of competitor information.[51]

Reward Systems

The importance of reward systems was discussed in Chapter 7. To be effective, rewards must be linked to specific results and behaviors that are deliberately articulated and managed. This link is created through performance management. Effective performance management systems involve the entire process of articulating goals, aligning goals up, down, and across the organization, identifying performance metrics, and then providing a compensation structure that rewards individual, and frequently team, effort. Just as publicly traded companies are rewarded in the stock market for results, a well-designed performance management system rewards individuals for a variety of results, financial and non-financial. The importance of an effective performance management system is worth repeating here where we focus on the reward system as a key component of the ethical culture and, in particular, the essential role it plays in alignment or misalignment of cultural systems.

DESIGNING A PERFORMANCE MANAGEMENT PROCESS THAT SUPPORTS ETHICAL CONDUCT Since people "do what's measured and rewarded," the best way for an organization to design a comprehensive performance management system is to spend time identifying which factors drive business results. This type of corporate soul-searching generally results in a list of factors, only some of which are financial and many of which are related to operational decisions that drive future financial performance. Just as *Fortune* magazine considers reputation when designing its famed "lists," many sophisticated companies understand that reputation, in many cases, drives financial results. However, many companies continue to design performance management programs that consider only financial results, ignoring the non-financial drivers that can actually serve as the underpinning of the numbers. These companies focus on "what" business results are delivered and they ignore "how" those results were achieved. That is probably the fastest way for an organization's ethical culture to get out of alignment.

Here's how performance management systems can be designed to get great results the right way. First, an organization needs to focus on the mechanics. For example, once an organization understands what is necessary to drive results, it needs to set goals to achieve those desired results and metrics to determine whether the goals are being met. Real success in this area comes when organizations effectively communicate those goals to every employee, helping employees identify how each person can create value for the organization and then rewarding employees fairly for their contribution toward achieving those corporate goals. Once the mechanics are in place, the next challenge is to marry the "what" with the "how," and that's where an organization's articulated values come in. Those values—probably concerning the importance of people and integrity and diversity and customer service, and so forth—need to be translated into metrics for which every employee is held accountable. When such a process is in place, high fliers who exceed all of their numbers can be held accountable for "how" they met those numbers because it is built right into their performance expectations and rewards process. A good example of this is an account executive with a leading consulting company who had a book of business in the millions and managed her firm's relationship with many of the largest companies in New York City. Her huge book of business would ordinarily be enough to ensure that she was named a partner in the firm. However, the senior management team was so upset at how she trounced the firm's stated value around "treating people with respect"—she was extremely abusive to her co-workers—that they repeatedly denied the promotion to her. Of course, one could argue that she shouldn't have a job at all. But at least her behavior—the "how" she was attaining her huge results—prevented her from being esteemed as a partner. Chapter 10 provides some additional examples of how companies are incorporating ethics into their performance management systems.

Pat Schaeffer, a founding principal of Talent Strategy Partners (and colleague of co-author Kate Nelson) and an expert in the design of performance management systems and compensation, says, "The use of stock options and other forms of stock-based compensation as key components of executive pay packages over the past 10 to 15 years has been justified as a way to align the interests of corporate executives with the interests of shareowners. In most companies, the stock components have been combined with incentive plans that provide senior executives with the opportunity to earn 50 percent or more of their base salary in the form of cash bonuses for hitting specific financial targets. What these compensation vehicles have done is focused company executives on delivering the financial results expected by Wall Street—and delivering those results in any way possible, including 'cooking the books.' The result of this lack of attention to the 'how' has been a crisis of investor confidence that has driven down the stock market and wiped out the nest eggs of thousands of honest, hard-working Americans."

REWARDING AND PUNISHING BEHAVIOR To understand the ethical conduct of individuals in the organization, we need to look more specifically at the behaviors that are rewarded and punished and at how this system aligns with (or doesn't align with) the rest of the ethical culture. When managers are asked about ethics in their organization, reward systems are frequently cited as a significant problem. They report that concern about the bottom line often conflicts with and overwhelms concern about ethics. Employees are rewarded for reaching a particular goal or for selling a certain amount of product, with little attention to how the goal is achieved. Because people tend to do those things that are rewarded, management must ensure that performance goals are realistic and can be achieved without resorting to unethical behavior. A classic case occurred at a GM plant several years ago. The plant manager had installed a device that periodically speeded up the assembly line beyond the rate agreed to in the union contract. When confronted, he pointed out that the firm's production specifications assumed that the line would run at maximum allowable speed 100 percent of the time. He installed the device to make up for inevitable downtime.[52]

Misalignment of the reward system with other aspects of the ethical culture is quite common. We frequently hear this from managers who work in an organization with a code of ethical conduct that isn't enforced. Think about what happens when these cultural systems conflict. For example, imagine an organization where everyone knows that the top sales representative's sales depend on unethical practices. Not only does the unethical conduct go undisciplined, but the sales representative receives large bonuses, expensive vacations, and recognition at annual sales meetings. Members of the sales force recognize that the reward system carries the "real" message, and so the code becomes meaningless, or worse yet, an example of top management's hypocrisy.

Recall from Chapter 7 that the reward system includes discipline as well as rewards. For an ethical culture to be in alignment, unethical behavior must be disciplined and disciplined equally across organizational levels. That means that the star executive who always makes the numbers must be punished for knowingly breaking the rules just as a lower-level employee would be disciplined. In fact, at that level, the discipline should probably be harsher because the higher in the organization one goes, the more responsibility one holds.

Coach Paterno, in our interview with him, was clear about the importance of rules and their enforcement with every player. "The players know what the penalties are. They have a pretty good idea of what's going to happen to them if they break the rules.... If I tell the players we have a rule, we have to enforce it and apply it to everyone. You can't say this is the rule and it's for everybody but your top quarterback." Paterno showed how he held players accountable when the Penn State team played its 1998 bowl game without two star players. One had academic problems, and the other had been accused of taking a gift from a sports agent. The team lost, but the program's integrity was intact. Interestingly, Paterno's rule enforcement extends to alumni and boosters who have gotten other football programs in big trouble with the NCAA. Penn State regularly sends letters reminding football game ticket holders of their responsibility to uphold the integrity of the football program. And, according to Paterno, some alumni have lost their rights to buy tickets because of past violations.

THE REWARD SYSTEM AND WHISTLE-BLOWERS The organization's treatment of whistle-blowers is a relevant reward system concern[53] and a frequent source of misalignment. In today's organizations, fewer employees are directly supervised. Therefore, organizations must rely more on their employees to report misconduct. However, as we all know, powerful norms exist against blowing the whistle. The words we use to describe this behavior, "tattling," "squealing," "snitching," "informing," and "ratting," all have negative connotations. In fact, there isn't a nice or even a neutral word to describe it.

As suggested in Chapter 3, whistle-blowers frequently suffer retaliation, particularly when they report managerial or organizational misconduct.[54] They're punished rather than rewarded for doing what they think is right. If an organization claims that it's attempting to develop an ethical culture, retaliation against a whistle-blower is a powerful example of misalignment. Again, the workers view this "punishment" of the whistle-blower as an example of the organization's "real" ethical beliefs.

Roger Boisjoly, a Morton Thiokol engineer, blew the whistle on his employer regarding O-ring safety and management problems leading to the space shuttle *Challenger* disaster. He lost his job as a result of his "ethical" behavior, sending the clear message to other employees that blowing the whistle gets punished. According to Boisjoly, "If you believe in practicing what you preach, it can mean career suicide."[55]

The ethical organization, however, should view the whistle-blower as an important cog in its control system and must find ways to make whistle-blowing a safe activity. Some organizations even reward whistle-blowing. For example, in 1996, *Fortune* magazine published memos from the chairman of Wall Street firm Bear Stearns. Two of the eight published memos concerned the importance of whistle-blowing and the company's policy to provide cash awards to whistle-blowers whose accusations are well-founded. This memo was addressed to senior managing directors, managing directors, and associate directors in 1993.

> We need your help. Please help us get a message out to every associate. It is essential that once again we stress that we welcome every suspicion or feeling that our co-workers might have about something they see or hear that is going on at Bear Stearns that might not measure up to our standards of honesty and integrity....
>
> We want people at Bear Stearns to cry wolf. If the doubt is justified, the reporter will be handsomely rewarded. If the suspicion proves unfounded, the person who brought it to our attention will be thanked for their vigilance and told to keep it up.
>
> Forget the chain of command! That is not the way Bear Stearns was built. If you think somebody is doing something off the wall or his/her decision making stinks, go around the person, and that includes me....
>
> *Get these messages out loud and clear.*
>
> We have had some senior people who resented "end runs." They quickly became associated with more conventional firms—you can draw your own conclusions about whether their career change worked out for the best.[56]

This leader sent a clear message that whistle-blowing was encouraged and rewarded. In the second memo, he shared information about a specific instance in which two administrative assistants detected that fictitious taxicab vouchers were being submitted by an employee. The employee was terminated, and the administrative assistants were provided an immediate cash award.

But most people don't expect or want a reward for doing the right thing. They just don't want to be punished for it. In an attempt to protect whistle-blowers, many organizations have installed hotlines and ombudspersons. Whistle-blowers can call these hotlines and speak confidentially and without fear of retaliation. Examples of how these work are included in Chapter 10. In addition, society has changed the laws, providing more protection to whistle-blowers under the Sarbanes-Oxley Act (see Chapter 3 for details).

Thus, organizational reward systems are important in themselves because they provide guidance about expected behavior, but they're particularly important in the sense that people look to them to reflect the "real" message about what is valued in the organization. Is there consistency between what the organization says (e.g., codes) and what it does (rewards and punishments)? Reward systems frequently represent the source of "cultural misalignment" that can lead to cynicism about organizational ethics.

Orientation and Training Programs

Socialization is often begun through formal orientation programs and reinforced through ongoing training. The organization's values and guiding principles can be communicated in orientation programs. More specific guidance in ethical rules and decision making can be provided in subsequent training programs. Recently, an increasing number of firms have added ethics to their list of training programs. Most *Fortune* 1000 firms provide some ethics training at least every few years.[57] In the 2000 Ethics Resource Center study,[58] 55 percent of people surveyed said that their employers provide ethics training and this training is generally mandatory. The percentage providing training is even higher for organizations with more than 500 employees—68 percent. More specifics about how ethics training is conducted in different firms will be covered in Chapter 10.

A former chairman and CEO of Allied Corporation said, "Through our ethics seminars, we encourage people to gain a broader perspective of their responsibilities at Allied. Our managers must be capable of recognizing the ethical dimensions of their business decisions."[59] By providing ethics training, the organization not only offers specific skills to managers, but indirectly communicates that ethical behavior is valued and that ethical dimensions should be considered in decision making. More specific examples of ethics training are included in Chapter 10.

The ethics training must be consistent with the ethical culture—how we really do things around here—because a training program that is out of alignment is thought of, at best, as a pleasant day away from the office. At its worst, the ethics training will be taken as a joke, when managers attempt to reconcile what they're hearing with their experience in the real organization.

Decision-Making Processes

Ethical decisions are influenced by the organization's formal decision-making processes. For example, managers may ignore the ethical dimension of decisions unless leaders state that ethical concerns must be a formal part of all decision making. This emphasis on ethics can also be reinforced by regularly addressing ethical concerns in meetings and by making them an expected part of managers' reports regarding new products or new business ventures. Environmental impact is now an expected and routine part of corporate decision making in many firms. Some organizations are also creating special high-level "ethics" committees charged with reviewing major organizational level decisions from an ethical perspective.[60] Others have advocated the implementation of moral quality circles, groups set up to assess the morality of business decisions.[61]

OVERRELIANCE ON QUANTITATIVE ANALYSIS Decision-making processes can also contribute to unethical behavior. For example, in Chapter 5, we discussed the decision-making process that kept the Ford Pinto from being recalled. In that situation, exclusive reliance on a quantitative cost/benefit analysis to the exclusion of moral considerations had disastrous consequences. In another example, Johns Manville, the former corporate giant and producer of asbestos, was brought down by decision-making processes that focused on the bottom line to the exclusion of worker health. More than 40 years ago, top management began to receive information implicating asbestos inhalation as a cause of severe lung disease in workers. Managers and medical staff suppressed the research and concealed the information from employees. During testimony, a lawyer reported on a confrontation with the corporate counsel about the failure to share X-ray results with employees. The lawyer reported asking, "You mean to tell me you would let them work until they dropped dead?" The lawyer replied, "Yes, we save a lot of money that way." It was apparently cheaper to pay workers' compensation claims than to develop safer working conditions. A New Jersey court found that the company had made a "conscious, cold-blooded business decision to take no protective or remedial action."[62] Obviously, organizational decision makers must rely on quantitative analysis in making business decisions. However, their reliance on numbers, to the exclusion of moral considerations, is problematic. Discussions about whether the decision is the "right" thing to do must accompany discussions about the effect of a particular decision on the bottom line. Important decisions should be subjected to a discussion of ethical concerns, especially potential impacts on stakeholders.

BURDEN OF PROOF In 1986, Beech-Nut Nutrition Corporation, the second-largest U.S. baby food manufacturer, pleaded guilty to 215 felony counts and admitted to selling apple products that were a blend of synthetic ingredients. How did this happen? There were many causes, among them the company's financial difficulties, the belief that other companies were selling fake juice (industry norms), and the belief that the juice was perfectly safe.

A chief cause may also have been the decision-making processes that were used. When Jerome LiCari, director of research and development, recommended changing suppliers in 1981 (because he suspected adulteration), Operations Head John Lavery turned the traditional burden of proof around. Generally, baby food manufacturers would switch suppliers if the supplier couldn't demonstrate that the product was genuine. In this case, Lavery said that if LiCari wanted to go with a more expensive supplier, he would have to prove that the concentrate they were buying was adulterated (rather than genuine). Given the technology available at the time, this was difficult, and the supplier was retained.[63]

A similar decision-making criterion was used in the decision to launch the space shuttle Challenger despite engineers' concerns about O-ring failure in cold weather.

In previous launches, engineers had been required to show evidence that the launch was safe (which would have been difficult, if not impossible). In the case of the *Challenger,* the burden of proof was changed. Engineers who balked at the impending launch decision were asked to prove that it was unsafe.

These examples suggest that it's relatively easy to alter decision-making processes to support whatever decision managers have already made. That's why it's extremely important that organizations design decision-making processes in good financial times and before a crisis occurs. Then, when trouble strikes, they can rely on these effective decision-making processes to guide them. The space shuttle *Challenger* might never have been launched if engineers had been required to prove that the launch would be safe, rather than unsafe. Managers must be particularly alert to changes in traditional decision-making criteria, particularly in times of crisis.

INFORMAL CULTURAL SYSTEMS

In addition to the formal systems described previously, organizational culture is kept alive informally and symbolically through informal norms, heroes, rituals, myths, and stories. Information about these is carried through informal communication systems such as the grapevine. In this way, people come to know what behaviors are "really" rewarded, how decisions are "really" made, and what organizational leaders "really" care about and expect. If messages from the formal and informal cultural systems differ, the ethical culture is out of alignment. And people are more likely to believe the messages carried by the informal system—the informal norms, for example. Recent research has found that employees' perceptions of informal cultural systems influence their ethics-related behavior more than the formal systems do.[64] Therefore, management of these informal systems is extremely important.

Norms: "The Way We Do Things Around Here"

Norms are standards of behavior that are accepted as appropriate by members of a group. They exert a powerful influence on individual behavior in organizations, and they can serve to support ethical or unethical conduct. For example, imagine an individual entering a computer software sales job who is told immediately by peers in the sales force that customers should always be dealt with honestly because long-term customer relations are so important to the firm. Here, the norm of honesty with customers supports ethical conduct. On the other hand, consider the individual who begins a new job and is told by his or her colleagues that making the sale is all that counts even if you have to lie to the customer about the capabilities of the software or delivery dates to make it. This norm supports unethical conduct. Either kind of norm (ethical or unethical) can become "the way we do things around here" in the organization.

Formal rules are often inconsistent with the informal norms that develop. For example, the salesperson described previously may have attended a mandatory ethics training session that taught rules of honesty in customer relationships. But if the message being sent on the job is to make the sale no matter what, the formal rule is overridden.

Similarly, at a fast-food restaurant, new employees may be told about a rule against eating food without paying for it. However, once on the job, they may see coworkers eating while the supervisor looks the other way. These coworkers may rationalize their behavior because of their low pay or poor working conditions, or because the supervisor doesn't seem to care or eats food himself or herself. Encouraged to join in, the new employee is likely to do so, having learned the "real" rules. Thus, despite formal rules, regulations, codes, and credos, informal norms are frequently the most influential behavior guides. And when informal norms are inconsistent with formal rules and codes, the organization is clearly out of alignment.

Heroes and Role Models

Heroes personify the organization's values.[65] They're symbolic figures who set standards of performance by modeling certain behaviors. These heroes can be the organization's formal leaders. For example, Bill Gates can be considered the hero of Microsoft and Herb Kelleher the hero of Southwest Airlines. Heroes can be founders who are no longer even present in the organization. As we noted earlier, Thomas Jefferson is still very much alive at the University of Virginia, and Walt Disney haunts the corridors at The Walt Disney Company. Stories about the values of these heroes continue to influence decision making. Thus, a hero who champions integrity and stands up for what is right may influence the behavior of many in the organization.

The organization's hero can also be someone who is not the president or chief executive officer. When asked to identify their organization's hero, Penn State students in a management class on organizational culture inevitably name football coach Joe Paterno. "Joepa" as he is affectionately known around campus, is not only the formal leader of the football team but a cultural hero as well. His values, including education first for college athletes and winning by sticking to the rules of the game,[66] are considered by many to extend far beyond the football program to permeate Penn State's culture. On campus, Joepa and his wife are also known for their philanthropy. Most recently, they showed their leadership in the fundraising campaign for a much needed university library addition, now known as the Paterno Library addition. Some say that Penn State is the only university whose sports arena is named after a former president while the library addition is named after its football coach.

Much socialization about ethics is informally conducted by role models and mentors who may be superiors or just more experienced co-workers. Mentoring is usually an informal process whereby a more senior person takes a junior person under wing, providing information, career strategies, and so on. Individuals who are passing through organizational "boundaries," such as new hires, or who are transferring from one part of the organization to another are most vulnerable to these socialization influences.[67] The mentor or role model may emphasize the importance of integrity and resistance to pressure to behave unethically, or the role model may indoctrinate the individual into accepted unethical practices, making it difficult for the individual not to go along.[68] The new accounting graduate who was told by his superior in a public accounting firm, "You're too honest to be an auditor," received a powerful message about ethics (or the lack thereof) in that organization. When looking for evidence of misalignment, ask whether the organization's heroes represent the values formally espoused by the organization or not.

Savvy executives understand the role that heroes play in forming or changing a culture. One CEO of a financial services firm was very serious about identifying and rewarding people who lived his organization's values. He challenged his executives to bring him stories of employees who were doing the right things in the right way, who were models of the culture. He collected these stories and sent personal, handwritten thank-you notes to those model employees. While a phone call might have sufficed, employees were so thrilled with his written recognition and praise that they displayed his notes in their offices. Those framed notes sent a rather loud message to other employees about what kind of behavior was valued at high levels. Of course, they also helped spread word of the "heroes" and their deeds.

Rituals

Rituals tell people symbolically what the organization wants them to do and how it expects them to do it.[69] Rituals are a way of affirming and communicating culture in a very tangible way.[70] For example, General Motors of Canada introduced a new vision and values by asking each manufacturing unit to create a small float representing one of the key values. These floats were part of a parade that kicked off a full day of culture-building ritual surrounding the theme "Customers for Life" and the motto "I Am GM." During the day, the CEO unveiled a large painting of the group vision and told a story about the company's future. To reinforce the "I Am GM" motto, employees were asked to see themselves as being responsible, at any moment, for the company, its products, and services. The day ended with the "GM Acceleration Song" performed by the 100-person Up With People singing and dancing group. The song had been revised to incorporate the new values created by the leadership team.[71]

Other companies have awards ceremonies that convey the values of the organization. What values are celebrated at these ceremonies? Is it success with integrity, or are only those who make their numbers celebrated? Ask whether the rituals are consistent with the formal rules and reward systems to help determine if the culture is in alignment.

Myths and Stories

Another extremely important way organizational culture is communicated and kept alive is through the informal communication network. People tell stories to give meaning to their world and life.[72] Organizational myths and stories explain and give meaning to the organizational culture. They're anecdotes about a sequence of events drawn from the organization's history. The story's characters are employees, perhaps company heroes, and the moral of the story expresses the organization's values.[73]

At IBM, a story that has been told and retold describes how a low-level employee denied Tom Watson, then IBM president, entry into a restricted area of the company because Watson was not wearing his IBM identification badge. Watson praised the employee, suggesting the importance of upholding company rules and applying them to everyone.

In his book, *Paterno by the Book*,[74] Paterno recounted a powerful story from the Penn State football program's history about a leader standing up for what he believes at a critical moment.

> The Miami game was a turning point for me.... Late that night, as we waited to board our charter plane, I strolled around the terminal replaying the joys of our victory when I saw something.... I looked again and sure enough two of our best players were standing at a not-too-visible spot of the airport bar, each fingering a glass of beer.... "You're in trouble," I told them. "You know that you're never to be seen standing at a bar." Naturally they protested that they were having only one, that they were coming down after the great game, that nobody around here knew them. "Never means never," I said. Nobody on the squad could possibly have the faintest doubt about my rule: We don't want a Penn State football player to drink in a public place.... He throws a bad light on the entire team, putting every member under suspicion. Furthermore, ... football players are public figures, watched and talked about. Also they're role models. I reminded the two guys of the one loophole in my rule: You can sit down with your folks privately and have a glass of wine. You can even have a couple of beers on a Saturday night—in private, with personal friends. That won't make you victims of hearsay. But if I see you standing at a public bar, you're in trouble.
>
> So now these two kids had forced the decision on me. One of them had previously got himself in a minor jam with the police. It made a mention in the paper. "You're gone," I said. That meant for good. Off the team. To the other I said, "This is the first trouble I know about. You get one more chance, but you're suspended for the next two games." On Monday evening the captains ... came to see me. The whole squad was meeting at that moment, they said, and had sent the captains to tell me that they felt the penalties were too harsh. They wanted me to take the first guy back and lift the suspension on the second—and they wanted to return to the meeting with my changed decision.
>
> There are moments in the life of a manager when his ability to maintain control teeters on a hair. He can only manage with the consent of the managed, unless he's a prison warden. On the other hand, he can only manage by unambiguous assertion of authority. Those are opposites, in a sense. If the manager, who sometimes has to choose in a split second, chooses the wrong one of those two, his effectiveness is finished.
>
> "Go back to your meeting and I'll be there myself in five minutes," I said. The sentence was harsh, I said to myself, but the rule they had broken was perfectly clear, defensible, and necessary. The morale and support of the entire squad hung in the air. If I backed off, the message was clear as a bell: I'm afraid of you guys. Ignore this rule. Ignore any rule that itches as much as this one does. And if there's a rule that itches less, try me on that, too.

Five minutes later, that squad room was a tableau of sullen, hard faces. I looked around, eye to eye, then talked. "A rule that protects us all was broken. The decision I made was the best one for all of us. I have no choice but to stand with it." Faces stayed frozen, waiting. I couldn't read them. "If anybody here can't live with it, go. Right now. If you stay, you do it my way, the right way, living by the rules. If you decide to stay and do it that way, we'll have a great football team. I'm going to walk out of here right now. A minute later I'm coming back in. Whoever's here, that's who we're going to play with."

As I walked bravely out of there, imitating John Wayne the best I could, my knees were shaking. In the promised minute, I returned. Every frozen face that was there during my first visit was still there, although still frozen.[75]

This story represents a critical event in the history of Paterno's tenure as Penn State's football coach. It symbolizes the idea that rules are valued and enforced in a culture of high integrity and accountability. To the extent that the story has become a part of the organization's culture, it serves to reinforce the culture's emphasis on the value of rules and represents alignment between the informal and formal cultures.

Language

Cultures develop and use language to communicate values to employees. The old joke that business ethics is an oxymoron suggests that many consider the language of ethics to be out of place in the business context. A number of the corporate ethics officers we interviewed suggested that the word "ethics" is "charged" and "emotional" for employees who often react negatively to any hint that their ethics might not be okay. When possible, they use other words to describe what they're trying to do. For example, employees seem to be more comfortable talking about integrity or shared values than ethics.

Research suggests that managers are reluctant to describe their actions in moral terms even when they are acting for moral reasons, a phenomenon referred to as moral muteness. This reluctance can be attributed to managers' avoidance of the interpersonal confrontation that may take place if they question an organizational practice or decision, to the value placed on "efficient" decision making such that moral talk can be thought of as a distraction, and to the desire to appear powerful and effective. Moral talk can appear idealistic and utopian and inconsistent with the expectation that managers can solve their own problems.[76]

Getting people to talk about ethics has also been likened to sex education. Although parents agree that sex education is a good thing, they find it difficult to broach the subject with their children. Similarly, managers may find it difficult to begin a conversation about ethics with other managers or with their subordinates. If these topics are typically not discussed, the manager who brings it up may feel like a goody-goody or a spoilsport.[77] But managers who become comfortable talking about ethics will be role modeling important behaviors for their subordinates.

Kent Druyvesteyn, one of the very first corporate ethics officers, told us an anecdote about the early development of ethics training at General Dynamics.

> Early on, at General Dynamics, we declared that our ethics training workshops were to be small and interactive, and that they were to be led by managers. And, we heard some complaints from managers who said, "We don't know anything about this." They thought we were going to have them teach Aristotle and Kant, but that's not what we were trying to do. We also had people in training say, "We can't have people in management do this. There won't be any quality control."
>
> At that point I said, "Let's consider what it is we're trying to do here. What we are trying to do is raise awareness, to increase knowledge of company standards and stimulate commitment to those standards. That's the most important thing." Here's an analogy I'd like you to consider. You have some small children and you decide that you want to teach them about sex. There are a number of ways that you could do this. You could hire an expert—someone who knows all about sex, who knows the right words to use, who knows all the latest terminology, who is pedagogically very skilled. You could hire this person to come into your home, sit down in your living room with your children, and teach them about sex. I mean, isn't that good management technique—to delegate it to someone? On the other hand, you could do it yourself. You may have limitations. You don't know everything. You might be embarrassed or tongue-tied. In the end though, who do you think would be more effective? To have the expert do it or for you to do it yourself? I have never had a person say that the expert would be more effective.

Top managers can also make ethics an acceptable topic of conversation by sending a message that it's not only OK, but expected, to talk about one's ethical concerns. They can do this by leading discussions about ethics, discussing the ethics code and its application in a video that is shown to employees, and otherwise openly discussing ethical problems with managers and employees. Senior managers can also build "moral talk" into the fabric of the organization by requiring routine discussion of moral issues and inclusion of ethical issues in business proposals.[78]

It's difficult to imagine discussing questions of organizational ethics without an acceptable vocabulary to support the discussion. Both educators and employers have a role to play in providing students and workers with the language that can be used to discuss and analyze organizational problems from an ethical perspective. It could be as simple as using words such as "right," "wrong," "honesty," "integrity," "values," and "character." How often does your organization ask whether the decision is the right one, in a moral as well as a business sense? Is this the "proper" thing to do for customers, suppliers, the community? How often is a job applicant evaluated for integrity, values, and character, in addition to performance? How often is potential harm to all stakeholders considered when making a business decision?

The use of ethical language may be related to decision-making behavior. In one study, individuals who discussed their decision-making process using the language of ethics were more likely to be the ones who made an ethical decision.[79] These people talked about ethics, morals, honesty, integrity, values, and good chara_ had made the unethical decision were more likely to recount the decision in _ traditional business language of costs and benefits. This research suggests a lm_ between language and ethical decision making. The implication for organizations is that their employees may need to be taught the language of ethics and its appropriateness for business decision making.

Special organizational language can also be used to avoid the moral implications of actions. For example, in Nazi Germany, the code names for killing and genocide were "final solution," "evacuation," and "special treatment." This use of euphemisms allowed people to avoid confronting the true meaning of their behavior.[80] Similarly, in recent years companies have created euphemisms to avoid the pain of decisions to layoff employees. "Downsizing," "rightsizing," "restructuring," and "targeted outplacement" are just a few of the terms we've encountered. It may be easier to impose a "targeted outplacement" than a layoff, but are the moral considerations as obvious with "targeted outplacement" as they are with layoffs? Recall from Chapter 4 that using moral language increases individuals' moral awareness. So, it's essential that moral language become a part of the organization's ethical culture.

DEVELOPING AND CHANGING THE ETHICAL CULTURE

We can conclude from this cultural analysis that ethics at work is greatly influenced by the organization's culture. Both formal and informal organizational systems and processes channel and reinforce certain kinds of behavior. Each of the systems on its own can support either ethical or unethical conduct. In addition, these multiple systems can work together or at cross purposes to support ethical or unethical conduct in the organization, leading to an organization that is in alignment or misalignment. Imagine an organization with an ethics code that forbids employees from accepting gifts of any kind, but a senior executive is known to have accepted box seats at the ball game from a client. This "we say one thing, but do another" approach leads to widespread cynicism. The code loses all credibility as workers pay more attention to what's done than to what's said. On the other hand, the organization that disciplines that executive visibly reinforces the code, supporting its ethical stance with all workers.

Developing or changing organizational ethics, then, involves simultaneously developing or changing multiple aspects of the organization's ethical culture. If the effort is to be successful, this ethical culture development or change should involve the alignment of all relevant formal and informal organizational systems. Obviously, this requires a major commitment from the most senior levels in the organization. Culture change attempted at lower levels is not likely to be effective unless it is fully supported and modeled by senior management.

Changing organizational culture is more difficult than developing it. In a new organization, workers are quite open to learning and accepting the culture of their new organizational home. However, anthropologists and organizational scientists agree that changing culture is an extremely difficult process.[81] This view is consistent with an idea basic to all organizational change and development efforts—that changing individual and group behavior is both difficult and time consuming. The human tendency to want to conserve the existing culture is referred to as "cultural persistence" or inertia. Culture has an addictive quality, perhaps because culture members are aware that culture components cannot be altered without affecting other, cherished values and institutions.[82] Also, an unethical culture tends to feed on itself. Why would successful (but unethical) managers want to change? They wouldn't. They would tend to hire people like themselves and perpetuate the culture that exists.

Most often, pressure for culture change comes from outside—from stockholders, the government, regulators, and other outside stakeholders. The public's general mistrust of business executives[83] and the threat of increased government regulation may encourage leaders to look more closely at their ethical cultures. In addition, organizations whose members have been "caught" engaging in unethical behavior, or those faced with costly lawsuits are prime candidates for such ethical culture change attempts. Finally, the government's sentencing guidelines for corporate crime turned the attention of many organizations to an evaluation of their ethical cultures during the 1990s. The same is likely true now as companies and their boards evaluate the impact of new legislation such as the Sarbanes-Oxley Act.

The influence of bad publicity and costly lawsuits extends beyond the targeted organization. Organizations scan the environment for information that is relevant to their concerns. When one organization in an industry is called on the carpet for a legal or ethical violation, other organizations in the industry take notice and act. Arthur Andersen's indictment for document shredding in the Enron case and its mishandling of multiple audits over a number of years has sullied the reputation of the entire auditing industry. And the finding that Merrill Lynch's analysts lied to customers about the quality of stocks has put the entire investment banking industry on alert. Thus, any organization that senses increased vulnerability to external pressure is also more likely to consider the need for attention to the management of its ethical culture.

The pressure to change organizational ethics can also come from within, but is not likely to occur unless the CEO decides that change is required. Sometimes, a new CEO must be brought in to lead the charge when change is needed. John J. Mack, a former Morgan Stanley president, became CEO of investment bank Credit Suisse First Boston in 2001 and set out to make the investment bank worthy of its clients' trust. He was brought in to clean up a troubled company that was being investigated for a variety of alleged legal and ethical missteps. Mack settled one case for $100 million and got busy changing the corporate culture. His first step—to get rid of the "cowboys" ("egomaniacal personalities who competed fiercely for deals often at the expense of their own clients and investors"). He has also reduced "star" salaries and perks, imposed strict codes of conduct, and overhauled every system so that clients' interests always come first. He has hired compliance officers who report directly to him and has held meetings with employees to "personally tell them to 'do the right thing.'" He has said, "I won't compromise values even if that means we end up with a firm half the size." Mack says that he "would rather lose a deal than a client's trust," and under Mack, CSFB has pulled out of 47 mergers and canceled or put off 11 equity and debt underwriting deals. According to one observer, "What's changed is that you have someone there who is saying the client counts.... It's like night and day."[84]

A CULTURAL APPROACH TO CHANGING ORGANIZATIONAL ETHICS

Any attempt to develop or change organizational ethics can benefit from an organizational change approach that includes a system-wide, long-term view. In addition, it should be based on the assumption that human beings are essentially good and capable of development and change.

A Cultural Systems View

The cultural approach relies on the idea that to be successful, any attempt to develop or change the organization's ethics must take the entire cultural system into account.[85] The change effort must target multiple formal and informal organizational subsystems. All of these must work together to create clear, consistent messages about what is and is not appropriate behavior in the organization. If subsystems conflict, confusion and mixed messages will result. Thus, the entire range of formal and informal subsystems must be analyzed and targeted for development and change.

This complex, multisystem approach to managing organizational ethics argues against any short-term, quick-fix solutions that target only one system. The idea that an organization could solve its ethics problem simply by establishing a code of ethics or by hiring a consultant to deliver a one-hour ethics training program becomes ludicrous when the complexity of the ethics culture is understood. The management of ethical conduct must be complex because it's influenced by multiple systems, each of them complex in itself. Thus, the complexity of the solution must match the complexity of the problem. A solution that isn't sufficiently complex will miss important information, make incomplete diagnoses, and produce overly simple and short-sighted solutions. The organization that creates a code of ethics in response to external pressure and files it away without making changes in other systems such as the reward system and decision-making processes is more likely making a negative statement about organizational ethics rather than a positive one. The informal message is that management is hypocritical and that the code of ethics serves no useful purpose beyond the creation of a false facade. The same can be said of lofty values statements. For example, many of these statements talk about valuing diversity. But what happens when people look around the organization and see few minority managers? Executives need to understand that when they put a values statement in writing, employees expect a commitment to follow through. The bottom line about systems thinking is understanding that, if an organization decides to get into the "ethics business" with a values statement, code, or training program, employees expect follow-through in other parts of the organization. A failure to follow through will be interpreted as hypocrisy.

A Long-Term View

The development of organizational culture takes place over a number of years. Effective culture change may take even longer, as much as 6 to 15 years.[86] It requires alterations in both formal and informal organizational systems that take time to implement and take hold. Resistances must be overcome. New rules and values must be reinforced via training programs, rites and rituals, and reward systems. Although not all organizational change efforts take this long, deep interventions in the organizational culture should be considered long-term projects.

Assumptions about People

Mainstream economics rests on the assumption that human beings are driven by self-interest and opportunism and are likely to shirk responsibility.[87] Acceptance of this assumption logically leads to change efforts focused almost exclusively on behavioral control.

We believe, however, that human beings are essentially good and open to growth and change. Most employees prefer being associated with a just organization that supports ethical behavior and disciplines unethical behavior. Given this type of environment, most individuals can be expected to choose ethical behavior. Individuals who engage in unethical behavior should not simply be labeled "bad" people. They are often responding to external pressures or are behaving according to organizationally sanctioned definitions of what's appropriate. Although unethical behaviors must be disciplined, the organization should also treat unethical behavior as a signal to investigate itself and the cultural context in which the behavior occurred. Through culture, the organization can change definitions of what is appropriate and inappropriate, and relieve pressures to behave unethically.

Diagnosis: The Ethical Culture Audit

Formal attempts to develop or change organizational ethics should begin with diagnosis. Diagnosing culture calls for time-consuming techniques, such as auditing the content of decision making, coding the content of organizational stories and anecdotes, and holding open-ended interviews with employees at all levels.[88] It also requires systematic analysis of formal organizational systems, such as the structure and criteria for rewards and promotion.

The framework presented in this chapter can provide guidance for an audit of the organization's ethical culture.[89] The audit should include probes into the formal and informal organizational systems that are maintaining the ethics culture in its current state. First, formal organizational systems can be analyzed in a number of ways. Through surveys, interviews, observation at meetings, orientation and training sessions, and analysis of organizational documents, perceptions of how formal organizational systems either encourage or discourage ethical behavior can be identified. A sample of the kinds of questions that can be asked are listed in Table 9.1.

Auditing informal systems is equally important. The culture can be analyzed to identify the organization's heroes as well as the behaviors that are reinforced through stories, rituals, and language. This can be accomplished through open-ended interviews, observation of organizational rituals, and analysis of the organization's stories. Some questions that might be asked in an audit of the informal system are offered in Table 9.2. The questions in Tables 9.1 and 9.2 are designed to suggest the general

Table 9.1 Selected Questions for Auditing the Formal System

1. How are organizational leaders perceived in terms of their integrity? Is ethics part of their "leadership" agenda?
2. How are ethics-related behaviors modeled by organizational leaders?
3. Are workers at all levels encouraged to take responsibility for the consequences of their behavior? To question authority when they are asked to do something that they consider to be wrong? How?
4. Does a formal code of ethics and/or values exist? Is it distributed? How widely? Is it used? Is it reinforced in other formal systems such as reward and decision-making systems?
5. Are whistle-blowers encouraged and are formal channels available for them to make their concerns known confidentially?
6. Is misconduct disciplined swiftly and justly in the organization, no matter what the organizational level?
7. Are people of integrity promoted? Are means as well as ends important?
8. Is integrity emphasized to recruits and new employees?
9. Are managers oriented to the values of the organization in orientation programs? Are they trained in ethical decision making?
10. Are ethical considerations a routine part of planning and policy meetings, new venture reports? Is the language of ethics taught and used? Does a formal committee exist high in the organization for considering ethical issues?

Table 9.2 Selected Questions for Auditing the Informal System

1. Identify informal organizational norms. Are they consistent with formal rules and policies?
2. Identify the organization's heroes. What values do they represent? Given an ambiguous ethical dilemma, what decision would they make and why?
3. What are some important organizational rituals? How do they encourage or discourage ethical behavior? Who gets the awards, people of integrigrity who are successful or individuals who use unethical methods to attain success?
4. What ethical messages are sent to new entrants into the organization—must they obey authority at all costs, or is questioning authority acceptable or even desirable?
5. Does analysis of organizational stories and myths reveal individuals who stand up for what's right despite pressure, or is conformity the valued characteristic? Do people get fired or promoted in these stories?
6. Does acceptable language exist for discussing ethical concerns? Is this language routinely incorporated and encouraged in business decision making?
7. What informal socialization processes exist and what norms for ethical/unethical behavior do they promote? Are these different for different organizational subgroups?

direction of an ethical culture audit. Specific questions that arise out of the particular system being analyzed must be developed to tap that system's unique problems and needs. Canned approaches to discovering culture that assume they can identify the relevant dimensions in advance are bound to fail.[90] In addition, the multisystem nature of organizational culture suggests that responses must be compared within and

260 ETHICAL PROBLEMS FACING ORGANIZATIONS

across systems to answer the key question of whether formal and informal systems are aligned within themselves and with each other.

As you may have determined by now, a full-fledged ethical culture audit is a complex process that the average manager is probably not prepared to conduct. Many large organizations will have human resources staff with the required expertise, and conducting such an audit within the firm can send a powerful message that the firm cares about ethics (assuming that the audit is followed up with action). But, other organizations that do not have the expertise in-house will need assistance with these diagnoses and intervention efforts. And in some firms, employees may be more willing to discuss sensitive ethical issues with a trusted outsider.

Understanding the cultural issues addressed in this chapter can help any manager become more sensitive to the complex nature of organizational ethics and the importance of cultural alignment. In fact, with a few changes, the questions in Tables 9.1 and 9.2 could be used to assess the ethics of an organization you're considering joining. You can ask your prospective manager or peers relevant questions and see how they respond. If they welcome such questions, and respond to them easily, that's a good sign that people in the organization are comfortable talking about ethical issues, a good first step.

Ethical Culture Change Intervention

Once the audit is complete, the data should be discussed with employees who can then be enlisted in the development of a culture change intervention plan. The plan will be guided by the diagnosis and the cultural, multisystem framework shown in Figure 9.2. Complementary changes in both the formal and informal organizational systems should be a part of any recommended change effort.

Though difficult, changing formal systems is a more straightforward process than changing informal systems. Gaps and problems identified in the diagnosis can be addressed in a number of ways. Structure can be altered to encourage individuals to take responsibility for their behavior and to discourage unquestioning deference to authority. Codes of ethics can be designed participatively, distributed, and enforced. Reward systems can be designed to punish unethical behavior. Performance management systems can be designed with an emphasis not only on "what" people do but also on "how" they do it. Whistle-blowers can be encouraged and provided formal communication channels and confidentiality.[91] Orientation programs can be designed to incorporate the organization's values, and training programs can be set up to prepare individuals to handle the ethical dilemmas they are most likely to face in their work. Integrity can be emphasized in selection and promotion decisions. Decision-making processes can incorporate attention to ethical issues by devoting time at meetings and space in reports.

It's more difficult to change the informal systems, particularly those that have been found to maintain unethical behavior in the organization. However, these changes must be undertaken if the total change effort is to be effective. These changes require attention to the "art" rather than the science of management and are consistent with ideas about the importance of "symbolic management." With symbolic

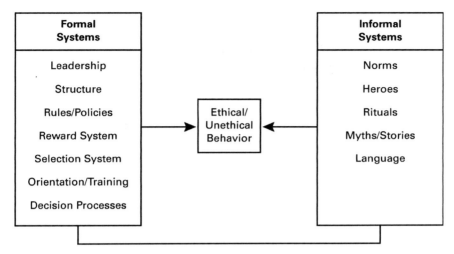

FIGURE 9.2 Developing and Changing Organizational Ethics—
A Multisystem Cultural Framework

management, organizational leaders and managers are encouraged to create rituals, symbols, and stories that will influence those they manage.[92]

The organization may have to be "remythologized" by reviving myths and stories of its founding and resurrecting related tales that can guide organizational behavior in the desired direction.[93] For example, Alexander Bell's comment, "Come here, Watson, I need your help," set up Bell's concept of service that was so important to AT&T's success for many years. However, myths must also be frequently evaluated for their continuing usefulness. New ones may have to be found or developed in order to fit the current needs and goals of the organization. Remythologizing should be done carefully and infrequently. Employees generally know what's "really going on" in the organization. If the revived myth doesn't fit with organizational reality, it will only increase their cynicism. Also, myths can't be changed frequently. Their strength and value in the culture come from their stability across time.

ETHICAL CULTURE CHANGE EVALUATION As with any organizational change and development effort, results should be evaluated over an extended period of time. Evaluation, like diagnosis and intervention, should be guided by the multisystem framework. Surveys and interviews can be repeated regularly to determine if norms have changed and to pinpoint potential problem areas. Documents can be analyzed to determine if ethical issues are being consistently considered. Other outcomes, such as number of lawsuits or reports of unethical behavior, can also be tracked. However, interpretation may need to go beyond simply the numbers. Increased reporting to a hotline, for example, may only mean that ethical sensitivity has been raised and can be viewed as a positive outcome rather than a negative one. This is probably the part of culture building that is most neglected. Most organizations are unwilling to make the investment in evaluation, and therefore they really can't calculate the effectiveness of their efforts.

THE ETHICS OF MANAGING ORGANIZATIONAL ETHICS

An effort aimed at changing organizational ethics requires us to face a particularly knotty ethical dilemma: Whose values or ethics are to prevail? We believe that a change effort that involves employees is not manipulative or coercive and is most consistent with a concern for the ethics of the change effort itself. Employees should participate in the problem diagnosis and planning process. They should be aware of what's happening and should take part in identifying problems and recommending solutions.

CONCLUSION

This chapter has proposed a cultural framework for thinking about ethical and unethical behavior in the organizational context. Although individual character traits may predispose a person to ethical or unethical behavior (as we learned in Chapter 4), the cultural context in the organization also has a powerful influence on the behavior of most employees. An organization that wishes to develop or change its ethical culture must attend to the complex interplay of formal and informal systems that can support either ethical or unethical behavior. Quick-fix solutions are not likely to succeed. A broad, multisystem approach to developing and changing organizational ethics was outlined to guide organizations in diagnosing and, if necessary, changing their ethical culture.

Although most managers are not prepared to conduct a broad culture change effort themselves, this chapter has provided managers with the understanding that organizational ethics is a complex cultural phenomenon. With this knowledge, the manager can begin to assess the ethical culture of their organization and will know what questions to ask the consultant who is brought in to help with a culture change effort. Individuals can also use these questions to help them assess their own organization and their fit with it.

DISCUSSION QUESTIONS

For the following questions, focus on an organization with which you are familiar. If you do not have significant organizational experience, discuss the questions with someone who is currently in a managerial role.

1. Does your organization address ethical issues in a formal, systematic way? If so, is it a cookie-cutter, one-size-fits-all approach, or has the organization customized an ethical culture to match its unique needs?
2. To the best of your ability, use the questions in Tables 9.1 and 9.2 to conduct an ethics audit of the formal and informal systems in your organization.
3. Having conducted the ethics audit, identify the formal and informal systems that are in need of attention. Where is the culture out of alignment? Design a

change program to address weaknesses and to align formal and informal systems into a strong ethical culture.
4. How would you change the culture audit questions if you were planning to use them to conduct an ethics culture audit of a firm you were considering joining?

CASE

VIDEOTEK CORPORATION

Jeremy Campbell is the chief executive officer and chairman of a relatively young, publicly held Boston high-tech company we'll call VideoTek (for video technology). VideoTek was founded in 1980 by Earl Mantz, who created a device that could convert black and white computer monitors into color monitors, which he sold for $85.

The company started with two people and grew quickly to a core of 35 people who respected Mantz as a visionary. Some in the founding group described him as a "deep-thinking, spiritual type of person, with high ethical standards." The company culture evolved naturally out of his style. It was a hard work/high trust culture. Good people were hired and trusted to work hard and well for the company, and they did. It was common for people to work 60 to 80 hours a week for VideoTek. They believed in what they were doing and they believed in their product.

The company grew explosively to 1,500 employees and over $200 million in sales in 1994. In 1989, when the company had achieved approximately $40 million in sales, it went public. A professional manager, Campbell, was recruited from a large company to bring operational sanity to this small company that was growing out of control. He was named president and CEO. Mantz, now a multimillionaire, happily became a member of the board.

Campbell brought in his own team—big company types—to manage the company. However, he recognized the value of Videotek's culture, and he vowed to perpetuate it. Management today still prides itself on the company's flat organizational structure (e.g., few layers of management) and efficient, open communication via the company's e-mail system originally set up by Earl. Just about everything that needs to be communicated within the company is communicated by e-mail. Employees who are on the road keep in touch via their laptops. In support of communication openness, a unique feature of the system allows messages to be sent anonymously.

But all is not rosy at VideoTek. Not long after Jeremy's arrival, long-time employees began to question top management's commitment to all aspects of the culture. They felt that he especially liked the "hard work" part, but what happened to "high trust"? Something was amiss. Jeremy seemed to be big on words but short on follow-through. He was doing some things that seemed highly questionable and supporting the questionable conduct of his friends. The key question seemed to be, "Could this top management team be trusted?"

Finally, the company has been experiencing a slowdown in growth. It needs new products to sustain its growth, but so far new products introduced under Jeremy's leadership have had disappointing results.

Following are two ethics-related e-mail messages. The first is a message sent to all employees by Jeremy Campbell in response to an incident of unethical behavior that the grapevine was buzzing about. The second communication is an electronic mail message also sent to all employees a month later by an anonymous employee.

E-Mail Communication From the Chairman and CEO:

From: JeremyCam@VTK 1-MAR-1999

To: All Staff

Subj: Ethical Conduct. Actions, Not Words.

The VideoTek Philosophy is a blueprint for action, a template for daily life at VideoTek. The second we forget that, we are vulnerable to internal challenges that threaten the very foundation of our continued success.

One precept of the VideoTek Philosophy must not be compromised under any circumstances: We live and work ethically. It is imperative to remind ourselves of certain key values which support this commitment:

The goal of any business is to make a sound profit. Our dedication to quality will help us realize that goal. We do not compromise our integrity in the name of profits.

VideoTek is changing the way people do business. Because we truly have an impact on people's lives, we must set a positive example of leadership and credibility in all things we do.

We are honest and fair in all transactions with our customers, suppliers, shareholders, and each other.

As specific challenges to these values have arisen, we have addressed them swiftly and decisively. In order to maintain focus on ethical behavior throughout the organization, I have formed a task force consisting of Joe Donaldson, Bill Sykes, Alan Golden, and Joyce Eldridge. This group will examine the following issues in depth and provide me with specific recommendations for corrective action:

- Relationships between VideoTek employees and customers and suppliers
- Outside business activities of VideoTek employees
- Protection of company assets and intellectual property rights

Beyond your own conduct, you have an obligation to report circumstances which you believe to be in conflict with VideoTek's ethical standards. Our ethics committee—composed of Joe Donaldson, Leslie Bolton, Alan Golden, and Joyce Eldridge—has been established to hear these reports and recommend the appropriate response.

VideoTek has been successful because of our ethics, not in spite of them. Only by remaining true to ourselves—resolute in our beliefs and consistent in our actions—will we continue to fulfill our mission. This requires both courage and wisdom, the very same qualities that have made us the company that we are today.

Jeremy

E-Mail Communication from Anonymous Employee

From: SECRET@VTK 1-APR-1999

To: All Staff

Subj: Preliminary Report from VideoTek Ethics Committee

The VideoTek ethics committee, consisting of Joe Donaldson, Leslie Bolton, Alan Golden, and Joyce Eldridge, has been meeting to ensure that all VideoTek employees act in the most ethical possible manner. We must all remember the timeless words of our president Jeremy Campbell: "One precept of the VideoTek Philosophy must not be compromised under any circumstances: We live and work ethically."

In light of this, we have prepared the 1992 Spearshaft of Ethics awards for cases of outstanding ethical behavior within VideoTek.

For instance, the ethics committee has received nominations from a few employees for one particular director of VideoTek who is also a major stockholder in one of VideoTek's customers, and whose son, a former employee of VideoTek, is also involved with this customer. Moreover, according to these employees, VideoTek has spent large sums of money and plans to spend even more to develop products for this customer, despite the fact that they have not lived up to the terms of their initial agreement with VideoTek. However, to avoid the slightest tiniest hint of a conflict of interest, the director in question stepped out of the meeting when the board of directors voted to approve the deal. Well, he didn't actually step out of the room, but he didn't vote on it, and that qualifies him for the Golden Spearshaft of Ethics. Even if VideoTek eventually loses money on the deal, we can still be proud to have lived by the highest of ethical standards.

From another employee who even read the annual report, we learned that the eight-person board of directors voted in 1992 to give all seven of the non-employee directors stock options. We think that it was very important that the directors get these stock options. The directors do not have nearly enough money. In fact, some of them are practically living on the brink of poverty, or at any rate on the brink of being merely well off. For the eight of them to generously give the seven of themselves these options was the least they could do. After all, the options are only worth $850,000 among them. Because of this generous and self-sacrificing move we are awarding the entire board of directors the Silver Spearshaft of Ethics.

Don't believe the rumor that top management has been inconsistent in ethical word and deed. The malcontents who are spreading this rumor are woefully misinformed about a recent incident. As everyone knows, Amy Masterson has been one of our finest sales representatives for several years. However, her commitment to the firm recently came into question when she steadfastly refused to release customer confidential information, even when encouraged to do so by some highly placed VideoTek managers, and even when releasing the information would have clearly contributed to VideoTek's bottom line. Nor would Amy accept the $150,000 top management offered her to go quietly. The entire top management team has been awarded a Bronze Spearshaft of Ethics for their unending support of unquestioning loyalty to the firm. (By the way, donations to help Amy defray her legal expenses on her unjust discharge lawsuit may be sent directly to her home.)

Sadly, it has also come to our attention that some employees have said that our Human Resources Policies do not live up to VideoTek's ethical philosophy. Nothing could be further from the truth. The Human Resources Policies have been reviewed and considered as broadly as possible within the company. For instance, the company policy on nepotism was carefully evaluated by both Jim and Dana Swift. The company policy on termination of employees was scrutinized by a tremendous number of VideoTek employees within the BW and TC Divisions [two new product divisions that have been shut down, resulting in millions of dollars in losses and hundreds of layoffs]. The ethics committee will also be inviting the employees who made the Spearshaft of Ethics nominations to personally review the termination policy, as soon as we can learn their names. Finally, VideoTek's policy on fair compensation was exhaustively studied by Jeremy himself, with the assistance of *Business Week* magazine, and he said he is fully satisfied that VideoTek is paying fair compensation.

In fact, the executive compensation committee has determined that the company's performance in 1992 was so outstanding that Jeremy has fully earned his compensation of $375,426 plus $50,000 bonus plus options, even though the company's performance was so average that it would be totally unreasonable for any employees to receive bonuses for 1992. In light of this, we are jointly awarding the Tin Spearshaft of Ethics to the entire human resources department and the executive compensation committee.

There are so many outstanding feats of ethical behavior within this company that we are sorry we can honor only an outstanding few. We hope that this will inspire everyone within the company to try harder in the coming year to live up to VideoTek's high ethical standards.

Lastly, we offer a few words from Jeremy himself: "I am personally chagrined that anyone could have any perception that any VideoTek employee would do anything unethical. Whoever you are, you had better just change your perception, Buster!"

Joe Donaldson, Leslie Bolton, Alan Golden, and Joyce Eldridge—NOT! April Fools!

Case Questions

1. Evaluate Jeremy Campbell's e-mail communication. Assume that this was the only "formal" communication employees had received from him regarding ethics (aside from a "Ten Commandments"–type brochure handed to every new employee at orientation). Do you think e-mail is an appropriate medium for this message? Why or why not? How would you evaluate the content of the communication itself?
2. Next, think about the anonymous e-mail communication. Assume that this communication represents the thinking of a large number of other employees, not just a lone dissenter. What does it say about the alignment or misalignment of VideoTek's ethical culture? For example, what does the communication say about the perception of ethical leadership, reward systems, honesty, and decision processes in the firm?
3. Shortly after this anonymous communication was sent, the ability to send anonymous communications was eliminated from the firm's e-mail system. What kind of symbolic message do you think that action sent?
4. Earl Mantz, the founder, was a cultural hero while he ran the company during its early years. He had created and maintained the hard work/high trust culture and had the respect of the people who worked for him. Now, however, many see him as someone who sold out, and a growing number of people from the original committed group are leaving to join other companies. In fact, less than five people remain from the original 35. They get together for a beer occasionally and reminisce about old times. Recently, one of them went on about how money and power can corrupt, "I wonder if the culture was ever real?" What has happened to the hard work/high trust culture? What happened to Mantz's ability to provide decision-making guidance? Is there any hope for culture change in this organization? For remythologizing?
5. What actions could the current CEO or a new CEO take, if any, to create, change, or maintain a desired ethical culture?

CASE

CULTURE CHANGE AT TEXACO

In 1999, Texaco settled a lawsuit that charged the firm with discriminating against African-American employees. Texaco paid $175 million, the largest settlement of this kind ever. The stock had fallen $3 per share after damning audiotapes became available to the public. Peter Bijur, then CEO, decided to stop fighting the lawsuit and settle. Minority employees received $140 million in damages and back pay, and $35 million was used to establish an independent task force to evaluate the firm's diversity efforts for the next five years.

Apparently, there had been very real problems throughout the Texaco organization. These included blatant racist language and behavior on the part of Texaco employees and managers, documented lower pay for minority employees (in some cases lower than the minimum for the job category), and comments such as the following overheard from a white manager: "I never thought I'd live to see the day when a black woman had an office at Texaco." Unfortunately for Texaco, and fortunately for minority employees, a Texaco official taped meetings about the lawsuit in which executives used racial epithets and discussed disposing of incriminating documents. The tapes were made available to *The New York Times* and, through them, to the public. To make matters worse for Texaco, a former senior financial analyst, Bari-Ellen Roberts, wrote a book detailing the humiliating experiences faced by many minority employees, including herself. One time, a white official referred to Roberts publicly as a "little colored girl." She also detailed how the organization regularly ignored grievance claims from minorities.

Bijur's unusual solution to the problem was to launch a complete culture change effort. During 1998 and early 1999, the company was in difficult financial straits due to low crude oil and natural gas prices. Revenues and earnings dropped precipitously and the number of employees was reduced from 27,000 to 18,500. At a time like that, another CEO might have put diversity issues aside in favor of a focus on the bottom line. But Bijur took advantage of the opportunity to "make us a better company." First, as leader, he made it clear that he would simply not tolerate disrespect and that those who didn't go along with the culture change would be dismissed. He even went outside the company, speaking to groups such as the Urban League, saying that "a real commitment must be more than a diversity checklist. It must be integrated into a company's business plan. It must guide our strategies for hiring, developing, promoting and retaining a diverse workforce. And it must extend beyond our corporate boundaries—not only to our customers and suppliers, but also to the communities in which we work and live."[94] Bijur hired African-Americans in key positions such as director of global business development, general counsel, and head of diversity for the company. All of these individuals said that they agreed to join the company because they were convinced of Bijur's personal commitment to real culture change. New recruiting systems were set up to increase the pool of minority candidates for every position. Women and minorities were included on all human resources committees. Search firms with success in minority hiring were brought in to help in the effort. For a longer-term solution, the company set up scholarship and internship programs to interest minorities in areas of study of importance to the firm. Next, Bijur set specific diversity goals and timetables and linked managers' career success and bonus compensation to their implementation of the initiatives. He included 360-degree feedback for all supervisors that included performance on diversity issues in evaluation criteria. He also established formal mentoring and leadership development programs to ensure that the company was preparing minorities for leadership positions. All employees were required to attend diversity training, and such training is now being incorporated into more general management training. And multiple methods were set up for filing grievances. These included hotlines, an alternative dispute resolution process with independent arbitration and mediation, and a confidential outside ombudsman. Finally, the company set up a Minority and Women Business Development Program to increase the number of minority wholesalers it works with. All of this is overseen by the independent task force set up as part of the settlement. The task force meets frequently with employee groups and monitors the firm's progress.

How is Texaco doing? Angela Vallot, director of corporate diversity initiatives, says "You're not going to change the way people think, but you can change the way people behave." Evidence suggests that changes in behavior are real. The new general counsel has few discrimination lawsuits to work on. In 1999, 44 percent of new hires and 22 percent of promotions went to minorities. The company spent over a billion dollars with minority and women-owned vendors in 1997 and 1998, exceeding a goal the firm set in 1996. Texaco even applied for inclusion in *Fortune* magazine's 1999 list of America's 50 Best Companies for minorities. It didn't make the list, but the application suggests that company officials were feeling pretty good about their progress. Weldon Latham, diversity expert at a Washington, D.C. law firm, says, "They are absolutely a model for how to approach one of the biggest problems facing this country."[95] Reports of the monitoring task force are posted on Texaco's Web site (www.texaco.com). In its third annual report, released in July 2000, the task force acknowledged the commitment of Texaco's leadership. "Through the values espoused by its leadership and its efforts to improve its employment practices, the Company continues to communicate effectively the message that it will not tolerate discrimination, harassment, or retaliation in its workplace and that equality and fairness for all employees are central to its mission as a highly competitive business enterprise." They also cited the ombudsman program as employees' preferred way to resolve grievances that might otherwise have become serious problems.[96] The task force's 2000 report cited more mixed results. Although the overall percentage of women and minority employees increased slightly, the percentage of new hires and promotions in both categories declined, and the representation of women and minorities in executive positions fell slightly as well. Nevertheless, the percentage of promotions in these groups exceeded the percentage represented in the overall Texaco workforce and this was viewed as a sign of continuing progress.[97] These reports note that there is much more work to be done, particularly after the firm's 2001 merger with Chevron. The new merged entity is being led by David O'Reilly, Chairman and CEO.

Case Questions

1. Identify the ethical culture problem at Texaco in the mid-1990s.
2. Based on the facts in the case, and what you have learned in Chapter 9, evaluate the culture change effort that is underway. What cultural systems have been targeted in the culture change effort? What systems are missing, if any? Does the culture appear to be in alignment? Misalignment? What else might management do that they haven't already done to make the culture change successful?
3. How long might such a culture change take?

CASE

AN UNETHICAL CULTURE IN NEED OF CHANGE: TAP PHARMACEUTICALS

In 1995, Douglas Durand was offered the position of vice-president for sales at TAP Pharmaceuticals. TAP had been formed 25 years before by Takeda Chemical Industries of Japan and Abbott Laboratories. Doug, 50 years old at the time, had married his high school sweetheart and worked for Merck & Co. for 20 years, working his way up in the sales organization to senior regional director. TAP offered him the opportunity to earn 40 percent more per year (in addition to a $50,000 signing bonus) and help the company move from niche player to mass market purveyor of ulcer and prostate cancer medicine. He took advantage of the opportunity and looked forward to the challenge.

But only a few months after arriving at TAP, he was shocked to find a very different culture from the one he had become accustomed to at Merck. Merck has long had a reputation for ethics and social responsibility and this had been borne out in Durand's two decades of experience. For example, at Merck, every new marketing campaign was evaluated by a legal and regulatory team before being launched, and drugs were pulled back if necessary. But TAP turned out to be very different. It quickly became clear that this was a culture where only numbers mattered. On his very first day on the job, Durand learned that TAP had no in-house legal counsel. The legal counsel was considered a "sales prevention department." At one point, Durand found himself listening in on a conference call where sales representatives were openly discussing bribing urologists with an up-front "administration fee" to doctors who prescribed Lupron, the company's new drug for prostate cancer. TAP sales representatives also gave doctors Lupron samples at a discount or for free, and then encouraged the doctors to charge Medicare full price and keep the difference. He overheard doctors boasting about their Lupron purchases of boats and second homes. TAP offered a big screen TV to every urologist in the country (10,000!), along with offers of office equipment and golf vacations. And reps weren't accounting for the free samples they gave away, as required by law. Durand knew that failure to account for a single dose can lead to a fine of as much as $1 million. Finally, rather than selling drugs based upon good science, TAP held parties for doctors. One such party for a new ulcer drug featured "Tummy," a giant fire-belching stomach.

Durand soon became frantic and worried about his own guilt by association. Initially, he tried to change the culture. After all, he had been hired as a vice president. But, everything he tried was resisted. He was told that he just didn't understand the culture at TAP. When he talked about the importance of earning physicians' trust, the sales reps just rolled their eyes. He then tried to influence change "the TAP way" by offering a bonus to reps who kept accurate records of their samples. The program actually worked, but then senior management discontinued the bonus, and, of course, the reps stopped keeping track. Over time, he found himself excluded from meetings and he felt trapped. What would happen to him if he left this new job in less than a year? He wouldn't collect his bonus and he wondered if anyone else would hire him. What would happen to his family? But he also worried about becoming the corporate scapegoat.

In desperation, Durand turned to an old friend he knew from Merck, Glenna Crooks, now president of Strategic Health Policy International. Appalled by what she heard, Crooks encouraged him to document the abuses he had observed and share the information with Elizabeth Ainslie, a Philadelphia attorney. Given the documented fraud against the U.S. government, Ainslie encouraged Durand to sue TAP under the federal whistle-blower program. Armed with documents, he filed the suit and federal prosecutors ran with it. Durand left TAP for Astra Merck in 1996. But under the whistle-blower program, investigations are conducted in secret. Neither TAP nor Astra Merck was supposed to know about it. The investigation took years and, when called to testify, Durand had to make excuses to take time off from his new job. He was uncomfortably living as a "double agent." In the end, TAP pleaded guilty to conspiracy to cheat the federal government and agreed to pay a record $875 million fine. In October 2001, Durand collected $77 million ($28 million went to taxes), his 14 percent share of the fine paid under the federal whistle-blower statute. He retired to Florida to be closer to his parents, but was still looking forward to the unpleasant task of having to testify against six TAP executives, some of whom had worked for him.

Case Questions

1. Analyze the ethical culture at TAP. Does the culture appear to be in alignment? Misalignment?
2. Based on the facts in the case, and what you have learned in Chapter 9, evaluate the culture change effort that Douglas Durand undertook. What cultural systems did he target in the culture change effort? What systems were missing, if any?
3. Why did his culture change effort fail? What would it take for it to succeed?

Source: Haddad, C. and Barrett, A. 2002. A whistle-blower rocks an industry. *Business Week,* June 24: 126–130.

NOTES

1. Byrne, J. 1992. The best laid ethics programs. *Business Week,* March 9: 67–69.
2. Murphy, P. 1989. Creating ethical corporate structures. *Sloan Management Review* 30 (2): 221–227.
3. Ibid.
4. Wesslund, P. 1992. Ethics are no substitute for the real thing. *Business Week,* April 7.
5. Murphy, Creating ethical corporate structures.
6. Barrett, R. A. 1984. *Culture and conduct: An excursion in anthropology.* Belmont, CA: Wadsworth.
7. Deal, T. E., and Kennedy, A. A. 1982. *Corporate cultures.* Reading, MA: Addison-Wesley. Louis, M. R. 1981. A cultural perspective on organizations: The need for and consequences of viewing organizations as culture-bearing milieux. *Human Systems Management,* 246–258. Martin, J., and Siehl, C. 1983. Organizational culture and counterculture: An uneasy symbiosis. *Organizational Dynamics* (Autumn): 52–64. Pettigrew, A. M. 1979. On studying organizational cultures. *Administrative Science Quarterly* 24: 570–580. Schein, E. H. 1985b. *Organizational culture and leadership.* San Francisco: Jossey-Bass. Smircich, L. 1983. Concepts of culture and organizational analysis. *Administrative Science Quarterly* 28: 339–358.

8. Smircich, Concepts of culture and organizational analysis.
9. Deal and Kennedy, *Corporate cultures.*
10. Morris, B. 1997. He's smart. He's not nice. He's saving Big Blue. *Fortune,* April 14: 68–81.
11. Deal and Kennedy, *Corporate cultures.*
12. Van Maanen, J., and Schein, E. H. 1979. Toward a theory of organizational socialization. In *Research in organizational behavior,* vol. 1, edited by L. Cummings and B. Staw. New York: JAI Press. Fisher, C. D. 1986. Organizational socialization: an integrative review. In *Research in personnel and human resources management,* vol. 4, edited by K. Rowland and G. Ferris. Greenwich, CT: JAI Press, 101–145.
13. Barrett, *Culture and conduct.*
14. Schein, *Organizational culture and leadership.*
15. Pettigrew, On studying organizational cultures. Schein, E. H. 1985a. How culture forms, develops, and changes. In *Gaining control of the corporate culture,* edited by R. H. Kilmann, M. J. Saxtion, and R. Serpa. San Francisco: Jossey-Bass, 17–43. Selznick, P. 1957. *Leadership in administration.* New York: Harper & Row.
16. Manley, W. W., II. 1991. *Executive's handbook of model business conduct codes.* Englewood Cliffs, NJ: Prentice-Hall.
17. Brooker, K. 2000. Can anyone replace Herb? *Fortune,* April 17: 186–192.
18. Schein, E. H. 1985a. How culture forms, develops, and changes. In *Gaining control of the corporate culture,* edited by R. H. Kilmann, M. J. Saxtion, and R. Serpa. San Francisco: Jossey-Bass, 1–743. Selznick, P. 1957. *Leadership in administration.* New York: Harper & Row.
19. Gunter, M. 2002. Has Eisner lost the Disney magic? *Fortune,* January 7: 64–69.
20. Treviño, L. K., Brown, M., and Pincus-Hartman, L. 2003. A qualitative investigation of perceived executive ethical leadership: Perceptions from inside and outside the executive suite. *Human Relations* 56(1): 5–37. Treviño, L. K., Hartman, L. P., Brown, M. 2000. Moral person and moral manager: How executives develop a reputation for ethical leadership. *California Management Review* 42(4): 128–142.
21. Neff, T. J. and Citrin, J. M. 1999. Lessons from the top: The search for America's best leaders. New York: Doubleday.
22. Treviño, Hartman, Brown. Moral person and moral manager.
23. Simpson, L. 2002. Taking the high road. *Training,* January: 36–38.
24. Paterno, Joe. 1989. *Paterno by the book.* New York: Random House.
25. Borden, R. C. 1989. Sherrill's termination released. *Bryan College Station Eagle,* March 3: 1. Hamilton, A. 1989. Switzer resigns. *Centre Daily Times,* June 20: D1. Status of sports investigations on college campuses. 1989. *The Chronicle of Higher Education,* June 7: A34.
26. Byrne, J.A. 1999. "Chainsaw," *Business Week,* October 18: 128–149.
27. Tidwell. G. 1993. Accounting for the PTL scandal. *Today's CPA,* July/August: 29–32.
28. Treviño, L. K., Weaver, G. R., Gibson, D. G. and Toffler, B. L. 1999. Managing ethics and legal compliance: What works and what hurts. *California Management Review* 41(2): 131–151.
29. Loomis, C. 2002. Whatever it takes. *Fortune,* November 25: 74–75.
30. Loomis. Whatever it takes. 75
31. Treviño, Weaver, Gibson, and Toffler. Managing ethics and legal compliance.
32. Brooker, K. 2000. Can anyone replace Herb? *Fortune,* April 17: 186–192.
33. Thompson, A. A. Jr. and Gamble, J. E. 1999. Starbucks Corporation. Case in *Strategic Management: Concepts and Cases,* 11th ed., edited by A. A. Thompson, and A. J. Strickland. NY: McGraw-Hill.
34. Weber, M. 1947. *The theory of social and economic organizations.* Translated by A. M. Henderson and T. Parsons. New York: Free Press
35. Sjoberg, G., Vaughan, T. R., and Williams, N. 1984. Bureaucracy as a moral issue. *Journal of Applied Behavioral Science* 20 (4): 441–453.
36. Milgram, S. 1974. *Obedience to authority: An experimental view.* New York: Harper & Row.
37. Treviño, L. K., Weaver, G. R., Gibson, D. G. and Toffler, B. L. 1999. Managing ethics and legal compliance: What works and what hurts. *California Management Review* 41(2): 131–151.
38. Jackall, R. 1988. *Moral mazes: The world of corporate managers.* New York: Oxford University Press.
39. Kanter, R. M. 1983. *The changemasters.* New York: Simon and Schuster.

40. Kelman, H. C., and Hamilton, V. L. 1989. *Crimes of obedience: Toward a social psychology of authority and responsibility.* New Haven, CT: Yale University.
41. Nelson-Horchler, 1991. The magic of Herman Miller. *Industry Week,* February 18: 11–12, 14, 17.
42. Seglin, J. L. 2000. The values statement vs. corporate reality. *New York Times* online (September 17), www.nytimes.com.
43. Thompson, A. A. Jr. and Gamble, J. E. 1999. Starbucks Corporation. Case in *Strategic Management: Concepts and Cases,* 11th ed., edited by A. A. Thompson, and A. J. Strickland. NY: McGraw-Hill.
44. Weaver, G. R., Treviño, L. K., and Cochran, P. L. in press. Corporate ethics practices in the mid-1990s: An empirical study of the *Fortune* 1000. *Journal of Business Ethics.*
45. Joseph, J. 2000. 2000 National Business Ethics Survey, vol. 1. Washington, DC: Ethics Resource Center.
46. McCabe, D., Treviño, L. K., and Butterfield, K. D. 1996. The influence of collegiate and corporate codes of conduct on ethics-related behavior in the workplace. *Business Ethics Quarterly* 6 (4): 461–476.
47. Weaver, G. R., Treviño, L. K., and Cochran, P. 1999. Corporate ethics practices in the mid-1980s: An empirical study of the *Fortune* 1000. *Journal of Business Ethics* 18 (3), 283–294.
48. Treviño, Weaver, Gibson, and Toffler. Managing ethics and legal compliance.
49. Bowers, W. J. 1964. *Student dishonesty and its control in college.* New York: Bureau of Applied Social Research, Columbia University. Campbell, W. G. 1935. *A comparative investigation of students under an honor system and a proctor system in the same university.* Los Angeles: University of Southern California Press. Canning, R. 1956. Does an honor system reduce classroom cheating? An experimental answer. *Journal of Experimental Education* 24: 291–296.
50. McCabe, D. L., and Treviño, L. K. 1993. Academic dishonesty: Honor codes and other situational influences. *Journal of Higher Education* 64 (5): 522–528.
51. Nel, D., Pitt, L., and Watson, R. 1989. Business ethics: Defining the twilight zone. *Journal of Business Ethics* 8: 781–791.
52. Labich, K. 1992. The new crisis in business ethics. *Fortune,* April 20: 167–176.
53. Graham, J. W. 1986. Principled organizational dissent: A theoretical essay. In *Research in organizational behavior,* vol. 8, edited by L. Cummings and B. M. Staw. Greenwich, CT: JAI Press, 152.
54. Glazer, M. P., and Glazer, P. M. 1986. Whistleblowing. *Psychology Today,* August.
55. Murray, T. J. 1987. Ethics programs: Just a pretty face? *Business Month* 130 (3): 30–32.
56. Greenberg, A. C. 1996. Memos from the chairman. *Fortune,* April 29: 173–175.
57. Weaver, Treviño, and Cochran, Corporate ethics practices in the mid-1990s.
58. Joseph, J. 2000. 2000 National Business Ethics Survey, vol. 1. Washington, DC: Ethics Resource Center.
59. Allied Corporation. 1984. Ethics education for managers. *Ethics Resource Center Report* 2: 1.
60. Schwartz, H., and Davis, S. M. 1981. Matching corporate culture and business strategy. *Organizational Dynamics* (Summer): 30–48.
61. Tiger, L. 1988. Stone age provides model for instilling business ethics. *Wall Street Journal,* January 11: 18.
62. Gellerman, S. 1986. Why "good" managers make bad ethical choices. *Harvard Business Review* (Winter): 15–19.
63. Welles, C. 1988. What led Beech-Nut down the road to disgrace? *Business Week,* February 22.
64. Treviño, Weaver, Gibson, and Toffler. Managing ethics and legal compliance.
65. Deal and Kennedy, *Corporate cultures.*
66. Paterno, *Paterno by the book.*
67. Van Maanen, J., and Schein, E. H. 1979. Toward a theory of organizational socialization. In *Research in organizational behavior,* vol. 1, edited by L. Cummings and B. M. Staw,.
68. Waters, J. A. 1978. Catch 20.5: Corporate morality as an organizational phenomenon. *Organizational Dynamics,* Spring: 319.
69. Deal and Kennedy, *Corporate cultures.*
70. Beyer, J. M. and Trice, H. M. 1987. How an organization's rites reveal its culture. *Organizational Dynamics* 15 (4): 524.

71. Channon, J. 1992. Creating esprit de corps. In *New traditions in Business; Spirit and leadership in the 21st century.* San Francisco: Berrett Koehler Publishers, 53–66.
72. Mitroff, I. and Kilmann, R. H. 1976. On organizational stories: An approach to the design and analysis of organization through myths and stories. In *The management of organization design; Strategies and implications,* edited by R. Kilmann, L. Pondy, and Slevin, D.P. New York: North-Holland.
73. Martin, J., and Siehl, C. 1983. Organizational culture and counterculture: An uneasy symbiosis. *Organizational Dynamics* (Autumn): 52–64.
74. Paterno, *Paterno by the book.*
75. Ibid.
76. Bird, F. B., and Waters, J. A. 1989. The moral muteness of managers. *California Management Review* (Fall): 73–88.
77. Berney, K. 1987. Finding the ethical edge. *Nation's Business* (August): 18–24.
78. Bird and Waters, The moral muteness of managers.
79. Treviño, L. K. 1987. The influences of vicarious learning and individual differences on ethical decision making in the organization: An experiment. Unpublished doctoral dissertation, Texas A & M University, College Station, Texas.
80. Kelman and Hamilton, *Crimes of obedience.*
81. Barrett, *Culture and conduct.* Uttal, B. 1983. The corporate culture vultures. *Fortune,* October 17: 66–71.
82. Barrett, *Culture and conduct.*
83. Ricklees, R. 1983. Ethics in America series. *Wall Street Journal,* October 31–November 3: 33.
84. Thornton, E. 2002. Can this man be a Wall Street reformer? *Business Week,* Sept. 23: 90–96.
85. Tichy, N. 1983. *Managing strategic change.* New York: John Wiley & Sons.
86. Uttal, The corporate culture vultures.
87. Nord, W. R. 1989. OD's unfulfilled visions: Some lessons from economics. In *Research in organizational change and development,* edited by R. W. Woodman and W. A. Pasmore. Greenwich, CT: JAI Press, 39–60.
88. Uttal, The corporate culture vultures.
89. Wilkins, A. L. 1983. The culture audit: A tool for understanding organizations. *Organizational Dynamics* (Autumn): 24–38.
90. Luthans, F. 1989. Conversation with Edgar H. Schein. *Organizational Dynamics* 17 (4): 60–76.
91. Near, J. P., and Miceli, M. P. 1987. Whistleblowers in organizations: dissidents or reformers? In *Research in organizational behavior,* edited by L. Cummings and B. M. Staw, 321–368.
92. Peters, T. 1978. Symbols, patterns, and settings: An optimistic case of getting things done. *Organizational Dynamics,* Autumn: 3–23.
93. McWhinney, W. and Batista, J. 1988. How remythologizing can revitalize organizations. *Organizational Dynamics* 17 (2): 46–79.
94. Chevron Texaco. 1998. "Texaco Chairman and CEO Tells National Urban League that Diversity Commitment Must be Worked on Daily." Press Release (August 4), Chevron Texaco Corporation.
95. Labich, K. 1999. No more crude at Texaco. *Fortune,* Sept. 16: 205–212.
96. Chevron Texaco. 2001. Fourth Annual Report of the Equality and Fairness Task Force for the Year ending June 30, 2001. Chevron Texaco Corporation.
97. Chevron Texaco. 2001. Fourth Annual Report of the Equality and Fairness Task Force for the Year ending June 30, 2001. Chevron Texaco Corporation.

MANAGING ETHICAL PROGRAMS AT THE ORGANIZATIONAL LEVEL

CHAPTER **10**

MANAGING ETHICS AND LEGAL COMPLIANCE

INTRODUCTION

Chapter 9 presented ethics as organizational culture. But it may have raised as many questions as it answered, such as "What are real organizations doing to create and communicate an ethical organizational culture?" This chapter is designed to help answer that question by focusing more narrowly on ethics and legal compliance programs in multiple large American corporations. These programs are designed to manage and communicate ethics in a variety of ways.

Whatever your organizational level, you should find the information in this chapter helpful. If you're at a high organization level, it should give you ideas about how to manage ethics and legal compliance in your firm. If you're at a lower or midmanagement level, it should help you to understand your own organization's approach to ethics management and how it compares to what other organizations are currently doing. If you're a student, it will help you to think about what to look for during the job search.

In preparing this chapter, we spoke with executives from seven companies in a variety of industries: American Express (travel, financial and network service provider), General Motors (automobiles), Lockheed Martin (defense), United Technologies (Otis elevators, Carrier air conditioners, Pratt & Whitney engines, Sikorsky helicopters), Merck (pharmaceuticals), Tenet Healthcare (hospitals), and USAA (insurance and financial services). We are grateful to these executives for their time. These companies range in size and ownership from USAA, a private, 4.8 million member-owned insurance and financial services company with 21,000 employees at six U.S. locations and two overseas offices, to General Motors, a public company with 355,000 employees in thirty countries. Merck has nearly 70,000 employees. American Express has 80,000 employees worldwide in about 160 countries. Tenet Healthcare has over 114,000 employees who work in 113 acute care hospitals across the United States. Lockheed Martin has 125,000 employees in 45 U.S. states and 56 nations and territories. United Technologies has over 150,000 employees, more than half outside the United States in 180 countries. Think about the challenge of managing ethics and legal compliance in these firms, many with employees at locations around the globe. All of the companies are engaged in a variety of efforts, but their approaches differ somewhat due to differences in industries and organizational cultures. For example, some industries (e.g., defense, financial services, health care) are more highly regulated than others. So, compliance with laws and regulations is an important goal and must be managed. For many of these companies, ethics and legal compliance is closely tied to the maintenance of the firm's reputation and brand value. For example, American Express aims to be "the world's most respected and valued service brand." In such an environment, integrity becomes a key driver of corporate action.

STRUCTURING ETHICS MANAGEMENT

Many businesses are allocating significant resources toward formal ethics and legal compliance programs. Tenet Healthcare spends $700,000 per year on ethics training alone. That's six dollars per employee per year. The increasing attention to formal ethics management programs has come about, in part, because of media attention to scandals in American business, management's awareness of the U.S. Sentencing Guidelines (see Chapter 2); because organizations such as the Conference Board have held business ethics conferences for a number of years at which formal ethics management systems are encouraged; and because some corporate leaders are simply committed to the importance of ethics in their organizations.[1]

Managing Ethics: The Corporate Ethics Office

Some organizations delegate ethics management responsibilities widely, finding that a strong statement of values and a strong ethical culture can bind the ethics management effort together. This approach may be particularly effective in smaller firms. However, most large firms find that ethics initiatives need to be coordinated from a single office to ensure that all of the program's pieces fit together and that all of the U.S. Sentencing Guideline requirements are being met (see Chapter 2).

The corporate ethics office concept can be traced to 1985 and General Dynamics, then the second largest U.S. defense contractor. The Secretary of the Navy, out of concern about the allowability of certain indirect expenses that had been billed to the government, directed General Dynamics to establish and enforce a rigorous code of ethics for all employees, with sanctions for violators. The company turned to a nonprofit consulting firm in Washington, D.C., the Ethics Resource Center, for help in developing the code. As part of this process, an ethics office was also set up and an ethics officer was hired.[2] In 1986, General Dynamics joined with other defense industry companies in the Defense Industry Initiative (DII, discussed in Chapter 2, see www.ussc.gov) to "embrace and promote ethical business conduct." The companies shared best practices, and these best practices provided much of the foundation for the U.S. Sentencing Commission requirements.

The 1991 U.S. Federal Sentencing Guidelines gave impetus to the move toward establishing formal ethics programs in many more firms outside the defense industry. The guidelines list seven requirements (see Chapter 2) for due diligence and an effective compliance program. The guidelines propose that organizations establish and communicate compliance standards and set up monitoring, reporting, and accountability systems. In addition, the guidelines call for the assignment of specific high-level individuals with responsibility to oversee legal compliance standards. This responsibility can be held by one executive, or it can be divided among a number of individuals such as the legal counsel, internal auditors, or human resource professionals. This requirement led to the development of a brand new role—that of the corporate ethics officer.

Ethics Officers

Until the mid-1980s, the title "ethics officer" didn't exist in American business. However, there are enough of these high-level ethics executives today that they now have their own professional organization, the Ethics Officer Association (EOA—see www.eoa.org). The association's stated mission is "to promote ethical business practices, serving as a forum for the exchange of information and strategies." The organization began in 1991 when over 40 ethics/compliance officers met at the Center for Business Ethics at Bentley College in Waltham, Massachusetts. The organization was officially launched later that year and began holding annual meetings in 1993. As of the end of 2002, the organization had over 800 members representing more than half of *Fortune* 100 hundred companies, non-profits, municipalities, and international members from around the globe. The organization also holds regular workshops and provides training for ethics officers and their staff.

Many firms designate their legal counsel as the ethics officer. Others create a title such as vice president or director of ethics, compliance, or business practices, director of internal audit, ethics program coordinator, or just plain ethics officer. Most firms locate the ethics officer at the corporate level, and these high-level executives generally report to a senior executive, the CEO, the board of directors, the audit committee of the board, or some combination. These individuals are expected to provide leadership and strategies for ensuring that the firm's standards of business conduct are communicated and upheld throughout the organization.

INSIDERS VERSUS OUTSIDERS An ethics or compliance officer may be an insider or someone brought in from the outside. We talked to past and present ethics officers who represent both categories. For example, Kathryn Reiman, senior vice president and chief compliance officer for American Express, was brought into the organization from outside because of her previous compliance and international experience at Lehman Brothers. It can sometimes be more difficult for an outsider to achieve credibility in the ethics or compliance role. But someone brought in from outside the company has the advantage of being able to evaluate the situation with a fresh eye and, if change is needed, may be better able to guide the organization through the change process. Most of those we interviewed believe that, if available, a respected and trusted insider who knows the company's culture and people is usually the best choice. Results of a 1995 survey support the insider preference.[3] Eighty-two percent of the firms responding to the question hired their ethics officer from inside the firm. The very best situation may be when the ethics officer is also a part of the senior management team. That's the case with Dennis Jorgensen of Tenet Healthcare. Jorgensen holds the title of Sr. Vice President, Ethics, Business Conduct and Administration. In addition to overseeing the firm's ethics and compliance efforts, he also oversees travel services, security operations, background screening services, aviation, and facility administration. In his multiple roles, Jorgensen interacts regularly with the senior management team and, most important, he has done so for years. That gives him a huge advantage compared with many other ethics officers. According to Jorgensen, when necessary, he can "tell the emperor he has no clothes!"

ETHICS OFFICER BACKGROUND The job of ethics officer has been called "the newest profession in American business."[4] These individuals come from many backgrounds. With insiders, the job is often assigned to someone in a staff function (e.g., someone in the corporate secretary's office, office of the legal counsel, audit, or human resources). According to the 1995 ethics officer survey, law was the most common background. That is true of most of our interviewees as well. Interestingly, some people believe that lawyers shouldn't be considered for the job because corporate lawyers are hired to defend the corporation and therefore can't objectively handle an ethical issue that calls the corporation's own behavior into question. But the ethics officers we interviewed agreed that what is most important is that employees respect the individual for being fair, trustworthy, credible, and discreet. The ethics program coordinator at USAA, Earnie Broughton, has training in industrial/organizational psychology and experience as a human resources generalist and line executive. Such a background is less common among ethics officers. But it's useful in an organization that is committed to making ethics management the responsibility of everyone from the CEO down. In fact, USAA's CEO recently circulated a letter identifying himself as the Chief Ethics Officer, a statement that any ethics officer would welcome. So, Broughton's office oversees the code and conflict of interest policy, ethics training, communication, and support. But at USAA, every executive, manager, and supervisor is considered to be responsible for ethics within his or her own area of responsibility. Broughton works closely with the "Ethics Council," a group of senior executives who meet regularly to talk about the ethics program and provide company-wide guidance on ethics issues.

The Ethics Infrastructure

Ethics offices can be centralized, decentralized, or some combination. The decision to centralize or decentralize may depend on the overall structure of the firm. For example, if the firm's other staff functions are highly decentralized, it may be difficult to centralize the ethics function. The structuring decision may also depend upon whether different business units have very different ethics management needs. For example, if one division of a firm deals in government contracts and others do not, that division may need a different approach that emphasizes compliance with government contracting regulations. So, local ethics offices might better meet the needs of different units that are in different businesses. But decentralized ethics offices can be difficult to manage effectively because they must communicate with each other constantly to ensure consistency and commitment to the organization's key values.

Even where different units have different requirements, it is usually helpful to have a central office that coordinates ethics and compliance activities and ensures management support for those activities. Most large organizations, such as the ones we talked with, have a headquarters ethics office that functions as the central point of communications for ethics and compliance activities. For example, the central ethics office at Lockheed Martin has about 11 staff people led by Nancy Higgins, ethics officer at Boeing before she joined the firm as vice president for ethics and business conduct in 2000. In addition, each of the four large business areas has a full-time ethics director who has responsibility for overseeing ethics and business conduct in his or her business areas. These ethics directors report to Higgins as well as to an executive vice president. Oversight is provided by the Ethics Steering Committee, chaired by the firm's chief operating officer, along with senior management representation from all business areas. In addition, Higgins reports to the Audit and Ethics Committee of the company's board of directors four times per year in written and oral form.

Ethics officers seem to agree that, whatever other reporting relationships exist, the ethics officer should have a direct reporting relationship to the CEO. They were particularly concerned about the ethics function being "stuck" under law, human resources, audit, or finance where it would be just another part of the "silo mentality" that still exists in many organizations. Ethics would then be perceived as audit's job or HR's job, rather than as part of the total culture. The person who leads the ethics office is in a much better position to "press the envelope" if he or she reports directly to the CEO. In fact, as with USAA, the best situation is likely when the CEO thinks of himself or herself as the "chief ethics officer" as well as the chief executive officer. In that situation, the CEO takes responsibility for managing ethics, with assistance from other individuals.

The Corporate Ethics Committee

In some organizations, ethics is managed by a corporate committee staffed by senior-level managers from a variety of functional areas. This committee is set up to provide ethical oversight and policy guidance for CEO and management decisions.[5] It also represents an affirmation that top management really cares about ethics.

At Lockheed Martin, the Ethics Steering Committee meets once every quarter and has done so since 1995. Members of the committee include the president of Lockheed Martin, the corporate chairman, the chief financial officer, and executives of large operating entities, plus vice presidents from functional areas such as human resources and communications. The two-way communication between the ethics office and these senior executives is essential. It provides the ethics office with information about what concerns these senior-level people, and it provides the firm's senior leadership with information about the types of problems that are coming into the ethics office from employees. The group's role is considered to be strategic. They think about how ethics fits into the company's culture. For example, at a recent meeting, the group discussed results from an employee survey. The group learned that some employees were afraid to go to their supervisors with ethical concerns. That led to the recommendation that the ethics office increase efforts to train front-line supervisors, providing them with a toolkit based upon real life scenarios—what to say and do (and not do) when an employee comes to you with an ethical issue.

COMMUNICATING ETHICS

Within the ethics infrastructure, good communication—downward, upward, and two-way—is essential if an organization is to have a strong, aligned ethics culture. The organization must evaluate the current state of ethics communication and initiatives. It must communicate its values, standards, and policies in a variety of formal and informal ways that meet its employees' needs. These communication efforts should be synergistic, clear, consistent, and credible. They also need to be executed in a variety of media, because people learn things in different ways. In general, the old advice to speechwriters still holds. "Tell 'em what you're going to tell 'em, then tell 'em, then tell 'em what you told 'em." In addition to downward communication from management, employees must also be provided opportunities to communicate their ethical concerns upward. Finally, an open communication environment must be created that says it's OK to ask questions and it's OK to talk about ethics. In the following section, we begin with some corporate communications basics—principles that should guide all ethics communication initiatives.

A number of the ethics officers we interviewed were sensitive to the negativity sometimes attached to the word "ethics." Employees can get defensive when they hear the word "ethics." They think to themselves, "Why are you here talking to me about ethics? Mine are fine." Kent Druyvesteyn, former ethics officer at General Dynamics, put it this way. "Using the word 'ethics' unfortunately implies that somebody has a deficiency. So, I would urge you not to use that word at least until you can make clear what you mean by it." This negative reaction to the word "ethics" may be more of a problem at some organizations than at others. Again, it depends upon the culture of the firm. Companies have used the term "values" or "business conduct" or "business practices" successfully. The key is to know your own company and to use terminology that sounds authentic within your organization's culture.

Basic Communications Principles

ALIGN THE FORMAL AND INFORMAL COMMUNICATION SYSTEMS When most people think of a corporate communications system, they think of the obvious—the company newspaper, Web site, and annual report. However, like culture, a corporate communications system consists of formal and informal components. Formal communications include all formal written and electronic communication such as newspapers, magazines, memos, recruiting literature, policy manuals, annual reports, Web sites, and advertising, as well as formalized oral communication such as meetings and speeches. But perhaps the most powerful component in a corporation's communications system is the informal component—the grapevine.

The grapevine—a continual stream of information among employees about "what's really going on"—exists in every organization. It contains news, rumors, impressions, and perceptions. Surprisingly, research has shown that from 70 to 90 percent of the information that passes through the grapevine is accurate.[6] In survey after survey of employees in numerous and varied businesses, the grapevine is where they said they received most of their information about their employer. (In those same surveys, most people said that they would rather receive information from their managers.) The grapevine can be examined to shed light on a corporation's credibility since most employees are plugged into it, it provides information fast and continually, and it contains the "inside" scoop on corporate events.

One way to determine corporate credibility on various issues—especially ethics—is to compare the messages on the formal and informal communications systems. For example, suppose that XYZ Company has a policy prohibiting employees from excessively entertaining customers. The policy is spelled out in a manual, and the president of XYZ has reinforced the policy in speeches to employees. Now imagine that XYZ's head of marketing repeatedly wines and dines clients. The costs of the lavish entertainment are detailed in expense reports that are approved by management and that are processed by clerical and financial control employees. In addition, other employees are invited along when the clients are entertained, and still more employees observe the head of marketing entertaining guests in expensive restaurants. Regardless of how strongly XYZ's formal communications system states the official policy, the informal communication system—the grapevine—will communicate what's really going on: XYZ is saying one thing and doing another. The company says it prohibits lavish entertainment, yet it condones that forbidden behavior in at least one high-level employee. As a result, XYZ's ethics culture is out of alignment, and it has no corporate credibility on the subject of customer entertainment. Furthermore, its credibility on other ethical issues is probably suspect.

Now, imagine another situation, ABC Company has a strongly worded policy regarding sexual harassment. Moreover, ABC's senior executives have frequently stated that sexual harassment will not be tolerated. Suppose a manager, Pat, is accused of sexual harassment. The charge is investigated, found to be accurate, and Pat is fired. The exact details of the incident may not be on the grapevine, but in most cases, just the bare bones of that story will send a strong message. The messages on the grapevine will match what's said by ABC's formal communications system. Employees will get the word very quickly that ABC means business on the issue of sexual harassment, and the corporation will have increased its credibility by "walking the ethics talk."

The importance of informal communications can't be overstated. Since truth and honesty are at the core of any ethics effort, if a company is saying one thing and doing another—if the messages on its formal communications system and its grapevine don't match—it has little or no credibility and probably shouldn't attempt a formal ethics communications effort until it has regained its credibility. How can you compare the formal and informal messages? Ask employees. Employee surveys and focus groups can provide feedback that will serve as the beginning of an effective comparison. How does an organization establish or regain credibility? Designing consistent policies and enforcing those polices are the only route an organization can take to gain credibility on ethics issues. If policies are enforced for only part of the employee population, or if there are different rules and treatment for different employees, there's little an organization can do to gain credibility until consistency is established.

ANALYZE THE AUDIENCE The first thing to do when designing a communications program is to analyze your audience's needs. Consider what employees already know, what they need to know, what biases and abilities they have, what the desired and required behaviors look like, when they should be asking questions, and where they can go to report their concerns and to ask for help.

When designing ethics communication for a typical employee population, organizations need to consider three kinds of people. (We use military jargon to describe the three types because it's easy to visualize and remember.)

GOOD SOLDIERS Group I are "good soldiers"—these people understand and follow the rules and policies of the organization, and they have good ethical compasses. They have the judgment or experience required to discern the difference between right and wrong, and they have the moral grounding to do the right thing. Be careful to note that these aren't just soldiers who follow orders, right or wrong. They know that "good" soldiers are expected to question an order they believe to be illegal or morally wrong and they would.

LOOSE CANNONS Group II is called "loose cannons"—they're people who may have good ethical compasses, but they don't know their corporation's policies, and they may not even be familiar with general ethical standards in business. Loose cannons may be inexperienced; or they may have transferred from another, unrelated industry with very different norms; or they may never have read a policy manual. Whatever the reason, loose cannons may be well meaning, but they're naive. Without guidance, ethics may not even be a consideration.

GRENADES Group III are "grenades," and they're neither ignorant nor benign. These people may or may not know the rules, but they don't care. They have their own agenda, and they lack any company or professional loyalty. We call this group grenades because their activities can blow up suddenly and severely damage the organization.

Although the communication needs of the three groups overlap, the emphasis for each specific group is clear. Good soldiers need support because good people often feel pressured to compromise in order to "fit in." Good soldiers need to know that their instincts are right and that their behavior is not the exception. It represents the organizational model. Loose cannons need to be educated; they need to know and understand basic norms of ethical conduct and specific company policy and standards. Grenades need to know unequivocally that ethical lapses will not be tolerated. They need to see good behavior rewarded and ethical lapses dealt with swiftly, consistently, and firmly.

There are probably a few grenades in any organization. But they surely exist everywhere, and the system must be prepared to deal with them. Good soldiers may account for a substantial portion of employees but perhaps not the majority. Since very few employees ever read a policy manual cover to cover, most people learn policy on a need-to-know basis. It is safest to assume that the majority of employees fit into the loose cannon category. The challenge in designing effective ethics communication programs is meeting the needs of all types of employees.

This focus on the ethics audience assumes that most employees don't come to the organization perfectly principled and perfectly prepared to make the right decision in every situation. Recall from earlier chapters that most employees are highly susceptible to influence from outside themselves, so the organization has to provide guidance, and, despite advances, the perfect integrity test hasn't been invented. Since polygraphs were outlawed for most types of employee screening in the United States, more organizations have turned to paper-and-pencil honesty or integrity tests to screen prospective employees. Most of these tests attempt to predict the prospective employee's propensity to steal from the organization, although others have a more general focus on workplace deviance. Integrity tests have been evaluated by the American Psychological Association and the government's Office of Technology Assessment. The two organizations' reports generally agree that research on integrity tests is improving and that evidence supporting the tests' ability to predict dishonest behavior has increased.[7] Nevertheless, many problems remain, and organizations will continue to have imperfect employees who need guidance on ethical issues.

Evaluating the Current State of Ethics Communications

Before beginning the actual design of an ethics communication program, it's essential to conduct an evaluation that asks the following questions:

WHAT KINDS OF ETHICAL DILEMMAS ARE EMPLOYEES LIKELY TO ENCOUNTER? In addition to common ethical dilemmas faced by employees everywhere, organizations need to identify the kinds of issues and dilemmas that might be unique to their particular industry. For example, a chemical company needs to pay special attention to environmental and safety dilemmas. A financial firm should pay extremely close attention to fiduciary, confidentiality, and conflict of interest issues. A manufacturing company may have to look at the ethical issues involved in worker safety, product quality, product liability, and labor relations. In addition to identifying issues specific to their industry, companies also need to examine the various jobs within their organization to uncover what specific professional dilemmas their communication program will have to address. For example, an internal auditor will face one set of dilemmas, whereas a manufacturing supervisor will face an entirely different set. Once typical dilemmas are identified, it's possible for an organization to develop a program that's useful for employees—one that shows them how to deal with the most common dilemmas.

WHAT DON'T EMPLOYEES KNOW? Is the company hiring numerous mid-career hires, who may come from other industries with different standards of conduct? Does the company regularly hire large numbers of recent college or business school graduates who may have little knowledge of business standards, much less specific corporate policy or industry standards? The communications program needs to target the specific needs of these different groups.

HOW ARE POLICIES CURRENTLY COMMUNICATED? How is policy communicated now? Does the policy manual weigh in at 40 pounds, or is it online and easy to search? When a manager has a policy question, what does he or she do—look it up in the manual, ask human resources, ask a colleague, search online resources, or guess? Is corporate policy ever discussed in orientation or training programs? No one is ever going to memorize a policy manual. Therefore, an ethics communications program needs to take a "snapshot" of key policies and concentrate on communicating those, as well as the message that employees need to know when to ask questions and that the organization encourages employees to inquire. Companies generally do a very good job of telling new hires how to succeed; what they usually don't do nearly as well is telling new hires how they're going to fail or get fired or worse. It's key that new employees understand their employer's standards. What does the company expect from them?

WHAT COMMUNICATIONS CHANNELS EXIST? How do employees receive messages from management? How does management receive messages from employees? Is "management by walking around" a common practice, or is senior management isolated from most employees? Is there a suggestion program? If so, do suggestions get responses? Are employees generally comfortable approaching their managers with problems, concerns, and questions? Is there a grievance process or a whistle-blowing procedure? Do most employees know where to go for help if their managers are unavailable or if their manager is part of the problem? Are human resources, legal, and audit professionals accessible to most employees? Analyzing the answers to these questions will give an organization a good idea of where effective communications channels exist, where they don't, and where to build new ones.

Multiple Communications Channels for Formal Ethics Communication

The company's ethics message can and should be communicated in a variety of ways. The most obvious ethics communication channels include a mission or values statement, a code of conduct, policy statements, a formal process for reporting concerns or observed misconduct, and communications from leaders. In addition to these, the ethics message needs to be reinforced in all formal communication materials, including recruiting and orientation materials, newsletters, magazines, annual reports, and Web sites. The following list suggests just some of the types of communications materials that can contain an ethics message:

WEB SITES The company's Web site is an important source of information about the company and its values and policies. Many companies are hesitant to include ethics information on their external Web site and instead, use their firm's intranet to convey the information. But stakeholders such as investors, potential employees, customers, and suppliers are likely to use the company's Web site to gather information about the company. So, if ethics is important to these relationships, it should be included on the external site. For example, Lockheed Martin includes a large amount of information about ethics on its external Web site (www.lockheedmartin.com) including its value statement, ethical principles, code of conduct, information about the Corporate Office of Ethics and Business Conduct, information about reporting problems to the Helpline, and information for suppliers and other business partners who are asked to be guided by high ethical standards and to respect the restrictions the firm places on its employees with regard to giving and receiving gifts, for example. The code, "Setting the Standard," is translated into fourteen languages. How many can you understand? United Technologies (www.utc.com) also includes information about ethics on its Web site. Click on "About UTC" and you'll see a tab for "ethics" that includes the code and other brochures in PDF format (also in multiple languages).

RECRUITING BROCHURES These can include the mission or values statement, a discussion of corporate values, and a description of how people in the organization succeed and fail. Ethical conduct can be highlighted. Many organizations also have a Web site location for those interested in finding out about careers within the firm and applying for jobs. On Merck's Web site (merck.com), prospective applicants are introduced to the company's values instilled by the son of founder, George W. Merck. These values should be familiar to readers of this book from Chapter 2 and the Merck River Blindness case. Recall that George Merck said, "We're driven by the idea that medicine is indeed for the people—and not for the profits. Whether we're discovering, developing, designing, marketing, or supporting, our work is ultimately aimed towards preserving and improving human life. We are all committed to the utmost standards of ethics and integrity as well as the highest level of excellence throughout the company." Prospective employees are then invited to click on the corporate mission and values statement (see below). The Web site goes on to highlight the intent focus on employee satisfaction and highlights Merck's many "awards and accolades," including being listed as one of the "100 Best Companies to Work For" by *Fortune* magazine, a regular honor for Merck, and being listed as one of the best companies to work for by *Working Mother* magazine. *Working Woman* magazine named Merck as one of the Top 25 Companies for Executive Women.

ORIENTATION MATERIALS These can include the mission or values statement, descriptions of common ethical dilemmas and advice for handling them, explanations of resources to help employees make ethical decisions, and how to raise an ethical issue or report an ethical concern. Organizations should pay particular attention to how orientations communicate values and expectations. New employees are eager to learn about their new employer and orientations provide a wonderful venue to communicate what an organization stands for and what it expects of employees. How *not* to introduce values and ethics during an orientation might best be illustrated by the manufacturing company's general counsel, who, when asked to address new hires on the company's ethics and compliance program, simply read the code of conduct aloud to the group of new employees.

NEWSLETTERS AND MAGAZINES These can include the mission statement, stories about corporate "heroes"—employees who illustrate the corporate values, and features that describe ethical dilemmas with comments from employees and managers about how they would deal with the problems. These can also be targeted to specific groups of employees with specific needs.

BOOKLETS These can vary given employees' need for information in particular areas of the business. The brief brochures can also be easily updated or added to, making the program flexible to the dynamic business environment.

A Novel Approach to Ethics Communication at USAA

USAA has developed a novel approach to ethics communication called the "Ethics Files." It provides employees an opportunity to learn about ethical issues in a fun, interactive, and ongoing manner, and keeps ethics "alive" in the organization. The ethics office has developed a character named Agent "Dewright" whose mission is to promote ethical business practices at USAA. Dewright regularly gets involved in ethical dilemmas that are published as top stories on the corporate intranet. Employees are invited to send in an appropriate response—What should Agent Dewright do?

Here is a sample ethical dilemma:

> Agent Dewright overheard an employee bragging about going on medical leave without needing to be on one. This employee found a doctor who would hand out medical notes for sick leave without question. What should Agent Dewright do?

Between 70 and 150 responses are received for each scenario. The above example generated 130 responses. The ethics program facilitator chooses 4 or 5 that illustrate the principle being conveyed and publishes those along with corporate guidance. These are available to all employees via the intranet. This method has turned out to be a great way to engage front line employees.

Here are some responses generated by employees:

> "If I knew the person had a phony sick leave slip, I would advise her to either confess or not use it. If she did not do this, I would contact the ethics office and report her. Then let the chips fall where they may. Having knowledge of the situation and not reporting it is just as bad as committing the fraud."

> "Let your manager know about what you 'heard'—understanding, of course, that what was heard may or may not be true. Since management and HR professionals are trained to look into these types of things, you can assume that this will happen, and whatever the truth of the matter may be, appropriate action will be forthcoming. Employees who are not here cannot contribute to the mission. Employees who take benefits from the company that are not earned, cost all of us."

"This should definitely be reported to management. This employee is committing fraud against the company and his fellow employees. By staying out for medical leave that is not warranted, he is contributing to the extra work that others have to pick up for him, not to mention the amount of money that is being paid for non-sickness if he is entitled to leave pay. I would not hesitate to report this or any other fraud that I observed. It not only affects the members, it affects all employees."

"Agent Dewright has an obligation to report such behavior by unethical employees. He should report what he overheard to the proper authority within the company and let someone investigate the matter to find out if it is actually true and for how long this has been going on. Once the investigation is complete, the proper authorities can evaluate the situation and proceed with an action. We are all adults and we know right from wrong. Why would anyone be willing to risk a job and reputation on doing anything that is unethical?"

"This is costing all of us! Hopefully you can find out the individual's name and contact the ethics department with this information. That office would be able to help identify the correct process and who to report this to. Not only does the employee need to be reprimanded, but the doctor needs to be called on the carpet for it as well."

Earnie Broughton and the ethics office offered the following message in reply:

"The best course of action for Agent Dewright is to report the incident to a supervisor, Employee Relations, the ethics office or one of the other resources available in the company to address this kind of problem. These people will take appropriate action to ensure that the allegation is being investigated."

The Code of Business Ethics and Conduct states "under no circumstances should false or misleading entries knowingly be made in any company report or record." This means that knowingly submitting a false medical statement to the company constitutes a violation of the USAA code of conduct—in fact, in this case, such an action constitutes fraud against the company in that the employee is claiming a benefit to which he or she is not entitled.

Some employees felt no action should be taken, since the case involved only a conversation that was overheard. Others were inclined to take matters into their own hands.

Unfortunately, doing nothing is not always the best strategy. According to the Code of Business Ethics and Conduct, "concealing or covering up an ethics violation is itself a major violation of the code." Addressing the situation directly with the employee is a personal decision. However, taking matters into your own hands could involve you in a situation that is more appropriately handled by others, such as a supervisor or Employee Relations.

This response was followed by a list of resources that are available at the company to deal with this type of issue.

Consider what this kind of communication tool can accomplish. Reporting a coworker is difficult to do. But employees' replies suggested that many of them believe it is appropriate. Reading those replies could help establish a new norm or standard of behavior in the organization. Reading the replies also offers rationales that an individual employee may not have thought about on his or her own. For example, the fact that such fraud is harming other employees was an important point brought out in more than one reply (for example, "this is costing all of us"). Further, the replies create expectations about role responsibilities. Not reporting is just as problematic as the fraud itself, so reporting is expected. Finally, the ethics office suggested that an individual is not expected to confront the employee or take any action other than to report the concern to appropriate authorities. So, by printing the appropriate replies and supplementing them with good information about expectations and available resources, the ethics office can reinforce many important messages on an ongoing basis.

A similar system was introduced in the early 1990s at Texas Instruments, but in this system, employees were encouraged to send in questions. This internal corporate communication tool called "Instant Experience," allowed employees to raise timely issues quickly and without a lot of bureaucracy, and it provided the ethics office with a constant line to the ethical pulse of the organization. The idea was the brainchild of Glen Coleman, a retired Air Force helicopter pilot and an aerospace engineer who worked for TI's ethics office at the time. Coleman admitted that, in Vietnam, he and his fellow helicopter pilots sometimes made potentially life-threatening mistakes. But on their return, they would freely enter their "stupid mistakes" into a book they called "Instant Experience" so that their buddies wouldn't make the same mistakes and lives could be saved.

In a variation of the idea that not everyone should have to get burned to find out that the stove is hot, Coleman reasoned that the ethics office could be a clearinghouse for ethical experiences that members of the organization were willing to share with others. As a result, these "instant experiences" were regularly transmitted to all employees on an electronic mail communication system and were retained on the system so that new employees could get up to speed and ongoing employees could check the system whenever they wished.

Here's an example of an anonymous question posed by a TI employee that was posted on the communication system.

> "Suppose I'm in a restaurant and I happen to overhear a conversation from behind me. It's two TI competitors discussing sensitive, competitive information that would be very valuable to TI. What do I do? Continue to listen? Put my fingers in my ears? Tell them to stop? And what should I do with the information that I've already heard? Forget it and pretend it never happened? Mark it TI STRICTLY PRIVATE and distribute it?"
>
> I didn't go out looking for the information and I couldn't change my table location to get away from the conversation. It seems a little ridiculous to just throw away an opportunity to use valuable information that I've acquired but didn't solicit in any way. What's the right course of action?"

And, here's how Carl Skooglund, TI's ethics director at the time, responded:

> "There is nothing illegal or unethical about accidentally being in the right place at the right time and overhearing a competitor's conversation. They must accept the responsibility for irresponsibly discussing sensitive information in a public place. If you have overheard the conversation, your best course of action is to document to your best ability what you heard and notify TI Legal, telling them how you acquired it. The TI employee who raised this question is correct. It would be ridiculous to pretend that you never heard the information. Under these circumstances you can share the information with TI. The competitor must accept responsibility for his carelessness. Our ethical principles do not exclude common sense."

Skooglund's response then took the issue a step further, inviting dialogue by asking TI employees if the response should be different if the TI employee had intentionally sat at a table adjacent to known competitors. Many employees responded, and over 95 percent of the responses agreed that intentional eavesdropping was clearly unethical. Here are some of their responses:

> "We are not in the spy business. It's totally unethical."
>
> "I was disappointed that you would even ask us this."
>
> "Spying is spying."
>
> "What happened to the golden rule?"
>
> "My grandmother told me that if something makes you feel guilty, don't do it."
>
> "If our customers knew about this, would their opinion of us suffer?"
>
> "I would be ashamed."
>
> "It's unmitigatedly unethical."
>
> "Would I be proud to have my TI badge on?"
>
> "Let's leave trickery to magicians."
>
> "Stay far enough away from legal limits so that TI's character is never questioned."

Skooglund agreed with the large majority of responses and assured the respondents that their ethical compasses were pointing in the right direction. This "Instant Experience" system allowed employees to openly share their ethics-related questions and experiences, and everyone in the organization learned from the open exchange. In an organization without such a system, this individual may have struggled silently with the issue or may have asked a few peers or a manager for advice. But with the system, the entire organization can learn from one individual's experience.

In addition to the weekly transmissions and interactions, a collection of the weekly articles was retained on the Instant Experience system as an archive with a chronological and a subject index. A survey of TI employees found that 30 to 40 percent were reading it every week and 70 to 80 percent read it at least monthly. Supervisors were also encouraged to print the messages and post them on a bulletin board.

This system was particularly effective because it fit TI's culture and was based on sound communication principles. First, electronic communication was an essential part of the high-tech TI culture. So, e-mail ethics discussions were a natural extension of that culture. Second, electronic mail is appropriate for "ethics" discussions because it allows for interaction with reflection. Ethical issues generally require some introspection, perhaps even a trip to the file cabinet to check the code of conduct. The "instant experience" system allowed employees to think about the issue and then participate in relatively informal discussions with other employees. Finally, research suggests that people are less inhibited when communicating electronically. Therefore, they may be more willing to discuss sensitive ethical issues electronically than they would be face to face, contributing to the "it's OK to talk about ethics" atmosphere.

Mission or Values Statements

In recent years, many corporations have developed mission or values statements. A mission statement, values statement, or credo is a succinct description of "how we do business"—the corporate principles and values that guide how business is to be conducted in an organization. A mission statement is a codification of essential corporate behavior. It's a sort of "Ten Commandments" for an organization. If it's to be effective, it should be short, memorable, and in plain language so that everyone can be clear about its message. It's also essential that the organization's own employees have input because a mission statement must accurately reflect the organizational culture. A mission statement scribed by outsiders just won't ring true and is likely to end up the subject of a Dilbert cartoon. But a mission statement that develops out of the firm's true values and history can be a mainstay of the corporate culture. Merck posts it s mission and values statements prominently on its Web site (www.merck.com):

> OUR MISSION
>
> The mission of Merck is to provide society with superior products and services—innovations and solutions that improve the quality of life and satisfy customer needs—to provide employees with meaningful work and advancement opportunities and investors with a superior rate of return.
>
> OUR VALUES
>
> 1. Our business is preserving and improving human life. All of our actions must be measured by our success in achieving this goal. We value above all our ability to serve everyone who can benefit from the appropriate use of our products and services, thereby providing lasting consumer satisfaction.
>
> 2. We are committed to the highest standards of ethics and integrity. We are responsible to our customers, to Merck employees and their families, to the environments we inhabit, and to the societies we serve worldwide. In discharging our responsibilities, we do not take professional or ethical

shortcuts. Our interactions with all segments of society must reflect the high standards we profess.

3. We are dedicated to the highest level of scientific excellence and commit our research to improving human and animal health and the quality of life. We strive to identify the most critical needs of consumers and customers, we devote our resources to meeting those needs.

4. We expect profits, but only from work that satisfies customer needs and benefits humanity. Our ability to meet our responsibilities depends on maintaining a financial position that invites investment in leading-edge research and that makes possible effective delivery of research results.

5. We recognize that the ability to excel—to most competitively meet society's and customers' needs—depends on the integrity, knowledge, imagination, skill, diversity and teamwork of employees, and we value these qualities most highly. To this end, we strive to create an environment of mutual respect, encouragement and teamwork—an environment that rewards commitment and performance and is responsive to the needs of employees and their families.

Obviously, it's possible to have a meaningless mission and values statement when the words are posted on Web sites and bulletin boards but aren't really a part of the organizational culture. To be meaningful, corporate values must guide corporate and individual decision making on a regular basis. Merck's commitment to its values was exemplified by its decision to pursue the research resulting in the discovery of Mectizan, the drug it is now giving away to treat River Blindness in the developing world (see case at the end of Chapter 2). And Merck employees tell us that these values are "drilled into them" and used on a regular basis. Also, the role of the "customer first" value that guided Johnson & Johnson's decision making in the Tylenol crisis (see Chapter 8) is perhaps the most famous single example of a corporate value being meaningfully applied.

Policy Manuals

A policy manual is important because it's the one place where all relevant company rules are housed. Generally, policy manuals describe not only laws and regulations pertaining to the company and its industry, but also all company policy, including human resources policy. Although it's critical for a corporation to define its policies and communicate them—it's one of the stipulations of the U.S. Sentencing Guidelines—most employees don't read policy manuals cover-to-cover, or scan every Web page if the manual is online. Employees consider policy manuals to be reference manuals, and, as a result, employees consult policy manuals in the way they use a dictionary—periodically and on a need-to-know basis. Many managers never consult a policy manual, however—it's much easier to ask someone than to look up the rules in a voluminous book—and, depending on whom they ask, they may or may not get the right answer.

The very nature of policy manuals—they're usually large and written in "legalese"—makes them a poor way to communicate important rules. Also, since all policy is detailed, all policy may be viewed as having the same importance. Obviously, some policies are much more important than others and should receive special emphasis.

When designing policy communications, analyze the audience. Who needs to know all the policy? Does some corporate policy only apply to a portion of the employees? What do employees really need to know, and what's nice for them to know? Here are some guidelines to follow:

COMMUNICATE RELEVANT RULES TO THE PEOPLE WHO NEED THEM Although there's certainly policy that applies to everyone, there's surely some policy that applies only to specific employee groups. For example, if accountants in the organization need specific policy, either separate it from the main manual under a specific heading, or leave it out of the main manual and distribute accounting policy only to accountants. If some policy applies to all employees, it can be incorporated into the code of conduct.

PRIORITIZE POLICY The material describing confidentiality is more important than a description of how to code a time sheet for sick time. Policy should be presented in a way that lets employees see, at a glance, what the most important rules are.

MAKE IT UNDERSTANDABLE First, eliminate the legalese—the only people who like legalese are lawyers. The rest of us like simple English. Second, tell employees what the policy means. Most policy manuals prohibit conflicts of interest, yet few employees can define what a conflict is. Give examples of conflicts and tell employees what a conflict looks like. If people can't tell you what a conflict is, it will be difficult for them to avoid one.

MAKE POLICY COME ALIVE Effective communication occurs not when you send the message, but when people receive it and understand it. Important policy needs to be communicated in short brochures that highlight important rules, and communicated in person in staff meetings, orientation programs, and training sessions.

Codes of Conduct

As stated in Chapter 9, a code of conduct is not a substitute for an ethics program; a code is only the start of an ethics effort. Codes come up frequently because most ethics programs, good or bad, have them. Codes vary substantially in length, content, and readability, but they're generally perceived as the main road map, the ground rules for ethical conduct within the organization.

It's probably fair to say that the longer the code, the fewer employees are likely to read it. On the other hand, the shorter the code, the broader and more abstract the guidelines. Reducing the number of pages represents acknowledgment that the company can't have rules to cover the hundreds of choices employees make every day. Rather, a focus on the values that should guide decision making can help employees make the best decisions in a wide variety of situations.

Many organizations deal with a longer code by dividing the code into parts. The first part provides the broad guiding principles. These are followed by a more detailed section that includes more specific application to cases, answers to commonly asked questions, and reference to more detailed policy manuals. Some organizations create separate booklets, in order to supplement a more general code, for workers in particular functions such as purchasing or human resources management. These can provide details and answers to questions that are likely to arise in that particular type of job, and the individuals in that job are more likely to read those details.

Code content may vary depending on the industry and the degree to which the firm has entered the global marketplace. Specific issues are addressed depending on the industry. Firms in the defense industry carefully outline the guidelines for charging one's time to particular government projects. If the firm is global, the code almost certainly deals with issues such as bribery. We'll talk more about this in the next chapter.

If the code is to be taken seriously, it should be updated regularly and redistributed throughout the organization. For example, at American Express the code is revised every two years and employees are given ethics training with each revision. Frequent communication refers to the code on an ongoing basis. Management and staff groups are conscious of what they call "labeling and linking." They label issues as ethics and compliance issues and refer back to the code. For example, the CEO sent a message regarding a new policy on money laundering and how American Express was responding. He referred to the code in his communication. At American Express, the code requires employees to report violations, and they are subject to discipline if they fail to do so. Because it is a global company with lots of little offices, it is impossible to watch everyone. Therefore, employees are expected to take responsibility for reporting misconduct. The system also empowers lower-level employees who might be asked to do something improper by a supervisor—they know they'll be protected. Every region where the company does business has an ombudsperson office that takes reports of violations. The system is secure and anonymous; the person who reports the violation is completely protected.

Many organizations ask employees to sign a statement acknowledging that they have read the company code and abided by it during the previous year. At GM, employee affirmation of compliance is handled through the intranet using a required electronic signatory process. Opinions differ as to whether such an annual requirement is a wise practice. Some see it as a necessary step that can convince workers that the company is serious about the code and expects it to be followed. Others see such statements as efforts by the organization to cover itself in case of a lawsuit. If workers also see it this way, they may end up with a cynical attitude toward the statement signing and the organization. Care should be taken to make the case that signing such a document is just one of many ways used to emphasize the importance of ethics in the organization.

Communicating Senior Management Commitment to Ethics

In *Corporate Culture and Performance,* Kotter and Heskett[8] pointed to one factor that could turn around a company that was heading in the wrong direction—a strong leader who could communicate the culture. They explained how the top managers of great companies lead.

> Visions and strategies were communicated with words—spoken simply, directly, and often—and with deeds ... they encouraged people to engage in a dialogue with them, not allowing the communication to flow in one direction only. In almost all cases, the leaders became living embodiments of the cultures they desired. The values and practices they wanted infused into their firms were on display in their daily behavior; in the questions they asked at meetings, in how they spent their time, in the decisions they made. These actions gave credibility to their words. The behavior made it clear to others that their speeches were serious. And successes, which seemed to result from that behavior, made it clear that the practices were sensible.

Without the buy-in and active support of senior management, ethics initiatives are doomed. But senior managers don't have a great track record in communicating a vision, ethical or otherwise. In a survey of professional and management employees, respondents revealed a lack of trust in their senior executives.[9] Most said that their company's leaders failed to communicate a "clear understanding of a corporate vision, mission, and goals." They also said that they trust their top management only about 55 percent of the time.[10] We suspect that the number may be even lower today given recent corporate scandals.

Nevertheless, most employees want to hear from senior executives. Another study of 14,250 employees in 17 companies in the United States and Canada found that "62 percent of employees list top executives as their preferred source of information, but only 15 percent say they actually get their company news from this source."[11]

What can senior managers do to establish better communications and more trust with employees? How can they begin to build an organization in which ethics are valued? They can take a look at the advice that Peters and Waterman[12] offered in their classic book, *In Search of Excellence.* "An effective leader must be the master of two ends of the spectrum: ideas at the highest level of abstraction and actions at the most mundane level of detail. The value-shaping leader is concerned, on the one hand, with soaring, lofty visions that will generate excitement and enthusiasm.... On the other hand, it seems the only way to instill enthusiasm is through scores of daily events." With this advice in mind, here are some concrete steps senior managers can take:

- Set high standards and communicate them loudly and repeatedly in public and in private.
- Act swiftly and firmly when someone violates the standards. Be consistent—don't have special rules for special people.

- Insist on complete candor from your direct reports. Tell them that you don't want to be protected from bad news.
- Never, never shoot the messenger.
- Talk to a wide variety of employees on different levels and in different locations. Get out there and find out what's really going on. Don't be satisfied with others' interpretations.
- In a crisis, take responsibility, be accessible, and be honest. Take the high road. If you do, the company will probably pull through the crisis with a minimum of damage. This is why Union Carbide received generally high marks for the handling of the Bhopal crisis (CEO Warren Anderson quickly flew to India) and why Exxon received bad marks for its handling of the *Valdez* oil spill (CEO Lawrence Rawls didn't visit Alaska until three weeks after the incident).
- Finally, put your money where your mouth is—fund and support ethics initiatives. Without supporting systems, most corporate value statements are collections of empty platitudes that only increase organizational cynicism.[13] To develop ethics initiatives, get help from your communications and training professionals. Don't leave your ethics strategy just to the lawyers.

At Merck, the CEO, Ray Gilmartin, is very vocal about the ethics program and very supportive of its efforts. In frequent face-to-face meetings with employees in the U.S. and overseas, he routinely weaves in messages about ethics—that results are important, but how the results are obtained is equally important.

At many firms, the code of conduct is introduced with a message from the senior executive. At UTC, George David, chairman and chief executive officer, introduces their code with the following message:

> Dear UTC Colleague: The subject of this booklet is ethics, and it is a subject about which all of us should have strong and aligned views. I can state mine simply: The employees of UTC must hold themselves to the highest ethical and legal standards of conduct. We must have a spotless, perfect record, period.

The message goes on to introduce the code and the business practices/compliance infrastructure.

At Lockheed Martin, the chairman recently instituted a "Chairman's Award." The award goes to someone who did something exemplary in the area of ethics, something over and above the call of duty, and it is given at the chairman's annual meeting that 250 senior managers attend. Nominations come from these senior leaders, each of whom is expected to nominate someone. The first winner was Ron Covais, a vice president in business development. He was "recognized for demonstrating the highest standards for integrity and ethical business conduct during the bidding phase of a significant new business opportunity with a foreign customer. Ron demonstrated our Corporation's values and set the standards with an international customer and the U.S.

Government by his willingness to walk away from an important contract." Covais had received an inappropriate "request for payment" by a foreign official. Lockheed Martin employees are expected to reject such bribes and Covais did. That, by itself, was considered to be routine and would not have merited the award. But this individual removed Lockheed Martin from the bidding process (and, consequently, walked away from an important contract), reported the problem to senior officials, and worked with both U.S. government officials and the foreign government to have the foreign official removed from the decision-making process. The customer subsequently agreed to conduct a new bidding process on ethical terms. Covais's action and his award were publicized, color photos and all, in "Lockheed Martin Today," the company newspaper that goes to every employee. The other nominees, one from each business unit and from corporate headquarters, were also named in the story. And, every top corporate executive witnessed the chairman giving the award. Think about the impact of such an event on the ethical culture. Every senior leader must expend effort each year to find examples of exemplary ethical conduct. The award ceremony itself is exactly the kind of "ritual" that helps to create an ethical culture. And the stories become part of the organization's cultural lore, the impact growing as the stories accumulate over time. This impact is particularly important to a company like Lockheed Martin that has had scandal in its past. Misconduct by Lockheed Martin's predecessor contributed to the passing of the anti-bribery Foreign Corrupt Practices Act (discussed in Chapter 11). It has become very important to the senior leadership of the firm to counteract any perception of the organization as unethical.

ETHICS TRAINING PROGRAMS Values statements, policy manuals, and conduct codes aren't enough. Organizations that are serious about ethics distribute these materials widely and then provide training in their meaning and application. Effective training programs are ongoing efforts to teach everyone from new recruits to high-level managers. We discussed in Chapter 1 whether ethics can be taught and we hope that, by now, you're quite convinced that it can. Ethics in organizations is about awareness of ethical issues and knowledge of appropriate conduct, and these can and must be taught to employees at all levels.

Training should be designed to suit the group of individuals being trained. A new employee needs different training from a manager who has been with the firm for ten years. An assembly-line worker might require only an hour of training, with regular refresher sessions, whereas a manager might require several days of training that address a variety of issues. Further, training needs to be based upon the goals of the program. Is the training supposed to increase awareness of ethical issues, convey knowledge of laws and policies, change attitudes or behaviors? Finally, ethics training need not be and probably should not be solely the province of the ethics office. Ethics training should be incorporated into leadership development and other programs so that it becomes integrated more fully into the culture of the organization.

TRAINING NEW RECRUITS Many firms provide ethics training to new recruits through new employee orientation. For example, every new Lockheed Martin employee gets several hours of training on ethical and legal issues as part of a 1–2 day training program for new employees. This training comes quite early and may be difficult to absorb because the new employee is given so much new information all at one time. The firm is working on ways to reinforce that training over time.

New consultants who are hired to work for Mercer HR Consulting are introduced to the firm's professional standards and ethics cases in a formal orientation program shortly after they are hired. Then, they attend quarterly training sessions in professional standards that include confidentiality, conflicts of interest, financial accountability, and the importance of peer review (a crucial practice in the consulting industry.) These training sessions are not conducted by ethics officers, but by the firm's senior consultants, who use customized videos and group discussion to introduce new hires and existing employees to common ethical issues and explain the firm's clear process for raising issues and getting help.

TRAINING EXISTING EMPLOYEES Training is also provided to existing employees and takes a variety of forms. Some companies provide a basic ethics training module to all employees. For example, every employee (125,000) at Lockheed Martin receives one hour of annual ethics awareness training. This training focuses on the firm's values and how those can and should be applied to one's work. Each year, the ethics office staff is challenged to make the training different and memorable—something that employees will talk with each other about after they leave the training session. Last year's training was entitled "Perspectives" and focused on the role of different perspectives in decision making. The goal is to get employees to recognize the value of considering the perspectives of all involved in a situation. Employees in a training session were divided into 3 or 4 teams of 3–6 individuals and given the ethics code. The session began with a video of the CEO saying, "I'm doing this training myself with my people and your manager will conduct yours." Each team then received the same ethical dilemma and a script that provided a different individual's perspective on the scenario. For example, one team might play the role of a plant manager, another a worker on the plant floor. A decision-making team listened to the perspectives as they were represented by the other teams and then had to decide what to do—should we delay shipment of a product or send it now and not do additional testing? The leader was given a facilitator's guide that provided suggested answers tied to company polices and the ethics code. This annual ethics awareness training has become integral to the Lockheed Martin culture. People expect it and look forward to what the ethics staff will create each year. The limitation of this year's training is that teams can get through only a few scenarios in a single training session. But the ethics office staff has created 25 scenarios and is making them available to managers for use in regular staff meetings.

In addition, Lockheed Martin is experimenting on the factory floor with PDA-based training. The business unit invests in the PDA (personal digital assistant) while the ethics group provides the content. The PDA can be passed around from workstation to work station, making it easier for factory employees to get the training they need. Five topics are mandatory for all employees (for example, diversity and a drug-free workplace) and others are specific to the job (for example, procurement and technical topics). The advantage is that thousands of employees can be trained relatively quickly and efficiently. But evaluation of this approach has not yet been completed.

Finally, based on information gleaned from a recent employee survey, Lockheed Martin is creating a new training program that focuses on front-line supervisors and offers them a toolkit for dealing with an employee who raises ethical concerns based on real-life scenarios. This is being incorporated into a broader leadership training program. Currently, about 600 people get this training a year. Since the company has 20,000 managers, they are working on ways to get this type of training to many more supervisors.

USAA has used an approach to training employees called "facilitated dialogue." The approach is used in groups sized from 12–15 people to groups as large as 30–50 (although smaller groups are preferred). In these training sessions, employees are first given a virtual tour of the company's intranet Web site and an introduction to the code of conduct. Then, participants are given customized scenarios that are relevant to their own work area. The groups discuss each scenario and refer back to the Web site when they have questions. The purpose is to familiarize them with the Web site and how it can be used to answer questions that arise in their work, as well as to promote other ethics resources.

General Motors recently launched a new Web-based interactive training program designed to raise employees' consciousness about its "Winning with Integrity Program." Every salaried employee in the U.S.—about 43,000 employees—is required to take this training. Each of about ten one-hour modules is focused on an individual topic such as workplace harassment. The training can be completed at home, but employees are given time to complete the training at work. Post-tests are included and employees must work with the module until they answer all of the questions correctly. The program also provides lots of links to related information on the Web site. The next step will be to expand the training to non-U.S. sites, but this will involve a lot of work, including translation and consideration of cultural issues.

TOP MANAGEMENT INVOLVEMENT IN TRAINING When organizations conduct ethics training for the first time, many of them begin the training at the top of the organization. "Cascading" is a term frequently used to describe ethics initiatives that begin at the top of the organization and work their way down, level-by-level. This technique is often used because of the importance of leadership to the credibility of ethics training. Each leader trains his or her direct reports, modeling the expected training behavior and the necessary commitment to integrity.

LOCAL MANAGEMENT INVOLVEMENT IN TRAINING Many organizations recommend having local management conduct the ethics training, using common everyday ethical dilemmas as the basis for discussion. Training sessions are thought to be more useful and effective if they address real ethical issues that people face every day in their own work setting. Examples of calls that have come in to the ethics office can be used as the basis for training. Employees make ethical decisions every day. Anybody who reports the time that they work or decides how to divide their time across different government contracts, or decides whether they are going to engage in some kind of an outside business activity that might be in conflict with their job, or has to decide what to tell a customer about a delayed order, is making an ethical decision. Using common everyday issues in training gives employees a feeling of comfort that the issue they've faced has faced others and that they're not some screwball who is worrying about something that doesn't matter.

At Tenet Healthcare, the ethics office has a commitment to transmitting the firm's values in a number of ways, but especially through orientation and ethics training sessions. Consider this—when Tenet made its first large acquisition, the firm added 35,000 new employees and all went through the two-hour orientation program in 120 days. In addition, an annual ethics refresher is held for each employee. What makes these unique is that they are conducted in face-to-face sessions of 30–40 individuals by 115 ethics facilitators drawn from around the company. The facilitators are trained in "train-the-trainer" conferences held twice each year. The facilitators conduct these refresher sessions in hospitals other than their own. They are given materials to use such as video vignettes, discussion guides, and policy and procedure statements. New materials are created each year to keep the program fresh. The vignettes are selected from real cases, preferably those that represent hot issues. For example, last year, the focus was on a single topic—retaliation/retribution for calling the Ethics Action Line. A video vignette was shown and discussed. Attendees were told how the case was handled. The session ended with a video message from the chairman reiterating his policy of "zero tolerance" for retaliation. The program was a big hit. Surprisingly, the ethics facilitators are provided no extra pay for this work beyond their regular salaries, although they are given release time supported by the office of the president. Even more surprising, there has been little turnover in the ethics facilitator ranks. These people become serious advocates of the ethics program and remain impressed that the company devotes so many resources to it. These sessions also make a statement about the values of the firm when the hospital CEO and one of the top three or four managers introduces each ethics class and explains why it is viewed as valuable to the hospital.

At USAA, the ethics office held a strategic planning conference with 45 ethics facilitators and other invited guests from across the enterprise. Modeled on a technique known as "Appreciative Inquiry" (developed by David Cooperrider and Suresh Srivastva at Case Western's Weatherhead School of Management) the session asked the participants to pair up, and to think about and share positive, memorable, peak ethics experiences they have had in their lives with their interview partner. Then, in groups, they thought about the conditions under which these kinds of peak experiences might happen more regularly. Finally, they considered what USAA might do to make such experiences even more the norm in the organization than they are today. Participants found the focus on the positive (rather than problems and deficiencies) particularly energizing. And their discussions led to some very specific suggestions that have been implemented. For example, the Agent Dewright idea discussed above emerged from this session.

To be effective, ethics training must be refreshed regularly. This doesn't necessarily have to be done in formal classroom training sessions. But regular updates are important for a variety of reasons: (1) people forget; (2) ethical issues change with changes in law, technology, and so on; and (3) refreshers send the signal that the organization is constantly thinking about ethics—it isn't a one-shot deal.

A TRAINING MODEL: THE ETHICS GAME A powerful example of how to communicate a corporate ethics message is through an ethics game. As mentioned in Chapter 1, Katherine Nelson, coauthor of this book, created the first corporate ethics game, "The Work Ethic: An Exercise in Integrity" when she was head of human resources communications at Citicorp in the late 1980s.

The game works like this: A group of employees is divided into teams; a facilitator then positions the exercise with the following messages:

> "We're playing a game about ethics because we want to make sure we get your attention."
>
> "We want to make sure you know integrity is important here."
>
> "This is an opportunity for you to practice making ethical decisions in a risk-free environment."
>
> "We're doing this to give you an overview of corporate policy and how things are done here."
>
> "We're also going to outline all of the resources available to you if you think you'd like some help or advice if you're faced with an ethical dilemma."

The facilitator presents the teams with a series of ethical dilemmas related to such topics as sexual harassment, reporting ethical concerns, responsibilities of customers, the need for confidentiality, and conflicts of interest. The ethical dilemmas are written so that they do not have a clear right answer.

For each issue, the teams take a few minutes to discuss what they think the appropriate action would be. Then, based on a consensus among team members, they choose one of four possible courses of action. Once the teams choose, the facilitator plays devil's advocate and questions the entire group on why they voted the way they did. The discussion can get very heated with participants and teams loudly defending their positions. The facilitator then reveals the scores for each course of action (scores are predetermined, preferably by the management of the organization where the game is being played). If the participants disagree with the scores, they can appeal them to an appeals board of senior managers. Again, the discussions get quite impassioned and lively. And the competition for the best scores keeps interest high.

The senior management appeals board is one of the most important aspects of the ethics game. The very presence of senior managers for 90 minutes or so sends a strong message that integrity and ethics must be important in this company, or all these executives wouldn't be spending so much time talking with employees about it. In addition, when discussing an appeal, the appeals board often communicates messages about company standards and expectations better than anything else. Along the way, employees can see how senior managers work through an ethical dilemma and what factors they consider important in making decisions.

Groups can disagree with the scoring of a question and appeal to these senior managers who have the power to change scores if they're convinced. This somehow "stamps" participating managers as approachable. Managers who participate in appeals boards frequently report a marked increase in the number of employees seeking them out and asking for advice. One manager described how he had been stopped in hallways, rest rooms, cafeterias, and even on the street to be asked advice by employees who had seen him as a judge on an ethics game appeals board. Most companies would do just about anything to have their employees seek advice from managers on ethical issues.

Senior managers can also learn a lot from participating in the game. It provides an opportunity for employees to raise issues directly to management. In one session, several male managers were made aware of how offensive young female trainees found any kind of sexual stereotyping. The young women were so determined to let management know how strongly they felt on this issue that the discussion continued at a reception after the game had officially ended.

Since the game usually raises more questions than it answers, it's crucial to have a debriefing. At the end of the game, the facilitator gives advice on how to solve ethical dilemmas and outlines the resources that are available to help people if they find themselves in need of advice.

The ethics game meets many communication and training goals, but it's especially effective in raising awareness, creating a dialogue, and describing expected dilemmas and how employees might handle them. However, in order for an ethics program to be effective over the long term, training and communications should continue over time. A game is an excellent beginning and can be used repeatedly with different dilemmas. However, it can't exist in a vacuum or be all things to all people. It needs to be part of an integrated ethics program with other media and complementary messages.

Although some may view an ethics game as heresy, those who have seen these training programs in action are quickly convinced of their effectiveness. Other companies have developed their own versions of the game and have used them successfully. For example, years ago, Lockheed Martin developed an ethics game modeled after the Citicorp game, but with a twist. At the time, the company received permission from Scott Adams, author of the Dilbert cartoons (popular with employees), to use the Dilbert character in their game. Then Chairman of the Board Norm Augustine appeared with Dilbert in an introductory video, and the game included a humorous "Dogbert answer" to each ethical question.

THE NORTHROP GRUMMAN "WHEN THINGS WENT WRONG" VIDEO

Northrop Corporation (now Northrop Grumman Corporation) surprised a lot of people when it created a case study called "When Things Went Wrong," which was about a devastating incident that took place in the late 1980s at a small 30-person Northrop site in Pomona, California. At the time, Northrop had about 46,000 employees. In the company's own words, "The incident shook the company to its roots and damaged its reputation." Because of testing irregularities, the facility was closed, the manager and engineer connected to the incident were fired and imprisoned, the division to which the facility reported was suspended from government contracting for two years, the company paid a $17 million fine, and it incurred legal and business costs in the many millions.

The company decided, however, that this painful incident could be used in a positive way to raise the ethical awareness and sensitivity of all Northrop employees. It also decided that the use of the case study would make it difficult for Northrop employees to claim that "it can't happen here." So the company created a videotape. In frank interviews, the CEO, Department of Defense representatives (the customer), and the managers of the parent division discussed the facts and the causes of the incident. These causes included an interplay of both individual and organizational factors. The video then identified what employees and the organization could do to prevent a recurrence.

In the early 1990s, thousands of employees viewed and discussed the video with their managers and co-workers. The response was overwhelmingly positive. "It helped heighten everyone's awareness of just what is needed from us as individuals when serious problems arise," one employee commented. This type of openness about ethical problems is rare. But it can be very healthy because it makes a clear symbolic statement that the company is willing to reflect on itself, confront mistakes openly, and fix the problems.

Since the early 1990s, Northrop has grown and continues to grow through mergers and acquisitions. Recognizing the relevance of the video's message, the company recently decided to begin using it again. It has been shown to all vice presidents to generate interest at a high level throughout the organization and has been shown to the company's business conduct officers. More showings are scheduled because its message about the importance of emphasizing ethical behavior and the consequences of ethical failure are as relevant today as they were ten years ago.

Formal and Informal Systems to Resolve Questions and Report Ethical Concerns

An organization with a strong ethical culture will be one where employees feel free to speak openly about ethical issues, question authority figures, and report concerns, and where managers are approachable and listen to their people. This may be the most important thing an organization can do to open up the communication lines and set up an environment of candor. Make sure people feel that they can discuss their opinions, their ideas, and their thoughts openly. Most important, set up an environment where people feel that they can sincerely bring up and resolve problems without being embarrassed or without fear of retribution. The first time you shoot the messenger who brings you bad news, you've taken the first step towards squelching ethics in the organization. News of the "dead messenger" will spread like wildfire on your organization's grapevine.

Although most organizations encourage employees to bring their concerns to their immediate supervisor first, employees sometimes want to ask a question anonymously, or they may have a concern about their supervisor's behavior. Also, the U.S. Sentencing Guidelines require that organizations "take reasonable steps to achieve compliance with written standards through monitoring, auditing, and other systems designed to detect criminal conduct, including a reporting system free of retribution to employees who report criminal conduct." As a result, many firms have established a more formal system for raising concerns. This generally takes the form of a telephone line employees can call to ask for help in resolving an ethical dilemma or to report an ethical problem or behavior they've observed in the organization. A number of names have emerged for these—"Communication Lines," "Guideline," "Open Line," "Helpline," "Hotline," "Ethics Action Line." These phone lines generally ring in the ethics office if there is one. For example, at Lockheed Martin, the Helpline is available 12 hours per day and rings centrally in the ethics office. Some large organizations provide separate reporting lines for each business unit. In a few firms, the line actually rings on the chairman's desk. Other firms have hired an outside consulting firm or law firm to take the calls at a toll-free number and then transfer the information to the company.[14] That's especially true in many global firms where a call can come at any time of the day or night because of time zone differences.

We believe that, where possible, it's best for ethics office staff to talk with callers directly because, as ethics office staff, they need to be in touch with what's going on in the organization. If they delegate the task, they lose the tone and perspective of the callers. For example, the nonverbal clues that come through on the phone can easily get lost in a paper report. One way to handle this is to answer calls during business hours and then contract with an outside firm for after-hours capability. Around-the-clock answering capability is essential for a global business. The ethics office can explain the decision to hire an outside contractor to employees as its solution to handling calls from around the globe. Organizations that have experience with telephone reporting lines find that a large majority of the calls represent requests for clarification. The individual says, "Here's what I want to do. Is it okay? Does it follow procedure?" The majority of calls in many organizations represent human resource-related issues such as fairness concerns. Some are relatively routine. But occasionally calls come in that represent serious breaches of the code of conduct or even illegal conduct. Managing these lines is no small feat. Tenet Healthcare's Ethics Action Line receives 5,000 to 6,000 calls per year.

One concern often raised about these reporting lines is that individuals will make invalid reports—"tattling" on people they don't like. But that's not the experience of the ethics officers we interviewed. Most people call about valid issues. Although their motives may not always be noble, the content is usually correct. Most of the people who use the communication line are using it because they sincerely have a question or concern about something or a question about something that they think is wrong. That's one reason why confidentiality is so important within the entire reporting and investigative system. The identity of both the reporter and the alleged violator must be protected throughout the process. The alleged violator must be protected because allegations can result from simple misunderstandings. The reporter must be protected from any retaliation from the accused.

Another relevant question concerns how to interpret the meaning of the number of calls and letters. Obviously, if an organization institutes and promotes an easy way to ask questions, express concerns, and report violations, the number of calls should increase dramatically. Does this mean that there are more ethical problems? Probably not. The executives who run these programs generally interpret such increases as evidence that their programs are working. However, in an ideal world, the ethics office should aim to put itself out of business. In other words, ethical conduct should become so institutionalized that there would be no reason for people to call. They would handle issues locally, with their managers. Like the Maytag repairman, the ethics officer would have a very boring job. On the other hand, a quiet telephone may also signal a number of other positive or negative conditions:

- Lack of concern or recognition of ethical problems (negative)
- An intimidating environment where people fear retribution (negative)
- Good problem solving at the local level (positive)
- No one knowing the ethics office exists (negative)

Ultimately, it is up to the ethics office to devise ways to determine what the numbers and changes in the numbers mean.

At USAA, Earnie Broughton monitors the Helpline for information about program effectiveness. He prefers to see a relatively low and stable level of allegations of misconduct and a higher level of advisory questions. That means that people are calling the Helpline for advice—a good thing. The question remaining is whether employees are willing to use the resources that are made available to them. USAA conducts an annual Internet survey of randomly selected employees in order to determine their awareness of the ethics office and its services, and their willingness to use those services—and if they are not aware or willing, why not.

Confidentiality and protection of reporters remains an important issue. Some firms use outside individuals often called "ombudspersons" who may answer the reporting line, provide information, investigate complaints, serve in an alternative dispute resolution role, and report problems to a corporate compliance or audit committee while maintaining the confidentiality of the reporter.[15]

Whether a telephone line, an ombudsperson, or some other formal procedure is most appropriate for a particular corporate culture, the important thing is to have some way for employees to raise issues without fear of retribution. If there's no way for employees to raise issues without such fear, the first time an executive hears about a problem may be from a district attorney, a regulator, or a newspaper reporter.

Finally, each of the firms we talked with has a system for investigating reports of misconduct. These are multi-stage processes that can be quite complex depending upon the seriousness of the allegation. Obviously, facts must be gathered to determine whether the allegation can be verified. Confidentiality must be maintained throughout these investigations, and they must be coordinated with other parts of the organization such as the legal, audit, security, or human resources department depending upon the problem. Then, depending upon a thorough analysis of the findings, recommendations must be made and actions taken to discipline employees and/or correct systemic problems in the organization.

USING THE REWARD SYSTEM TO REINFORCE THE ETHICS MESSAGE

Recall from Chapter 9 that the reward system is key to alignment in an ethical culture. At Lockheed Martin, the Performance Recognition System instituted in 2002 rates employees not just on objectives of the job such as increased sales or profits.

Employees are also rated on "how you got there." This part of performance evaluation is tied to the corporation's values: ethics, excellence, can do, integrity, people, and teamwork. Each of these attributes is explicitly defined. For example, *ethics* is defined as "Is honest and forthright. Embraces truthfulness. Knows regulations, rules, policies, and compliance requirements, and actively demonstrates compliance. 'Always does the right thing.'" *Integrity* is defined as "Acts with integrity. 'Walks the talk.' Is reliable, and holds self accountable for actions and results. Is a good steward of Lockheed Martin resources. Credits others' contributions as appropriate." *People* is defined as "Treats others with respect and dignity. Values and encourages diverse perspectives. Consistently professional in all dealings with others, and demonstrates good interpersonal skills. Builds trust through interactions. Partners with others in setting priorities, solving problems, and improving quality. Demonstrates continuous, consistent, and clear communications. Actively listens." Managers are asked to provide specific behavioral examples of each attribute. They are required to base their salary increase recommendations on these attributes (along with bottom-line performance expectations) and to put those recommendations in writing.

At Tenet Healthcare, an "ethics modifier" has been a formal part of the annual incentive plan for about five years. All bonus-eligible managers (about 1,000 people) are reviewed by a subgroup of the Corporate Integrity Committee twice each year for their ethics and compliance behavior (this committee meets quarterly to review ethics/compliance issues and includes the chief operating officer, chief corporate officer, senior vice president for ethics, general counsel, senior vice president of audit, senior vice president of patient financial systems, vice president of quality management, executive vice president of human resources, and the divisional executive vice presidents). Each individual is discussed, and managers who the subgroup believes have "wavered off the ethical plane" can have their annual bonus adjusted downward between 5 and 25 percent as a result. They are given warnings at their mid-year evaluations so that they have an opportunity to fix problems that have been identified. Those who don't make adjustments are docked—and managers have had their bonuses docked for this reason every year that the program has been in existence. Those who have demonstrated extraordinary ethical courage or proactive ethical behavior can have their bonus adjusted up by a similar amount. For example, a CEO made a tough decision to remove a very successful surgeon from the medical staff because of an ethical issue. The decision to remove the surgeon negatively affected the hospital's bottom-line performance because the surgeon was a heavy admitter of patients. Therefore, the CEO's bonus (tied to bottom-line hospital performance) was negatively affected by his ethical decision. The committee saw this as courageous and the right thing to do, even though not in his personal interest. He was awarded about a 20 percent increase in his bonus by the committee. The committee also gives individuals commendation letters for their personnel files. Over the years of the program, the balance has shifted from more downward modifiers because of ethical problems to more positive modifiers because of proactive or courageous behavior.

At Otis Elevator Co. (a subsidiary of United Technologies Corporation), Stephen Paige, then president and now UTC's vice chairman and chief financial officer, wrote a letter to employees making it clear that Otis seriously disciplines breaches of integrity. In his words:

> Our company is making substantial changes in the way we do business. I am writing today to highlight what has not changed, and never will change: our commitment to the highest ethical standards and business practices.
>
> We know that Otis employees are honest, mature, independent, and scrupulous in their conduct at work. We know that Otis employees care about ethics and our company's reputation. And we know that employees support sanctions for any colleague whose behavior shows he or she does not hold these fundamental Otis values.
>
> Our ethics program grows out of this knowledge. We provide training and communications programs to all employees in our Code of Ethics, which offers guidance in how to behave in specific business situations. Through our worldwide network of business practices officers (BPOs), we also provide expert advice to employees who have questions or who face ethical dilemmas.
>
> But for those few who do not care about ethics; who think they can cut corners; who violate the law, our policies or our standards, there is no place in Otis. To our regret, we have had to terminate the employment of nearly a dozen colleagues this year alone for violations of our Code of Ethics—a record that is simply unacceptable. Unlawful or unethical conduct can only harm our company and we will take whatever actions are necessary to prevent that from happening.
>
> Our actions reflect our fundamental belief: Otis would rather lose business than compromise our standards of conduct.
>
> Please take this opportunity to refresh your knowledge of our Code of Ethics, and to recommit yourself to its guidelines and principles. We have so much to be proud of at Otis, and our reputation as an ethical company stands in the first rank of our accomplishments. We are determined to protect this priceless asset.
>
> Thank you for your continued support.

This letter confirms the company's willingness to take firm action to uphold standards through discipline when necessary, and is likely welcomed by the company's many ethical employees (see Chapter 7 for information about the appropriate use of discipline).

EVALUATING THE ETHICS PROGRAM

Many organizations have committed significant resources to their ethics efforts—hiring high-level executives, developing values statements and codes, designing and implementing training programs, and more. Few organizations, however, have systematically evaluated these efforts because doing so presents many challenges. For example, as suggested earlier, more calls to the telephone line can mean different things and can be interpreted in a variety of ways. And asking employees at an ethics training program whether they "liked" it or not doesn't tell you much about the quality of the ethics program. Many employees will respond affirmatively just because they "liked" the idea of a few hours or a day away from the office. Whether or not they "liked" it should be secondary. The most important question should be, is the program accomplishing its goals?

Otis has gone the extra mile in the area of evaluation. Otis has over a million elevators in operation in more than 200 countries around the world! You may not have thought much about it, but all of us depend on the integrity of a company that provides many of the elevators we ride daily. As part of a toolkit provided to each of its companies, Otis requires a self-assessment process that involves regular evaluations of program effectiveness including training, communication, work practices reviews, instances of misconduct, corrective actions, reports and records. Companies are also asked to identify strengths and weaknesses of their programs and to implement changes to overcome weaknesses. Finally, they are asked to share their successes, program strengths, and lessons learned with the rest of Otis.

Organizations that are members of the Defense Industry Initiative are often at the forefront on evaluation because the DII asks each of its member organizations each year to certify that the firm is complying with the six DII principles. These self-certifications are available to all members, and a report is published and sent to the U.S. Congress annually.

Surveys

Surveys are probably the most common approach to evaluation. Many organizations already conduct regular employee attitude surveys; some have added ethics to the list of survey topics and some conduct separate ethics surveys. Surveys can target knowledge, attitudes, skills, and behaviors. For example, if ethics training has been recently required of all employees, surveys can evaluate the extent to which employees understand the company's expectations and standards. Baseline data can be collected before ethics training is begun, and then several months after it's completed to analyze whether positive change has occurred. Surveys can help to evaluate employees' skill at recognizing and resolving ethical issues, and they can measure the extent to which employees observe unethical conduct in the organization. Finally, attitudes toward ethics management programs and processes can be evaluated. It's important to survey regularly so that changes and progress can be evaluated. A final suggestion about surveys—don't ask questions if you're not willing to accept the answer. Employees will expect action based upon survey results. If you've asked them to take the time to complete a survey, you should communicate the results and planned action.

The most famous ethics-related survey is likely Johnson & Johnson's credo survey. Then-chairman James Burke had been on the board of IBM Corporation in the 1980s and became impressed with IBM's employee survey program. He decided that one way to keep the Johnson & Johnson credo alive would be to survey employees about how the company was doing relative to the credo. The survey went through a number of iterations after being tested on employees at a variety of locations. The first survey was conducted in the United States in 1986–1987. The first international survey was conducted the following year. The first part of the survey contains 118 items and takes about 25 minutes to complete. It asks employees to rate things like the company's "customer orientation" on five-point scales. The second section is open-ended for written comments. One of the findings has been the impact of top leadership and corporate culture on survey results. For example, former Chairman Burke had emphasized the customer above all. President David Clare emphasized safety first. In an analysis of the survey results, ratings on these two survey dimensions were highest. Most of all, the survey is viewed as a way to keep the credo alive, a way of "closing the loop on this thing called the Credo."[16]

Lockheed Martin conducts an employee survey every two years so that the firm can gauge whether ethical principles are being applied, whether employees have observed wrongdoing, and, if so, whether they have reported it. The survey also allows the firm to assess the impact of ethics programs, and areas in need of attention. All 125,000 employees are surveyed every two years in a voluntary survey. The participation rate has increased each survey period and is now about 50 percent. Results of the survey are published in the company newspaper in great detail and are certified by the Ethics Resource Center, a not-for-profit consulting firm that conducts the survey for the company. In 2001, the company reported an analysis of surveys from 61,000 employees. The 2001 survey was available online, making it easy to complete. Paper copies were sent to employees without e-mail addresses. Most results were positive and showed improvements over previous surveys. For example, a high percentage of employees reported that they know what constitutes ethical business conduct, how to obtain guidance on ethical issues, and how to report misconduct. However, a few areas of concern were noted and those are being addressed.

On top of its annual survey, Lockheed Martin's internal audit department conducts an annual review of the ethics office and its operations, reporting its findings to senior management. That serves to keep the ethics program staff on its toes.

VALUES OR COMPLIANCE APPROACHES

Formal corporate ethics initiatives can be categorized as emphasizing either a values or compliance approach to managing ethics. The values approach is proactive and aspirational. It emphasizes expected behavior and an effort to achieve high standards represented by the spirit of the law and organizational values. It relies on such techniques as leader communication and role modeling to affirm the organization's commitment to its stated ethical values and goals. Employees learn that these are not empty words, but words that organizational leaders believe and live by. Ethics becomes a point of pride in the organization. "We're so good we don't have to cheat!" The response to a values-oriented program is generally good until violations occur. Then, employees expect that commitment to be backed up with sanctions against the violator(s).

With a compliance emphasis, the focus is more on required behavior—obeying the letter of the law rather than aspiring to lofty ethical principles. Disciplinary procedures for violators are also important to compliance efforts. Many organizations that are motivated by the U.S. Sentencing Guidelines mandate a compliance approach. Employees are told that compliance with the law is essential and that employees who break the law will be punished. The danger with a compliance-only focus is the possibility that employees will believe anything goes as long as there isn't a rule against it, or that the company is interested only in protecting itself, not in helping them.

An effective program should have both values and compliance components. By themselves, abstract values statements can appear hypocritical to employees. "Management makes these lofty statements, but they don't tell us what we should do." Values must be translated into rules for behavior, and, to give the rules meaning, violators must be disciplined. Employees welcome information that reduces ambiguity about what they can and can't do. And if enforcement is applied consistently across all organizational levels, they are likely to perceive the system as fair and just.

On the other hand, employees often view a strictly compliance-oriented program with cynicism. Without a strong values base, compliance programs seem to focus on catching employees doing something wrong rather than on aspiring to do things right. Employees translate this emphasis into mistrust and a "CYA" approach. Either "the organization doesn't trust its employees," or "the organization is just out to protect its own behind." The best programs aim to focus on aspiring to a set of values first and foremost, supported by just and fair enforcement of the rules.

At American Express, the emphasis is on legal compliance because, as a financial services firm, compliance with the law is heavily tied to the brand and its image as "the world's most respected and valued service brand." There are 150 employees who focus on legal compliance full time, and lots of other people have compliance as part of their jobs. Although it is considered a compliance program, it works with the firm's values and both are tied together through the code of conduct.

At Merck, development of a formal ethics program was driven by its longstanding values-based culture. Interestingly, Merck did not have a formal ethics code until 1999. In rolling out the code initiative, the firm was careful to position it as simply a continuation of the good things the company was already doing. They also worked hard to get participation and buy-in through focus groups and surveys. This is typical of values-based programs where employee buy-in and support are essential.

Tenet Healthcare operates in the highly regulated hospital industry, where compliance with laws and regulations is very important. Therefore, at Tenet, legal compliance is essential. The compliance program is separate from the ethics program and focuses on legal/regulatory issues such as contracts, billing, and federal payer programs, conducting its own web-based training on these issues. The ethics program focuses more on values. Recent events suggest that the distinction between ethics and compliance may be problematic and the connection between the two needs strengthening. As this book went to press, Tenet Healthcare was addressing accusations and federal investigations on two fronts. First, the firm has admitted that it achieved huge profits from "aggressive Medicare billing" by making use of a loophole in the Medicare law. The firm apparently adhered to the letter of the law rather than the spirit of the law in this case, and its compensation system has been targeted for scrutiny. Hospital CEO bonuses were tied largely to "exceeding profit and revenue growth targets," accounting for half of all hospital CEO compensation in 2001. In the first quarter of 2003, these "outlier" Medicare payments dropped to $40 million from $191 million in the same period in 2002.[17] In addition, Tenet was highlighted in a *60 Minutes* segment alleging that two doctors with privileges at a Tenet-owned hospital in California were performing unnecessary coronary bypass surgeries. Physicians are not Tenet employees, but the hospitals grant them the privilege to practice and can influence them through compensation agreements. The physicians involved in the investigation have lost their privileges and the hospital has stopped performing cardiac surgeries until new doctors can be brought in. Multiple lawsuits have been filed against the hospital and more are likely. Senior management has warned that earnings for the rest of 2003 will be lower than expected. The firm's chairman and CEO, Jeffrey Barbakow, resigned in May 2003.[18] Other senior officers have also resigned or retired. Tenet stock has dropped precipitously in response to the scandals. Executives are now focused on a "top-to-bottom review of pricing, compensation, and ethics."[19]

GLOBALIZING AN ETHICS PROGRAM

In the next chapter, we will talk about business ethics in a global environment. What sets United Technologies Corporation (UTC) apart is the extent to which its ethics and compliance efforts are truly global. Recall that United Technologies has over 150,000 employees, more than half outside the United States in 180 countries. Imagine how difficult it must be to design systems and programs to effectively reach such a wide audience across multiple cultures. UTC's program rests on three coordinated efforts: the Ombuds program, the DIALOG program, and a worldwide business practices organization.

The Ombuds program at UTC offers employees a series of toll free numbers (one for each of the five business unit ombudspersons, and one for the corporate ombudsman's office) worldwide that are answered by UTC ombudspersons. UTC ombudspersons use an outside language interpreter service to help when employees call using a language unfamiliar to the ombudsperson. The ombudsperson's job is to serve as a neutral point of contact for employees who have a concern. Employees who call one of the toll-free numbers can be completely anonymous to the organization, a commitment the company goes to great lengths to keep. For example, an assistant to a senior business-unit executive called with concerns about expense report behavior. If investigated openly, the source of the information would have been identifiable. Instead, the company chose to audit all expense reports of people at the same level. In that way, they protected the reporter's identity. They found the problem, fired the executive, and no one was the wiser. However, ombudspersons do not conduct investigations. If the issue requires investigation or intervention, it is turned over to people in other areas (e.g., human resources, business practices) for further action. Ultimately, the ombudsperson reviews the answer from the company. If it doesn't completely and fairly address all of the issues raised by the employee, it goes back to management with the suggestion that it be fixed.

The written DIALOG Program is also a global program. Postage-paid forms are available in every UTC facility. Employees are invited to comment, complain, compliment, or question. Since its inception in 1986, the firm has received about 60,000 completed forms. In the early years of the program, most came from North American locations, but the number from overseas locations has been growing. These represent questions about benefits, working conditions, and other human resources issues. But occasionally, more serious issues are reported through the system: for example, sexual harassment or allegations of fraud or other financial abuse. A designated administrator at each unit receives these, removes identifying information, and sends the messages to the appropriate management person for a response. The goal is to have a response from management within 14 days. The response is then sent to the employee. UTC has launched a similar Internet-based program that allows employees to submit inquiries via an encrypted site. The inquiry is accessible only to DIALOG administrators, who edit the inquiry and send it to management for response. Only the employee and the ombudsperson or eDIALOG coordinator who processes the inquiry have access to the file.

The business practices organization is led by Patrick Gnazzo, a lawyer who was chief trial attorney for the U.S. Navy, and then held a variety of significant positions at UTC before becoming vice president for business practices in the mid-1990s. Gnazzo is one of the top executives in the company. He reports to the senior vice president and general counsel, as well as to the audit committee of the board of directors with whom he meets at least twice a year. Gnazzo supervises a network of senior business practice officers at each business unit larger than about 300 employees. Although he doesn't appoint these individuals, he can veto appointments. Most have at least several years of experience in the company and have a familiarity with internal controls and the company culture. They are considered high potential people who generally come from staff functions such as finance or quality assurance. Good communication skills are considered a must for business practices staff, along with the ability to pick up the ball and run with it when a problem arises. These people are trained in regional training programs led by Gnazzo and his staff. For example, a recent regional training brought about 100 business practices officers together in Singapore. These individuals turn over about every two years, a rate that is considered to be both a boon and a bane. It's a boon because these individuals move on to other senior positions in the firm and they take their business practices training and experience with them, essentially becoming champions for the business practices organization in their new senior management roles. The bane is that training new people is a constant challenge.

The business practices unit manages UTC's Code of Ethics (in place since 1990), a companion Policy Statement on doing business with the U.S. Government, and the corporate policy manual. The goal is to keep the number of policies from spiraling out of control. Anyone who drafts a new policy must explain why it's needed. The culture is built upon the assumption that the firm hires people who can exercise good judgment and don't need a policy to cover everything. The Code applies to UTC employees worldwide and includes a section entitled "Worldwide Communities" that specifically addresses ethical issues relating to doing business abroad. But the Code is not ethnocentric, allowing some adaptation to the cultural mores of different cultures. However, it is also made clear that this flexibility does not permit violations of U.S. or local laws. Employees are encouraged to consult with the business practices/compliance officer in their unit for clarification. The business practices unit conducts between 150 and 200 investigations each year and aims to close cases within the calendar year if possible. Serious allegations about criminal behavior are investigated, and, if warranted, referred to the government for action.

CONCLUSION

This chapter has offered specifics about how ethics is managed in large business organizations. Large businesses that are committed to ethics are likely to have formal ethics management systems such as an ethics office, ethics officer, explicit ethics training, a telephone counseling/reporting line, and a system for investigating and following up on reports of misconduct. However, the specifics of these systems vary with the context and culture of the firm. Some companies in highly regulated industries may focus more on legal compliance. Others that have a longstanding values-based culture will want to make sure that the ethics management system is designed with a heavy emphasis on values and aspirations. Research has found that the best of these formal ethics management programs have an overarching values-based approach that incorporates legal compliance within the framework of a broader set of company values. Smaller firms with a strong commitment to ethics are less likely to have separate formal ethics management structures and systems. Whether large or small, the keys to effective ethics management are commitment to ethics from the very top of the organization, involvement of leaders and employees at every level, and recognition that ethics management is an ongoing effort requiring continuous reinforcement and integration into the larger corporate culture.

DISCUSSION QUESTIONS

1. Imagine that it's your responsibility to select an ethics officer for your organization. What qualities, background, and experience would you look for? Would you ever be interested in such a position? Why or why not?
2. What are the advantages of having an ethics office or officer report to a company's chief executive officer, the legal department, human resources, or audit? What are the disadvantages?
3. Think about an organization where you've worked. What kinds of ethical dilemmas are unique to that organization? To that industry? What might be the best way to prepare employees to deal with those dilemmas?
4. Which of the following exist in the organization: mission or values statement, policy manual, code of conduct, ethics training (who conducts it), hotline? Are they consistent and credible?
5. Is senior management committed to ethics? How do you know? What could they do differently or better?
6. Are leaders at all levels held accountable for their ethical conduct? If so, how? If not, why not? What would you recommend?
7. What recommendations would you make for handling frivolous calls to the hotline?

8. Does the organization evaluate its ethics initiatives? How? If not, why not?
9. Would you characterize the ethics efforts in this organization as taking a values, compliance, or combination approach? Is it effective? Recommend improvements.
10. How would you raise an ethical concern in this organization? List all of the resources available to you. Which ones would you be likely to use? Why or why not?
11. Imagine that you're the CEO of a small manufacturing company. An employee has dumped toxic waste in a nearby stream. Who would you call into your office, and what would you want to know? Develop a short-term and long-term action plan for dealing with the crisis. Who would you communicate with and why?
12. Evaluate the ethics program at your organization from the perspective of "fit." Has the ethics program been designed to "fit" the organization's overall culture? If so, how? If not, what could be done to make the program a better fit?
13. Think about your own positive, memorable, "peak experiences" when it comes to ethics. Be prepared to discuss those with others in your class and to think about the conditions that would make it possible for such experiences to happen more regularly at work. Or, if you don't have much work experience yourself, interview someone who has and ask these questions. Be prepared to report back what you learned from the interview.

SHORT CASE

WHAT'S WRONG WITH THIS PICTURE?

You're a management consultant who has been asked by Green Company to help design an ethics communication and training program for all Green Company employees. Your meetings to date have been with the head of human resources, and your contract with the company has been negotiated with him. Once the papers have been signed, you begin your research and are quickly stymied by Green's corporate counsel. He says that you will not be allowed to ask employees about ethical dilemmas that have occurred at Green. He specifically asks that you get your information from other sources such as press accounts of problems in the industry, or from other organizations with which you've worked. In addition, the head of human resources has told you that you'll be unable to meet the three most senior executives because they're busy negotiating a large acquisition. You will have access to other high-level managers who can tell you what they think the seniors want. You're instructed to write a code of conduct for the company and a mission statement, and prepare presentations for the senior managers to give to employees sometime next month on corporate expectations and values.

Case Questions

1. Based on what you know about developing ethical cultures and programs, identify the problems presented by this case.

2. Why do you think the corporate counsel has responded in this way? What will be your response to him, if any?
3. As a consultant, what are your ethical obligations, if any?
4. How will you proceed?

NOTES

1. Weaver, G., Treviño, L. K., and Cochran, P. 1998. Corporate ethics programs as control systems: Managerial and institutional influences. Unpublished working paper.
2. Personal communication, Kent Druyvesteyn, 1994.
3. Weaver, G., Treviño, L. K., and Cochran, P. 1999. Corporate ethics practices in the mid-1990s: An empirical study of the *Fortune* 1000. *Journal of Business Ethics,* 18 (3): 283–294.
4. Austin, N. K. 1994. The new corporate watchdogs. *Working Woman,* January: 19–20.
5. Towne, P. L. 1991. Training employees and communicating ethical standards. In *Corporate ethics: Developing new standards of accountability.* Conference Board Report No. 980. New York: The Conference Board, 25–26.
6. Simmons, D. G. 1985. The nature of the organizational grapevine. *Supervisory Management* (November): 39–42.
7. DeAngelis, T. 1991. Honesty tests weigh in with improved ratings. *APA Monitor,* 7. Ones, D. S., Ziswesvaran, C., and Schmidt, F. 1993. Comprehensive meta-analysis of integrity test validities: Findings and implications for personal selection and theories of job performance. *Journal of Applied Psychology,* 78: 679–703. Sackett, P. R., Burris, L. R., and Callahan, C. 1989. Integrity testing for personal selection: An update. *Personal Psychology,* 42: 491–529.
8. Kotter, J. P., and Heskett, J. L. 1992. *Corporate Culture and Performance.* New York: Free Press.
9. Smith, A. L. 1991. *Innovative employee communication: A new approach to improving trust, teamwork and performance.* Englewood Cliffs, NJ: Prentice-Hall.
10. Ibid.
11. Ibid.
12. Peters, T. J., and Waterman, R. H., Jr. 1982. *In search of excellence: Lessons from America's best-run companies.* New York: Harper & Row.
13. Hammer, M., and Champy, J. 1993. *Reengineering the corporation: A manifesto for corporate revolution.* New York: HarperCollins.
14. Powell, J. M. 1994. Pinkerton responds to the Federal Sentencing Guidelines. *Corporate Conduct Quarterly* 3(1): 10.
15. Miller, S. S. 1991. The ombudsperson. In *Corporate ethics: Developing new standards of accountability.* Conference Board Report No. 980. New York: The Conference Board, 29–30.
16. Johnson & Johnson's credo survey: Genesis and evolution. 1993. *Ethikos* 7, No. 2 (September/October): 2.
17. Pollack, A. 2003. Tenet Healthcare reports $55 million quarterly loss. *The New York Times,* April 11.
18. Ibid.
19. Weintraub, A. 2002. A scandal-ridden Tenet stands by its man. *Business Week,* November 25: 46.

INDEX

A. H. Robins, 201, 203–205
Abbott Laboratories, 32, 270
abuse, sexual, 25. *see also* harassment
accountability
    corporate, 34–36
    management, 3–6
    organizational culture and, 225–227, 239
Adelphia Communications, 7, 34–35, 44, 126
advertising, 70, 72–73, 205–207, 337
age discrimination, 62–64
altruism, 23
American Precision Components, Inc., 41
antitrust regulation, 41
Archer Daniels Midland, 7
Arthur Andersen
    conflict of interest in, 198–199
    corporate crime and, 41
    deregulation and, 34–35
    ethics and, 7
    fiduciary responsibilities and, 73, 126–127
    organizational culture of, 10
    trust and, 44
authority
    management and, 179–181
    organizational culture and, 238–239
    personal responsibility and, 181–185
awareness, moral
    decision-making and, 15–16
    legality and, 133
    personal responsibility and, 110–119, 181–185

banking and corporate fraud, 200–201, 213–215
barriers to ethical judgment, 120–124
Bear Stearns, 47, 246
behavior
    assigned roles and, 175–178
    authority, obedience to, 179–181
    business ethics and, 161–162
    control, locus of, 119–120
    cross-cultural, 318–322
    cross-cultural ethics and, 321–323
    decision-making and, 15–16
    discipline and, 142–143
    environment and, 13–14
    financial performance and corporate, 37–38
    global business ethics and, 330–333
    group norms and, 173–175, 249–250
    individual, 9–12
    industry initiatives and corporate, 26–27
    organizational culture and, 225–226, 228–230
    personal responsibility and, 181–185
    principles of, Caux Round Table, 348
    reward and punishment systems, 165–173
    script processing and, 120–122
    self-interest and, 23, 28
    situational ethics and, 162–165
    stereotypes and, 62–63
beliefs. *see* values
bias, 120–124, 139–140
bribery
    conflict of interest and, 68–69
    cross-cultural ethics and, 323–329, 340–341
    fines and punishment of, 41
    Lockheed Martin, 296
    pharmaceutical companies and, 5
    principles on, Caux Round Table, 349
    Royal Dutch Shell and, 344–345
Buffett, Warren, 79, 214
burden of proof, 248–249
bureaucracy, 238–239
business. *see also* corporations; international business; organizations
    assigned roles and, 175–178
    conflicting interests in, 195–197
    cost vs. benefit, 122–123
    cross-cultural ethics and, 328–329, 340–346
    ethical decision-making and, 94–100
    global environment and, 310–312, 316
    individualism vs. collectivism, 319
    policy and global, 330–333
    principles of, Caux Round Table, 347–351
    situational ethics and, 162–165
    social responsibility and, 6–7, 36–40
    trust in, 219
Business Week
    on corporate reputations, 24
    on financial rankings, 37
    on global business, 334
    on investor confidence, 35
    on whistle-blowers, 83

Caremark decision, 42
Carnegie, Andrew, 33

INDEX 317

cascading, ethics training by, 298
case studies
   A. H. Robins, 203–205
   advertising and product safety, 205–207
   Enron Corporation, 198–200
   ExxonMobil, 24, 217–218
   Ford Motor Company, 105–109, 120–123, 129–132
   Johns Manville, 33, 177, 208–210
   Johnson & Johnson, 36, 44, 202–203, 233, 240
   Lincoln Electric Company, 212–213
   Merck & Co., 35, 51–52, 342
   Northrop Grumman Corporation, 301–302
   Salomon Brothers, 40–41, 47, 79, 213–215, 236
   Scott Paper Company, 210–212
   Sears, Roebuck and Co., 186–189
   TAP Pharmaceuticals, 42, 270–271
   Texaco, 7, 64, 151–152, 267–269
   Texas Instruments, 29–30, 288–290
   Union Carbide, 26–27, 215–217
   USAA, 286–288
   VideoTek Corporation, 263–267
case study exercises. *see also* gaming as a training model
   advertising, 221
   authority, 189
   communication, 313
   confidentiality, 70, 109
   conflict of interest, 67, 85, 102, 220
   corporate policy, 347
   corporate resources, 75–76, 86
   customer confidence, 85–86
   decision-making, 88–89, 92
   discipline, 142
   discrimination, 62–63
   diversity, 147, 159
   environmental protection, 222–223
   family issues, 149–150
   fiduciary responsibilities, 73
   financial resources, 76–77
   harassment, 65, 148–149
   hiring and work assignments, 138–146
   honesty, 156
   human resources, 85
   moral judgment, 111, 114, 134
   performance evaluation, 140
   personal ethics, 53
   product safety, 71, 220–221
   relationships, team, 159
   sexual harassment, 65
   shareholders, 221–222
   termination, 144
   whistle-blowers, 79
Caux Round Table, 341, 347–351
character, 9–12, 99
charities, 24–25

cheating, 3, 12, 242
Chemical Manufacturers Association, 26–27
Citigroup. *see also* Salomon Brothers; Salomon Smith Barney
   Enron scandal and, 200
   management ethics in, 235–237
   organizational culture and, 228–229
   stakeholders at, 214
citizenship, corporate, 37
Civil Rights act of 1964, 32, 63–66
code of conduct. *see also* compliance programs; honor code; industry initiatives
   assigned roles and, 175–178
   communication of, 292–293
   ethics and, 13
   global business ethics and, 330–333
   industry initiatives for a, 26–27, 35–36
   Malden Mills, 39
   organizational culture and, 240
   responsibility and, 32
   trust and, 44–45
code of ethics. *see also* honor code
   business behavior and, 6–8
   changing corporate culture and, 260–262
   conflict of interest and, 70
   cynicism and, 4
   decision-making and, 100–101
   integrity and, 126–127
   laws and, 16–17
   organizational culture and, 226–227, 230, 241–243
collectivism, 319, 328–329
commitment, 29–30, 294–296
communication
   changing corporate culture and, 258–262
   compliance programs and, 275–280
   corporate, 216, 280–296
   grapevine, 171, 280–283
   organizational culture and, 226–227, 239, 253–254
   regulation, 218
   systems of, 284–293, 302–304
community. *see* stakeholders
competition and regulation, 34–36
compliance programs. *see also* code of conduct; industry initiatives; law
   communication of, 241
   corporate values and, 308–310
   costs of, 42–43, 276
   ethics and legal, 275
   evaluation, 306–308
   Health Care Compliance Association, 42
confidentiality, 70–71. *see also* privacy
conflict of interest
   advertising and corporate, 205–207
   cross-cultural ethics and, 328–329
   employment contracts and, 60–61
   human resources and, 67–70

laws and, 16–17
organizations and, 198–201
conscience, 183
consequences
    decision-making and, 89–90, 97–98, 124–125
    personal responsibility and, 181–185
    product safety and, 204–205
    worker safety and, 209–210
conspiracy, 199
consumer. *see also* customer service; stakeholders
    global business and the, 335
    principles on, Caux Round Table, 349
    protection, 197–198, 340
    rights, 7, 197
contracts, employment, 60–62
control, locus of, 119–120
corporate citizenship, 37
corporate crime, 40–43, 199, 204
corporate culture, 213. *see also* organizational culture
corporate policy
    decision-making and, 100–101
    discrimination and, 62
    global business ethics and, 330–333
    interpretation of, 152–155
    manuals, 291–292
    organizational culture and, 240–241
corporate resources, use of, 74–78
Corporate Social Responsibility (CSR), 30–34, 36–40. *see also* social responsibility
corporations. *see also* business; organizations
    assigned roles and, 175–178
    compliance programs and, 276–280
    diversity and, 146–152
    ethical decision-making and, 94–100
    global environment and, 310–312, 333–340
    human resources and, 138–146
    relationships, team, 155–158
    reputations of, 24–25
    role models in, 152–155
    social responsibility and, 6–7, 36
    volunteerism in, 46–48
    whistle-blowers and, 78–84
corruption, foreign bribery and, 324–329. *see also* bribery
cost/benefit analysis, 248. *see also* decision-making
costs
    compliance program, 276
    corporate scandal, 194–195, 214
    environmental, 34–36, 216–218
    stakeholders and corporate, 218–219
    worker rights, 146
    workplace theft, 28
Credit Suisse First Boston, 40–41, 200, 256
crime, corporate, 40–43, 204, 349

culture. *see also* globalization; international business; organizational culture
    behavioral consistency and, 321–322
    bribery and, 324–328
    ethical standards and, 328–333
    global business ethics and, 330–333
    global environment and, 318–319
    homogeneity and, 322
    individualism vs. collectivism, 319
    negotiations in a foreign, 323–324
    perception, selective, 320
    power distance and, 319–320
    similarity and, 322–323
customer service, 70–74, 240. *see also* consumer; stakeholders
cynicism, 3–6, 19, 226, 240

decision-making
    behavior and, 113–119
    bias in, 120–124
    consequences of, 124–126
    cross-cultural ethics and, 328–329
    disclosure rule in, 93–94, 99, 102, 345
    emotion and, 128
    ethics and, 15–17, 88, 161–162
    fact gathering in, 123–124
    groupthink in, 182
    integrity and, 126–127
    intuition and, 127–128
    organizational culture and, 247–249, 254–255
    personal responsibility and, 181–185
    prescriptive approach to, 89–94
    psychological approach to, 110–112
    steps to ethical, 94–100
    stock price and earnings in, 194–195
Defense Industry Initiative (DII), 26, 276, 307
deregulation. *see* regulation
Dilbert, 240, 301
disability discrimination, 62–64
discipline, 142–143, 165–173
disclosure rule and decision-making, 93–94, 99, 102, 345
discrimination. *see also* diversity; stereotypes; women
    costs of, 146
    cross-cultural ethics and, 340
    global environment and, 319–323
    human resources and, 61–64, 138–140
    racial, 7, 16
    Texaco and, 267–269
discussion topics. *see* case study exercises
diversity, 64, 146–152. *see also* discrimination; women
Doonesbury, 9
Dow Corning, 24, 227
downsizing, 144–146, 210–213
dress codes, 147–148

due care theory, 197, 222–223
duties and decision-making, 91–93

economy, 31–32, 194–195
education, ethics, 7–11
ego. *see* self-interest
electronic communication, 288–290, 297–298
emotion, 128
employees. *see* workers
employment, 60–62, 74–78, 138–146, 210–213
Enron Corporation
    Citigroup and, 236
    conflict of interest and, 67
    corporate crime and, 41
    deregulation and, 34–35
    ethics and, 7
    organizational culture of, 10
    situational ethics and, 163–164
    trust and, 4, 44
    whistle-blowers and, 82–83
environment. *see also* organizational culture
    behavior and, 10
    compliance programs, 42
    cross-cultural ethics and, 329
    ethics and, 13–14, 161–162
    globalization and business, 310–312, 316
    principles on, Caux Round Table, 349
    protection, 215–218
    workplace, 61
Environmental Protection Agency (EPA), 42, 215, 219
Equal Employment Opportunity Commission (EEOC), 63–66, 146, 218
equality. *see* discrimination
ethical responsibility, 31–33
ethics, defined, 13, 38, 305. see also case studies
Ethics Officer Association, 42, 277
Ethics Resource Center, 4, 6, 7–8, 276, 342
euphemisms, use of, 255
evaluation
    communication, 283–284
    compliance program, 306–308
    performance, 61, 140–142, 155–158, 261–262, 304–306
exercises. *see* case study exercises
expatriate managers, 317–323
ExxonMobil, 24, 217–218

facts in decision-making, 123–124
False Claims Act, 82
Federal Bureau of Investigation (FBI), 83
Federal Communication Commission (FCC), 218
Federal Reserve Board, 194, 218
Federal Trade Commission (FTC), 218
fiduciary responsibilities, 70, 73–74, 127
financial performance, 36–40, 40–43
financial responsibility, 30–31

Food and Drug Administration, 218
Ford Motor Company, 7, 105–109, 120–123, 129–132
Fortune
    on Citigroup, 235–236
    on code of ethics, 241–243
    on corporate reputations, 24–25, 37
    on Enron Corporation, 198
    on General Motors, 128
    on Malden Mills, 38–39
    on media cynicism, 4
    on organizational culture, 228
fraud, 41, 199–200

gaming as a training model, 2, 76, 300–302. *see also* case studies; case study exercises
Gates, Bill, 34, 250
General Dynamics Corporation, 14, 233, 254
General Electric Company, 44, 231
General Motors, 4, 33, 128, 197
globalization. *see also* culture; international business
    cross-cultural ethics and, 340–346
    ethics and business, 316, 330–333
    managers and business, 317–323
Goldman Sachs, 40–41, 46
government. *see also* politics in global business; regulation
    changing corporate culture and, 256
    Corporate Social Responsibility (CSR) and, 32, 34–36
    ethics scandals in, 7–8
    foreign bribery and, 324–329
    regulation, 7, 34–36, 218–219
    whistle-blowers and, 79–84
    worker protection and, 146
grapevine, 171, 280–283
groups
    business stakeholders as, 195–197
    consistency and homogeneity of, 321–323
    individualism vs. collectivism in, 319
    norms and behavior, 173–175, 249–250
    organizational culture and, 228
    shareholders as, 213–215
groupthink, 182

harassment. *see also* sexual abuse; women
    costs of, 146
    cross-cultural ethics and, 329
    human resources and, 61
    management and, 148–149
    sexual, 7, 64–67, 168–170
health. *see also* safety
    asbestos and, 22, 33, 177, 248–249
    Bill & Melinda Gates Foundation, 34
    global environment and issues of, 333–335, 337
    government regulation and, 34–36

privacy and, 206
product safety and, 205–206
worker safety and, 208–210
Health and Human Services, Department of, 35–36
Home Depot, 33, 334
homogeneity, cultural, 322
honesty. *see also* integrity
   business standards and, 219
   corporate resources and, 76–78
   cross-cultural ethics and, 323–329, 328–329
   global environment and, 337
   job performance and, 156
   organizational culture and, 226–227
   personal values and, 3, 27–28
   role conflict and, 175–178
honor code, 3, 178, 242. *see also* code of conduct; code of ethics
hotlines, 302–304
human resources
   compliance programs and, 276–280
   employment contracts and, 60–62
   management of, 138–146
   organizational culture and, 237
human rights, 334–343

individualism, 319
industry initiatives
   Caux Round Table, 341
   Chemical Manufacturers Association, 26–27
   compliance programs and, 42, 276–280
   global business and, 333–340
   Health Care Compliance Association, 42
   organizational ethics and, 26–27
inequality. *see* discrimination
integrity. *see also* honesty; reputation
   cross-cultural ethics and, 323–329
   decision-making and, 98–99, 126
   defined, 165, 305
   personal values and, 5, 27–28
   Royal Dutch Shell and, 344–345
   testing, 283
   virtue ethics and, 93–94
intellectual property, 111
internalization, organizational culture and, 229–230
international business. *see also* culture; globalization
   bribery and, 324–329
   child labor and, 330–331
   cross-cultural ethics and, 340–346
   ethical standards and, 329–333
   management and, 317–323
   nationalism in, 332–333
   principles of, Caux Round Table, 347–351
   relativism vs. ethical imperialism, 330
International Business Machines (IBM)
   integrity and, 171–172

9-11 United Services Group, 46–47
   social responsibility and, 36
   trust and, 44
intuition, 100–102, 127–128
investment banking, 200–201, 213–215, 256
investment, social responsibility and, 40

Jefferson, Thomas, 99, 230, 250
job performance. *see* performance, job
job security, 210–213
Johns Manville, 33, 177, 208–210
Johnson & Johnson, 36, 44, 202–203, 233, 240
JP Morgan Chase, 47, 200
judgment, moral
   behavior and, 11–12, 113–119
   cost vs. benefit and, 122–123
   decision-making and, 15–16, 96, 110–119
   law and, 133

kickbacks. *see* bribery; conflict of interest

labor, 340, 342. *see also* workers
law. *see also* compliance programs; government; regulation
   business ethics and, 16–17
   consumer protection, 197–198
   copyright and patent, 111
   corporate crime and, 40–43
   Corporate Social Responsibility (CSR) and, 32
   cross-cultural ethics and, 324–329
   discrimination and, 62–64
   global environment and, 333–340
   moral judgment and, 133
   regulation and, 7
   reward and punishment systems and, 168–169
   whistle-blowers and the, 82–84
layoffs, 144–146, 210–213
leadership
   cascading training and, 298
   compliance program, 276–280
   ethics and corporate, 18, 27–28, 294–296
   group norms and, 173–175
   organizational culture and, 230–237
learning theory, social, 168, 171
legal responsibility, 31–33
Levi Straus & Co.
   business strategy and, 37
   corporate responsibility and, 32
   global ethics of, 330–331, 334, 336–337
   values and, 27–28
Lincoln Electric Company, 212–213
Lockheed Martin, 36, 296
locus of control, 119–120
loyalty
   assigned roles and, 175–178
   authority, obedience to, 179–181, 238

employment contracts and, 74–75, 212–213
group norms and, 3, 173–175
worker behavior and, 28–29

Malden Mills, 38–40
management. *see also* case studies; case study exercises
  accountability, 3–6
  authority, obedience to, 179–181
  behavior and, 14–17
  changing corporate culture and, 255–262
  communication, 280–296
  compliance programs and, 275–280
  discipline and, 142–143
  diversity and, 146–148, 151–152
  economic responsibilities, 32
  ethical behavior and, 161–162
  family and personal issues, 149–152
  global business ethics and, 330–333
  global environment and, 316
  harassment and, 148–149, 151–152
  human resources functions of, 138–146
  individualism vs. collectivism, 319
  integrity, 344–345
  international, 317–323
  job security and, 210–213
  judgment, obstacles to, 120–124
  moral development and, 118–119
  moral leadership and, 28
  organizational culture and, 10, 230–237, 294–296
  performance, 243–247
  reward and punishment systems, 165–173
  role models and, 152–155
  structures for compliance, 276–280
  team relationships and, 155–158
  terminations and, 144–146
  whistle-blowers and, 78–84
McKinsey & Company, 46, 61
media
  business ethics and, 7–8
  cynicism and, 4
  organizational ethics and, 24–25
mentoring, 250–251. *see also* role models
Merck & Co., 35, 51–52, 342
Merrill Lynch
  conflict of interest and, 200
  9-11 United Services Group, 46–47
  product safety and, 72
  trust and, 4, 40–41
Microsoft Corporation, 33–34
mission statement. *see* values
Mitsubishi Motors, 7, 66–67
models, role. *see* role models
Money-laundering, 41
money-laundering, 199
monopoly regulation, 34
Monsanto, 24, 333–334

morals. *see also* values
  behavior and, 113–119
  business ethics and, 161–162
  communication of, 253–254
  cross-cultural ethics and, 329
  decision-making and, 15–16, 88, 96, 110–119, 248–249
  gender and, 117
  judgment and, 11–12
  judgment, reasoning and, 122–123
  organizational culture and, 230–234, 242–243
  personal responsibility and, 181–185
  philanthrophy and, 33–34
  virtue ethics and, 93–94
motivation, 23
myths, 251–252

newsletters, 286
Newsweek, 163–164, 169
Nike, 338–340
9-11 United Services Group, 45–50
non-profit organizations, 48–50
norms
  cross-cultural, 321–323, 323
  group, 173–175, 249–250
Northrop Grumman Corporation, 301–302

obedience to authority
  management and, 179–181
  organizational culture and, 238–239
  personal responsibility and, 181–185
obligations and decision-making, 91–93, 98–99
obstacles to ethical judgment, 120–124
Occupational Safety and Health administration (OSHA), 208, 219
Organization for Economic Cooperation and Development (OECD), 340–341
organizational culture. *see also* culture; environment
  auditing, 258–262
  behavior and, 10
  communication principles and, 280–296
  defined, 225, 228
  environment and, 13–14, 161–162
  ethics and, 18
  global environment and, 316
  mission statements and, 290–291
  systems for changing, 255–257
  systems of, formal, 230–249, 259, 302–304
  systems of, informal, 249–255, 259, 302–304
organizational ethics
  industry initiatives for, 26–27
  management and, 28
  social responsibility and, 6
  values and, 3
organizations. *see also* business; corporations

assigned roles and, 175–178
behavior and, 14–17, 23
business ethics and, 7–10, 161–162
compliance programs and, 275–280
cross-cultural ethics and, 340–346
cynicism and, 3–6
decision-making and, 94–100
euphemisms and, 255
global environment and, 316, 319, 333–340
non-profit, 24–25, 48–50
social responsibility and, 6–7
whistle-blowers and, 78–84
orientation. *see* socialization
Otis Elevator Company. *see* United Technologies Corporation

paternalism, 27
Paterno, Joe
  on cynicism, 5
  on enforcing standards, 234
  on recruitment, 237
  on rule enforcement, 27–28, 245, 252–253
  on values and philanthropy, 250
payoffs. *see* bribery
peer pressure, 173–175, 175–178
perception, 320, 327–328
Performance, job
  compliance programs and, 304–306
performance, job
  discipline and, 142–143
  employee evaluation and, 140–142
  family and personal issues, 149–152
  global business ethics and, 330–333
  human resources and, 61
  organizational culture and, 243–247
  personal responsibility and, 181–185
  team relationships and, 155–158
  terminations and, 144–146
performance management, 243–247, 260–262
philanthrophy, 24–25, 31–34, 164
Polarfleece, 38–40
policy. *see* corporate policy
politics in global business, 333–340
power, cross-cultural, 319–320
prejudice. *see* discrimination
price fixing, 7
principles and decision-making, 91–93
privacy, 61, 206. *see also* confidentiality
product safety. *see* safety
profiling, 63, 140
profit, Corporate Social Responsibility (CSR) and, 32
proof, burden of, 248–249
public relations, cynicism and, 3–4
public trust. *see* trust
punishment. *see* reward and punishment systems

quantitative analysis, 248. *see also* decision-making

racial discrimination, 7, 16, 62–64. *see also* discrimination
rationalization, 173–175
reasoning, moral, 11–12, 96, 113–119
recruitment, 285
Reebok Corporation, 337–338
regulation. *see also* government
  bribery and, 324–329
  compliance programs and, 275–276, 308–310
  corporate reputation and, 213–215
  Corporate Social Responsibility (CSR) and, 32, 34–36
  costs of, 218–219
  global environment and, 333–340
  government, 7, 34–36
  industry initiatives and, 26–27
  trust and, 44–45
  whistle-blowers and, 79–84
reinforcement theory, 166–168
relationships
  compliance programs and management, 276–280
  control, locus of, 119–120
  cross-cultural, 317–322
  customer confidence, 70–74
  decision-making and, 100–101
  employment, 60–61
  ethics and, 18
  team, 155–158
  workplace, 30
religion, 25, 149, 328
reputation. *see also* integrity
  banking and, 213–215
  behavior and, 30, 37–38
  business standards and, 219
  compliance programs and, 275–276
  environment and, 215–218
  global business, 334–335
  Johnson & Johnson, 202–203
  organizational, 24–25, 74–76, 232
  performance management, 243–247
  Texas Instruments, 29
  trust and, 43–45
responsibility
  advertising and corporate, 205–207
  Caremark decision and corporate, 42
  global, 333–340
  management, 294–296
  morals and personal, 181–185, 219
  organizational culture and, 238–239
  principles of, Caux Round Table, 348
  social, 6–7, 30–36
  stakeholders and corporate, 202–203, 218
retention, worker, 61
reward and punishment systems
  changing corporate culture and, 260–262

INDEX **323**

compliance programs and, 304–306
global business ethics and, 330–333
management of diversity, 165–173
organizational culture and, 225–227, 243–247
risk, 125
rituals, 251, 258–262, 296
role models
    authority, obedience to, 180–181
    changing corporate culture and, 258–262
    global business ethics and, 330–333
    management as, 152–155
    organizational culture and, 250–251
    situational ethics and, 161–165
roles, assigned, 175–178
Royal Dutch Shell, 343–345

safety. *see also* health
    asbestos and, 22, 33, 208–210, 248–249
    automobile, 7, 120–123, 129–132, 183
    consumer protection and, 197–198
    corporate responsibility and, 32–33
    health and, 22, 205–206
    product, 70–72, 201–205
    workplace, 208–210
Salomon Brothers, 79, 213–215
Salomon Smith Barney, 40–41, 47, 236. *see also* Citigroup
Sarbanes-Oxley Act, 35, 82–83, 246, 256
scandal
    business ethics and, 4, 7–8
    deregulation and, 34–35
    Doonesbury on, 9
    industry initiatives and, 26–27
    organizational reputation and, 24–25
    trust and, 44–45
    Watergate, 7
Scott Paper Company, 210–212
Sears, Roebuck and Co., 186–189
Securities and Exchange Commission (SEC), 194, 218
self-discipline, 99
self-interest
    behavior and, 23, 28
    changing corporate culture and, 258
    consequences and, 125
    social responsibility and, 30
September 11, 2001
    cynicism and, 5–6
    reflections on, 45–50
    Southwest Airlines and, 25
    whistle-blowers and, 83
sexual abuse, 25. *see also* harassment
sexual harassment. *see* harassment
shareholders. *see* stakeholders
similarity, cultural, 322–323
situational ethics, 162–165
60 Minutes, 39, 179, 310

social concensus and group norms, 173–175
social learning theory, 168, 171
social responsibility. *see also* Corporate Social Responsibility (CSR)
    corporations and, 6–7, 30–31
    cross-cultural ethics and, 329
    financial performance and, 36–40
    global business and, 333–340
    Malden Mills and, 38–40
    principles of, Caux Round Table, 348
    Royal Dutch Shell and, 343–345
    worker behavior and, 30
social science, 3
socialization
    communication, 285
    ethics training and, 296–297
    organizational culture and, 229, 247, 250–251, 260
society
    Corporate Social Responsibility (CSR) and, 32–33
    cross-cultural ethics and, 328–333
    decision-making and, 124–126
    ethics and, 18, 27, 30–31
    human rights and, 334–335
    individualism vs. collectivism, 319
    organizational culture and, 228
    philanthrophy and, 33–34
    power distance and, 319–320
    regulation and, 34–36
    self-interest in, 23
Southwest Airlines, 25, 230–231, 237
stakeholders. *see also* consumer; customer service
    changing corporate culture and, 255–262
    community as, 95, 215–218
    defined, 195–197
    global environment and, 316, 333–334
    principles of, Caux Round Table, 348–351
    protection, 218–219
    responsibility and, 213–215
standards. *see* corporate policy
stereotypes, 62–63, 140, 318–323. *see also* discrimination
stockholders. *see* stakeholders
student exercises. *see* case study exercises
subordinates. *see* workers
systems, formal and informal, 230–255, 259, 302–304, 308–310

Tailhook Association, 168–170
TAP Pharmaceuticals, 42, 270–271
teamwork, management of, 155–158
termination, 144–146
Texaco, 7, 64, 151–152, 267–269
Texas Instruments, 29, 30, 288–290
theft, 28, 74–78
theory

consequentialist, 89–90
deontological, 91–93
due care, 197, 222–223
reinforcement, 166–168
social learning, 168, 171
tobacco industry
  advertising and the, 207
  global ethics of, 334–335
  health and ethics of, 7
  RJR Nabisco, 133
  secrecy and the, 98
training
  cascading, 298
  changing corporate culture and, 260–262
  compliance program, 277
  cross-cultural, 323–329
  ethics and values, 7–10, 11–12, 226, 296–302
  foreign assignment, 317–322
  socialization, 247
  values, 2
transcultural corporate ethics, 340–346
Trudeau, Gary, 9
trust
  business standards and, 219
  conflict of interest and, 69–70
  group norms and, 173–175
  organizational reputation and, 25, 43–45
  personal reputation and, 30
truth
  in advertising, 70, 72–73
  global environment and, 337
  relativism vs. ethical imperialism, 330
Tyco, 34–35, 44

U. S. Chamber of Commerce, 28
U. S. Department of Health and Human Services, 35–36, 42
U. S. Sentencing Commission, 41–43, 56–57, 142, 241, 276
  compliance programs and, 302, 308–309
  policy manuals and the, 291–292
Union Carbide, 26–27, 215–217
United Nations, human rights and, 341–342
United Technologies Corporation, 305–306, 310–312
USAA, 286–288
utilitarianism, 89–90, 97–98

values. *see also* morals
  communication, 290–291
  compliance programs and, 43, 308–310
  conflict in personal, 3, 161–162
  cross-cultural ethics and, 328–329
  cynicism and, 5

decision-making and, 88–89
diversity and, 64
language and, 253–254
Levi Straus & Co., 27
non-profit organizations and, 48–50
organizational culture and, 225–227, 240
role models and, 250–251
teaching, 7–10
VideoTek Corporation, 263–267
virtue ethics, 93–94, 126–127
volunteerism, 47–48

Waste Management, 41, 126
weaknesses in ethical judgment, 120–124
Web sites, 284–285, 298
whistle-blowers
  communication systems and, 302–304
  corporate change and, 260
  cross-cultural ethics and, 329
  procedure for, 78–84
  retaliation and, 299
  reward systems for, 245–247
  role of, assigned, 178
women. *see also* discrimination; diversity; harassment
  discrimination and, 62–63
  moral development and, 117
  product safety and, 204
  Working Mother and, 37
  Working Woman and, 29
workers. *see also* labor
  authority, obedience to, 179–181
  business ethics and, 161–162
  child labor as, 330–331, 335, 337
  communication with, 282–283, 302–304
  corporate resources and, 74–78
  employment contracts, 60–62
  hiring, 237
  job security and, 210–213
  organizational ethics and, 23, 29–30
  principles on, Caux Round Table, 349–350
  product safety and, 208–210, 248
  reputation, 30
  responsibility and, 181–185
  rights, 207–208
  team relationships and, 155–158
  worker behavior and, 28–29
World Trade organization (WTO), 24, 349
WorldCom
  Citigroup and, 236
  corporate crime and, 41
  deregulation and, 34–35
  trust and, 7, 44
  whistle-blowers and, 83